# FIFTH EDITION

# AMERICAN BUSINESS VALUES

## A Global Perspective

D0061279

**Gerald F. Cavanagh, S.J.**

*Charles T. Fisher III Chair of Business Ethics*
*Professor of Management*
*College of Business Administration*
*University of Detroit Mercy*

PEARSON

Prentice
Hall

Upper Saddle River, NJ 07458

**Library of Congress Cataloging-in-Publication Data**

Cavanagh, Gerald F.
  American business values: a global perspective / Gerald F. Cavanagh.—5th ed.
    p. cm.
  Includes bibliographical references and index.
  ISBN 0-13-146706-9 (alk. paper)
    1. Business ethics—United States.   2. Industries—Social aspects—United States.   3. Social
responsibility of business—United States.   4. Free enterprise—United States.   I. Title.

HF5387.C379 2006
174'.4'0973—dc22

                                                                          2005045888

**Editorial Director:** Jeff Shelstad
**Senior Acquisitions Editor:** Michael Ablassmeir
**Associate Editor:** Melissa Yu
**Assistant Editor:** Richard Gomes
**Marketing Manager:** Anke Braun
**Marketing Assistant:** Patrick Danzuso
**Managing Editor :** John Roberts
**Production Editor:** Renata Butera
**Permissions Supervisor:** Charles Morris
**Manufacturing Buyer:** Michelle Klein
**Design Director:** Maria Lange
**Cover Design:** Bruce Kenselaar
**Cover Illustration/Photo:** Getty Images, Inc.
**Manager, Print Production:** Christy Mahon
**Composition:** Integra Software Services
**Full-Service Project Management:** BookMasters, Inc.
**Printer/Binder:** R.R. Donnelley–Harrisonburg
**Typeface:** 10/12 Times Ten

Credits and acknowledgments borrowed from other sources and reproduced, with permission, in this textbook appear on appropriate page within the text.

Pearson Education LTD.
Pearson Education Singapore, Pte. Ltd
Pearson Education, Canada, Ltd
Pearson Education—Japan

Pearson Education Australia PTY, Limited
Pearson Education North Asia Ltd
Pearson Educación de Mexico, S.A. de C.V.
Pearson Education Malaysia, Pte. Ltd

10  9  8  7  6  5  4  3  2  1
ISBN 0-13-146706-9

# Contents

# Preface

*American Business Values: A Global Perspective* probes the ethics and values of business people and business itself. A person's ethics and values have a pivotal influence on other people and on business. Ethics and values influence the effectiveness of leadership, innovation, product quality, on-the-job relationships, and government regulations. Moreover, work and business are so central to our lives that they are a major influence on our personal values, goals, and lifestyles. Our primary focus here will be on American business values, but we will also examine how those values are influencing people and businesses throughout the world, and how American values are in turn being affected by other peoples.

More specifically, the purpose of this book is to enable each reader to:

- Clarify and articulate her/his personal goals, ethics, and values.
- Distinguish between ethical and unethical behavior within the firm, and to examine how it influences people, products, and the work environment.
- Know the language, tools, and applications for ethical analysis, and to understand how good moral habits can be developed.
- Comprehend the values, ethics, and beliefs that provide the foundation for free market systems of production and exchange, and to identify their strengths and weaknesses.
- Critically assess the complex, responsible relationships among business, government, and society.

Business and government managers both must take a long-range view in order to meet the needs of people in the global marketplace. This, in turn, requires effective long-term planning that respects the needs of all stakeholders. Policies and plans that benefit the firm in the long term require a consensus of people within that organization. That consensus can be built when they understand the mission and values of the firm. Creativity and innovation gives business its energy and success, but we also recognize the influence of historical traditions and values. Hence, we will discuss both traditional business values and objections to these values.

The free enterprise system has been immensely successful in providing jobs, goods, and services to billions of people on the planet. Energetic and creative entrepreneurs, managers and workers with a long-term perspective have made business effective. However, there is an ethical value that is sometimes in tension: the central importance of *each* individual person. To be ethical, every business decision, action, and policy should be made considering all who are touched by that decision, whether they be employees, customers, suppliers, shareholders, neighbors, or community. Shareholders are important, but they are only one of many stakeholders of the firm. Not to be forgotten are the poor, unemployed, and unskilled; they are stakeholders of society, and thus indirectly also stakeholders of the firm.

On a personal note, I was Academic Vice President and Provost of University of Detroit Mercy for six years. I helped develop a new mission statement, select new deans and vice presidents, and oversaw 250 volunteer faculty and staff who worked on 30 committees to redesign the curriculum, standards, and structure of the university. I saw how a clear and compelling mission, empowering leaders, commitment to ethics, wide consultation, and good communication brought energy and success to the university.

This fifth edition of *American Business Values: A Global Perspective* retains the best elements of the fourth, yet adds essential new features. We attempt to clarify the changing values of industrialized peoples, especially Americans. Moreover, we also spotlight the way that a firm's values influence one's personal values, and the way that the values of the individual can influence the organization. Chapter 1 examines outsourcing, advertising and the media, free market fundamentalism, financial and ethical bankruptcies, and restoring trust to business. Chapter 2 examines how we develop moral maturity, as well as the stress we face in life and at work. Chapter 3 provides models and skills to make ethical decisions, shows how ethical behavior benefits the firm, and how virtue can be developed. Chapters 4 and 5 probe the influential historical roots of American business. Chapter 6 investigates the principal weaknesses of the free market system, along with more cooperative alternatives. Chapter 7 examines personal values and beliefs and how they are influenced by the organization. Chapter 8 analyzes how values and ethics affect the performance of the firm. Chapter 9, a new chapter, studies the global marketplace, along with sweatshops, speculation, and global codes of conduct. Chapter 10 investigates mission statements, business planning, and projects some shifts in future business values and beliefs. At the end of each chapter are questions for discussion, brief cases, and exercises that will help the reader better understand the issues.

I thank the following who have given me many insights, face-to-face and through their writings. Thanks to colleagues and good friends over the decades: Tom Bausch, John Boatright, George Brenkert, Marty Calkins, Archie Carroll, Phil Cochran, Richard DeGeorge, Andre Delbecq, John Dienhart, Tom Donaldson, Tom Dunfee, Georges Enderle, Ed Epstein, John Fleming, Bill Frederick, Ed Freeman, David Fritzsche, Kathy Getz, Al Gini, Ken Goodpaster, Allen Grey, Kirk Hanson, Ed Hartman, Michael Hoffman, LaRue Hosmer, Tobias Karcher, Daryl Koehn, Jeanne Liedtka, Jeanne Logsdon, John Mahon, Dennis Moberg, Pat Murphy, Les Myers, Laura Nash, Michael Naughton, Richard Neilson, Lisa Newton, Karen Paul, Moses Pava, Jim Post, Lee Preston, Prakash Sethi, John Steiner, Lee Tavis, Manuel Velasquez, Sandra Waddock, Gary Weaver, Jim Weber, Patricia Werhane, Oliver Williams, Duane Windsor, Rich Wokutch, and Donna Wood. I am sure I have forgotten some cherished colleagues, and for that I apologize. I believe that we are part of a global learning community that shares a common passion: how to help business managers be better citizens to more people in this ever smaller world. I owe each of you much for your insights and friendship.

More immediately, this book is the result of research and enriching dialogue with business people, scholars, and students. The following provided helpful comments and suggestions for this fifth edition: Charles Fornaciari, Mary Ann Hazen, Mark Bandsuch, John Steiner, Dan Saint, Larry Ruddell, E. Leroy Plumlee, William Vitek, Jim Evans, Diana Walsh, and Mike Whitty. Graduate research assistants Preeti Mascarenhas from India, Sandy Kizi from Iraq, Romero Tavares from Brazil and Bernadette Kakooza from Uganda helped with research, and Preeti did the index. Thanks to the University of Detroit Mercy and Dean Bahman Mirshab and the faculty of the College of Business Administration for their support for this project. Thanks to editors Michael Ablassmeir and Melissa Yu as well as project director Jennifer Welsch for their help on this fifth edition.

Gerald F. Cavanagh, S.J.

*Charles T. Fisher III Chair of Business Ethics*
*Professor of Management*
*College of Business Administration*
*University of Detroit Mercy*
*Detroit, Michigan*

# CHAPTER I

# Free Markets Need Ethical Norms

Is it enough for Harvard to attract the brightest students, if we do not excel in making them caring, active, enlightened citizens and civic leaders?
DEREK BOK, PRESIDENT, HARVARD UNIVERSITY, FAREWELL ADDRESS

The serious or complex problems we face cannot be solved by the consciousness that created them.
ALBERT EINSTEIN (1879–1955), NOBEL PRIZE–WINNING PHYSICIST

Entrepreneurs and business managers set the tone for our society. Their firms provide the jobs, products, and services that we need. Bill Gates, Warren Buffet, and Michael Dell are successful and highly rewarded businesspeople. Their goals, attitudes, and activities heavily influence our personal goals and values. A businessperson's values influence relationships with colleagues, customers, suppliers, and shareholders; affect the amount of leisure time the businessperson has; and ultimately determine the person's success or failure. Business has more influence over most of us than government or church, and, in some cases, even more than our own family; it is the dominant institution in our society. Businesspeople in most nations are models for behavior, both good and bad. Because globalization is pushing free markets throughout the world, many other people are now being pulled, often reluctantly, toward these same values. Let us examine the case of the late Sam Walton and the company he founded, Wal-Mart.

Sam Walton changed our purchasing habits and our values. Not only does Wal-Mart provide products, services, and jobs that we need, but its methods have an important influence on our lives. Wal-Mart is the largest, most successful, and most profitable retailer in the world. Its business methods—low price, customer service, control of inventory—have become a model that is followed by business firms throughout the world. In 2004 it was listed as one of "America's Most Admired

I

Companies."[1]The successes and limitations of Wal-Mart tell us much about the goals and values of business and businesspeople in the United States today.

## WAL-MART AS A MODEL OF BUSINESS VALUES

Sam Walton founded the first Wal-Mart store in 1962, the same year that Kmart and Target began. Walton heard about the new discount stores in the early 1960s, and copied winning strategies from around the world. Walton started with the principle, "Give people high value, low prices, and a warm welcome." He visited each store and told his associates who work there, "I want you to promise that whenever you come within 10 feet of a customer, you will look him in the eye, greet him, and ask if you can help him." Walton's strategy has proved to be an immense financial success. There are more than 1.4 million associates—more than the number of employees working at General Motors (GM) Ford, General Electric (GE) and IBM combined—working at nearly 5,000 Wal-Mart stores and wholesale clubs (Sam's Club) across 10 countries. These stores had $286 billion in annual revenue and almost $9.1 billion in profits in 2003.[2] Wal-Mart is the world's largest employer and retailer, with sales 50 percent greater than Target, Costco, Sears Roebuck, and Kmart combined. Some estimate that more than one-tenth of U.S. productivity gains have come because of Wal-Mart's press for lower prices.

Wal-Mart has mastered information technology and global supply chain management, and these practices contribute to the success of the "everyday low prices" policy. Labor costs are also low, reflecting Walton's belief that "No matter how you slice it in the retail business, payroll is one of the most important parts of overhead, and overhead is one of the most crucial things you have to fight to maintain your profit margin."[3] Wal-Mart may reflect its Bentonville, Arkansas roots with its belief that it has a responsibility not to contaminate the culture. It refuses to carry music or computer games with mature ratings, forces some magazine publishers to hide racy covers, and in some stores it refuses to carry the "morning after" contraceptive pill. However, most locations do carry inexpensive firearms.

Most of Wal-Mart's stores have been in small towns, but now it is expanding to cities. It plans to open 40 new stores in California. The strategy suffered a setback, however, in the case of a proposed store in the Los Angeles suburb of Ingelwood. The city council rejected Wal-Mart's request for a building permit. Wal-Mart then hired people to gather petitions to put the question on the ballot, but 60 percent of the voters rejected the proposal to put up the store and to exempt it from environmental review, traffic studies, and public hearings with regard to building the store. Wal-Mart has 38 stores in cities of more than 1 million people, a small

---

[1]"America's Most Admired Companies: Recent Bad Press Hasn't Dimmed the Business World's Affection for Wal-Mart," *Fortune,* March 8, 2004, pp. 27–30.
[2]From Wal-Mart Web site: www.walmartstores.com, accessed November 12, 2004.
[3]Simon Head, "Inside the Leviathan," *New York Review of Books,* December 16, 2004.

proportion of its total stores, but that number will undoubtedly increase. When it locates in an inner city, such as southwest Los Angeles, Wal-Mart provides much-needed low cost goods, jobs, and tax revenue, and often uses a facility that has been abandoned. Wal-Mart acknowledges that it too often has been insensitive to local needs, and promises that it will do better in the future; critics say it still has a long way to go.[4]

When Wal-Mart comes to a new community, it has an immense advantage in its purchasing power and efficiency over local retailers, and thus may force many local retailers to close. Moreover, when setting up a new store, Wal-Mart generally obtains substantial local subsidies and tax breaks, as the community builds new roads and water and sewer lines. When coming to a new town, Wal-Mart claims that it will add new jobs and new tax revenue. However, data show that most often this is not true. The local community often ends up with about the same number of jobs and about the same tax revenue. In some locations, such as Cathedral City, California, Wal-Mart left the town when the tax breaks expired. This left the city with a hollowed-out downtown, a large empty building, lost jobs, and huge short-falls in public revenues. A report found that Wal-Mart has collected more than $1 billion in state and local government subsidies during its decades-long expansion. The report finds some value in subsidizing inner-city sites, but questions the use of public money when Wal-Mart's salaries and benefits force other retailers to reduce their own salaries and benefits in order to compete.[5]

In the wake of its success, Wal-Mart has stirred backlash and criticism. Some of the complaints are it pays full-time associates wages that are below the poverty level; it discriminates against women in pay and promotion; it relentlessly forces suppliers to cut prices; and when it opens a store it forces dozens of small mom-and-pop stores in the town's older downtown area out of business, thus gutting the downtown. Wal-Mart's low wages have pressured supermarkets and other competitors to lower their own wages and benefits.[6] Wal-Mart's low wages also contribute to its 44 percent annual worker turnover. Wal-Mart is sued roughly 12 times each day, making it the most sued institution in the United States, after the federal government. The lawsuits come from customers, employees, and constituents from many of their other groups of stakeholders.[7] While Wal-Mart's size partly explains the volume of lawsuits, these lawsuits also indicate that many customers and associates feel exploited.

Wal-Mart shares much information on customer preferences with suppliers. It also demands the ability to influence the design of products and how they

---

[4]Robert McNatt, "Who Says Wal-Mart Is Bad for Cities? Underserved Neighborhoods Welcome Its Jobs, Low Prices and Tax Revenue," *Business Week,* May 10, 2004; Ann Zimmerman, "Defending Wal-Mart: CEO Scott Rebuts Critics of Pay Scales, Outlines Workplace Diversity Moves," *New York Times,* October 6, 2004, p. B1.

[5]Barnaby J. Feder, "Wal-Mart's Expansion Aided by Many Taxpayer Subsidies," *New York Times,* May 24, 2004, p. C7.

[6]For an account of a Wal-Mart associate trying to pay living expenses on her wage of $7 per hour, see Barbara Ehrenreich, *Nickel and Dimed: On (Not) Getting by in America* (New York: Holt and Co., 2001).

[7]O. C. Ferrell, "Business Ethics and Customer Stakeholders," *Academy of Management Executive,* 18, no. 2 (2004): 126–129.

are made, and that savings be passed along to Wal-Mart and its consumers. Generally, a supplier must sell to Wal-Mart, simply because it controls such a huge segment of the market. As a result, it dominates suppliers. As one supplier put it, the second worst thing a manufacturer can do is to sign a contract with Wal-Mart; the worst thing is not to sign one.[8] Wal-Mart's unrelenting insistence that its suppliers lower their costs has coerced many firms to relocate their manufacturing to China, where wage rates are a small fraction of those in the United States.

Wal-Mart is currently involved in a class-action lawsuit for sex discrimination brought by some 1.6 million female associates. Plaintiffs analyzed the data obtained from Wal-Mart. The data show that, for example, although women make up 93 percent of the cashiers and 68 percent of the salespeople, they constitute only 14 percent of the managers, and 36 percent of the assistant managers. Competitor stores have 57 percent women managers. On average, women receive their first promotion 4.4 years after joining Wal-Mart, while men receive their first promotion after only 2.9 years. Moreover, women's pay for the same job with the same seniority is substantially less. Wal-Mart argues that it has decentralized management, so decisions are made locally and disputes should be settled locally; therefore, a class action suit covering all of Wal-Mart is not appropriate.[9] Wal-Mart's claim of a decentralized management seems to be contradicted by the compensation that its CEO H. Lee Scott received in 2003. Scott was among the highest paid executives in the United States when he "walked away with $23 million,"[10] certainly the salary of a central manager.

Wal-Mart's health benefits do not measure up to those of its competitors. A Georgia survey found that more than 10,000 children of Wal-Mart associates were in the state's health program for poor children, which cost taxpayers $10 million annually. A North Carolina hospital found that 31 percent of 1,900 patients who said they were Wal-Mart associates were on Medicaid, and another 10 percent of those patients had no insurance at all. Wal-Mart says 23 percent of its associates are not eligible for health insurance, and that it provides for 58 percent of its associates who are eligible. Those who do receive insurance are asked to pay 33 percent of the cost. Average pay for a full-time sales clerk is $1,000 a month (below the U.S. government poverty level for a family of four). From that, the clerk must pay an average of $200 each month for insurance, and many employees cannot afford that after paying for basic food and lodging for a family. In contrast, one of Wal-Mart's competitors, Costco, pays the entire cost of insurance for 96 percent of its eligible workers. Wal-Mart responds that their internal survey found that 90 percent of its employees have health insurance—many from spouses or parents. Wall Street approves of Wal-Mart's lower labor cost, and disapproves of Costco's high labor

---

[8]Jeffrey E. Garten, "Wal-Mart Gives Globalism a Bad Name," *Business Week,* March 8, 2004, p. 24; Anthony Bianco and Wendy Zellner, "Is Wal-Mart Too Powerful?" *Business Week,* October 6, 2003, pp. 100–110.
[9]"Wal-Mart Trial by Checkout: Facing a Giant Sex Discrimination Suit," *The Economist,* June 26, 2004; "No Way to Treat a Lady? As Sex Discrimination Suit Unfolds, Studies of Wal-Mart Practices Show a Big Gap in the Status of Men and Women," *Business Week,* March 3, 2003; "Attention Wal-Mart Plaintiffs: Hurdles Ahead," *New York Times,* June 27, 2004, p. BU5.
[10]"Another Stellar Year for Honchos," *Business Week,* December 27, 2004, p. 14.

costs, and it is reflected in both stock prices.[11] California suffered a long and bitter strike at several supermarket chains in 2004 when the older supermarkets attempted to cut health benefits and create a lower wage scale for entering employees in order to compete with Wal-Mart and avoid bankruptcy. Finally, Wal-Mart family heirs are the richest in the world, with a net worth estimated at $95.8 billion, and yet among philanthropists they are the most miserly; in their lifetime they have contributed only 1 percent of their wealth to charities, a small fraction of what many other wealthy persons or families have given.[12]

In summary, Wal-Mart is very popular with consumers and investors. Wal-Mart has even been given credit for keeping inflation down. It shares much information with suppliers. In the last few years, as its reputation began to suffer, it has begun to contribute to community projects. Wal-Mart provides low-wage jobs and few medical and retirement benefits. Its low-cost strategy has forced competitors to cut back on wages and medical and retirement benefits. Wal-Mart and other low-cost retailers are responsible for gutting the downtown small shopping areas of thousands of towns and cities across the United States. Low-cost goods are a notable benefit to purchasers, but one may question if this benefit is worth the price of so many "associates" being paid such low wages with few, if any, health or retirement benefits. It also seems fair to ask if Wal-Mart takes unfair advantage of its workers and suppliers.

## INFLUENCE OF BUSINESS VALUES

Wal-Mart and other firms have a strong influence on our goals, values, and lifestyles. People in other countries often consider American business the archetype of business. English has become the language of commerce. The United States has the largest markets, and has a strong influence on global business and personal values. Attitudes and values vary from one country to another. We will here focus on American business values, so that American and other businesspeople may better understand their own goals and values.

The goals, values, and ethics of business and businesspeople are important. Whether one can trust a handshake without a contract, or how one will be treated as a worker, depends on managers' ethics and values. Business ethics and values have a profound influence on our lives, including new products, workplace design, relationships among colleagues at work, and government regulations. People's ethics and values hold together the fabric of a firm and a culture. Moreover, work and the business firm are so central to our lives that they in turn strongly influence our personal goals and lifestyles. In the last few years we have seen in the headlines how the lack of ethics of some executives caused the collapse of dozens of firms, which resulted in the loss of hundreds of thousands of jobs, billions of dollars in savings and pensions, and widespread trust in business.

---

[11]Reed Abelson, "States Are Battling about Wal-Mart over Health Care," *New York Times,* November 1, 2004, pp. A1, A13.
[12]"The Most Generous Philanthropists," *Business Week,* November 29, 2004, p. 89.

In this first chapter we will explore ways in which values and ethics influence our lives and businesses. Later chapters will go into detail about how we develop moral maturity and make ethical choices, as well as the history behind the business values we hold today. For a definition of some terms that we will be using, see Figure 1-1. Values govern our personality and our actions. They undergird and direct the important decisions that each of us make. Whether we realize it or not, values profoundly influence our choices and our lives. To know our values allows us to possess greater control over our own actions and future.

A value system is at the foundation of personal and business decisions. Yet values become so much a part of us that we are generally unaware of their content and impact. An analogy might help. Consider the way we use a personal computer. As we learn to use the various programs, the procedures becomes habitual or automatic. Operating the computer—for word processing, accounting, inventory control, and other needs—becomes so much a part of us that we become explicitly aware of it only when we reflect on our actions, perhaps to

---

**FIGURE I-I**   Business, Values, and Ethics Terms

| | |
|---|---|
| *CEO* | Chief executive officer of an organization |
| *CFO* | Chief financial officer of an organization |
| *Common good* | The well-being of all the members of the community; the good of the entire society taken as a whole |
| *Conflict of interest* | A situation in which a person may gain personal benefit from actions she or he may take based on obligations the person is entrusted to manage |
| *Ethics* | The principles of conduct governing an individual or a group, and the methods for applying them |
| *Free market* | An unregulated economic market operating by free competition of buyers and sellers |
| *Goal* | The result toward which effort is directed; the end to be pursued |
| *Ideal* | An ultimate goal that an individual or a society holds for itself; a standard of perfection |
| *Ideology* | A cluster of values integrated into a comprehensive, coherent, motivating statement of purpose |
| *Market fundamentalism* | That all economic, social, and human interactions are contract-based and are measured by money |
| *Moral* | Dealing with or capable of distinguishing right from wrong |
| *Norm* | Criterion for distinguishing what is right from what is wrong, and what is correct from what is incorrect |
| *Morality* | The rightness or wrongness of principles, practices, and activities, along with the values and rules that govern them |
| *Value* | A lasting belief that a certain goal or mode of conduct is better than the opposite goal or conduct. |

teach another. Yet without knowing the procedures, it is impossible to accomplish the task. In a parallel fashion, not understanding personal values prevents us from fully understanding our own actions and the actions of others. In this chapter we examine some business firms and current business practices, focusing on the values that undergird them.

Free enterprise values are familiar to each of us. For example, freedom is a foundation value of the economy—free markets, free movement of people, free entry into new business, freedom to take or leave a job. This freedom parallels the freedom that we cherish in political life—democracy. The free enterprise system, stimulated by economic and political freedom, provides a multitude of benefits to Americans:

- An immense output of goods and services
- New jobs in the United States and around the world
- High standards of living available to the majority
- Great rewards for many, stemming from the skill, new ideas, and initiative of entrepreneurs
- The promotion of flexibility and innovation among people
- Reinforcement of the value of personal freedom

The many successes of free markets do not change the fact that serious problems exist in the free market system. It is vital to be aware of and find the root causes of these problems, if we expect to improve our businesses and our lives. The unethical and even criminal actions of some business managers which have been brought to light over the last decade have sobered our expectations and demanded that we try to understand what happened, so as to make such actions less likely in the future.

## Ethical and Financial Breakdowns

It seems that stories about ethical and legal business failures appeared almost daily in newspapers and on TV during the early years of the twenty-first century. The long list of executives that abused their power and position, committed fraud, and attempted to gain unearned personal wealth, has caused businesspeople and all Americans disappointment, embarrassment, and anger. Most American executives and firms have integrity. However, the list of those who do not is too long to ignore. The following is a partial list of some of those errant business executives. At Adelphia, John J. Rigas, founder and chief financial officer (CFO), and Timothy Rigas, CFO, were both convicted of securities, wire, and bank fraud. Andrew S. Fastow, CFO of Enron, pleaded guilty to fraud and is in prison; he is one of more than 20 former Enron executives who have either pled guilty or been indicted. Scott D. Sullivan, CFO of WorldCom, pled guilty to accounting fraud and is now in prison. WorldCom CEO Bernard Ebbers was convicted in federal court of fraud, conspiracy and filing false reports. Samuel D. Waksal, chief executive officer (CEO) of ImClone, pled guilty to securities fraud and insider trading and is serving 7 years in prison. Martin L. Grass of Rite Aid is serving 8 years for conspiracy and obstruction of justice. Frank P. Quattrone, key investment banker with Credit Suisse First Boston (CSFB), was convicted of obstruction of justice. Michael Sears, CFO of Boeing, pled guilty to bribing an Air Force procurement officer with a $250,000 a year job, so that she would steer $23 billion in contracts to Boeing.[13] CEO Martha Stewart and her broker Peter Bacanovic were both convicted and went to jail for conspiracy and obstruction of justice over selling Stewart's shares of ImClone. Indicted and awaiting trial at the time of this writing are Enron's Kenneth L. Lay, CEO, and Jeffrey K. Skilling, president;[14] and Richard M. Scrushy, CEO of HealthSouth. The trial of Tyco CEO Dennis Koslowski and CFO Mark H. Swartz ended in a mistrial.

Most of the previously mentioned executives participated in schemes involving hundreds of millions or even billions of dollars; Martha Stewart's lie was to cover up the $300,000 she received by selling ImClone stock before it fell. These are but a few of the more visible figures who have been involved in corporate crime in recent years. These well-educated and privileged people were more concerned with share price, growth, and their own power and wealth than with truth, honesty, and trustworthiness.[15]

Some say that these executives are but a few bad apples; however, lying and corruption seem to be widespread. Thus, others maintain that we have a more basic problem, due to the structure of the corporation itself, because it is given vast power and limited liability under U.S. law.[16] Even firms which ought to be the watchdog of ethics, such as accounting firms, seem to fall victim. Each of the major accounting firms had a conflict of interest in the affairs of the previously-mentioned corporations: The firms provided a clean audit to companies that were paying the auditing firms large consulting fees. Arthur Andersen was forced out of business because it gave a clean audit to numerous firms that reported false profits, such as Enron, WorldCom, and Waste Management.[17] General Motors unilaterally decided that it would no longer give its audit firm, Deloitte Touche Tohmatsu, consulting business, because of potential conflict of interest.[18] The accounting oversight and lobbying group, the American Institute of Certified Public Accountants, opposed many of the measures that eventually became law, thus losing much of its moral stature in the eyes of the public. Moreover, each of the major accounting firms sold tax avoidance to firms, as one more way to increase profits.[19]

Taxes are necessary to provide the public services that benefit all of us. Taxes are the price we pay for civilization; one cannot have a civilized society without

---

[13]Tim Weber, "Ex-Boeing Financial Chief Pleads Guilty to Felony: Conflict of Interest in Pentagon Dealings," *New York Times,* November 16, 2004, p. C2.

[14]Mimi Swartz with Sherron Watkins, *Power Failure: The Inside Story of the Collapse of Enron* (New York: Doubleday, 2003).

[15]Thomas L. Carson, "Self-Interest and Business Ethics: Some Lessons of the Recent Corporate Scandals," *Journal of Business Ethics* 43 (April 2003): 389–394.

[16]Ted Nace, *Gangs of America: The Rise of Corporate Power and the Disabling of Democracy* (San Francisco: Berrett-Koehler, 2003).

[17]For an account of the Arthur Andersen demise, see Barbara Ley Toffler, *Final Accounting: Ambition, Greed, and the Fall of Arthur Andersen* (New York: Broadway Books, 2003).

[18]Cassell Bryan-Low, "GM to End Consulting Projects with Deloitte Touche Tohmatsu," *Wall Street Journal,* April 7, 2003, p. 8.

[19]Lynnley Browning, "Suit Accuses KPMG and Others of Selling Illegal Tax Shelters," *New York Times,* August 17, 2004, p. C3.

the funds to pay for it. Even though government is often inefficient, it does provide necessary services. And yet many people in the United States try to avoid their taxes. Wealthy people and business firms have the power and influence to place provisions in the tax code that exempt them from paying their fair share of taxes. That leaves working poor and middle-class Americans to pay the bill for public services and defense. Corporations have benefited mightily from loopholes and tax avoidance schemes. A U.S. General Accounting Office investigation released in 2004 found that more than 60 percent of U.S. corporations, doing $2.5 trillion of business, paid no federal tax during the boom 1996–2000 years. Some 71 percent of foreign firms, having $750 billion of business in the United States, paid no U.S. taxes. The legislated U.S. corporate tax rate is 35 percent of profits. In the year 2000, among corporations with assets of at least $250 million, 45 percent paid no taxes, and another 35 percent paid less than 5 percent tax. By 2003, total tax revenue from corporations was 7.4 percent of federal tax receipts, the lowest rate since 1983 and the second lowest since 1934. In a parallel fashion, wealthy individuals pay little or no tax because they can hire advisors who use loopholes in the tax code to limit tax liability. Many object that it is not fair to give rich individuals and corporations special benefits to allow them to avoid their fair share of taxes.[20]

Still another public scandal involves the mutual fund industry, which has been guilty of a variety of unfair practices, from misleading investors to illegally providing hedge funds and other large investors better prices and access. These mutual funds also generated fees for themselves by excessively trading stocks at the expense of long-term investors. This places the average individual investor somewhere between being a second-class citizen and the victim of a scam. Bank of America and Fleet Boston, for example, paid $675 million in penalties for illegal investment procedures. New York Attorney General Eliot Spitzer noted that mutual fund companies have been penalized $1.65 billion so far. However, this sum amounts to only 2 percent of their forecasted combined earnings this year, and no senior executives of the firms have been held liable.[21]

Another industry manifesting corruption is Wall Street and financial firms. Huge financial firm salaries and bonuses testify to how they generate enormous fees for themselves, at the expense of their clients. The firms have been involved in a conflict of interest between the investment bank activities and their own financial analysts. Analysts have provided glowing reports on a firm's financial future, so that their bank could obtain the lucrative merger and acquisition investment business. Analysts and investment bankers have turned investing into

---

[20]See David Cay Johnson, *Perfectly Legal: The Covert Campaign to Rig Our Tax System to Benefit the Super Rich—and Cheat Everybody Else* (New York: Penguin, 2004); Mortimer Zuckerman, "An Intolerable Free Ride," *U.S. News and World Report,* May 17, 2004, p. 80; John D. McKinnon, "Over 60 Percent of Corporations Didn't Pay Taxes," *Wall Street Journal Online,* March 5, 2004.
[21]"America's Mutual Fund Scandal: A Big Legal Settlement Has More Bark Than Bite," *Economist,* March 20, 2004, p. 83; Paula Dwyer, "Breach of Trust: The Mutual-Fund Scandal Was a Disaster Waiting to Happen, an Inside Look at How the Industry Manipulated Washington," *Business Week,* December 15, 2003, pp. 98–108.

a game in which they always win and ordinary investors lose. The investment firms also have bribed CEOs with early shares of hot initial public offerings (IPOs), so that the business leaders will send them business. This has fueled a vast transfer of wealth from ordinary investors to Wall Street bankers and their CEO clients. Some examples: Merrill Lynch and CSFB agreed to pay $100 million to settle their cases. J.P. Morgan Chase, Morgan Stanley, Goldman Sachs, and Citigroup have all been involved in similar unfair activities.[22] Citigroup is the world's largest financial services company with 200 million customers in 100 countries and approximately 300,000 employees. It was ordered to close its private banking unit in Japan for a variety of violations of Japanese law, including money laundering. In the United States Citigroup has agreed to pay $2.65 billion to settle a suit by WorldCom shareholders who maintained that Citigroup's support gave WorldCom credibility in spite of its fraud. Citigroup has yet to settle with Enron shareholders. However, many are worried that the settlements will do little to change the culture of Wall Street.[23]

These scandals are not restricted to the United States. The European Union's major dairy provider—Italy's Paramalat—claimed to have $5.5 billion in a Bank of America account in the Cayman Islands that never existed; it is now in bankruptcy. Dutch Ahold, Japanese Snow Brand Milk Products, and others, including French, German, and Irish firms, have been involved in similar scandals.[24] These unethical and criminal activities are so widespread that many worry that they will undercut trust in business and the market system itself. Many thus ask: Is this the end of the flood of scandals, or are these high profile cases merely the beginning of an era marked by reduced ethics in business?

Americans were publicly warned several years earlier that the scandals were coming. Arthur Levitt, then chair of the U.S. Securities and Exchange Commission (SEC) saw the problem posed by "managed earnings" (falsification of accounting records), and warned that auditing firms were approving such false reporting. He tried to implement new SEC regulations that would have prevented some of the scandals, but most of his proposals were rebuffed.[25] He ran into a powerful lobby made up of corporations, stock analysts, and institutional investors that derailed the proposed regulations. Approximately a year after Levitt left the SEC, the Enron and WorldCom scandals broke, and almost all of his proposals were enacted into legislation.[26] Without trust, the market system does not work well, and may even collapse. Hence it is essential that we understand why these

---

[22]"Senators Question Effectiveness of $1.4 Billion Settlement," *New York Times,* May 8, 2003, p. C8.
[23]"Will It Matter: The Global Settlement," *Business Week,* May 12, 2003, pp. 30–34, 114; "It's Cleanup Time at Citi: A New CEO Aims to Overhaul the Superbank's Culture," *New York Times,* November 7, 2004, Sec. 3, p. 1; "Citi Starts to Settle," *Business Week,* May 24, 2004, p. 52.
[24]"Parma Splat: What Are the Lessons from the Scandal at Europe's Largest Dairy-Products Group?" *Economist,* January 17, 2004, pp. 59–61; and "The Year of Nasty Surprises: Suddenly the Continent Is Awash in Accounting Scandals," *Business Week,* March 10, 2003, pp. 48–49.
[25]On the fear, Kurt Eichenwald, "Could Capitalists Actually Bring Down Capitalism?" *New York Times,* June 30, 2002, pp. 1, 5; on the early ignored warning, Carol J. Loomis, "Lies, Damned Lies, and Managed Earnings: The Nation's Top Earnings Cop Has Put Corporate American on Notice: Quit Cooking the Books," *Fortune,* August 2, 1999, pp. 74–92.
[26]For his more recent reflections, see Arthur Levitt with Paula Dwyer, *Take on the Street: What Wall Street and Corporate America Don't Want You to Know* (New York: Pantheon, 2002).

scandals happened—for the sake of building a working and healthy market system, and to prevent such scandals in the future. Let us examine the case of CEO Dennis Kozlowski of Tyco, who appears not to have violated generally accepted accounting principles (GAAP). His first trial ended in a mistrial.

## Tyco and Dennis Kozlowski

Dennis Kozlowski grew up in a poor, integrated neighborhood in Newark, New Jersey, that has since been demolished. He graduated from Seton Hall University in 1968 with a major in accounting, and joined Tyco in 1975. Kozlowski was quickly promoted; as president of Tyco's Grinnell Fire Protection, Kozlowski cut salaries, but paid large bonuses to managers who produced improved earnings. He presented awards to the best performing managers and identified the worst performers at an annual company-wide banquet.

Kozlowski was made CEO of Tyco in 1992. For 27 years, Kozlowski was an effective and enterprising manager. His idol was Jack Welch of GE, who built share value by acquiring firms and cutting any unit that was not profitable enough. Kozlowski lowered Tyco's U.S. taxes from 35 percent of income to 18.5 percent by moving Tyco's headquarters to Bermuda. He also set up more than 100 finance subsidiaries for sheltering interest, dividends, royalties, and other income; thus Tyco could brag that in 2001, while it had 65 percent of its revenue from the United States, only 29 percent of its taxable income came from the United States.[27] Kozlowski appeared on the cover of *Business Week* in 2001, the feature of an article titled "The Most Aggressive CEO," and was named one of "America's Most Powerful People" by *Forbes*. In 1995 Kozlowski moved corporate headquarters from a small wooden building in Exeter, New Hampshire, to an expensive Manhattan office with spectacular views of Central Park. He also used Tyco funds to purchase a $16.8 million apartment for himself in Manhattan. Yet, for many years afterward, he told outsiders that the small Exeter building was corporate headquarters, and he bragged that in this low-cost corporate office, even the CEO did not have a reserved parking spot. Tyco's revenues increased an average of 48 percent annually from 1997 to 2001 and its pretax operating margins averaged 22 percent. As a reward, Kozlowski's own compensation went from $9 million in 1997, to $67 million in 1998, then to $170 million in 1999; this made him the second highest paid CEO in the United States.

Kozlowski grew Tyco's revenues by means of acquisitions, and he used numerous accounting tricks to inflate Tyco's earnings. One of the gimmicks involved firms about to be acquired. Before the acquisition Kozlowski arranged to reduce revenues for the firm and also charged not-yet-due expenses; thus after the acquisition Tyco could show artificially large revenues and lower expenses. From 1999 to 2001 Kozlowski acquired more than 700 companies, so that this trick added much to the bottom line. Another gimmick shifted funds from one account to another; this inflated the company's profits by $186 million from 1999

---

[27] Anthonly Bianco, William Symonds, and Nanette Byrnes, "The Rise and Fall of Dennis Kozlowski: How Did He Become So Unhinged by Greed?" *Business Week,* December 23, 2002, pp. 64–77.

to 2001, according to an internal Tyco report that was prepared for the board of directors after Kozlowski was arrested and fired.[28]

Kozlowski's personal expenditures drew much attention: examples are his $6,000 shower curtain for his apartment, the $110,000 hotel bill for a 13-day stay in London, and the $2 million birthday party for his new wife on the island of Sardinia—all charged as expenses to Tyco. By 2000 Kozlowski had homes in Boca Raton, Florida; Nantucket Island, Massachusetts; Beaver Creek, Colorado; and New York City. "Kozlowski laid out $29.8 million to build a mansion in Boca. . . . He topped off his collection of airplanes and speedboats by shelling out $15 million for a rare . . . vintage yacht."[29] He tried to avoid New York City's sales tax by shipping a $3.9 million painting destined for his New York apartment to New Hampshire, which has no sales tax. He divorced his wife of 29 years and in 2000 married the restaurant waitress for whom he threw the previously-mentioned birthday party.

Tyco now has a new CEO. Most of its businesses were salvageable. Kozlowski seems not to have committed the egregious fraud that we see among the CEOs at Enron, WorldCom, Global Crossing, and other firms, but he did engage in accounting "tricks" to fool investors. He also used Tyco funds for many personal expenses and illegally tried to avoid taxes. Moreover, while he claimed to be living simply—working out of a small wooden headquarters building in New Hampshire—he allowed himself to be caught up in an extravagant and greedy lifestyle. Which of Kozlowski's actions are those of a good CEO and which are not? From what you know, how would you evaluate his ethics? His moral maturity? From the Tyco example, can it be said that even accounting that follows the stated GAAP rules might still be unreliable at best and unethical and dishonest at worst?

## PROFITABILITY AND MARKETS

The press for greater efficiency, shedding businesses that are not profitable enough, and shifting businesses overseas to obtain lower labor costs characterizes most business in the previous decade. This has been done aggressively but perhaps legally by Wal-Mart; semi-legally and with accounting "tricks" at Tyco; and illegally by Enron, WorldCom, and Adelphia. In each of these instances, the impact on the people who were fired, outsourced, or lied to seems not to have been an important or determining consideration for managers. Does this mark a shift in ethics and values over this period? Is this shift a benefit to citizens in the United States? Is it a benefit to citizens in other countries?

### Shareholder Value

The principal objective of Sam Walton at Wal-Mart, Dennis Kozlowski at Tyco, Jack Welch at GE, and Bernard Ebbers at WorldCom was to increase shareholder

---

[28]"Tyco Admits That It Used Various Accounting Tricks to Inflate Its Earnings," *New York Times,* December 31, 2002, pp. A1, C2; Mark Maremont, "Finally, a CEO Faces a Jury: Kozlowski," *Wall Street Journal,* September 25, 2003, pp. C1, C10.
[29]Bianco et al., "The Rise and Fall of Dennis Kozlowski," p. 74.

value. Wall Street and investors demand this steady increase, and indeed force it as a goal on executives of publicly held firms. Wall Street analysts and the demand that the share price move steadily upward exert an extraordinary pressure on executives, their policies, and their actions. Institutional investors—mutual funds, pension funds, and endowments—represent the interests of more than a hundred million Americans, and they, also, press for constantly increasing returns. However, focusing on increasing shareholder value as the primary purpose of the firm leads managers to neglect their responsibilities to other stakeholders: employees, customers, suppliers, and the community.

Making increased shareholder value the primary purpose of the firm leads to a focus on short-term goals, and the neglect of long-term investment in people, plant, research, and development, even though the latter are essential to long-term growth and value creation.[30] Moreover, such focus elevates the role of shareholders above that of all other stakeholders of the firm.[31] For example, Jack Welch and Al Dunlap, CEOs at GE and Sunbeam, found that one way to keep shareholders happy was to lay off workers.

## Outsourcing Jobs and Layoffs

Until recently layoffs were considered to be a last resort for a firm, to be used only when every other strategy had failed and the firm could not pay the wages. Executives now tell their workers that their firm does not have a responsibility for their employment but only for their "employability." They encourage workers to keep their skills fresh, so that they may readily move to a new job. But during the boom period executives found that they could increase their share price by simply laying off workers to cut costs. These strategic layoffs have led to a break-down of the traditional employment contract that gave an employer loyalty and good performance in return for the employer's promise of employment, career, and retirement security.

Layoffs and outsourcing have several negative effects. First, lost jobs bring a loss of family income, increased anxiety, and health problems for the wage earner and for the entire family.[32] Social networks at work are destroyed, and marriages break up, triggered by the loss of jobs and income.[33] Second, layoffs reduce loyalty to the firm. From the time of the first layoff, people in the firm feel less security and have less long-term commitment to the organization. Workers continue to ask: Who is going to be next? Third, people who survive a layoff are expected to pick up the extra work. They are given "stretch goals" and are asked to "work smarter" with no new resources. Their tasks require more hours to accomplish, which often means they must work overtime at no extra pay. This then leaves less time for other human needs and interests, such as spouse, children, and

---

[30]Allan A. Kennedy, *The End of Shareholder Value: Corporations at the Crossroads* (Cambridge, MA: Perseus, 2000).
[31]Marjorie Kelly, *The Divine Right of Capital: Dethroning the Corporate Aristocracy* (San Francisco: Berrett-Koehler, 2003).
[32]Angelo J. Kinicki, Gregory E. Prussia, and Frances M. McKee-Ryan, "A Panel Study of Coping with Involuntary Job Loss," *Academy of Management Journal,* 43, no. 1 (2000): 90–100.
[33]Priti Pradhan Shah, "Network Destruction: The Structural Implications of Downsizing," *Academy of Management Journal,* 43, no. 1 (2000): 101–112.

recreation. Steve Kerr was GE's chief training officer; he called such additional demands on managers immoral, as in most cases the remaining workers were not provided the additional tools they needed to do the job.[34]

On the other hand, the few firms which have a no-layoff policy are doing well. Southwest Airlines has had such a policy for 30 years and is doing better financially than any other major airline. Southwest's president, James F. Parker, says, "We are willing to suffer some damage, even to our stock price, to protect the jobs of our people."[35] Other firms with a no-layoff policy include S.C. Johnson, Pela, FedEx, Lincoln Electric, and AFLAC. Executives at these firms argue that their no-layoff policy brings loyalty, higher productivity, and the motivation to suggest more efficient ways to do the job. Otherwise workers, fearing for their jobs, are afraid to make suggestions to improve their efficiency. Moreover, these firms also have an edge in recruiting talented workers. When layoffs are necessary, some firms have a policy that provides training and helps laid-off workers find other jobs. When Cisco Systems was forced to lay off 6,000 of its workers, the firm was innovative. If a laid-off worker agreed to work for a local nonprofit organization for a year, Cisco would provide one-third of their salary plus benefits and stock options, and that person would have priority to be rehired when business picked up.[36]

Using layoffs as a first solution to financial problems raises a question about the very purpose of the corporation. Should executives be responsible to workers, families, and the communities that share their risks, as well as to stockholders? "Any reform package that fails to rebalance power by addressing the legitimate needs and rights of employees to monitor executive behavior and protect their human capital investments fails to complete the job."[37] Reform legislation has largely been designed to correct accounting and financial problems. But the social capital and the competitive advantage that workers provide a firm are not recognized in the U.S. legislation that has been enacted so far.

In the United States we are narrowly focused on financial returns, and we measure that by increased wealth. Yet David Korten points out that real wealth actually resides in our resources: the people, the earth, and communities. He then shows how in the United States, we have been so intent on increasing the amount of money in hand that we have destroyed much of our real wealth. In the name of increasing wealth or shareholder value, we destroy not only social capital in the loyalty of workers, but also natural capital when we strip-mine, deplete forests and fisheries, or dump hazardous wastes; and communities in the way we design our cities and the individualistic manner in which people live.[38]

Competition in domestic and global markets is also a source of pressure for greater efficiencies. We witness the benefit of this at Wal-Mart, where "everyday low prices" enable us to purchase products at considerable savings. These low

---

[34]Interview with Steve Kerr, "Stretch Goals: The Dark Side of Asking for Miracles," *Fortune,* November, 13, 1995, pp. 231–232.

[35]"Where Layoffs Are a Last Resort," *Business Week,* October 8, 2001, p. 42.

[36]"Pink Slips with a Silver Lining," *Business Week,* June 4, 2001.

[37]Thomas A. Kochan, "Addressing the Crisis in Confidence in Corporations: Root Causes, Victims, and Strategies for Reform," *Academy of Management Executive,* 16, no. 3 (2002): 140.

[38]David Korten, "The Difference Between Money and Wealth: How Out-of-Control Speculation Is Destroying Real Wealth," *Business Ethics,* January 1999, p. 4.

prices are possible because Wal-Mart purchases products that are manufactured in low-wage countries. Global competition also stimulated the improved quality of the U.S.-made automobile. Two decades ago Japanese manufacturers achieved major market share in the United States largely because of better quality. In the face of that competition, Ford and GM have increased quality, offered warranties, and have largely bridged the quality gap. (The financial Gap was covered by tariffs)

Market pressures have encouraged the outsourcing of jobs by U.S. firms. This outsourcing involves everything from sweatshops making garments, shoes, toys, and other labor-intensive products to highly-trained people writing software for Microsoft in India. India has a surplus of well-educated young people. They speak English, and wage rates in India are a fraction of what they are in the United States.

Well-paying jobs are being lost, and labor unions, which protect workers' rights, yuck! now have less influence in the United States. Moreover, many of the jobs that are being added are in the low-paying service sector, such as hospitality—workers in restaurants, motels, and taxi drivers. Furthermore, even a well-paying job is not as secure as it was two decades ago. In the United States, skilled and unskilled workers are on notice that they should develop their abilities and keep themselves flexible. Being good workers is not enough to guarantee that their employer will keep them and provide for their retirement. Many technical jobs are also being sent overseas. Research and development activity is being outsourced by U.S. and European firms. Note that such outsourcing of jobs presents another danger: Sending design jobs to China or India risks the loss of intellectual property. Often the developed country's technology is taken and used to compete against the firm itself.

On the other hand, a person in India or Kenya needs a job perhaps even more than does the U.S. citizen. On a larger scale, the future stability of the world depends on the prosperity of people in many poorer nations, and prosperity comes with having a job. For example, one of the underlying causes of unrest and terrorism in Middle Eastern countries is the lack of jobs for the immense number of young, energetic males. The challenge is to encourage job and income growth that benefits both people in the United States and poorer people of the world.

For the sake of a healthy U.S. economy, incentives are called for—tax and otherwise—to keep many highly skilled jobs in the United States. Otherwise, American citizens will not be motivated to spend many years in graduate education, especially in the sciences and engineering, paths which are difficult and time consuming. Why spend 5 to 7 years obtaining a doctorate in these difficult fields if there is little prospect of obtaining a job and a decent salary? A shortage of talented people with these credentials would further the downward economic spiral for the United States.

This situation with all its difficulties has been summarized with stinging clarity by William Frederick, a preeminent business scholar and former dean of the University of Pittsburgh Graduate School of Business:

> Global free market capitalism is rampant, violating cultural borders as it has long done, repeating many of 19th century capitalism's worst excesses, at times exploiting Third World workers, raping the globe's environments, stripping away ecological diversity, overworking the earth's fertile soils,

amassing and hoarding and wielding mammoth fortunes, recruiting the West's armed might to secure existing markets and to open new ones, manipulating world financial institutions to promote market-centered economics, resisting full-scale, good-faith United States participation in regional and international environmental compacts and supporting various saber-rattling and saber-wielding policies of governments here and abroad. Clearly, one cannot treat business actions as if they are separated from today's major geopolitical struggles, because the actions taken by governments often mirror the interests of business.[39]

Frederick wrote this shortly before September 11, 2001 and the bankruptcy of Enron that wiped out jobs and pensions for most of the 20,000 worldwide employees of the firm. The largest bankruptcy in U.S. history, WorldCom, occurred just a few months later. These, plus many other fraud revelations, shocked the nation and the world, and give additional weight to Frederick's warnings.

## LIVING SHORT TERM

Americans consume much and save little. We purchase fashionable clothes and autos, and go into debt to pay for them. We enjoy the convenience of our credit cards, but then are often unable to pay the amount due. Average American credit card debt is now more than $4,000. Providing the consolidation of credit card debt, using a home as collateral, is a huge new industry. When we hear radio ads for obtaining cash "even if your credit is not perfect," we rightly should worry about the high interest rates and the indebtedness that follows. Advertising and social pressure stimulate our need to possess things and thus to demonstrate to others that we are successful. We make our success clear to our neighbors by means of the goods we have: a larger house, a bigger car, and more expensive clothes. After the many products and services we buy, we have little to save. Yet savings are essential to the economy.

Savings are the lifeblood of the business system. Savings provide the funds for investment in new plants, research, and creativity. But our American propensity to use almost all of our discretionary income to purchase goods provides us minimal savings. After the September 11, 2001 attack on New York and Washington, Americans were told to buy more goods to pull the economy out of its lethargy. Thus in 2003 the savings rate of U.S. households fell to 0.6 percent of after-tax income, which is close to an all-time low.[40] This also presents a problem for the future of families, because many do not have adequate pension plans. Some have no pension funds at all. And, given takeovers and bankruptcies, those who do have a pension cannot always depend on it.

---

[39]William C. Frederick, "Notes for a Third Millennial Manifesto: Renewal and Redefinition in Business Ethics," *Business Ethics Quarterly,* 10, no. 1 (2000): 156–157.
[40]James C. Cooper and Kathleen Madigan, "The National Piggy Bank Is Going Hungry: A Low Savings Rate Threatens Boomers' Retirement—And Long-Term Growth," *Business Week,* September 20, 2004, p. 29.

Growth in productivity requires new investment, but new investment is limited by the amount of capital available. The lack of personal savings means that less capital is available for investment. Too, the U.S. federal government currently demands increasing amounts of capital, because of its large budget deficits, so that of the capital available, less is available for private investment. This spawns an increase in interest rates, and borrowing thus becomes more expensive for business, individuals, and government. Because of the demand for capital and lack of savings in the United States, we must borrow more than two-thirds of the capital we need from abroad. If productivity in the United States declines because of a lack of capital at affordable interest rates, the entire economy will likely slow, thus threatening future jobs and pensions. Increased personal consumption, minimal personal savings, increased federal deficits, and larger personal and federal debt cause both short- and long-term problems for individuals and for the nation. Both personal and government behavior stems from short-sighted, self-interested values that might be characterized as an attitude of "let someone else worry about it."

## Managers Measuring Progress

In a large firm, it is difficult for top management to be acquainted with specific products, markets, or employees. Given the greater distance from customers, new product ideas, production, and the public, executives turn to what they *can* understand—the control mechanism at their fingertips—"the numbers." Managers largely rely on share price, return on equity, market share, total capitalization, and other numerical indices of success. Focusing on short-term measurable results can lead managers to reduce funding on elements that may benefit the firm in the long term, such as research, risk-taking, and training programs.

In sum, a principal cause of fraud, lack of loyalty, lack of innovation, and short-sighted management is an emphasis on short-term goals. Managers, like all of us, are tempted to take the easy way out; they prefer short-term, measurable results so that their personal record looks good. Short-term, self-centered motives also breed unethical behavior.

## Trust in Corporate Executives

Americans have little confidence in corporations or in corporate executives. On the one hand, this should not come as a surprise, given recent fraud and scandals. On the other hand, trust is essential for any institution and for that institution's leaders, especially in a democracy. When Americans are asked, not many institutions gain much support, but the low point to which business has fallen is notable. Two polls show this lack of confidence. In 2003 only 6 percent of Americans had "a great deal" of confidence in large corporations; in 2004, only 12 percent expressed "a lot of confidence in executives of large corporations."[41] Business cannot exist without trust, and such a low level of trust spells trouble for business and business executives.

---

[41]The first poll in 2003 was reported in "How Much Confidence Do You Have in These Institutions?" *Trusteeship,* November/December 2003, p. 9; the second in 2004 was done by Barna Research Group.

**TABLE 1-1** Attitudes of Graduate Business Students on Issues Underlying the Business System

| | *Percentage Agreeing\** | | | | | |
|---|---|---|---|---|---|---|
| | *1974* | *1981* | *1983* | *1988* | *1996* | *2004* |
| 1. Business is overly concerned with profits and not concerned enough with public responsibilities | 75% | 70% | 51% | 66% | 69% | 60% |
| 2. Our foreign policy is based on narrow economic and power interests | 70% | 75% | 54% | 53% | 38% | 64% |
| 3. Economic well-being is unjustly and unfairly distributed | 80% | 34% | 34% | 42% | 38% | 51% |
| 4. The real power in the United States rests with | | | | | | |
| a. the Congress | 52% | 61% | 69% | 61% | 66% | 56% |
| b. the giant corporations and financial institutions | 81% | 88% | 87% | 89% | 88% | 79% |
| c. the public | 43% | 45% | 56% | 50% | 50% | 40% |

\* *Graduate business students from author's classes at Wayne State University (1974), at the University of Detroit (1981, 1983, 1988), and at the University of Detroit Mercy (1996, 2004).*

Graduate business students' attitudes on some of these issues are shown in Table 1-1. Among these students only 40 percent now indicate that the real power in the country rests with the public. This is the lowest this number has been in the last 30 years, and it indicates a significant feeling of powerlessness. Also noteworthy is the 51 percent who feel that "economic well-being is unjustly and unfairly distributed." This is the highest percentage of graduate business students that have felt this way since the "rebel" years of the early 1970s. Almost two-thirds feel that "U.S. foreign policy is based on narrow economic and power interests." This attitude is stronger than it has been in more than 20 years. The percentage of business students that have consistently said that the real power in the United States rests with giant corporations and financial institutions remains high in spite of the scandals and the resulting loss of confidence in business. These students indicate that they believe corporate executives have the most power in the United States, and that it is being exercised for the executives' own interests.

Cynicism among these students is as apparent now as it was in the 1970s. These business students average 28 years of age, and most have worked at several full-time jobs. If these graduate business students are so disillusioned, the general population is probably even more so. This cynicism is promoted by advertising, since advertising claims are often exaggerated and sometimes untrue. We have become accustomed to consumer products being glamorized beyond what is believable.

## ADVERTISING AND MEDIA SHAPE VALUES

Abercrombie & Fitch (A&F), the clothing retailer, published a racy magazine/catalogue beginning in 1997. Its target audience was teenagers and young adults. The magazine included photos of nude and nearly nude young models. Its 280-page

*Christmas Field Guide* in 2003 featured the title "Group Sex" on its cover. To push its line of apparel, the *Guide* rarely pictured clothing, but used images of listless, barely-clothed young people in an attempt to project an image of cutting-edge counterculture. Pro-family and feminist groups protested the *Guide,* and called for a boycott of A&F. In the wake of the protests, A&F withdrew the *Guide* in 2004. A&F sales have been dropping steadily for more than a decade.

The president of Citizens for Community Values placed an ad in the *Wall Street Journal* urging people to sell their A&F stock. When he learned that A&F had dropped the *Guide* he said that it "doesn't change a thing … They have a track record of sexual exploitation and there are many different ways to continue that campaign." He and leaders of other groups have asked to meet with executives of A&F to discuss their advertising, but executives have refused. A&F judged that its magazine would give it a cutting-edge image, but found that "in terms of its racy content, it became harder and harder to outdo themselves, to provoke, to generate reaction, and to create the excitement of the past."[42] Is this another type of "race to the bottom" in order to obtain the attention of the potential purchaser? What does this tell us about sexually explicit advertising? Do such actions hurt the common good? Let us examine the purpose of advertising.

Advertising is the communication link between retailer and consumer. Without advertising, the prospective purchaser is not aware of the price, quality, and availability of goods and services that might be of benefit. A free market requires a free flow of information, and advertising provides a major portion of the information that is essential to consumers.

Looking at advertising from the consumer's viewpoint, the purpose of advertising is to provide information that will help that consumer make or refuse to make a purchase decision. From the standpoint of the seller, the purpose of advertising is to convince people to purchase the product or service. As an example, one wonders why the consulting firm Accenture placed so much of its advertising budget into pictures of professional golfer Tiger Woods. Does golfing have anything to do with consulting? Is a prospective client of Accenture going to believe that there is a connection? Perhaps we are more gullible than we care to believe. The success of advertising is demonstrated by the fact that $160 billion is spent on it each year in the United States; more than $400 billion is spent annually on advertising worldwide.

Advertisers use a variety of approaches as they attempt to influence the purchasing decisions of consumers. Some advertising is informative and tasteful, and supports the values of individual responsibility, family, community, and sustainability. Note the British Petroleum (BP) and Shell ads on how they are investing in renewable sources of power and clean air. GE now advertises its commitment to wind and solar energy, and GE diesel and jet engines that use less fuel and produce less noise and pollution. Recall the Gallo TV ads which feature birthdays, weddings, baptisms, and other family-oriented activities. On the other hand, some advertising is self-oriented and sexist, encouraging anti-women macho attitudes.

---

[42]David Carr and Tracie Bozhon, "Abercrombie & Fitch to End Its Racy Magazine," *New York Times,* December 10, 2003, pp. C1, C8.

Some ads are deceptive, crude, and demeaning. People become suspicious and cynical about products that are thus advertised.

## Children Are Targets

Advertisers target children, knowing that this is a successful technique. Many school lunchrooms are like fast-food courts lined with soft-drink dispensers containing products which contribute to obesity among young people.[43] Moreover, 40 percent of U.S. teens get TV news and ads piped into their classrooms. Also, firms influence curricula by providing free materials. Exxon tells students that solar and wind energy is costly and unattainable, and the American Coal Foundation tells them that "the earth could benefit rather than be harmed from increased carbon dioxide."

By the age of 2, children begin to ask for products by their brand name. Marketers want these children to nag their parents for their products. Though 98 percent of the requests may be denied, the ad campaign pays off if the other 2 percent result in purchases of the product. The average child sees 40,000 commercials and receives 70 new toys each year. Children then want more and more things. Some parents report that they have had to expand their home to hold new toys. Marketers know that kids are now big business; in 1984 kids 4 to 12 years old spent $4.2 billion a year, but in 2004 they spent $35 billion—much of it at stores designed just for them. Marketers have developed a new vocabulary to describe kid marketing. Some examples: *Nag Factor* (or *Pester power, nudge factor, leverage*) refers to kids nagging parents to the point of purchase. *Shut-up toys* are toys costing $5 or less which are bought in desperation to pacify a child begging for something more expensive. *Viral marketing* uses cool kids to persuade their peers to purchase a product. Polls of parents show that 70 percent say kids are too focused on buying things, and 85 percent would like more limits on advertising to kids.[44] Some people applaud these techniques, saying that they simply demonstrate the freedom and creativity of the market system. But most people believe that such marketing takes advantage of uncritical children at an impressionable age and makes them victims of strategies designed to exploit them.

Marketers even pay cool alpha boys to push products, and find "It" girls to host slumber parties and then urge their friends to purchase products. Researcher Juliet Schor calls such marketers "predatory." These marketers' subtle message to children is that their meaning and self-worth comes from acquiring and owning. However, Schor's research shows that the more involved children become in the world of buying goods, the more likely they are to be depressed, anxious, have lower self-esteem, and have more psychosomatic complaints and poorer relationships with parents.[45]

---

[43]Neil Buckley, "Health Lobby Aims to Burst School Soft-Drinks Bubble: School Boards Have Come to Rely on Income from Exclusive Sales Deals," *Financial Times*, August 3, 2003, p. 12.
[44]Katy Kelly and Linda Kulman, "Kid Power: We All Want the Best for Our Children. But When They're Driving the Shopping Cart, How Much Is Too Much?" *U.S. News and World Report*, September 13, 2004, pp. 47–31.
[45]Juliet B. Schor, *Born to Buy: The Commercialized Child and the New Consumer Culture* (New York: Scribner, 2004).

Numerous other firms have self-centered advertising themes geared to children and their elders. Burger King claims, "Sometimes, you gotta break the rules." Neiman Marcus says, "Relax, no rules here." Bacardi Black Rum promises to take the drinker to a tipsy night where anything goes: "Some people embrace the night because rules of the day do not apply." Do these ads of Burger King, Neiman Marcus, and others promote, as one critic put it, "self-obsession, narcissism, and contempt for all rules"? Do they "strike at the sense of connectedness that any society needs to cohere and to care about its common problems and least fortunate members?"[46] These advertising strategies encourage materialism and self-centeredness and make it more difficult for us to develop common values in order to face our common problems.

In spite of its goal of global dominance of sports equipment and its immense marketing budget, Nike was not an official sponsor for the 1996 Olympic games in Atlanta nor for later Olympic games, where it cost up to $40 million to become an official sponsor. Nevertheless, Nike did run a series of TV ads during the Atlanta games in which Olympic athletes it had under contract were featured in Olympic-looking surroundings. IBM sponsored the official Web site. But before the Olympics, Nike announced a "sports-oriented official Web site cunningly called @lanta." The Atlanta committee for the Olympic games considered suing Nike for its deceit and attempt to get free exposure at the Olympic games at the expense of legitimate sponsors.[47] Nike's cheap antics with regard to the Olympic games, its self-centered advertising themes, and the sweatshop wages that it early supported are examples of the values that Nike communicates to us.

Calvin Klein runs a series of ads in magazines and on buses with young teens posing in "what looks like opening scenes in a porn movie." In one ad, a girl is shown lying down with her skirt up, exposing her panties. In another shot a young curly-headed boy is shown gazing out sadly from his crotch, as if looking for his next sexual relationship.[48] Sex is offered casually and as a commodity, but this is normal advertising copy for Calvin Klein. What effect does such advertising have on our values and morals?

## Advertising Affects Values

Given the magnitude and pervasiveness of advertising, its effect on our values and the values of our children should concern us. However, it is difficult to clearly demonstrate that advertising affects our values. Advertisers do try to convince us that if we feel unattractive, ill, or unhappy, they have just the right product for us; something we can buy can solve our problems. In order to sell, advertisers often intentionally appeal to materialism, lack of self-esteem, social status, and fear of ridicule.

Marketers have been accused of being creators of dissatisfaction. They present the handsome, immaculately dressed woman or man as an ideal to strive for; yet the ideal does not exist in the real world. Striving for such an ideal can result

---

[46]John Leo, "Not Too Calvinist," *Responsive Community,* Fall 1995, pp. 12–14.
[47]"Is Nike Playing Olympic Games?" *Business Week,* July 1, 1996, p. 4.
[48]Leo, "Not Too Calvinist."

in unattainable expectations and frustrations, especially for the young and impressionable. Is it not shallow and dehumanizing to judge a person by the style of his or her clothes? Moreover, such advertising sets persons up to be grievously disappointed when they discover that money, possessions, and power do not bring happiness.

Obviously, advertising does encourage consumption.[49] Marketing and advertising in their promotion of an affluent lifestyle present an image of Americans as materialistic, superficial, and self-centered. This image is projected throughout the world, so it is not surprising that people in Asia, Africa, Latin America, and the Middle East see Americans as materialistic, selfish, and interested largely in ourselves and not in others.

Marketing firms sell not only products, but political candidates as well. Advertising firms provide pictures of a political candidate in a 30-second TV ad in order to get us to vote for him or her. In place of seeing a political leader giving an explanation of a complex issue, we are subjected to carefully crafted images, with carefully chosen film footage and sound overlays. We are not introduced to a person, but rather presented an image, and are expected to vote on the basis of that image. Just as troubling, such a strategy communicates that complex issues are simple and easy to resolve, given a certain ideology. This is not only false but it implicitly denies that citizens need to be informed. It also undermines the patience to do the hard work that is required to intelligently vote in a democracy.

Advertisers tell us that they do not create values; they merely build on the values that they find already present. Successful advertising does appeal to our existing values. Nevertheless, advertising can reinforce and solidify childish, self-centered, and materialistic values latent in all of us. It does this especially among the less mature. In addition, advertising promotes national brands, so it encourages people to value Coke over juices, Fritos over vegetables, Porsches over people, fashionable clothes over art, and soap operas over reading. Along with its positive contributions of information in the free market, advertising also promotes shallowness, acquisitiveness, and egoism.

Advertisers also tell us that they do not influence our values. They say they are professionals, and they merely offer their skills without regard to the merits of a particular product or firm. However, this is an unacceptable moral position. Products, firms, and advertising strategies differ widely. Some products are worthwhile; others are trivial or even dangerous. Some firms treat customers and employees well; others do not. Some advertising campaigns are informative and humane, while others are manipulative and even deceptive.[50] Video games can be educational, or violent and anti-social; the number of "mature" games is increasing. One game, "Grand Theft Auto: Vice City," sold 1.5 million copies in its first three days on sale. It casts the player as a gangster gunman with complete disregard for any laws.[51]

---

[49]Thomas Princen, Michael Maniates, and Ken Conca, eds., *Confronting Consumption* (Cambridge, MA: MIT Press, 2003).
[50]See Gene R. Laczniak and Patrick E. Murphy, *Marketing Ethics: Guidelines for Managers* (Lexington, MA:Lexington Books, 1985).
[51]"Video Games: Strong Players," *Economist,* December 14, 2002, p. 60.

Television and films are major vehicles for advertising. TV advertising supports programming and enables networks to be profitable. When a specific product is given a prominent place in a film, the film producer is usually paid, because marketers know that if you see a certain brand of beer or car in a film, you are more likely to purchase it. CBS carried the 2004 Super Bowl. At halftime, Janet Jackson and Justin Timberlake sang. At the end of the song, Timberlake tore off Jackson's top, exposing her breast. The Super Bowl has an immense number of viewers—many of them children. Many people were shocked at the exposure. CBS and Viacom said that it was a surprise to them, and they had not pre-approved the action. Yet prior to the halftime show both had hyped the coming show as "shocking." The event set off Congressional hearings and a Federal Communications Commission (FCC) investigation. In the wake of threatened FCC and legislative sanctions, CBS and the other networks promised to clean up their programming. Such manipulative programming and advertising contributes to people's cynicism and distrust of business. Indeed, a worldwide poll revealed that 45 percent of executives conceded that their corporations did not deserve the loyalty of their customers.[52]

*pure loyalty*

## WHY SOME FAIL

Let us return to the values of free enterprise. We have sketched that free enterprise encourages competition, innovation, and growth, and at the same time short-term, self-centered, materialistic attitudes. The intrusion of government brings about inefficiencies and additional costs, and also discourages flexibility and creativity. The growth of a sense of personal entitlement encourages laziness, often expressed as "I have a right to an education and/or a job." The self-interest of businesses seems to encourage personal self-interest, so that some people feel that they should do the least amount of work for the best possible pay. These attitudes undermine business and our society in the minds of many.

A distinguishing feature of democratic capitalism and the entrepreneurial spirit is that they encourage individuals to be the principal source of social and economic activity.[53] In fact, the past success of democratic capitalism in North America and Western Europe put those countries in a vulnerable position: They are envied by poorer peoples and criticized as exploitative. Moreover, affluent parents who grew up in poverty do not know how to raise their children in affluence, and these children can become pampered and lazy. Both heavy-handed government and a personal sense of entitlement (or excessive self-interest) blunt the spirit of innovation and the attitudes that encourage the entrepreneur and business in general.

### Self-Interest as a Personal Goal

Business ideology holds that when individuals and firms pursue their own self-interest, market forces and the "invisible hand" bring about the most efficient use

[52]"The Stat," *Business Week,* March 8, 2004, p. 14.
[53]Michael Novak, "Toward a Theology of the Corporation," in *Business and Society: Dimensions of Conflict and the Corporation,* ed. P. Sethi and C. Falbe (Lexington, MA: Lexington Books, 1987), pp. 1–20; see also Novak's *The Spirit of Democratic Capitalism* (New York: Simon & Schuster, 1982).

of resources and result in the greatest satisfaction of peoples' needs. According to this ideology of self-interest, the best that Intel can do for society is to provide quality chips at a low price and, in so doing, provide a good return to shareholders. This is Intel's contribution to society. If Intel fails in this, it is a failure as a business firm.

The ideology of self-interest has worked well for generations in the United States. And on many counts, it is still working well. It is justified by economic theory and blessed by the Protestant ethic, which we will examine in Chapter 4. Individuals and businesses pursuing their own self-interests have brought goods and services, jobs, family income, and wealth to Western Europe, Japan, the United States, and now China, India, and other nations. Acquisitiveness, coupled with creativity, has made these economies successful. The ideology of self-interest acknowledges that people tend to be selfish. Capitalism, or free enterprise, builds on this self-centered motivation and directs it to work for the benefit of the entire society. Nobel Prize–winning economist Milton Friedman is still the intellectual  spokesperson for the ideology of self-interest, and we will consider his views in greater detail in Chapter 6.[54]

Many claim that economic goals—that is, increasing productivity, personal income, gross national product, and the availability of more and better goods and services—are the most important goals of our society. As U.S. President Calvin Coolidge put it just before the Great Depression of the 1930s, "The business of America is business." One of the most valuable features of the free market is the potential for creating jobs. In a noteworthy case, Mohammad Yunus and his vision of micro-lending have provided work and income for 60 million poor, illiterate women in developing countries, as we will see in Chapter 9. Most jobs are created by entrepreneurs who are creative, who plan for the long term, and who take risks.[55]

On the other hand, self-interest as a personal motivation has its negative aspects, and can even become pathological. Note this graphic description of how this motivation can be perverted:

> Bald, disrespectful, and single-minded aggressiveness that is understood to be destructive in other circumstances has become celebrated in corporate trenches as "competitiveness." Angry egocentric lust for power that would qualify as tyranny in politics has been elevated to "strategic mastery" and "leadership" in business. And a runaway greed has been sanctioned as "wealth creation," making heroes out of billionaire workaholics.[56]

Given the greed and fraud among business executives early in the twenty-first century, is this an accurate description of those aggressive, competitive business managers, or is it one-sided and biased?

---

[54]Milton Friedman and Rose Friedman, *Free to Choose: A Personal Statement* (New York: Harcourt Brace Jovanovich, 1980).

[55]For examples, see Jim Collins, *Good to Great: Why Some Companies Make the Leap and Others Don't* (New York: HarperCollins, 2001).

[56]John Dalla Costa, *The Ethical Imperative: Why Moral Leadership Is Good Business* (Reading, MA: Addison-Wesley, 1998), p. 37.

Two of the major problems spawned by business and industrialization are sweatshops and pollution, and both continue to be serious problems. We will discuss both issues in later chapters, but for now let us point out that exploitative workplaces and trashing the environment reduce costs, and so are bred by short-term self-interest. It is in the short-term best interest of firms to use cheap child labor and not to pay for the safe disposal of toxic waste, even though these actions injure people and society. The pursuit of self-interest generates these problems, so one can hardly expect that same motive to bring a solution. Thus we must find more complete goals and values in order to have decent workplaces and a livable environment. To narrow the purpose of the firm to making a profit for shareholders is short-sighted. Kenneth Mason, when president of Quaker Oats, said that making a profit is no more the purpose of a corporation than getting enough to eat is the purpose of life. Getting enough to eat is a requirement of life. Life's purpose is broader and more challenging. It should be possible to say the same about business and profit.

Moreover, an exclusive focus on self-interest can breed a selfrighteousness in pursuing narrow goals that result in indifference to consequences. These attitudes are described flippantly as "creative greed." Consider the values and tactics of men we will examine later: Charles Hurwitz of Pacific Lumber, Jack Welch of GE, and Sanford Weil of Citigroup. Each of these men looked to short-term self-interest, and their actions injured many other people. Critics note that our society idolizes men who are aggressive in their greed; it rewards them with money, power, and status, and thus reinforces selfishness and narrowness of vision.

Some corporate CEOs perceive MBA graduates as self-centered and not to be trusted. James Burke, a Harvard MBA himself who was CEO of Johnson & Johnson, says:

> In my business I'd as soon take a python to bed with me as hire a [Harvard MBA]. He'd suck my brains, memorize my Rolodex and use my telephone to find some other guy who'd pay him twice the money ...  The problem begins with the selection process. If you lean heavily on test scores, you necessarily end up with people who are very adept at quantification. And human nature being what it is, people who are good at numbers tend to put a lot of faith in numbers. Which means that kids are coming out of business schools with less and less language skills, less and less people skills, and more and more to unlearn. The really important decisions don't have anything to do with quantification, as everyone figures out — eventually.[57]

Defenders of the ideology of self-interest respond that they speak of "enlightened" self-interest: that is, self-interest taken over the long term. They maintain that it is in the long-term self-interest of a manager and a firm to produce high-quality goods in order to maintain the loyalty of customers. Similarly, it is in the long-term

[57]Laurence Shames, *The Big Time: The Harvard Business School's Most Successful Class and How It Shaped America* (New York: Mentor, 1986), pp. 181–182.

self-interest of a manager and a firm to provide healthy and open working conditions that help to hold able workers. Financial contributions to universities and community groups are justified on the basis that they will eventually provide a benefit to the firm and the firm's community. Indeed, evidence shows that a firm that obeys the law, is more socially responsible, and contributes more to charities does have better financial performance.[58]

Money and wealth are instruments to help people live a happier life. Business is the mechanism that brings jobs, goods, and services to people. Therefore money and business are not ends in themselves. When money and wealth become ends in themselves, ethics and priorities are bent to serve those goals. Spelling out the cost of this skewing of purpose: "Capitalism without a context in a humane community would seem to inevitably shape people into greedy and insensitive human beings."[59]

## Free Market Fundamentalism

George Soros, who made billions on hedge funds, is convinced that the problems discussed in this chapter stem largely from the elevation of self-interest to a moral principle, and that this has corrupted business, politics, and personal decisions. Self-interest as a guiding principle—an ideology—for personal and group activities has become dominant, especially in the United States. This ideology Soros calls "market fundamentalism." He defines market fundamentalism as: All social activities and human interactions are viewed as transactional, contract-based relationships and valued in terms of a single common denominator, money. All economic and social activities should be regulated only by the invisible hand of profit-maximizing competition, and by government as little as possible. Market fundamentalists are convinced that markets are self-correcting and that any attempt to ensure the common good or the collective interest of the community distorts the market mechanism, reduces efficiency, and is ultimately ruinous.

Soros is convinced that the incursions of such market ideology even into fields far outside business are having destructive social effects. As an example, he makes a distinction between "making the rules" and "playing by the rules," which is instructive for both the individual citizen and the business manager. Making the rules involves the decision of the group in an attempt to determine what is best for the public interest or the common good; in a democracy this is done through the political process. Market behavior is guided by playing by the rules. But Soros says:

> Unfortunately the distinction is rarely observed. People seem largely to vote their pocketbooks and they lobby for legislation that serves their personal interests. What is worse, elected representatives also frequently

[58]Michelle Conlin, Lauren Gard, and Jessi Hempel, "America's Top Philanthropists," *Business Week,* November 29, 2004, pp. 86–94; Richard E. Wokuch and Barbara A. Spence, "Corporate Saints and Sinners: Philanthropy, Crime and Organizational Performance," *California Management Review* 29 (Winter 1987): 62–77.

[59]Oliver F. Williams, C.S.C., "To Enhance the Common Good: An Introduction," *Common Good and U.S. Capitalism* (Lanham, MD: University Press of America, 1987), p. 5.

put their personal interests ahead of the common interest. Instead of standing for certain intrinsic values, political leaders want to be elected at all costs—and under the prevailing ideology of market fundamentalism, or untrammeled individualism, this is regarded as [a] natural, rational and even perhaps desirable way for politicians to behave.[60]

This results in the corruption of the political process, which in turn lessens respect for government. This then paradoxically becomes the strongest argument in favor of giving markets even freer reign. Soros acknowledges that markets are more efficient than the political process. Or, put another way, the failure of politics "is much more pervasive and debilitating than the failure of the market mechanism"; yet one of the principal reasons for the failure of the political process is self-centered individualism. Soros's principal concern is that global markets and global capitalism are not working well. He is convinced that the failures he describes have rendered global capitalism unstable, and he has devoted much of his effort and great fortune to encouraging the establishment of a more open society that is available to all.[61] We will discuss his critique as it applies to global free markets in Chapter 9. Let us now turn to how we might restore trust in business.

## RESTORING TRUST TO BUSINESS

Concentrating on freedom and personal self-interest makes cooperation, commitment, and community more difficult. One of the most basic human needs is to share joys, problems, and hopes with others. Our deep-rooted values of individualism and self-interest, which support a free enterprise system, can nevertheless fracture community and turn the individual in on itself.[62] The business firm values the person who is mobile, energetic, creative, and ambitious. People like this were attracted to the New World and thrived here in succeeding generations. However, we have rarely acknowledged the negative qualities of such people. Granted, the New World gained the energetic and the daring; but it also drew more than its share of the rootless, the unscrupulous, those who value money over people, and those who put self-interest before love and loyalty. These values encourage people who, when faced with a difficult situation, abandon it all and flee to a new environment. The qualities that we value so highly—mobility and willingness to take risks—encourage us to flee the difficult situation in the hope of leaving our problems behind when we begin again. We have all seen lives and careers shattered when a person walks out on a firm, on friends, or on family. Note the large number of biological fathers who are delinquent in their child support payments. It is easier to escape long-term responsibility in the tolerant, freedom-loving United States, if one has a mind to do so.

---

[60]George Soros, *The Crisis of Global Capitalism* (New York: Public Affairs, 1998), p. xxvi.
[61]George Soros, *Open Society: Reforming Global Capitalism* (New York: Public Affairs, 2000).
[62]Paul Krugman, *The Great Unraveling: Losing Our Way in the New Century* (New York: W.W. Norton, 2003).

## Integrity and Sanctions

Returning to the corporate financial scandals and frauds: How could so many businesses and executives have failed so grievously even during the overheated late 1990s? The Enron and WorldCom bankruptcies, and most of the others, were the results of deliberate attempts to obscure the truth—so that the firm looked more profitable and healthy than it actually was. There is a powerful incentive in the free market to look profitable, even if one is losing money. As long as analysts and investors can be convinced that profits are steadily increasing, share price also increases. Increasing share price means that the firm can borrow more in order to acquire more firms, and thus increase revenue. What values were present that brought about these failures?

A root cause of the previously-mentioned financial and ethical failures was a lack of honesty. Chief financial officers at each firm found themselves with a conflict of interest. They were willing to hide expenses and invent or exaggerate revenues. There was a short-term incentive for them to make the firm look more profitable. A second motivation was greed. In most of the previously-mentioned instances, the executives had lucrative stock options, which made their lying profitable to them personally. It also increased their performance bonuses, since the "results" looked so good. Arthur Andersen audited both Enron and WorldCom. Moreover, Andersen had large consulting contracts with both firms, and Andersen determined it could not afford to lose them; this provided a powerful incentive for the auditor to overlook accounting misdeeds, again a conflict of interest.[63]

Another root cause of the failures is Wall Street's obsession with quarterly earnings. Daily and even hourly TV and radio report stock movements. These reports often are given at the same time as the state's announcements of the daily lottery winners, and both are examples of people trying to make money on speculation. Some maintain that the American obsession with short-term earnings and the lottery has turned us into a "casino society"—that is, it is easier to make money by speculation than by working.

The purpose of the free enterprise system is to provide goods, services, and jobs. Profit is an essential, but not exclusive, measure of the success of a firm. If a firm is not profitable, it will fail and will cease providing jobs and goods. However, placing exclusive emphasis on profitability ensnares a firm in the difficulties that destroyed Enron and WorldCom. Such emphasis also leads a firm like Wal-Mart to pressure its suppliers to use low-wage, sweatshop manufacturers for its goods, and to pay low wages, along with poor health and retirement benefits, to its workers.

Legislation passed in the wake of the U.S. scandals, the Sarbanes-Oxley (SOX) Bill, is designed to lessen some of the conflicts of interest discussed previously. It restricts an auditing firm from also consulting with the same company, and the auditing firm must rotate its lead auditor every 5 years. The audit committee of the company being audited must be composed totally of outside directors. The company's lawyers must report evidence of securities fraud to the CEO and the

---

[63]Marianne M. Jennings, "Preventing Organizational Ethical Collapse," *Journal of Government Financial Management,* 53 (Spring 2004): 12–19.

board. And the CEO and the CFO must each personally certify the quarterly financial reports. Meanwhile the Securities and Exchange Commission has written new regulations on conflict of interest between investment bankers and analysts, and has set up a board to oversee the accounting firms. A conflict of interest that was not addressed is the common case when the CEO is also the chairperson of the board, the very group that oversees and evaluates the CEO's performance. It is difficult to do an adequate performance appraisal of the CEO, if the CEO is chair of the group doing the evaluation.

The SOX legislation is intended to lessen conflicts of interest. Each element is designed to make it more difficult for an individual to benefit himself — generally financially — at the expense of other people who are less informed. Take the requirement that the CEO must certify quarterly financial reports. Ken Lay, CEO of Enron, has consistently maintained that he did not know the details of the various off-the-books accounts in which Enron hid their expenses.[64] One might respond that he did know, in which case he lied and is responsible. Or one might argue that he did not know, and he then disregarded his responsibility as chief executive to be informed of all such major actions.

Two current trends in political life accelerate the loss of a sense of the common good in the United States: Narrow special interests are now stronger and more vocal, and there is a paralyzing lack of consensus regarding national priorities. In many arenas, the confrontational mode of dealing with others is a part of the American way. Not only do we use the adversary system in courts of law, but we have institutionalized much conflict (e.g., labor versus management, business versus government, environmentalists versus growth). The rhetoric is one of "battle" and "struggle," "win or lose," as if a loss for one group is a win for another. Special interest groups gather in Washington, D.C. to push for their narrow objectives. These include the American Medical Association (physicians), National Rifle Association, National Education Association (public school teachers), auto dealers, pro-choice feminists, and the Religious Right. Some militant special interest groups even work to defeat members of Congress who are not to their liking. The media then give unwarranted attention to protests, scandals, and conflicts; viewers love a fight! Negotiation and building a consensus are hard work and are not glamorous, and thus do not make the headlines. Therefore, poor communication, distrust, and cynicism grow at a time when listening, cooperation, and compromise are badly needed.

When Americans agree on an issue, the agreement is often about being against something: taxes, bureaucrats, censorship, big government. But we Americans find it harder to tell others what we stand *for* — what kind of a society we favor. We find it difficult to express social ideals and we lack the vocabulary to do so. We are not helped by our political discussions, which appeal to simplistic ideologies and do not help us to sort out priorities and balance the resulting tradeoffs. Yet it is essential to discuss our priorities, both personal and national, if we are to determine what kind of society we want. These failures in the political

---

[64]Mimi Swartz and Sherron Watkins, *Power Failure: The Inside Story of the Collapse of ENRON* (New York: Doubleday, 2003), pp. 287–289, 298–300, 369–371.

forum encourage Americans to be deaf to and distrustful of those with differing views; this distrust was made worse in the 2004 national election. Finding a common bond and developing a sense of community are now both more important and more difficult.

However, as we will see in later chapters, many executives in Europe, Japan, and the United States are developing a new sense of global ethical responsibility. These executives seek to (1) avoid legal and financial problems (risk management), (2) align their firm with its proclaimed values and also encourage commitment and trust within the organization (organizational functioning), (3) establish a good reputation with customers and suppliers (market positioning), and (4) be regarded as good corporate citizens in their community (civic positioning).[65] Moreover, a firm is not penalized financially if it is more responsible. In fact, as mentioned previously, firms that are ethically and socially responsible tend to be more successful financially.[66] This more responsible attitude is a value shift for executives, and they are broadening the measures of firm performance beyond financial to also include social and environmental criteria. The remaining chapters of this book will expand on these issues and help us to clarify our personal and business goals, better understand our successes and failures, and plan our future.

## SUMMARY AND CONCLUSIONS

During the last decade, the U.S. economy has witnessed success in providing jobs and a multitude of low-price goods and services for people. This sparks pride because the successes are built on traditional values of free markets, competition, self-interest, and innovation. On the other hand, recent business scandals—financial fraud; "managing the numbers" to suit the analysts and shareholders; preferential treatment given by banks, mutual funds, and insurance companies to their largest customers; and executives using company funds to purchase personal homes or furniture—are often justified by the same values of competition and self-interest.

Self-interest motivates business and many people. Advertising and the media encourage self-interest. Yet excessive self-interest undermines loyalty, family, community, and helping others. If competition and self-interest are not moderated by integrity, trust, and moral values, free enterprise is at risk of collapsing, because business requires trust. Moreover, it will be impossible for Americans to achieve fulfilling and happy lives if most of us remain self-centered. If self-interest becomes an acceptable moral norm in all decisions, government, health care, and schools will deteriorate even further. For government to operate effectively and to provide adequate education and health care for all requires that we determine our goals as individuals and as a society. Then the hard part of democracy begins: dialogue, negotiation and compromise.

---

[65]The categories are those of Lynn Sharp Paine. See her *Value Shift: Why Companies Must Merge Social and Financial Imperatives to Achieve Superior Performance* (New York: McGraw-Hill, 2003).
[66]M. Orlitzky, F. L. Schmidt, and S. L. Rynes, "Corporate Social and Financial Performance: A Meta-Analysis," *Organization Studies* 24, no. 3 (2003): 403–441. The researchers analyzed more than 50 published studies and found the positive correlation.

The following chapters will examine personal moral development (Chapter 2), ethical behavior (Chapter 3), the historical roots of American business values (Chapters 4 and 5), and the effect of those values on society (Chapter 6), in the workplace (Chapter 7), and in the global marketplace (Chapters 8 and 9). As we will see in Chapter 2, we are born self-centered and become more concerned about others as we mature.

## DISCUSSION QUESTIONS

1. Are the benefits of Wal-Mart's "everyday low prices" worth the cost of so many "associates" receiving low wages with few, if any, health or retirement benefits? Does Wal-Mart take unfair advantage of its workers and suppliers?
2. List the principal benefits of a healthy free enterprise business system.
3. What is a conflict of interest? Describe a conflict of interest for a: purchasing agent, government official, auditing firm, investment banker, mutual fund, and for businesses paying taxes.
4. How would you evaluate Dennis Kozlowski's ethics? His moral maturity? How did he change during his last decade at Tyco? Can accounting that follows the stated generally accepted accounting procedures (GAAP) still be unreliable?
5. List the (a) strengths and (b) weaknesses of viewing the purpose of the firm as increasing shareholder value. When this results in a short-term view, what are the results for the firm?
6. Are "managed earnings" common in financial reporting? What is the problem with them?
7. Do you think that business scandals are now at an end, or are these high profile cases the beginning of a new era marked by a lack of ethics and values in business?
8. When U.S. jobs are "outsourced" to increase profitability, outline the advantages and disadvantages to U.S. citizens.
9. List the negative effects of layoffs. When a firm finds it necessary to "downsize," what are its responsibilities to the affected people?
10. How do we judge the impact of jobs that are being created in developing countries against the loss of jobs for Americans? Are Americans able to sustain themselves more easily than people in poor countries?
11. Cite the evidence for the loss of confidence in business and in business executives. How might this affect the efficiency of business operations?
12. Is it fair to target young children in advertising? Why do we see so many sexually explicit advertisements? Is this an example of a "race to the bottom" in order to obtain the attention of the potential purchaser? Do such actions hurt moral standards and the common good?
13. Do many ads promote self-obsession and contempt for rules, and fracture the sense of connectedness that any society needs to cohere and to care about its common problems and least fortunate members?
14. In what way do advertising and the media influence values? Do you think each presents honest or deceptive images of people and what brings them happiness?
15. Is it shallow and dehumanizing to judge a person by the style of his or her clothes or the car he or she drives?
16. Is self-interest the primary motivation of most businesspeople, as you experience them?

17. Is self-interest an adequate motivation for businesspeople? When is it effective? When is it not adequate?
18. What analogy does Kenneth Mason, former president of Quaker Oats, use in rejecting Milton Friedman's position that the purpose of the corporation is to maximize returns to shareholders?
19. Does self-interest as a goal for business people necessarily cast government into the role of a regulator? Explain.
20. Describe market fundamentalism. According to Soros, why is self-interested behavior appropriate when purchasing but not when voting? Is self-interest already a moral norm?
21. What values brought about the failures of Tyco, Enron, and WorldCom?
22. Do you think that new legislation and regulation will restore trust to business? Is anything else needed? If so, what?

# CASES

## Case 1-1      College Test

Kathy Blankenship and Joe Fontana are juniors at Lincoln University's business school. Both are taking their first course in finance taught by Dr. Hugh Sikora. Kathy is in the Honors Program. Joe is an outgoing young man, and is a "C" student. On the first exam, Kathy scored the second highest grade in the class and Joe failed. The next exam, more heavily weighted, was three weeks later. During the exam Sikora noticed Joe glancing in the direction of Kathy's paper several times. When grading the papers, Sikora noted all fifteen multiple-choice answers were identical on both Joe's and Kathy's papers, including two responses that were incorrect.

1. You are a student sitting behind Joe, and you see what he is doing. Do you have any responsibility to speak to Joe? To the instructor?
2. As the instructor, you notice Joe's activities during the exam. What should you do? Why?
3. As you grade the papers, you note the identical answers on the exams. What should (or would) you do?
4. What ethical issues are involved here? ■

## Case 1-2      Cynthia Cooper, WorldCom Internal Auditor

Cynthia Cooper grew up in Clinton, Mississippi, headquarters of WorldCom. She worked there for 10 years and rose to be vice president of internal auditing. In Spring 2002, she found that WorldCom had billed $500 million to capital expenditures that had not been authorized. Cooper alerted WorldCom board members, and informed CFO Scott Sullivan of the irregularity. Sullivan told her that WorldCom's auditing firm approved the audit, and he asked her to delay her inquiry for one quarter. Cooper was suspicious, but was stonewalled in her effort to find further information. So she and her team worked late at night to check WorldCom's operational and financial accounting records.

Because of fierce competition in long distance and wireless businesses, by 2000 WorldCom's revenues were dropping and thus not able to meet analysts' expectations. In order to bolster revenues, WorldCom charged many expenses from operations to capital expenses in order to bolster profitability. The actions were approved by CFO Sullivan and by the outside auditor,

Arthur Andersen. On June 24, 2002, the board audit committee told CFO Sullivan that he was fired. The next day WorldCom announced that they had inflated profits by $3.5 billion over the previous five quarters. The internal auditors' discovery triggered the largest bankruptcy in U.S. history and resulted in the loss of jobs for thousands of their co-workers. Sullivan and a dozen others pled guilty to accounting fraud. CEO Bernie Ebbers in 2005 was convicted of fraud in federal court. During bankruptcy WorldCom was reorganized and is now MCI.[67]

1. Was it professional for Cooper and her team to pursue their suspicions so vigorously? Was it ethical for her to do so? Was it wise?

2. Should she have given Sullivan and WorldCom more time to correct the situation as he requested, and perhaps have saved thousands of jobs?

3. Is Cooper typical of internal auditors in her willingness to pursue her suspicions, even though it meant not following the orders of her CFO boss, and working late on her own time?

4. What would you have done if you were in Cooper's position? What would you have done if you were in Sullivan's position, given WorldCom's declining revenues? ■

---

# Case 1-3     Confidentiality of E-Mail

Alana Shoars, an e-mail administrator for Epson America in Los Angeles, arrived at work one morning to find her supervisor reading e-mail messages that had been sent between employees. She protested, and was fired. Although Epson had no stated policy on the privacy of messages, they argued that the network was their property and was for company business only. Bank of Boston found one employee using e-mail to bet on horses, and another was running an Amway business from office e-mail.

1. Does a firm have a right to monitor employees' e-mail?

2. Does a firm have an obligation to inform employees of their policies on e-mail?

3. Comment on the ethics involved in the situation at Epson and Bank of Boston. ■

---

[67]Jesse Drucker, "Ebbers to Face Criminal Charges for Role in WorldCom Scandal," *Wall Street Journal,* March 2, 2004, p. A1; Susan Pulliam and Deborah Solomon, "How Three Unlikely Sleuths Discovered Fraud at WorldCom," *Wall Street Journal,* October 30, 2002, p. 1; Amanda Ripley, "The Night Detective," *Time,* January 6, 2003, pp. 44–50.

## Exercise

### Personal Goals and Values Inventory

This exercise is intended to help you clarify your own personal goals and values, and to see how your life goals support or conflict with your values and personal experiences.

1. **Procedure:**
   a. Rank order the values on the value survey below (sixteen long-range values).
   b. Complete the life goal inventory. Reflect on and record your major goals for the next 1 to 2 years in each of the areas indicated.
   c. Write a paper (maximum of six double-spaced typed pages) examining and comparing your life goals, your most important values, and your experiences.

2. **Criteria** for evaluating the paper include the demonstration of your ability to analyze and articulate your own goals, values, and experiences:
   a. Clarity of analysis of goals, values, and experiences.
   b. Ability to recognize and deal with the meaning of support and conflict among goals, values, and experiences, and their significance for future career and life decisions.
   c. Quality of your paper, including life experiences, correct writing, and examples.

3. **Suggestions** for writing the paper:
   a. Write in the first person, not the third person. It may help to think of this as a letter to yourself, to a very close friend, or as a diary entry.
   b. Describe your personal history in a paragraph or two, including what generated your goals. What specific events in your life have affected your goals and values?
   c. Discuss briefly each of the seven goals but describe only your most important values or clusters of values.
      1. Do your values support your goals? Or do some conflict?
      2. To what extent have your life experiences up to this time been guided or influenced by your goals and/or your values?
      3. Compare your present job, activities, and life, and your goals and values.
      4. Is there any particular satisfaction in your life that might be explained by support from your goals and values?
      5. Is there any frustration that might be explained by conflict among them?
      6. Clarify the points you make with specific personal experiences and examples.
   d. Your listing of your goals and values is intended to help you with your analysis. It is merely an aid to help you write your paper.
   e. Write reflections honestly and straightforwardly. No one but the instructor will see your paper. It is confidential, and will be returned quickly.
   f. Use clear language and good grammar. Choose directness and clarity over elaboration.
   g. It is not necessary to turn in the completed order of personal values or the completed life goal inventory. If you do, include only as an appendix.

4. Apologies for intruding into your personal values. However, experience indicates that most of us do not take time to reflect on our goals and values unless (1) we are asked to do so, or (2) a crisis arises in our lives. The exercise and paper will enable you to gain a better understanding of your goals before a crisis arises.

## EXERCISE

### Rank Ordering of Personal Values

Rank the following sixteen long-range personal values[68] in the order of importance to you, that is, insofar as they are guiding principles in your life. Study the list of values carefully. Place *1* in front of the value that is most important in your life, *2* in front of the next most important, and so on. The least most important value for you should be ranked 16. If you change your mind, feel free to change the ranking.

    When you are finished, the list should roughly indicate the importance of the various values in your life.

_____ Achievement (promotions at work)
_____ Beauty (natural and artistic beauty)
_____ Cooperation
_____ Dollar rewards (money and salary)
_____ Family security (taking care of and being with loved ones)
_____ Freedom (independence)
_____ Justice (equal opportunity for all; concern for the disadvantaged)
_____ Love, friendship, and intimacy
_____ Physical health and well-being
_____ Pleasure (sensually and sexually enjoyable personal life)
_____ Possessions (good car, clothes, home, many material goods)
_____ Recognition (respect, admiration from others)
_____ Self-respect (a good self-image, self-esteem)
_____ Sense of accomplishment (making a lasting contribution)
_____ Spirituality (prayer, meditation, striving to be a good person)
_____ World at peace (lessening of war and conflict)

## EXERCISE

### Life Goal Inventory

This inventory[69] is designed to help you examine your life goals. Describe as fully as you can your aims and goals in all areas of your life. List all goals that are important to you, whether they are fairly easy or difficult to attain. Be honest in this assessment; only then will the inventory be useful to you. For example, if your major goal is to enjoy leisure satisfactions, indicate this, so as to better understand and evaluate yourself. In your own words, describe two to five goals in each of the following areas over the next year or two. The categories are a guide; feel free to change them to suit your own goals.

*Career* (goals in employment or career; situation aimed for).

   **1.**

   **2.**

   **3.**

---

[68]Adapted from Milton Rokeach, *The Nature of Human Values* (New York: Free Press, 1973).
[69]Adapted from Joyce S. Osland, David Kolb, and Irwin Rubin, *Organizational Behavior: An Experiential Approach,* 7th ed. (Upper Saddle River, NJ: Prentice Hall, 2001).

*Relationships with People* (goals with friends, parents, spouse, colleagues, others).

**1.**

**2.**

**3.**

*Status and Respect* (goals in your social circles; people from whom you seek esteem).

**1.**

**2.**

**3.**

*Leisure* (vacations, sports, hobbies, other interests).

**1.**

**2.**

**3.**

*Learning and Education* (knowledge, skills, experiences to learn, areas to study).

**1.**

**2.**

**3.**

*Spiritual Growth and Religion* (goals: peace of mind, prayer, meaning, giving self to others).

**1.**

**2.**

**3.**

*Material Rewards and Possessions* (goals in income, wealth, possessions).

**1.**

**2.**

**3.**

# CHAPTER 2

# *Maturity and Moral Development*

No one can be poor that has enough; nor rich, who desires more than he has.
LUCIUS ANNAEUS SENECA (4 BC–65 AD), *Roman philosopher and playwright*

You have the most powerful weapons on earth—love and prayer.
JOHN MARX TEMPLETON. FOUNDER, TEMPLETON FUNDS

We are not born with moral maturity. We learn a sense of right and wrong from parents, friends, churches, schools—and from experiences like those we reviewed in Chapter 1. In this chapter we will examine: (1) the moral development of the individual person, (2) the stress that stems from an absence of personal values and goals, (3) methods of making personal values explicit, and finally (4) the reasons for considering ethics when making all business decisions. To be successful today, it is essential for us to clarify our personal goals, to stay mentally alert and engaged during a 50-year working life, to know in which sort of organization we can work best, and to constantly try to improve our own competency.[1] Before we consider these essentials for success, let us examine some examples of people, including executives, who found themselves under stress.

Katy Spivak, a student at Emory University, yielded to ads and the gifts that were offered to sign up for 14 credit cards. Within three years she had a debt of $9,000. She now works two jobs and has paid down her debt to $7,500. However, 118,000 other young people under 25 have filed for bankruptcy. The adult credit card market has matured, and firms find college students to be easy targets as new customers.[2]

Lee Iacocca was president of Ford and later chairman of Chrysler, but he reported that he flunked retirement. He says his life was so structured and isolated

---

[1]Peter F. Drucker, "Managing Oneself," *Harvard Business Review,* March–April 1999, pp. 67–74.
[2]"Congratulations, Grads—You're Bankrupt: A Marketing Blitz Buries Kids in Plastic and Debt," *Business Week,* May 21, 2001, p. 48.

as CEO, that he was not able to handle the flexibility of retirement. He partici-pated in the hostile and ill-fated attempt to take over Chrysler. His third wife of three and one-half years maneuvered him to move to California, and then fought him in a nasty divorce six months later.[3]

James E. Olson was chairman and chief executive officer of AT&T. He oversaw the largest corporate restructuring in American history—the breakup of AT&T into numerous smaller systems. In the process, he cut $1 billion from AT&T's costs, largely through layoffs. One year later at age 63 he died suddenly.[4]

Eli Black, CEO of United Brands, broke the window of his 44th floor office in Manhattan and jumped to his death. Two months later the Securities and Exchange Commission revealed that United Brands had paid a $1.25 million bribe to a government official in Honduras for a reduction in the export tax on bananas. Black knew about the bribe.

Each of these people faced stress, anxiety, and a conflict in values. Their sto-ries demonstrate the strains and anxieties that face businesspeople every day. This chapter will examine the sources of these conflicts, the anxiety and stress that accompany them, and some strategies that will aid in avoiding conflicts and stress.

## LACK OF MATURITY BRINGS STRESS

People whose moral development manifests maturity (for definitions, see Figure 2-1) are generally more relaxed, enjoy life more, are able to more fully utilize their talents, and are generally more liked and respected by their families and peers. Moreover, they are also considered wise and are more often consulted by others. Even a mature person in a difficult situation—for example, an honest accountant in a firm that is misstating income or a pacifist in a time of war—possesses a basic stability and composure. On the other hand, crises,

**FIGURE 2-1**  Moral Development Terms

| | |
|---|---|
| *Character* | A stable, organized personality with a composite of good and bad moral habits within a person |
| *Common good* | Good of the group as a whole; general welfare |
| *Community* | Any group sharing goals, interests, work, and so on |
| *Maturity* | State of being fully developed as a person |
| *Moral development* | Increased ability of a person to distinguish right and wrong and to engage in good behavior |

---

[3]"How I Flunked Retirement," Lee Iacocca interviewed, *Fortune,* June 24, 1996, pp. 50–61.
[4]*Business Week,* May 2, 1988, p. 34.

stress, and illness often plague the person who has failed to achieve mature moral development.

## Midlife Crisis

If we have not internalized our own moral values, we often must be faced with important life and career decisions that demand clarifying goals or examining alternatives. Even when we have clear goals early in life, these goals may change, perhaps through new experiences or disappointments. Either situation often leads to a midlife crisis.

> Adrienne Glasgow was manager of international finance at Borden at the age of 35. However, she quit her job, because, she said, she was not fulfilled. She is now consulting.[5] Two-thirds of women engage in a mid-course correction, and those who fall short of their career goals even after such a correction are more likely to be depressed.[6]
>
> John Z. DeLorean was vice president in charge of General Motors car and truck divisions in North America. DeLorean quit because he felt that the GM committee system was too unwieldy. It dispersed authority and responsibility, and he felt that as a result no one could show initiative. DeLorean may be correct in his assessment, or he may not, but his case is not unique. The *Wall Street Journal* and *Fortune* have run articles on scores of people who left well-paid corporate jobs to do something quite different at a fraction of their former pay. These men and women found their work in the corporation to be unsatisfying, and many have turned to a simpler and less-structured life.
>
> Typical is Ross Drever, age fifty-two, who quit as director of Amsted Industries' research division at a $140,000/year salary. He now works in a cranberry bog in Three Lakes, Wisconsin. He says, "I have a lot of suits and shoes I'll never use again."

These managers, and others like them, felt they were giving too much time to a job that gave them little satisfaction. They made a radical change; they left comfortable jobs, homes, and friends to carve out a new life. These women and men show us how some at midlife examine their values and goals and act on what they find. They found that they could not have it all at once; they found it necessary to make choices. The challenge for each of us is to make the right kind of choices—ones that enable us to grow and at the same time satisfy our own internal morality.

---

[5]Betsy Morris, "Executive Women Confront Midlife Crisis," *Fortune,* September 18, 1995, pp. 60–86. This article chronicles a dozen such cases. See also Abigail J. Stewart and Joan M. Ostrove, "Women's Personality in Middle Age: Gender, History, and Midcourse Corrections," *American Psychologist* 53 (November 1998): 1185–1194.

[6]Deborah Carr, "The Fulfillment of Career Dreams at Midlife: Does It Matter for Women's Mental Health?" *Journal of Health and Social Behavior* 38 (December 1997): 331–344.

This reassessment often occurs around the age of 40. People look around and ask if this is the way they would choose to spend the rest of their life. Time is running out, they feel—there may be only two decades of healthy work life left, or maybe even less.

A midlife crisis can be traumatic—to family, to fellow workers, and to the person experiencing it. On some occasions the person experiencing the midlife transition panics and seeks a dramatic change. The individual sometimes breaks all connections to the past, leaves spouse and children behind, and goes off accompanied by different friends. This sort of radical break can cause disruption and hurt to families, neighbors, and co-workers. Such a reaction to the midlife reassessment is desperate, and not mature. However, the frequency of these sharp midlife breaks show that not many of us have sufficiently probed our own goals in order to take charge of our lives. Rather than setting our own goals, we often choose the job that has the highest salary and allow this single criteria to determine our career and goals.

In an effort to help his own professional school graduates set priorities that will give them long-term satisfaction, the dean of Harvard Business School gave them this advice:

> There is no success in business that can compensate for failure at home. Invest first at home, and think of that as your most important investment in your lives. The most important work you do in your whole lives will be inside the walls of your home."[7]

Too often businesspeople spend disproportionate hours at work, and in the process neglect their most important relationships—those within their families.

The midlife journey can be a gradual, life-giving reassessment, especially if a person has internalized his or her own goals and values. The journey can become a crisis if goals and values have not been examined and if the course of life has been determined by salaries and status, instead of by enlightened choices.[8] The objective should be to consciously take possession of our own goals and values. The more clearly we recognize what our heartfelt goals are and what brings us real happiness, the greater the chance that our midlife reassessment will be gradual and peaceful.

## Stress and Anxiety at Work

Self-esteem depends on the candid feedback a person receives from others. Those who gain the esteem of their peers consider themselves successful in the American culture. Such people are typically competent, goal-oriented, conscientious, ambitious, humble, and hard working, qualities which stem from the Protestant ethic, as we will see in Chapters 4 and 5.

---

[7]*Business Week,* June 26, 2000, p. 83.
[8]Denise Lyons, "Freer to Be Me: The Development of Executives at Midlife," *Consulting Psychology Journal* 54 (Winter 2002): 15–27.

The culture, through families, schools, churches, business, and government, communicates its values to the individual. A culture thus gives people direction. Without this socialization process, it is not possible to know what one person may expect of another in everyday dealings. We will examine the socialization process within the firm in Chapter 7.

Job performance, self-esteem, and satisfaction at work and at home are influenced by the values that Americans share, such as the importance of work and wealth, individualism, self-interest, and time thrift. These same values can also cause conflict and stress. We are stressed by our ideals and the expectations we have for ourselves, and it is this stress that drives us forward. Nevertheless, we must be careful lest our expectations drive us too far and too hard, and negatively affect how we treat ourselves, our families, colleagues, and fellow citizens. These values, taken to extremes, promote competitiveness, self-interest, desire for control, and frequent job changes—all of which can place us under greater stress.[9]

Stress occurs when we face a constraint, demand, or opportunity related to what we desire and for which the outcome is both important and uncertain.[10] The vast majority of U.S. workers feel stress on the job; 62 percent say their workload has increased and 53 percent say work leaves them "overtired and overwhelmed." In addition, 42 percent say that job pressures are harming their personal relationships, and 35 percent say that their jobs are harming their physical and emotional health. Workplace stress is estimated to cost the United States more than $300 billion each year in health care and missed work. Moreover, this stress seems to be increasing.[11] This stress has a variety of causes, among them pressure to finish a job, fear of losing one's job, and lack of control over outcomes. In addition, many Americans are working harder and longer hours as their co-workers are laid off and those left are asked to pick up the extra work. At present, workers in America put in more time on the job than do workers in any other nation. Japan held first place until 1995, when American workers surpassed Japanese workers in total hours worked. Workplace demands and stress are not limited to the United States and Japan, though. Half of the workers in the European Union complain that they must work at very high speed, face tight deadlines and monotonous tasks, and have no opportunity to rotate tasks.

For most of us, success in business is considered important, and people who are not deemed successful in the workplace are often judged inferior by others. This lack of work-place success is often a source of stress. Further job-related stress is caused by conflict and confusion over a person's responsibilities, or when

---

[9]Michael Peterson and John F. Wilson, "Work Stress in America," *International Journal of Stress Management* 11 (2004): 91–113.
[10]Adapted from R. S. Schuler, "Definitions and Conceptualization of Stress in Organizations," *Organizational Behavior and Human Performance* (April 1980): 189; see also Stevan E. Hobfoll, *Stress, Culture and Community: The Psychology and Philosophy of Stress* (New York: Plenum Press, 1998).
[11]Bruce Cryer, Rollin McCraty, and Doc Childre, "Pull the Plug on Stress," *Harvard Business Review* (July 2003): 102–107; Arthur Schwartz, "Always on the Job, Employees Pay with Health," *New York Times,* September 5, 2004, p. B1; "Attitudes in the American Workplace VII" (Harris Poll, 2001).

the job calls for actions that run counter to a person's ethics.[12] In the latter case, either a compromise is reached or something is sacrificed, either of which can cause stress and frustration.

Those who are judged successful according to the prevailing norms (i.e., viewed as wealthy, ambitious, and hardworking) may by that very fact suffer anxieties. Successful corporate workers are mobile. They are often asked to leave their present jobs and homes in order to move on to "better" positions. Psychologists tell us that anxiety is caused by moving from the known to the unknown. Having mastered one environment, it is unsettling to be asked to move to a new one. Executives now tout workplace flexibility as a desirable quality. But in the process of moving from job to job, firm to firm, and city to city, loyalty to both firm and community is lost.[13] It is true that in order to mature, one must take risks and change. Yet being uprooted every few years—leaving behind not just the confidence built in mastering a job but also friends, relatives, and knowledge of the community—can undermine the willingness to commit oneself to a new job or neighborhood. These mobile managers place demands on their spouses and children, who undergo the same cyclic trauma of arriving and departing, and the accompanying pain and anxiety it causes. People in such situations may be forced to depend more on their aggressiveness than on the help and cooperation of co-workers, friends, and neighbors. In some cases (fortunately, probably the minority of cases) destructively narcissistic managers who narrowly focus on themselves, devalue others, and impair an organization's morale and performance add to workplace stress. On the whole, stress, especially stress whose primary source is the workplace, appears to be increasing. In addition, there is the stress caused by work-family conflict, especially with the increase in the number of families where both spouses work.[14] If this is true of those whose mobility is caused by their success, it is even more true when the cause is that a person has been laid off.

The unknown, and even more the uncontrolled, produce anxieties. Ulcers and other physical symptoms are often manifestations of anxiety; they can result when there are conflicting demands on the individual. Neuroses have been experimentally induced in animals exposed to ambiguous stimuli. After the same or very similar stimuli, the animals were sometimes rewarded and sometimes not (or sometimes rewarded and sometimes punished). Gastric ulcers developed in

---

[12]See Peter J. Frost, *Toxic Emotions at Work: How Compassionate Managers Handle Pain and Conflict* (Boston: Harvard Business School Press, 2003), pp. 36–55, 92–93. See also the comprehensive overview in James Quick, Jonathan Quick, Debra Nelson, and Joseph Hurrell, *Preventive Stress Management in Organizations* (Washington, D.C.: American Psychological Association, 1997).

[13]Richard Sennett, *The Corrosion of Character: The Personal Consequences of Work in the New Capitalism* (New York: W. W. Norton, 1998).

[14]Timothy Judge and Jason Colquitt, "Organizational Justice and Stress: The Mediating Role of Work-Family Conflict," *Journal of Applied Psychology* 89 (June 2004): 395–404; Ray Labit, "The Long-term Organizational Impact of Destructively Narcissistic Managers," *Academy of Management Executive* 16, no. 1 (2002): 127.

caged laboratory rats who spent one month subjected to ambiguous stimuli. During 47 hours of every 48-hour period, they had to endure an electric shock every time they went to the food box or the water cup. They needed the food, but also feared the shock. Furthermore, because they were not shocked during the remaining hour, they were never sure whether they would get a shock as they ate their food. The conflict of wanting the food and yet being afraid of the pain, plus a lack of control over the situation, produced the ulcers. Control rats, which were simply deprived of food and water for 47 of the 48 hours, did not develop ulcers.[15]

Cats that were first fed and then shocked following the same buzzer exhibited a wide variety of aberrant physical activities, such as restless roving, clawing at wire cages, butting the roof with their heads, and ceaseless vocalizing—all indicating a high degree of anxiety. These cats were then given the opportunity to drink milk that contained alcohol. Half the animals quickly learned that the alcohol relieved the symptoms of their anxiety, and they invariably chose the 5 percent alcohol mixture served in a distinctive cocktail glass. The cats preferred the alcohol as long as their tensions persisted and they remained neurotic. When the animals experienced psychic pain because of lack of control, they sought relief in withdrawal, and their neurotic symptoms disappeared under the influence of the alcohol.[16]

People, too, attempt to escape from the pain that arises from uncertainty and the inability to control their immediate environment. That escape can be manifested in healthy ways, or it can show itself as a refusal to face the issues that are causing the problem. The stress that ensues can trigger addiction to alcohol or drugs, and/or it can cause illness, such as ulcers, high blood pressure, heart attacks, or even cancer. Job-related stress has become a vital concern for business, because unmanaged stress can cause poor job performance.[17] Stress, and the illness, absenteeism, and health care costs that result from stress, have become immense expenses for business.

Anger, irritability, and aggressive competitiveness are some of the factors that cause heart disease. The person with a "Type A" personality—hard-driving, harried, competitive—is more likely to suffer from heart disease because of stress. Children who get neither unconditional love from or much physical contact with loving parents are more likely to become adults who are cynical and easy to anger.

Time off from work can lessen stress. However, the United States ties Japan for having the fewest average annual vacation days (10), even though a vacation could be a possible time of renewal. Most European countries have two to three

---

[15]Nancy G. Vogeltanz and Jeffrey E. Hecker, "The Roles of Neuroticism and Controllability/ Predictability in Physiological Response to Adverse Stimuli," *Personality and Individual Differences* 27 (1999): 599–612; Bernard Berelson and Gary A. Steiner, *Human Behavior: An Inventory of Scientific Findings* (New York: Harcourt, Brace & World, 1964), pp. 276–279.
[16]*Ibid.*
[17]Victoria Doby and Robert Caplan, "Organizational Stress as Threat to Reputation: Effects on Anxiety at Work and at Home," *Academy of Management Journal* 38, no. 4 (1995), 1105–1123.

times as many vacation days.[18] In addition, in a few notable court cases, firms have been held responsible for work-related stress. Not all stress, however, is bad for the individual or for job performance. In fact, a moderate amount of stress is linked to better job performance; the "fight or flight" response releases a moderate amount of stimulants and thus enables persons to better achieve their objectives. Social support, regular non-competitive exercise, and relaxation will reduce stress to manageable levels. Firms such as Bank of America, IBM, GM, Xerox, Johnson & Johnson, and many others provide wellness programs for their people, knowing that such programs will pay off in healthier and happier workers.[19]

Stress can also lead people to seek quiet places in order to reflect on themselves and their goals, thus enabling them to emerge from the stressful situation healthier and in better control of their lives. Quiet time, reflection, meditation, and prayer are being "rediscovered." These are effective tools for moderating normal stress and for helping people to grow in moral maturity. We will discuss spirituality in the workplace in Chapter 7. The need for businesspeople to take charge of their own lives and to actively pursue their own moral development is underscored by the fact that Steven Covey's books emphasize this and have been best sellers for decades.[20] Stress and anxiety are lessened when people are explicitly aware of their own values. In the process of becoming aware of their own values, people become more morally and emotionally mature.

## MORAL DEVELOPMENT

We know people who are willing to work unselfishly for the benefit of others, even when it requires personal sacrifice. Some people in every community spend their lives providing food and shelter for the sick and homeless. Some executives habitually take into account the effect of their decisions on "the little guy." Some leaders take the blame for the blunders of subordinates. We consider such people to be morally good; they have a high level of moral development.

On the other hand, we also know people who consider only themselves. For example, we note some colleagues who are polite and helpful to superiors but who are harsh and demeaning to subordinates. Some are well-educated and articulate, and thus skillful in hiding their self-centeredness; others are straightforward and blunt in their greediness.

Let us examine the moral development of some graduate business students. Business students often display conventional thought patterns and lack clear

---

[18]"Yankees: Nose to the Grindstone," *Business Week,* September 4, 1995, p. 28; Kevin Williams and George Alliger, "Role Stressors, Mood Spillover, and Perceptions of Work-Family Conflict in Employed Parents," *Academy of Management Journal* 37, no. 4 (1994): 837–868; Wayne F. Cascio, *Costing Human Resources: The Financial Impact of Behavior in Organizations* (Boston: Kent, 1982).
[19]William M. Kizer, *The Healthy Workplace: A Blueprint for Corporate Action* (New York: Wiley, 1987).
[20]Steven Covey, *The 7 Habits of Highly Successful People: Powerful Lessons in Personal Change* (New York: Fireside, 1990); Covey, *Principle-Centered Leadership* (New York: Fireside, 1991).

personal goals. At Harvard Business School, an examination of students' values found that:

> Many students came in the door, as it were, repeatedly espousing such credos as "The important thing is to act—whether you are right or wrong" or "I must do my personal best." The implications of these credos tend to flow something like this:
>
> INTERVIEWER: When all is said and done, what would you like your life ultimately to be about?
>
> STUDENT: I would like to achieve my personal goals.
>
> INTERVIEWER: What might some of those be?
>
> STUDENT: I guess that would depend on what company I was with.
>
> INTERVIEWER: What kind of company would you like to work with?
>
> STUDENT: It wouldn't really matter.

The examiners concluded that the graduate business students' "primary values are those of achieving success, however it is defined by the prevailing culture, and involve little self-reflective choice. And if this is the case, we must assume that such students are extremely vulnerable to becoming the victims of inadequate and ill-considered goals."[21] Is this troubling judgment too severe?

Moral development is somewhat like physical development. People grow physically, psychologically, and morally. As an infant's body develops, it must physically progress through the stages of creeping, crawling, toddling, walking, and finally running. Similarly, a person progresses morally through certain identifiable phases. As a result of moral development, the person has an increasing ability to recognize moral issues and to distinguish right from wrong. This ability to make moral judgments and to engage in moral behavior increases as maturity increases. People are not born possessing moral skills; moral skills must be cultivated and developed, much like skills of other kinds.

Scholars have observed moral development for centuries and have classified the stages of development in various ways.[22] Child psychologist Jean Piaget was the first to collect data from observing and interviewing children. Psychologist Lawrence Kohlberg investigated moral development over the life span of a person, and his work is the starting point for most current research on moral development.[23]

---

[21]Sharon Daloz Parks, "Is It Too Late? Young Adults and the Formation of Professional Ethics," in *Can Ethics Be Taught? Perspectives, Challenges and Approaches at Harvard Business School* (Boston: Harvard Business School Press, 1993), pp. 24–25; see also Frederick P. Close, "The Case for Moral Education," *Responsive Community,* Winter 1993/1994, 23–29.

[22]See, for example, Craig A. Wendorf, "History of American Morality Research, 1894–1932," *History of Psychology* 4 (August 2001): 272–288.

[23]John Dewey, "What Psychology Can Do for the Teacher," in *John Dewey on Education: Selected Writings,* ed. Reginald Archambault (New York: Random House, 1964); Jean Piaget, *The Moral Judgment of the Child* (Glencoe, IL.: Free Press, 1948); Lawrence Kohlberg, "The Cognitive-Developmental Approach to Moral Education," in *Readings in Moral Education,* ed. Peter Scharf (Minneapolis: Winston Press, 1978), pp. 36–51.

## Stages of Moral Growth

Kohlberg found that moral development proceeds through three levels, each level consisting of two stages. Let us now examine these levels and stages.

### Level I: Self-Interest

At this level a child is able to respond to rules and social expectations and can apply the labels *good, bad, right,* and *wrong.* The child sees rules (1) as something imposed from the outside and (2) largely in terms of the pleasant or painful consequences of actions or in terms of the power of those who set the rules. The child views situations from his or her own point of view. The child does not yet have the ability to identify with others, so the child's point of view is largely one of self-interest.

**Stage 1: Punishment**    —I won't do it, because I don't want to get punished.—[24] The child does the right thing to avoid punishment or to obtain approval. There is little awareness of the needs of others. The physical consequences of an act determine its goodness and badness regardless of the wider consequences.

**Stage 2: Naively Egoistic**    —I won't do it, because I want the reward.—
The child is now aware that others also have needs and begins to defer to them in order to obtain what he or she wants. Right actions are those which satisfy the child's own interests. "You scratch my back, and I'll scratch yours"; and, on the other hand, "If someone hits you, you hit them back." Right is what is fair, an equal exchange, a deal. Human relations are viewed as being like the relations of the marketplace.

### Level II: Approval

Maintaining the expectations of one's family, peer group, or nation is viewed as valuable in its own right, regardless of the consequences. The person at this level does not merely conform to expectations but is loyal to the group and attempts to maintain and justify association with the group. The person is now able to understand another's point of view and assumes that everyone has a similar point of view. The person conforms to the group's norms and subordinates his or her own needs to those of the group.

**Stage 3: Interpersonal Relations: "Good Boy—Nice Girl"**    —I won't do it, because I want people to like me.—
Good behavior is conduct that pleases or helps close family and friends and is approved by them. Right action is conformity to what is expected within the family. Behavior is frequently judged by intention: "He means well." One earns approval by being a good brother, mother, or worker. Being good means keeping mutual relationships positive through such methods as loyalty, trust, respect, and gratitude. The moral behavior of members of social fraternities, sororities, and adolescent gangs is often no higher than this stage of moral development. Young men in Al Qaeda are likely also at this stage.

---

[24]For this adaptation of Kohlberg's model, thanks to William Damon, "The Moral Development of Children," *Scientific American,* August 1999, pp. 73–78.

**Stage 4: Law and Order**     —I won't do it, because it would break the law.—

Right behavior consists of doing one's duty, showing respect for authority, and maintaining the social order for its own sake. Loyalty to the nation and its laws is paramount. The person now sees other people as individuals, yet also as part of the larger social system which gives them their roles and obligations. Hence order and laws are essential. The person enters this stage as a result of experiencing the inadequacies of stage 3.

### Level III: Autonomous, Principled, or Abstract Ideals

The person no longer simply accepts the values and norms of the groups to which she or he belongs. There is an effort to find moral values and principles that impartially take everyone's interests into account. The person questions the norms and laws that society has adopted and redefines them so that they make sense to him or her. Proper laws and values are those to which any reasonable person would be committed whatever the society or the status held within that society.

**Stage 5: Social Contract**     —I won't do it, because moral law obliges me not to.—

The individual is aware that people hold a variety of conflicting views, but rules must be upheld in the interest of the social contract. Laws are agreed on and must be followed impartially, although they can be changed if need be. Some absolute values, such as life and freedom, are held regardless of differing individual values or even majority opinion. Utilitarianism ("the greatest good for the greatest number") is the characteristic ethical standard. The morality of this stage is the "official" morality of the U.S. government and the Constitution.

**Stage 6: Conscience and Principle**     —I won't do it, because it's not right, no matter what others say.—

Right action is defined by decisions of conscience that flow from universal ethical principles that are chosen by the person because of their comprehensiveness, universality, and consistency. These ethical principles are not specific, concrete moral codes like the Ten Commandments. Instead they are based on the belief that people are ends in themselves and should not be used merely as means, and the universal moral principles respecting the dignity of individual human beings, the equality of human rights, justice, and public welfare. The person's motivation for doing right is built upon care for fellow human beings and a belief in the validity of universal moral principles plus a personal commitment to these principles.[25]

## Reasoning and Caring in Moral Development

Observations of morally mature people show that *all* people move through these stages. Individuals are not able to move to a higher stage until they have passed through the lower stages. An example of one who has moved through the earlier stages to Level III might be Sen. John McCain (R, AZ). McCain is

---

[25]F. C. Power, A. Higgins, and L. Kohlberg, *Lawrence Kohlberg's Approach to Moral Education* (New York: Colombia University Press, 1989).

more statesmanlike and less partisan than many of his fellow members of Congress. He follows his conscience about his duties to others and the need to sacrifice for a cause that is larger than his own self-interest. In the U.S. Congress, McCain risked the displeasure of members of his own party by sponsoring the Climate Stewardship Act to reduce carbon dioxide emissions and the resulting global climate change. He has also worked to lessen waste in government, and to make elections more fair by reducing the excessive money required to be elected to national office. Whether or not one supports his political positions, it cannot be disputed that McCain is working from principle to achieve what he perceives to be the good of all.

Another example of a morally developed person is Farooq Kathwari, CEO of furniture retailer Ethan Allen. Born in Kashmir, India, and a Muslim immigrant to the United States, Kathwari has made the Ethan Allen chain of stores profitable. In selling goods, Kathwari refuses to give "big box" retailers discounts, because to him it would be unfair to the smaller retailers. In addition, he takes on responsibilities beyond his business. He has formed a group of experts in an attempt to bring peace to Kashmir. The project is highly respected by Indian, Pakistani, and U.S. governments. After the September 11, 2001 terrorist attack on the United States, he took out ads in major newspapers calling for "fostering unity among people of all faiths."

Note that the motivation for both McCain and Kathwari goes beyond pleasing others (stage 3), or even obeying the "rules of the game" (stage 4). They pursue the "greatest good of the greatest number" (stage 5), and they even seem to be seeking the overall welfare of *all the people* (stage 6). Their principles lead them to use their talents and energy in order to help all—perhaps especially those who are disadvantaged or have less voice.

However, Kohlberg found that few people reach the highest stages of moral development. Most Americans remain stuck at stage 3 or 4 for their entire lives.[26] For example, Kohlberg says that former President Richard Nixon never got beyond moral stage 3 or 4. According to him, Nixon did not understand the U.S. Constitution, which is a document built on a stage 5 foundation. World renowned psychiatrist Karl Menninger, founder of the Menninger Psychiatric Institute, agrees with Kohlberg's assessment of Nixon, but goes farther and adds Nixon to the list of men that Menninger calls evil, which includes Adolph Hitler, Lyndon Johnson, and James Watt (President Reagan's anti-environmental secretary of the interior, who served time in jail).[27]

Some people claim that schools should be value-free and not try to encourage moral development. Kohlberg responds that this is nonsense. All teaching communicates values. Choosing to be value-free is itself taking a value position. Then the question is: What are the values that *are* communicated? And what values *should be* communicated? Supporting Kohlberg is the finding that level

[26]*Ibid.,* p. 38.
[27]"Famed Psychiatrist Karl Menninger Analyzes the World, Finds It Needs Help," *Wall Street Journal,* December 23, 1985, pp. 1, 8; see also Karl Menninger, *Whatever Became of Sin?* (New York: Hawthorn Books, 1972).

of education is positively related to moral development. On the other hand, business students are more conventional, less reflective, and seem to be less ethical than other students.[28]

A study of a group of managers and their actual handling of moral dilemmas found that "managers typically reason at stages 3 or 4." These mid-level business managers, 86 percent of whom were male, were interviewed and asked how they would respond to three moral dilemmas. Managers in smaller organizations (less than 250 employees) or self-employed managers were more likely (54%) to reason at stage 4. Managers in larger organizations were more likely (again 54%) to reason at stage 3.[29]

Many ask if moral development can be influenced during the education and rearing of children. Researchers note that in communities that have reached a consensus about values, such as honesty and integrity, "Teachers did not tolerate cheating on exams, parents did not let their children lie and get away with it, sports coaches did not encourage teams to bend the rules for the sake of a win, and people of all ages expected openness from their friends." However, in communities that are divided on these issues: "Coaches espoused winning above all else, and parents protested when teachers reprimanded their children for cheating or shoddy school-work. Under such circumstances children learned not to take moral messages seriously." Stanford University youth moral development expert William Damon says that in order to achieve moral development in young people, people should work to achieve shared standards in harmonious communities. He calls this a "youth charter," which is developed for the sake of the children.[30] But a question arises: Can harmony and shared values be achieved in a pluralistic society which places such a high priority on freedom and individual rights?

In his earlier research, Kohlberg used only males for his data. To complete the model, Carol Gilligan examined the moral development of women. She found that, especially in the later stages, women's moral development differs from that of men. Whereas men tend to judge good and bad on the basis of reasoning and principles, women more often consider relationships, caring, and solidarity. Women (and in many cases men) at the higher stages of moral development often decide right from wrong on the basis of what effect the proposed action would have on relationships, love, and caring.[31] Because of these insights, ethicists have identified

---

[28]Anthony J. Daboub, Abdul M. A. Rasheed, Richard L. Priem, and David A. Gray, "Top Management Team Characteristics and Corporate Illegal Activity," *Academy of Management Review* 20 (January 1995): 155.

[29]James Weber, "Managers' Moral Reasoning: Assessing Their Responses to Three Moral Dilemmas," *Human Relations* 43, no. 7 (1990): 687–702.

[30]William Damon, "The Moral Development of Children," *Scientific American,* August 1999, pp. 72–78; see also Damon, *The Youth Charter: How Communities Can Work Together to Raise Standards for All Our Children* (New York: Free Press, 1997).

[31]Carol Gilligan, *In a Different Voice: Psychological Theory and Women's Development* (Cambridge, MA: Harvard University Press, 1982). Robbin Derry found justice and caring moral orientations in both men and women and so did not verify the sex differences; see Robbin Derry, "Moral Reasoning in Work Related Conflicts," in *Research in Corporate Social Performance and Policy,* ed. William C. Frederick, vol. 9 (Greenwich, CT: JAI, 1987), pp. 25–49. See also Andrew Wicks, Daniel Gilbert, and Edward Freeman, "A Feminist Reinterpretation of the Stakeholder Concept," *Business Ethics Quarterly* 4 (October 1995): 475–497.

caring as an additional norm for making ethical decisions. Caring, as well as the ethical norms of rights and duties, justice, and utilitarianism will be discussed in the next chapter.

Kohlberg has carefully studied moral development and has provided a useful model.[32] These theories of moral development have been both supported and challenged, but even most challengers agree that moral development takes place roughly in the way described.

The stages of moral development described by Kohlberg are similar to those described by Dewey and Piaget. Edward Stevens uses Kohlberg's levels of moral development, and proposes that some popular ethical theories can be explained by the fact that their originators were stuck at one of Kohlberg's lower levels. He finds that both social Darwinism (see Chapter 4) and Ayn Rand's objectivism flow from a primitive, self-interest stage of moral development (see Table 2-1).

Kohlberg found that moral judgment is the single most important factor in moral behavior. It is impossible to be morally mature without the ability to address various options and to make intelligent judgments on the rightness and wrongness of each. Moral judgment depends on moral reasoning, and we will discuss both moral judgment and moral reasoning in the next chapter.

## Individualism and the Common Good

Ethical acts and moral development presuppose that there exists a moral good and that there is some agreement on what it is. Robert Bellah and his coauthors investigated the American view of a good society.[33] They interviewed a wide variety of Americans from coast to coast and found that society places obstacles in the path of determining the moral good and of achieving a national consensus on important issues. The principal value for most Americans is freedom, as we saw in Chapter 1 and will see again in later chapters. Hear the authors:

> Freedom is perhaps the most resonant, deeply-held American value. In some ways, it defines the good in both personal and political life. Yet freedom turns out to mean being left alone by others, not having other people's values, ideas, or styles of life forced upon one, being free of arbitrary authority in work, family, and political life. What it is that one might do with that freedom is much more difficult for Americans to define. And if

---

[32]See, for example, Gerald Baxter and Charles Rarick, "Education for the Moral Development of Managers: Kohlberg's Stages of Moral Development and Integrative Education," *Journal of Business Ethics* 6 (April 1987): 243–248; see also Thomas Lickona, "What Does Moral Psychology Have to Say to the Teacher of Ethics?" in *Ethics Teaching in Higher Education,* ed. Daniel Callahan and Sissela Bok (New York: Plenum Press, 1980), pp. 103–132. For a detailed description of maturity, including Kohlberg's moral development model, see Robert Kegan, *The Evolving Self: Problem and Process in Human Development* (Cambridge, MA: Harvard University Press, 1982), esp. pp. 50–71.

[33]Robert N. Bellah et al., *Habits of the Heart: Individualism and Commitment in American Life* (New York: Harper & Row, 1985).

**TABLE 2-1**  Moral Development and Ethical Theory: An Overview

| *Theories of Moral Development and Corresponding Stages*[1] | | | *Ethical Theories Corresponding to Stages of Moral Development*[2] |
|---|---|---|---|
| *Jean Piaget's Theory* | *John Dewey's Theory* | *Lawrence Kohlberg's Theory* | *Edward Stevens's Theory* |
| 0. Premoral | | 0. Premoral | Group A<br>1. Social Darwinism |
| 1. Heteronomous (age 4–8) | I. Preconventional | I. Self-interest<br>1. Punishment | 2. Machiavellianism |
| 2. Autonomous (age 8–12) | | 2. Naively egoistic | 3. Objectivism (Ayn Rand) |
| | II. Conventional | II. Approval<br>3. Interpersonal relations: "good boy–nice girl" | Group B<br>4. Conventional morality |
| | | | 5. Legalistic ethics |
| | | 4. Law and order | 6. Accountability model of ethics |
| | III. Autonomous | III. Autonomous and principled<br>5. Social contract | Group C<br>7. Pragmatism<br>8. Marxism |
| | | 6. Conscience and principle | 9. "Economic humanism" |

[1]*Adapted from Lawrence Kohlberg, "The Cognitive-Development Approach to Moral Education,"* in Readings in Moral Education, *ed. Peter Scharf (New York: Winston Press, 1978), pp. 36–37.*
[2]*Adapted from rough congruence presented by Edward Stevens,* Business Ethics *(New York: Paulist Press, 1979).*

the entire social world is made up of individuals, each endowed with the right to be free of others' demands, it becomes hard to forge bonds of attachment to, or cooperation with, other people, since such bonds would imply obligations that necessarily impinge on one's freedom.[34]

Making freedom such an important value has given Americans a respect for other individuals and has encouraged creativity and innovation. However, it also has its costs:

It is an ideal freedom that leaves Americans with a stubborn fear of acknowledging structures of power and interdependence in a technologically complex society dominated by giant corporations and

---

[34]*Ibid.,* p. 23.

an increasingly powerful state. The ideal of freedom makes Americans nostalgic for their past, but provides few resources for talking about their collective future.[35]

Such a sense of freedom leaves both the person and society having little inclination or vocabulary to address common concerns. The traditional term *common good* refers to the good of society as a whole; that is, all people taken together. The fact that now we so rarely use the term speaks volumes about the primary concerns of Americans. Ironically, the more diverse the United States becomes, the more tolerance is stressed. Yet tolerance is a personal virtue, and it does not contribute to a commitment to improve society.

This emphasis on freedom is generally hostile to older ideas of the moral order. The center of our current moral order is the individual, who is given full freedom to choose careers, commitments, and a life, not on the basis of obligations to others or of truths outside the individual, but on the basis of self-satisfaction as the individual judges it. Commitments—from marriage and work to political and religious involvement—are made as a way to enhance individual well-being rather than out of obedience to moral imperatives. If it is satisfying to me, I will do it; if it is not satisfying, I will withdraw. In a word, what is good is what one finds personally rewarding. If preferences change, so does what is considered good. Even the most fundamental ethical virtues are treated as matters of personal preference. Hence, the basic ethical rule is that individuals be able to pursue whatever they find rewarding as long as they do not interfere with the actions and values of others.[36] Note that this is the child-like Level I of moral development.

Individuals often elevate their subjective view of themselves and their world and declare it reality. It is true that our personal goals and values are a bedrock and upon them we build our life, our friends, and our future. We are responsible before God to the extent that we have been true to our own conscience. Nevertheless, personal values are rarely sufficient for society to use as a foundation in order to construct a mutually beneficial future together.

An individualistic value system makes it very difficult to discuss issues that face groups of people. It provides no "public philosophy," no means of addressing large value questions. If every person is "defined by their preferences, but those preferences are arbitrary, then each self constitutes its own moral universe, and there is no way to reconcile conflicting claims about what is good in itself."[37] We thus turn away from the moral norms of Abraham Lincoln, Mahatma Gandhi, Nelson Mandela, Martin Luther King, and the Protestant ethic. Feeling good takes the place of being good; self-expression uproots authority; utility displaces duty. Not only are our common values few, but often we do not even live out the ideals that we do possess. Our individualistic values make it more

---

[35] *Ibid.,* p. 25.

[36] *Ibid.,* pp. 6, 47. For a discussion of the meaning of freedom in business, see Michael Keeley, "Freedom in Organizations," *Journal of Business Ethics* 6 (May 1987): 249–263.

[37] Bellah et al., *Habits of the Heart,* pp. 76–77.

difficult to cooperate to develop a consensus on such community issues as peace, a clean environment, public health, public transportation, or working and living areas that are good for the group. Working for the common good would find fewer people saying "I want this" and more saying "This would be good for the community to which we belong."[38]

Americans have lost much of their "social capital"; they tend to choose individual pursuits rather than group activities. Over the past generation, television, two-career families, and suburban sprawl have all contributed to the fact that fewer of us are engaged in community groups. "Our growing social capital deficit threatens educational performance, safe neighborhoods, equitable tax collection, democratic responsiveness, everyday honesty, and even our health and happiness." One method that has been found to increase social capital is the implementation of community service programs. Well-designed service/learning programs "improve civic knowledge, enhance citizen efficacy, increase social responsibility and self-esteem, teach skills of cooperation and leadership, and may even reduce racism."[39]

We also find that the gap between our moral ideals and what we actually do is often large. In public opinion polls of Americans, 94 percent say that voting is an important obligation, yet only 60 percent voted in the high turnout 2004 election. Keeping fully informed about news and public affairs is said to be important by 92 percent, yet only 52 percent read a newspaper daily. Three quarters of working people say that excessive emphasis on money in the United States is an "extremely serious" or "serious" problem, yet 47 percent say that making a lot of money is "absolutely essential" or "very important." Finally, 83 percent say tolerance is an important personal guiding principle, yet 48 percent would not approve of an interracial marriage.[40] Our ideals do not much affect our actions, so our moral development is stunted. Our goals tend to be personal, so we are less likely to take actions for the sake of the community or the common good.

Postmodernism, deconstructionism, and even some aspects of feminism are cited as contributing to confusion over morals in the United States. These intellectual trends, popular in many universities, also undermine the effort to build character. Some intellectuals are convinced that it is necessary to lessen the influence of the current power elite (e.g., business, government, religious, and education leaders), because their control bends society to the elite's own benefit.[41] Their critique has much truth and is worth considering, but it also undermines efforts to develop common moral principles and a consensus-based public policy. If these philosophies were fully implemented, each of us would then have even less help in developing ethical principles and character in ourselves and our children.

---

[38]David Hollenbach, S. J., *The Common Good and Christian Ethics* (Cambridge, MA: Cambridge University Press, 2002.)
[39]Robert D. Putnam, *Bowling Alone: The Collapse and Revival of American Communities* (New York: Simon & Schuster, 2000), p. 367; see also Robert Putnam and Lewis Feldstein, *Better Together: Restoring the American Community* (New York: Simon & Schuster, 2004).
[40]"Moral State of the Union," *Responsive Community,* Winter 1994–1995, pp. 76–77.
[41]Clarence C. Walton, *Archons and Acolytes: The New Power Elite* (New York: Rowman & Littlefield, 1998).

Each person thus decides what is the moral good for him- or herself, and there is little common ground for judging moral issues. A person becomes his or her own private judge on the most important questions in life. Our individualistic notion of the moral good is thus isolated from the influence of family values, religious values, and the values of the Founding Fathers, the U.S. Constitution, and our own history (see Chapters 4 and 5). When these sources no longer provide values, it is more difficult to build personal or common goals for moral development. As a result, three out of four Americans think we are in moral and spiritual decline. However, some effort has been put forth to probe our shared values, common goals, and even the common good in U.S. business life.[42]

## Wealth and Status as Goals

Young people choosing a potential career and hence a college major are faced with a dilemma: Should I choose a college major that will afford the best salary, or should I choose a major that really satisfies me? Students and parents debate this issue, and it is not easy to resolve. Some occupations—such as engineering or accounting—offer higher starting salaries. However, some worry that college students will make career choices that provide higher initial salaries, but which will not satisfy them later in their lives.[43] To what extent should greater salary and wealth be one's personal goal? Let us provide some background.

Wealth and status are individualistic goals. They are sought out of self-interest; sometimes enlightened self-interest. However, a word of caution is in order here. Evidence is accumulating that people who focus on goals of personal financial success, social recognition, or an appealing appearance have no better and often, in fact, poorer psychological and physical health than do those who believe that such materialistic pursuits are less important. Except for those living in absolute poverty, increased wealth does not bring about greater happiness or satisfaction. One researcher followed 5,000 U.S. adults over a 9-year period. Those that had a large increase in wealth during those 9 years did not show a significant increase in happiness or satisfaction.[44] A parallel study found that 22 individuals who won large amounts of money in the lottery had no greater general satisfaction than poorer neighbors of similar background to whom they were compared. In addition, those focused on material goals report "more headaches, backaches, sore muscles and sore throats than individuals less focused on such goals."[45] These findings hold true whether people are wealthy or poor, and have been validated in many countries across the globe.

---

[42]See John W. Houck and Oliver F. Williams, eds., *Is the Good Corporation Dead? Social Responsibility in a Global Economy* (Lanham, MD: Rowman & Littlefield, 1996); see also "Where Have Our Values Gone?" *U.S. News & World Report,* August 8, 1994, p. 100; "Appealing to the 'Better Angels,' " *U.S. News & World Report,* February 7, 1994, p. 88; Robert B. Dickie and Leroy S. Rouner, *Corporations and the Common Good* (Notre Dame: University of Notre Dame Press, 1986).
[43]David Koeppel, "Choosing a College Major: For Love or for Money?" *New York Times,* December 5, 2004, p. BU1.
[44]E. Diener, E. Sandvick, L. Seidlitz, and M. Diener, "The Relationship Between Income and Subjective Well Being: Relative or Absolute?" *Social Indicators Research* 28 (1993): 195–223.
[45]Tim Kasser, *The High Price of Materialism* (Cambridge, MA: MIT Press, 2002), p. 11.

Those who are successful in accumulating additional wealth or status often find that this does not satisfy them. They see that there is more to obtain, so happiness eludes them. When increased wealth comes, individuals and even nations of people may experience short-term improvement in happiness, but that happiness often does not last. When the attainment of material goals does not bring happiness, these people think that more money or status will do so; but this is not the case, according to the data. While engaged in this materialistic pursuit, they receive less satisfaction of their needs for competence and esteem, and thus fail to address the underlying psychological issues that lead to feelings of emptiness and unhappiness, the very feelings they are trying to ameliorate with greater materialistic possessions.

People in the United States who possess a strong materialistic orientation are more likely "to watch a lot of television, compare themselves unfavorably to people they saw on television, be dissatisfied with their standard of living, and have low life satisfaction."[46] Moreover, strong materialistic values are linked to depression and anxiety, accompanied by physical problems such as headaches, and personality disorders such as narcissism and antisocial behavior.

In his extensively documented book, *The Loss of Happiness in Market Economies,* Robert Lane points out that people who live in poverty do gain in their sense of general well-being when their incomes rise. But for the advanced market democracies of the world, the spirit of unhappiness and depression haunts them:

> ... a postwar decline in the United States in people who report themselves happy, a rising tide in all advanced societies of clinical depression, increasing distrust of each other and of political and other institutions, declining belief that the lot of the average man is getting better, a tragic erosion of family solidarity and community integration together with an apparent decline in warm, intimate relations among friends.[47]

Psychological findings help us to explain some of the above sobering conclusions. When one pursues wealth and status, such pursuit often makes the achievement of personal relationships and connection to others more difficult. Materialistic goals generally lead one to invest less time and energy in relationships and communities, and this is reflected in low-quality relationships "characterized by little empathy and generosity, and by objectification, conflict, and feelings of alienation."[48] Behavior that flows from such values undermines caring, marriage, families, and local communities. We will return to the influence of our personal goals on our sense of well-being when we examine these issues within the organization in Chapter 7. However, for now let us point out two ironic conclusions to this issue which may be a surprise to some. First, economic growth

---

[46]Kasser, *The High Price,* p. 55.

[47]Robert E. Lane, *The Loss of Happiness in Market Democracies* (New Haven: Yale University Press, 2000), p. 3.

[48]Kasser, *The High Price,* p. 72; see also Mihaly Csikszentmihalyi, *Good Business: Leadership, Flow, and the Making of Meaning* (New York: Viking, 2003) and Martin E. P. Seligman, *Authentic Happiness* (New York: Free Press, 2002).

in affluent countries has provided no apparent boost to human happiness and morale. Second, for the individual person to achieve a better sense of well-being, having fewer rather than more personal material needs is more likely to bring one happiness.[49]

## Leaders Build Shared Values

Shared values for colleagues who work together is one of the most important characteristics of successful firms. Leaders of organizations, including business firms, have a unique responsibility to formulate and articulate shared values.

It is essential that leaders understand explicitly what they themselves stand for. Their values set the standards and impact the behavior of everyone in the organization. Moreover, great energy and initiative result when the values of leaders and those in the organization coincide. The most admired leaders easily and proudly speak of high ethical aspirations. They know that work colleagues want to live up to these aspirations. They do this by means of carefully chosen language, metaphors, and stories.

Examination of business leadership shows that shared values:

1. Foster strong feelings of personal effectiveness;
2. Promote high levels of company loyalty;
3. Facilitate consensus about key organizational goals and stakeholders;
4. Encourage ethical behavior;
5. Promote strong norms about working hard and caring; and
6. Reduce levels of job stress and tension.[50]

When people do communicate and cooperate better in the workplace, it generates "social capital" (alongside financial and physical capital), and this social capital is as important for the organization as are financial and physical capital. Communities that have greater social capital have been found to be more efficient and productive, and their people more motivated and happier.[51] In Chapter 8 we will see examples of successful organizations in which the leaders articulate clear and inspiring values for their colleagues within the organization.

President Abraham Lincoln was one of the most effective and inspiring leaders in U.S. history. Lincoln faced the potential end of the United States during the U.S. Civil War. Note how he combines his own values and a deep concern for others and for future generations:

> It is not merely for today, but for all time to come that we should perpetuate for our children's children this great and free government,

---

[49]David G. Myers, *Exploring Social Psychology* (Boston: McGraw-Hill, 2000), p. 319; see also Myers, "The Funds, Friends, and Faith of Happy People," *American Psychologist* 55 (January 2000): 56–67; Myers *The Pursuit of Happiness: Who Is Happy and Why?* (New York: William Morrow, 1992), pp. 39–41.
[50]James M. Kouzes and Barry Z. Posner, *The Leadership Challenge: How to Get Extraordinary Things Done in Organizations* (San Francisco: Jossey-Bass, 1987), pp. 192–193.
[51] "The Ties That Lead to Prosperity: The Economic Value of Social Bonds," *Business Week*, December 15, 1997, p. 153.

which we have enjoyed all our lives. I beg you to remember this, not merely for my sake, but for yours. I happen temporarily to occupy this big White House. I am a living witness that any one of your children may look to come here as my father's child has. It is in order that each of you may have through this free government which we have enjoyed, an open field and a fair chance for your industry, enterprise, and intelligence; that you may all have equal privileges in the race of life, with all its desirable human aspirations. It is for this the struggle should be maintained . . . That nation is worth fighting for.[52]

A leader's good values are an inspiration for developing virtue and character, and are an important part of the contribution of an effective leader.

## PERSONAL VALUES OF BUSINESSPEOPLE

The value profile of the business student has for generations been more pragmatic, materialistic, and self-centered than that of other students. For more than a generation, concern for people has been a value of less importance to business managers.[53]

The values of managers from five countries—Japan, Korea, India, Australia, and the United States—were measured and compared.[54] The value systems of these managers in widely varying cultures were more similar than different. Among the minor differences, the Japanese were more pragmatic and more homogeneous in their values and Indian managers were more moralistic.

There were significant differences between the values of younger and older managers. Compared to their senior peers, younger managers across all cultures tended to:

1. Place less importance on organizational goals
2. Place less importance on co-workers and more on themselves
3. Place less importance on trust and honor
4. Place more importance on money, ambition, and risk
5. Be slightly more pragmatic

This study was done several decades ago, but even then we can note the younger managers' slippage in values from their seniors. These younger managers have since become executives at Enron, Global Crossing, WorldCom and Arthur Andersen. Another study of moral judgment revealed that business

---

[52]Donald T. Phillips, *Lincoln on Leadership: Executive Strategies for Tough Times* (New York: Warner, 1992), pp. 164–165.
[53]Gordon Allport, Philip Vernon, and Gardner Lindzey, *Study of Values* (Boston: Houghton Mifflin, 1931); for the values of business managers, see William D. Guth and Renato Tagiuri, "Personal Values and Corporate Strategy," *Harvard Business Review* 43 (September–October 1965): 126.
[54]George W. England, "Managers and Their Value Systems: A Five-Country Comparative Study," *Columbia Journal of World Business* (Summer 1978): 35.

students in a developing country, Belize, showed a "higher stage of moral judgment" than U.S. business students.[55]

The picture that emerges is of the competitive gamesman, someone focused on his or her own life and career and less concerned about the organization, trust, honor, or other people. Since this survey, the values of businesspeople as a whole have shifted more in the same direction; the values of the then younger managers are now predominant.

A more recent extensive study examined the CEOs of firms that have been highly successful compared to peer companies. These leaders tend to be humble. They do not take credit themselves for the accomplishments of their very successful firms, but rather give credit to other people. Their ambition is for their firms, not for themselves.[56]

## Measuring Personal Values

Another examination of the values of working people found six distinct clusters of values: conformist, manipulative, sociocentric, existential, tribalistic, and egocentric.[57] The first four of these value sets were most common among managers. The conformist set was common among older, lower-level, and less-educated managers. The manipulative set was found most often among the well-educated, high-income workers in large retail organizations in the northeastern United States. Those who possessed sociocentric values tended to be well-educated, well-paid company presidents over 60 years of age.[58]

One paradox of this study is worth our attention. Company presidents tend to have sociocentric values: They encourage the development of cooperative, friendly relationships between people. For them, working with people toward a common goal is more important than getting caught up in a materialistic rat race.[59] Ironically, sociocentric managers are significantly underrepresented in jobs just two levels below the presidency. Upper level managers focus on long-term goals, and younger managers are more likely to have short-term goals of being recognized and getting ahead. Therefore, the values that get a person to within sight of the top job are not the same values that will push her or him along further. Those searching the organization for potential successors to the CEO will find *few* candidates among many in the best preparatory slots in the organization: division managers, directors, and parallel positions.

In every examination of values, managers are shown to be pragmatic—focused on efficiency and productivity. Interestingly, 61 percent of all managers say that an improvement in the quality of life in the United States will come by

---

[55]Richard Priem et al., "Moral Judgment and Values in a Developed and a Developing Nation: A Comparative Analysis," *Best Paper Proceedings — '95,* ed. Dorothy P. Moore (Vancouver: Academy of Management, 1995), pp. 401–405.
[56]Jim Collins, *Good to Great* (New York: HarperCollins, 2001), pp. 21–37.
[57]Vincent S. Flowers et al., *Managerial Values for Working* (New York: AMACOM, 1975).
[58]For a comprehensive review of research on personal, work, institutional, and group values, see Bradley R. Agle and Craig B. Caldwell, "Understanding Research on Values in Business," *Business and Society,* 38 (September 1999): 326–387.
[59]Collins, *Good to Great,* pp. 36–37.

means of a return to basic values, especially commitment and integrity. Overall, 80 percent of managers believe that their company is guided by "highly ethical standards." However, this belief is stronger among top management, and more cynical views are held by those of lower rank.[60] Clear, strong, engaging values are essential to good leadership. "A leader needs a philosophy, a set of high standards by which the organization is measured, a set of values about how employees, colleagues, and customers ought to be treated, a set of principles that make the organization unique and distinctive."[61] Indeed, where members of a firm share values, the members tend to be more ethical. Or, looking at it from the other side, where values are not shared, managers are more likely to take bribes, falsely report earnings, and steal company secrets.[62]

The above value probes of managers show that younger managers are more concerned about themselves and less about the organization. Most firms now encourage cooperation and concern for customers, fellow employees, and teamwork; therefore these attitudes of younger managers present a problem for business. Since most young people coming into business are more self-centered, it will be a challenge to choose those who respect their peers and can work in teams, and to socialize them to have greater concern for other people.[63] The exercise at the end of Chapter 1 is designed to help individuals clarify their own goals and values.

## Personal Experience Gives Direction

In earlier generations, children growing up in a family would witness their father and mother working in or near home, whether as shoemaker, baker, or farmer. They saw not only the skill and effort required in work but also the joy of accomplishment. Because commercial work is now generally done away from home, children do not often directly witness it and only hear about it through comments, often complaints.

The attitudes of all people, especially the young, are influenced by the media. Consider business as it is presented on TV and in films. Most TV and film writers have no direct experience in business. As a result, their portrayal of business professionals is often caricatured or stereotyped. Recall the TV show *The Apprentice,* in which Donald Trump goes through the process of hiring one apprentice from a pool of competing applicants with his signature phrase "you're fired." Notice how the businessperson is generally pictured as shallow, grasping, narrow, and petty, focusing only on wealth and status. When did you last see a TV program or film that presented the joy of work or useful accomplishments in business?

---

[60]Warren H. Schmidt and Barry Z. Posner, *Managerial Values in Perspective* (New York: American Management Association, 1983), pp. 29–41.

[61]James M. Kouzes and Barry Z. Posner, *The Leadership Challenge* (San Francisco: Jossey-Bass, 1987), p. 187.

[62]Barry Z. Posner, James M. Kouzes, and Warren H. Schmidt, "Shared Values Make a Difference: An Empirical Test of Corporate Culture," *Human Resources Management* 24 (Fall 1985): 299.

[63]To compare the humble CEO that Jim Collins found with the Gen X manager, see Jay A. Conger, "How 'Gen X' Managers Manage," *Strategy & Business,* First Quarter 1998, pp. 21–29.

When we try to develop good moral habits, which we will discuss in Chapter 3, TV is a major hindrance. It relentlessly presents materialism, status, sex, and violence. A task force of psychologists reported that the average child witnesses at least 8,000 murders on TV by the time she leaves *elementary* school. Another group estimates that ABC, CBS, NBC, and FOX displayed more than 10,000 sexual incidents. For every scene depicting sexual intercourse of married partners, the networks showed 14 scenes of sex outside marriage. TV pushes materialism and immediate gratification by means of its roughly 20,000 commercials a year.[64] Thus the shallow, greedy, and biased view of life as shown on cable and network TV forms the values of children and others.

In sum, although the value tests described above support some of the media stereotypes of businesspeople, these same evaluations show that older managers have strong religious and social values and that successful top executives have more balanced values and are more humble. Yet these latter facts are rarely reflected in the media. Biased perceptions have a powerful influence on all of us, especially the young and impressionable.

## Helping Behavior

It is not merely businesspeople and business students who hold social values in relatively low esteem; this is reflected in the values of much of American culture. As laboratory experiments have shown, people are heavily influenced by the values and activities of others. In any culture, norms of right and wrong are inculcated by the family, media, the neighborhood, and the workplace. But the attitudes of bystanders in the immediate vicinity have a large influence on whether our social values influence our personal values. Several laboratory experiments were prompted by the early morning 1964 murder of 28-year-old Kitty Genovese in New York City. She was stabbed to death in full view of many apartment dwellers. Later investigation showed that at least 38 people saw or heard the attack but not one person tried to help; no one even phoned the police. This story shocked the country, and some researchers decided to try to uncover what elements influence helping behavior.

In one experiment, each subject was led to believe that several other subjects had been placed in adjoining rooms connected by an interoffice phone.[65] Sometimes the subject was told there was one other subject, sometimes that there were two other subjects, and sometimes that there were five. In reality, the subject was the only person involved. During a discussion over the phone on a topic of current interest, one "participant" suffered what seemed to be an epileptic seizure; that person choked, stuttered, and called out for help. The greater the number of people the subject thought were present, the less likely the subject would be to help and the slower the subject would be to help. Apparently, the subject felt the problem could be left to others. If the subject thought no other

---

[64]"The War over 'Family Values,' " *U.S. News & World Report,* June 8, 1992, p. 36.
[65]Leonard Berkowitz, *A Survey of Social Psychology* (New York: Holt, Rinehart and Winston, 1980), pp. 374–375.

person was there to help, the subject was more likely to feel the responsibility to respond to the participant calling for help.

Similar results were obtained when individuals were placed in a room and asked to fill out a questionnaire. Subjects were either alone in the room, accompanied by two other subjects, or two confederates who were instructed to remain impassive. After a few minutes, smoke began to pour into the room through a small wall vent. Results of this experiment again showed that when other individuals are present, persons are less likely to respond in a socially responsible way. When subjects were alongside passive confederates, they reported the apparent fire only 10 percent of the time.

It seems clear that individuals will act responsibly when they personally feel the responsibility. When another, unknown person is present, they are not as likely to act responsibly. Nevertheless, these and other studies show that people will help others, even if they don't expect anything in return. Furthermore, people respond more quickly and responsibly if they have been the recipients of help themselves or if they have previously been successful in helping others. This data suggests that people working in small firms and in smaller work groups are more likely to feel responsibility for others in the work group.

Data show that volunteering to help other people has a significant positive effect on the giver's health. Researchers have found that "doing regular volunteer work, more than any other activity, dramatically increased life expectancy (and probably vitality). Men who did no volunteer work were two and a half times as likely to die during the study as men who volunteered at least once a week."[66] The results were not so dramatic for women, perhaps because most women already have close personal, helping relationships. In an attempt to explain the results, researchers point out that when one performs volunteer service there are physiological changes in the brain, which may explain the feeling of warmth when one helps another. Moreover, researchers theorize that people have evolved to depend upon others. They say that evolution has less regard for the individual than the survival of the species, and so sets up an instinct for helping others. A suggested exercise that integrates service work helping others into an academic course is included at the end of this chapter. Let us now examine the need for businesspeople to develop a greater ability to identify ethical issues so as to more easily engage in moral behavior.

## NEED FOR ETHICS IN BUSINESS

No society can long exist without some agreement about mutually held moral values. Without a level of trust and concern for others, it is impossible to live and work together. Nevertheless, more than three-quarters of Americans (78%) think that the state of moral values in the United States is now weak. Americans worry even more about moral values (53%) than about the economy (38%). Even more

---

[66]Eileen Rockefeller Growald and Alan Luks, "Beyond Self: In the Body/Mind Economy, the Benefits of Helping Other People Flow Back to the Helper," *American Health,* March 1988, pp. 51–53.

surprising, 60 percent think that the government ought to be involved in promoting moral values.[67] The 2004 national elections demonstrated the importance of moral values to the majority of Americans. Managers recognize the need for ethical norms to guide their everyday actions. Actions at every level of the firm are influenced by ethics, such as subordinate and peer interactions, use of company property, quality of work, worker and product safety, truth in advertising, and use and disposal of toxic materials.

Managers understand that without ethics the only restraint is the law. Without ethics, business agreements not written in contract form cannot be trusted. Government regulation can limit freedom, but without regulation managers must exercise better ethics in their ordinary business actions. If ethical standards do not exist, it requires more regulation, as we see in the Sarbanes-Oxley legislation enacted after the business scandals of 2001 and 2002. Moreover, without reasonable regulations, unscrupulous managers could engage in activities such as marketing unsafe drugs and dumping toxic wastes in lakes and rivers. Because of unethical managers, business agreements must be delineated by detailed contracts, insurance, reports, and lawyers. One might ask: Shall we be honest and free or dishonest and policed?

Business managers do act ethically under the following conditions: (1) when they believe that a moral principle has a bearing on a situation, and (2) when they perceive themselves as having power to affect the situation.[68] This is true not only of top managers but also of middle managers—both groups in general act ethically when they understand the ethical issues and see that they have some influence on the outcome. However, as a group, middle managers are almost twice as likely to be unethical as either top managers or lower-level managers.[69]

Fraud is stealing by concealment, and it is the most common unethical business act. Losses to business from fraud may be in the hundreds of billions of dollars annually. Fraud raises costs, lowers profits, and accounts for 30 percent of business failures. Fraud is more likely if a person is under financial pressure, if the opportunity for fraud exists, and if the person can rationalize the crime as justified, harmless, or temporary.[70]

The fraud and misdeeds of Tyco, Qwest, Computer Associates, HealthSouth, ImClone, Arthur Andersen, and so many other firms at the beginning of the twenty-first century remind us of the need for ethical managers. Unfortunately, such unethical behavior is not new. In the previous 20 years, a surprisingly large number of American firms were involved in both unethical and illegal activities. During one 10-year period, 11 percent of the largest U.S. firms were convicted of bribery, criminal fraud, illegal campaign contributions, tax evasion, or price fixing.

---

[67]Data from a Gallup/CNN Poll quoted in *USA Today,* August 6, 1996, p. 4A.
[68]See the field research reported in the series of three articles by James A. Waters and Frederick Bird: "Everyday Moral Issues Experienced by Managers," *Journal of Business Ethics* 5 (October 1986): 373–384; "The Nature of Managerial Moral Standards," *Journal of Business Ethics,* 6 (January 1987): 1–13; "The Moral Dimension of Organizational Culture," *Journal of Business Ethics,* 6 (January 1987): 15–22.
[69]"Middle Managers Most Likely to Be Unethical," *Management Accounting,* December 1987, p. 3.
[70]W. Steve Albrecht, Gerald W. Wernz, and Timothy L. Williams, *Fraud: Bringing Light to the Dark Side of Business* (Burr Ridge, IL: Irwin, 1995).

Firms that had two or more convictions include Allied, American Airlines, Bethlehem Steel, Diamond International, Firestone, Goodyear, International Paper, J. Ray McDermott, National Distillers, Northrop, Occidental Petroleum, PepsiCo, Phillips Petroleum, Rapid-American, R. J. Reynolds, Schlitz, Seagram, Tenneco, and United Brands. Leading the list are firms that had at least four convictions each: Braniff International, Gulf Oil, and Ashland Oil. Both large pay-offs to government officials and smaller "facilitating" payments divert resources, undermine competition, and hinder economic development.[71] But crime and immorality are punished when the market price of a firm's stock collapses as the news of the criminal act is made known.[72] The ultimate punishment was meted out to the worst offenders when Braniff went bankrupt and Gulf and Ashland Oil were taken over. Management fraud in the early part of the twenty-first century ended in bankruptcy for Enron, Adelphia, WorldCom, and Arthur Andersen.

Most of the large U.S. petroleum firms have contributed illegally to presidential election campaigns: Standard of California, Exxon, Sun, Ashland, Gulf, and Getty. The chairman of Phillips personally handed Richard Nixon $50,000 in Nixon's own apartment. Managers in many firms also made multimillion-dollar foreign bribery payments: Exxon, Lockheed, McDonnell Douglas, United Brands, Mobil, Gulf, and Phillips. When Congress learned of this, they passed the U.S. Foreign Corrupt Practices Act (see Chapter 8). The chief executives of Gulf, American Airlines, and Lockheed lost their jobs because of the unethical payments. On the other hand, the CEOs of Northrop, Phillips, and Exxon, who were just as guilty, were excused by their boards. Firms in the U.S. are not alone in engaging in bribery and other unethical behavior. Executives from the Japanese electronics firm Hitachi stole trade secrets from IBM. After being caught, the firm and executives pled guilty and agreed to pay damages to IBM.[73] Other Asian, as well as German and French, firms have also been guilty of bribery and stealing trade secrets.

## Personal Greed or Corporate Pressure

Embezzlement and fraud are committed to benefit the individual and are motivated by personal greed. Bribery, price fixing, and compromising product and worker safety are often responses to pressure for bottom-line results. According to the perpetrators, they are done "for the sake of the firm." A study of the ethics of managers showed that 59 to 70 percent felt "pressured to compromise personal ethics to achieve corporate goals."[74] This perception increased among lower-level managers. A majority felt that most managers would not refuse to market

[71]"The Destructive Cost of Greasing Palms," *Business Week,* December 6, 1993, pp. 133–138; Irwin Ross, "How Lawless Are Big Companies?" *Fortune,* December 1, 1980, pp. 56–64; see also Robert K. Elliott and John J. Willingham, *Management Fraud: Detection and Deterrence* (New York: Petrocelli Books, 1980).
[72]Wallace Davidson and Dan Worrell, "The Impact of Announcements of Corporate Illegalities on Shareholder Returns," *Academy of Management Journal* 31 (March 1988): 195–200.
[73]"IBM Data Plot Tied to Hitachi and Mitsubishi," *Wall Street Journal,* June 23, 1982, p. 4; David B. Tinnin, "How IBM Stung Hitachi: Espionage," *Fortune,* March 7, 1983, pp. 50–56.
[74]Archie Carroll, "Managerial Ethics," *Business Horizons,* April 1975, pp. 75–80.

below-standard and possibly dangerous products. Even so, it is encouraging to note that 90 percent supported a code of ethics for business and the teaching of ethics in business schools. They presumably sought a level playing field where they would not be pressured into unethical acts. Pressures to act unethically occur in many firms, but especially in large firms that are operating in a dynamic and competitive environment.[75]

Pressure and organizational culture can dull the ethical judgment of managers. Behavior that the manager finds unethical at home or before taking a job is often considered acceptable on the job. Laboratory research shows that unethical behavior increases as the culture becomes more competitive and that it increases even more if such behavior is rewarded. Conversely, a threat of punishment tends to deter unethical behavior. Whether a person acts ethically or unethically is also very strongly influenced by the individual's personal ethical values and by informal organizational policy.[76]

Instances of unethical behavior by managers point to the need for:

**1.** Good character, nourished by a sensitive and informed conscience;
**2.** The ability to make ethical judgments; and
**3.** A business culture that rewards ethical behavior and punishes unethical behavior.

In simpler societies, people daily deal face-to-face with others whom they might be tempted to cheat, and this provides a built-in safeguard against unethical behavior. In large organizations, in complex societies, and when people contact one another largely by telephone or e-mail, developing ethical sensitivities and good character is far more important in preventing wrongful actions.

## Enlightened Self-Interest and Ethics

Advocates of free markets argue that the pursuit of enlightened self-interest (for definition, see Figure 2-2) by managers results in greater honesty and better ethics among businesspeople. They argue that high ethical standards are in the long-term best interest of the firm. Such a simplistic, straightforward position sounds reasonable. However, it does not always work very effectively.

One problem with this view is that *enlightened* is an elastic term and does not have the same meaning for everyone. Also, even if agreement existed on the meaning of *enlightened,* self-interest in action can easily slip into selfishness. Our normal human selfish desires (many call it original sin) distort our perceptions of what is in our long-term interest. Making the problem worse, the selfish manager, such as "chain saw" Al Dunlap (who laid off tens of thousands, ruined several firms, and yet took millions of dollars in compensation for himself), is sometimes excused by free enterprise ideologies.

---

[75]Melissa S. Baucus and Janet P. Near, "Can Illegal Corporate Behavior Be Predicted? An Event History Analysis," *Academy of Management Journal* 34 (February 1991): 9–36.
[76]W. Harvey Hegarty and Henry P. Sims, Jr., "Unethical Decision Behavior: An Overview of Three Experiments," in *Academy of Management Proceedings,* 1979, p. 9.

**FIGURE 2-2** Self-interest Terms

| | |
|---|---|
| *Altruism* | Concern for the welfare of others and less concern for self |
| *Enlightened self-interest* | Norm for assessing self-interest, used by a mature, enlightened person, viewing the long-term |
| *Individualism* | A view that all values, rights, and duties originate in the individual and that the community has no value not derived from individual constituents |
| *Self-interest* | Norm for thinking and acting that focuses on the benefits and advantages accruing to oneself and/or one's own personal interests |
| *Selfishness* | Concern for one's self without regard for others |

Experience shows that for a mature person to operate effectively in any environment, some altruism is necessary. That is, contrary to the self-interest endorsed by Ayn Rand, one must also consider the benefits and harms that others will experience, and one must even be willing on occasion to sacrifice one's own personal benefits for the sake of others. Altruism encourages personal virtue and good character; it is a protection for the individual and for society as a whole. On the other hand, in many instances, enlightened self-interest can provide a shortcut method of solving problems effectively and efficiently but, like all shortcuts, it cannot handle all cases. In addition, when one chooses enlightened self-interest as an ideology, one feels compelled to justify every action by pointing out how it will increase the profitability of the firm. Financial analysts and shareholders may be pleased, but this subordinates people and ethics to money, and places managers in a rigid, simplistic mind-set.

Instances arise when ethical treatment of others, perhaps people outside the firm, will be at a net cost to an individual or firm. Since many popular forms of free market ideology do not permit consideration of others for their own sake, businesspeople who hold such positions are in danger of falling over the cliff into immorality. Moreover, as we have seen, many do fall, and they are more likely to fall if they hold that enlightened self-interest should always be the motivation for one's actions. Examples of ethically good behavior and of selfish behavior among managers will be presented in Chapter 8. In sum, enlightened self-interest will take one a long way toward being more efficient and even more ethical, but it falls short of taking one the entire distance.

When considering the ethics of a situation, each person takes a basic stance toward other people. There are five possible ways one can consider oneself in relation to others:[77]

---

[77]Adapted from Garth Hallett, *Reason and Right* (Notre Dame, IN: Notre Dame Press, 1984).

1. Self alone
2. Self first
3. Self equally as others
4. Others first
5. Others alone

People who consider only themselves alone are selfish egoists. People who consider themselves first but also consider others are more enlightened. Equitable consideration of oneself and others is suggested by the Golden Rule ("Do unto others as you would have them do unto you"). Considering others first or others alone are generous forms of altruism.[78] Good parents consider their children first. When such selfless action is not, for example, co-dependency, but is done in a mentally healthy way, it is morally mature. Consideration only of others is the attitude of an unselfish, generous, saintly person (e.g., Mother Theresa). Such saintly people are rare, and are heroes and models of behavior for many people.

## Customs, Bias, and Culture

Even though managers recognize the importance of ethics, in the mind of the average person ethics is hard to distinguish from culturally determined attitudes. When ethics are not distinguished from culturally determined attitudes, difficult ethical dilemmas are resolved arbitrarily, for there seem to be no objective values or norms that can be used to help judge the issues. We noted the effect of the predominant American value of freedom earlier in the chapter (see "Individualism and the Common Good"). If each person uses his or her own unique ethical norms, it is impossible to decide that one action is ethical and another is less so. Moreover, even experts in ethics differ among themselves, thus encouraging the popular notion that ethics is not an objective discipline and no common norms exist.

Almost everyone recognizes the need for ethical norms for use by all, yet it is also clear that developing these norms is no easy task. Facing us are different value systems, various perceptions of facts, and different judgments on tradeoffs. Moreover, even if we could develop adequate ethical decision-making norms, this would not necessarily make decisions easy. Ethical issues are not easily framed in terms of measurable data, unlike financial (return on investment) or marketing (share of market) issues. Nevertheless, a developed sensitivity to other people's concerns and an understanding of ethical principles provides a foundation for making good ethical judgments. Moreover, it is effective insurance against serious ethical blunders, such as, for example, Enron and WorldCom lying about income, ITT helping to overthrow the elected democratic government of Chile, and Lockheed bribing top Japanese and Dutch government leaders. Making the

---

[78]For an argument that altruism is not common, see George Loewenstein, "Behavioral Decision Theory and Business Ethics: Skewed Trade-offs Between Self and Other," in *Codes of Conduct: Behavioral Research into the Firm*, David M. Messick and Ann E. Tenbrunsel, eds., (New York: Russell Sage Foundation, 1996), pp. 214–227.

behavior of managers more ethical also can enable a firm to be a better producer, employer, and citizen and thus a more trusted and valued member of society.

The moral growth of organizations, which can be compared to the moral growth of people, is one aspect of corporate culture, and it is the responsibility of the leaders of the organization.[79] A multitude of personal ethical decisions provides the foundation for both the moral growth of people and the moral growth of organizations. Speaking of the growth of an organization in general and its moral growth in particular, Moses Pava says:

> This growth is hardly natural. When it does occur, it is the outcome of lit-
> erally thousands of large and small decisions on the part of the organiza-
> tional members and other stakeholders who can impact the organization.
> When the decision outcomes are more or less correct, organizational
> growth follows; otherwise, organizations are stymied, corporate decline
> sets in, and organizational survival is put in jeopardy.[80]

From the above we can conclude the following:

1. A sense of what is right and wrong, plus ethical norms for making judgments, is essential for any person, including business managers.
2. Ethical norms are not easily derived. Moreover, there is often disagreement about the facts of a particular case, the relevant norms, and the various tradeoffs.

We thus recognize both the importance of the task and the difficulty in accomplishing it.

## Young People and Morals

Writers like Rousseau and Emerson (see Chapters 4 and 5) believe that human beings are by nature good, and thus hold that young people are good until tarnished by modern civilization. The data indicate otherwise. The earlier section of this chapter on moral development presents evidence that infants are born self-centered and that individuals must mature in their ethical skills.

Moreover, studies show that many young people are involved in unethical acts. A large-scale study of more than 3,000 Illinois teenagers done over a 6-year period revealed some startling facts. One-third of all 14- to 18-year-olds had been involved in a serious crime. Thirteen percent admitted taking part in a robbery, 40 percent acknowledged keeping stolen goods, and 50 percent admitted shoplifting. Moreover, many of the conventional "predictors" for criminal behavior did not hold true. Except for the most violent behavior, the delinquent was just as likely to be a girl as a boy, to be white as black, to come from a small town as from an inner city. Peers had more influence on these young people than their parents did. In fact, in 80 percent of the cases, parents did not know about the offenses their children

---

[79]For some suggestions, see Helen J. Alford, O.P. and Michael J. Naughton, *Managing as If Faith Mattered* (Notre Dame, IN: Notre Dame University Press, 2001).
[80]Moses L. Pava, "The Path of Moral Growth," *Journal of Business Ethics,* 38 (June 2002): 43–54.

had committed. One research team member spent two years alongside youths in a wealthy Chicago suburb and reported a "near vacuum of morality enclosed by the perimeter of the edict to achieve. Anything that jeopardizes their occupational future is bad. The rest really doesn't matter." Peer pressure has a strong influence on adolescent attitudes and conduct.[81] In a similar and frightening reminder, the parents of the two Columbine murderers, Klebold and Harris, had little knowledge of their son's activities leading up to the 1999 shooting of a dozen classmates and a teacher in Colorado.

Considerable unethical behavior also occurs in colleges and universities. A study of 6,000 students in 31 colleges and universities around the United States indicated that more than two-thirds acknowledged that they had cheated on a test or major assignment while undergraduates. The lowest percentage of admitted cheaters were in schools of education (57%), the highest percentage (76%) were in graduate business schools.[82] Once they got into the business world, 66 percent of all students in another survey said that "they would consider lying to achieve a business objective." Roughly the same proportion would "inflate their business expense report."[83] Such attitudes, consistent over several decades, present a problem for business firms, business schools, and society as a whole.

## Need for Ethics in Business and in Business Schools

Both business schools and business firms know that ethics and moral values are vital to any business enterprise. When they considered introducing ethics into the curriculum, Harvard Business School faculty studied the ethical needs of graduate business students. They found that:

> ... these talented, highly motivated students have a strong sense of interpersonal accountability—of being trustworthy—in immediate face-to-face situations with colleagues and superiors. Yet perhaps because many of them have been insulated from diversity and failure, and have not heretofore been encouraged to critically reflect upon some of the important issues before them and their societies, they only have a limited sense of what is at stake. As a consequence, most do not yet articulate a vision by which they believe they could positively affect our collective life—signaling an absence of worthy myths and dreams. Unless they are effectively initiated into the public purposes and ethical norms of their profession, they will be ill-prepared to provide managerial leadership capable of engaging complex relationships

---

[81]Donna R. Clasen and Sue Eicher, "Perceptions of Peer Pressure, Peer Conformity Dispositions, and Self-reported Behavior Among Adolescents," *Developmental Psychology* 22 (April 1986): 521–530; on earlier data, see "Kid Crime: Host of Juveniles Admit Serious Acts," *Detroit Free Press,* January 24, 1977, pp. 1, 2.

[82]Donald L. McCabe, "The Influence of Situational Ethics on Cheating Among College Students," *Journal of Sociological Inquiry* 63 (1992): 365–374.

[83]Rushworth M. Kidder, *How Good People Make Tough Choices: Resolving the Dilemmas of Ethical Living* (New York: William Morrow, 1995), pp. 48–50.

among conflicting loyalties within a vision of the common good. They will not be able to provide ethical leadership in public life.[84]

The resulting first year ethics course at Harvard, and the halting efforts of other business schools to integrate ethics into the curriculum will be discussed in Chapter 3.

In his pleading for more attention to ethics and character education in colleges and universities, Arthur J. Schwartz, the director of character education programs at the John Marx Templeton foundation, provides—a bleak assessment of the current situation: "Only a relatively few institutions usually small liberal arts colleges or those that are religiously affiliated or faith inspired—have a wide and comprehensive commitment to character development in all dimensions of college life." This is unfortunate, since business is now looking for people of good ethics and character.[85]

Recent fraud, jail sentences, and the negative publicity on corruption in business have damaged the reputation of business and have increased the felt need for ethics and ethics education. In opinion polls, nearly 75 percent of Americans say that you cannot be too careful in dealing with CEOs of large corporations, and almost 80 percent believe that top managers will take "improper actions" to help themselves at the expense of their firms. Only 23 percent of Americans believe that CEOs of large corporations can be trusted, and 39 percent see Big Business as a threat to the nation's future.[86]

On the other hand, and even before the fraud publicity, business executives and the actions of their firms demonstrated the importance of ethics. Almost two-thirds of executives are convinced that high ethical standards strengthen a firm's competitive position. Almost all U.S. firms and a vast majority of non-U.S. firms have a code of ethics.[87] More than 100 boards of directors of large firms have established an ethics or social responsibility committee of the board. CEO speeches, annual reports, and special social and environmental responsibility reports stress the importance of ethics in business decisions. Groups such as the Aspen Institute and the World Resources Institute have devoted resources to encouraging additional studies of ethics in business school curricula.[88] We will present additional information on ethical corporate governance in Chapter 8.

In sum, the need for ethics in business is clear. The daily news stories of unethical activities remind us of the need for ethical managers. Most executives and managers try to be ethical. However, many business students and

---

[84]Parks, "Is It Too Late?", p. 19.
[85]Arthur J. Schwartz, "It's Not Too Late to Teach College Students About Values," *Chronicle of Higher Education,* June 9, 2000.
[86]Gallup/CNN/*USA Today* Poll, July 16, 2002. Additional data is available on both the Gallup and the *USA Today* Web sites.
[87]Ronald E. Berenbeim, "Corporate Ethics Practices: Corporate Ethics Codes" (New York: Conference Board Report, 1992); see also R. Edward Freeman and Daniel R. Gilbert, Jr., *Corporate Strategy and the Search for Ethics* (Englewood Cliffs, NJ: Prentice Hall, 1988).
[88]See *Beyond Grey Pinstripes—2001: Preparing MBAs for Social and Environmental Stewardship* (Washington, D.C.: Aspen Institute, 2001).

businesspeople have shallow personal goals and are ill-equipped to recognize and to decide ethical problems. They do not possess the sensitivity, the concepts, or the models for effectively resolving ethical difficulties. The next chapter will provide concepts, norms, and models to aid managers in solving ethical dilemmas and building character.

## SUMMARY AND CONCLUSIONS

Emphasis on success and winning can cause stress and serious physical ailments. Particularly prone to heart disease, stroke, ulcers, and other illnesses are the irritable, cynical, and aggressively competitive Type A managers. The ambition of aggressively competitive managers pushes them ahead rapidly in the organization, but it is ultimately a barrier to getting to the top. Most chief executives generally are patient, humble, and have the ability to listen, weigh alternatives, and work cooperatively.

Maturity and moral development go hand in hand. In the same way as people grow emotionally and psychologically, so do they grow morally. Without maturity and moral development, people risk traumatic challenges in middle age. On the other hand, people who have reflected on and owned their goals and values do not face the same anxiety, stress, and the debilitating diseases that stem from stress; rather they confidently confront the changes that come during the midlife reassessment. By being aware of their own personal goals and values and how they relate to others, they are better able to live, love, and enjoy life and work.

The morally developed person is better equipped to face ethical dilemmas. That person has the maturity and skills necessary to gather the facts, search for the most appropriate ethical norms, and make a reasoned ethical judgment. We will detail that process in Chapter 3.

Recent business fraud speaks loudly of the need for ethics in business. The prevalence of corporate crime and unethical and greedy acts by individuals, as well as the lack of ethical skills among Americans, argues for developing our ethical sensitivities and our ability to make ethical judgments. The next chapter presents some methods and models that have proven to aid ethical decision-making and character development.

## DISCUSSION QUESTIONS

1. What are the symptoms of a midlife crisis? Under what conditions will the effects of the midlife transition be less traumatic?
2. Why do you think that the dean of Harvard Business School found it necessary to advise his graduates about the importance of their home lives? Was that advice appropriate and wise?
3. What causes anxieties and stress? What physical ailments do these lead to? What do the above described experiments using rats and cats tell us? What role does alcohol play?

4. What is the relation between moral development and maturity? What is the relation of moral development to ethics?

5. What did Harvard Business School find regarding the need for ethics and a moral vision among its students? Do you think these values are typical of other graduate business students?

6. Describe the differences between a person at Kohlberg's Level I and another at Level II. Describe the differences between a person at Level II and another at Level III. At what level are most people?

7. What are the strengths and the weaknesses of the American view that freedom is the most important value? In what way is freedom a moral good?

8. How is this view of freedom an obstacle to discovering the "common good" or encouraging community values?

9. Why does the pursuit of wealth and status generally not bring happiness to people who have already met their basic needs? What physical and psychological illnesses does such pursuit often bring? Why is this so?

10. According to William Damon, in order to help children develop moral maturity, a consensus is required in a community (parents, school, coaches). Does this present a conflict with the American view of freedom and individual rights? Is there a solution to this conflict? Explain.

11. Business executives tend to have less social concern than others. What processes tend to perpetuate their lack of concern?

12. Under what circumstances is an individual more likely to come to the aid of another person? Describe the results of the experiments on coming to the aid of another.

13. What events of the last decade underscore the need for business ethics? List the ways that firms have responded positively to this need.

14. What are the principal limitations of free enterprise or self-interest ideology? How do the limitations differ for self-interest that is "enlightened"? Does enlightened self-interest ensure that a person will act ethically? Why? Give an example.

15. Is inflating costs or selling poor-quality goods less bad if the individual making the decisions to do so does not profit?

16. What do the surveys show about the ethics of young people compared to the ethics of their elders? What accounts for the difference?

# CASES

## Case 2-1      Inflated Résumé

Alex Albertson has performed well as a manager for 4 years at Sentel Systems. Because he has applied for promotion to director of his unit, his résumé is checked by Human Resources. He claims to have an MBA from Santa Clara University. However, HR finds out that he dropped out of the program within two courses of finishing when he accepted this current job.

1. Would you continue to consider Alex for the promotion?
2. Would you fire him?
3. Would you discipline him? Explain.
4. What ethical norms help you in your decision? ∎

## Case 2-2      Drug Test

Karen Matthews, 38, was working in her laboratory when her supervisor made a request. Her supervisor handed her a small bottle and told her to produce a urine sample. Karen refused. The next day Karen was fired for her refusal.

1. Was Karen correct to refuse?
2. Does the company have the right to ask for a urine sample? ∎

## Case 2-3      Bank Deposit Insurance

In an economic downturn investors worry about the safety and security of financial institutions. Perceptions that banks are unstable could cause investors to withdraw their money, and thus cause the failure. Hence, bank deposits up to $100,000 are insured by the Federal Deposit Insurance Corporation (FDIC).

Branch managers are responsible for maintaining deposit totals in their branch offices. You are an assistant branch manager and you have just heard your manager explaining the FDIC coverage to a customer who maintains more than $300,000 in your bank. The customer was obviously very concerned about the safety of her funds. The bank manager misinterpreted the FDIC guidelines and reassured the customer that her life savings are properly insured when they are not.

The manager's annual performance review and salary increase are partially based on the dollar amount of total deposits in that office. The manager knows that the customer will withdraw the funds that are not insured by the FDIC and that the branch will lose the deposits. You tell the manager that her assurance to the customer was in error. The manager tells you not to be concerned, since the customer does not understand the financial soundness of the bank and is worried only because of a mistaken fear that banks will close as they did during the Great Depression.

Discuss the ethics of the case.

1. Since the customer does not understand the intricate workings of the banking system, is the manager justified in allowing the customer to believe her funds are safe?
2. Is the bank manager's explanation acceptable? ■

## EXERCISE

### Service-Learning in the Community

Doing service work for people in need in agencies in the city provides an opportunity for experiential learning. Service-learning also enables you to gain insights into some of the issues that you will be studying in this course: personal values, moral development, work place diversity, poverty, ecology, moral responsibilities of management, and corporate social policy. In addition, repairing the weaknesses in our society is in the best interest of business; healthy people, families, and neighbors provide good employees and customers to business. Service-learning is a part of dozens of graduate business programs in the United States.

In order to participate in the service-learning project, you are asked to:

1. *Do service* for at least 12 hours during the term in an agency that you and the instructor agree upon. This should be an agency that serves the poor, such as a homeless shelter, soup kitchen, an organization that tutors inner-city youth, or one that delivers food to the disabled and elderly in the inner city.
2. *Write a journal* entry of your own reflections after each session of volunteer work.
3. *Participate in a reflection session* that will help you to reflect on your experiences. Some questions to consider for the reflection session:
   a. Describe your experience (agency, setting, etc.) of service-learning.
   b. What about the experience was most troubling?
   c. What was most inspiring or empowering?
   d. What in society has brought about this problem (e.g., homelessness, inability to get a decent meal, lack of affordable housing)? What are the social and political causes of the problem? What might be done to address the problem? What initiative would make this agency unnecessary?
   e. What did you learn?
   f. Were you affected or changed in any way? How?
   g. Describe at least two concepts from the course that are illustrated in your service experience.

h. Has this service-learning increased your awareness of responsible leadership in our communities? How?

4. *Write a 6-page reflection paper* on your service-learning experiences. The reflection paper is due on the second-to-last class.

An alternate plan: The service-learning project can be done in teams of four to five, and can be the subject of an end-of-the-term presentation in place of the paper.

# CHAPTER 3

## Ethical Behavior in Business

A billion dollars doesn't go as far as it used to.

J. PAUL GETTY (1892–1976), FOUNDER, GETTY OIL COMPANY

No one was ever honored for what he received. Honor has been the reward for what he gives.

CALVIN COOLIDGE (1872–1933), PRESIDENT OF THE UNITED STATES, 1923–1929

The ethical failures of Enron, Arthur Andersen, WorldCom, and Tyco underscore the need for ethical behavior in business. To be an ethical adult requires moral maturity and the ability to make ethical judgments along with a developed habit of doing so. We examined moral development in the last chapter. In this chapter we will (1) provide the tools for making ethical judgments, and (2) describe how the individual person develops good moral habits, virtue, and character. In the first portion of the chapter we will ask: How does one make a judgment about what is morally right and wrong? What norms, models, and techniques are available for helping us to make ethical decisions?

Ethics can be defined as the principles of conduct governing an individual or a group, and the methods for applying them. Ethics provides the tools to make moral judgments. Let us provide a few examples of situations that call for ethical judgments.

Andrew S. Fastow, former chief financial officer of Enron, with an MBA from Northwestern University, pleaded guilty to two counts of fraud. He admitted to setting up false accounts to hide losing transactions of billions of dollars from investors and employees and enriching himself.[1]

---

[1]Jack Hitt, "American Kabucki: The Ritual of Scandal," *New York Times,* July 18, 2004, sec. 4, pp. 1, 3.

Jason Stacy, a graduate student in California, uses Napster to take music from the Internet for his own use. He gives some of that music to friends, and also sells it to fellow students.

In a study of managers' ethics, 47 percent of top executives, 41 percent of controllers, and 76 percent of graduate business students were willing to commit fraud by understating write-offs that cut into their companies' profits. In addition, 29 percent of teenagers say that one has to "bend the rules to succeed" in business.[2]

Nearly two-thirds (62%) of high school students admitted that they cheated on an exam at least once in the past year; 27 percent acknowledged stealing something from a store during this same period, and 40 percent said that they would sometimes lie to save money. Yet, showing an inconsistency, 74 percent rated their character as higher than their peers, and 98 percent said that it was important for them to be a person of good character.[3]

A Pennsylvania man advertised "Blank receipts, 100 restaurant receipts, 50 styles, $5.98. Satisfaction guaranteed." The blank receipts are attractively designed to look like the receipts of restaurants anywhere in America: Captain's Table, Trophy Room, Village Green, P.J.'s, and so on. The idea is that the purchaser, after filling in a date, a number of diners, and a total bill, can use these faked receipts in reporting expenses. An IRS spokesperson says that selling blank receipts is not illegal.

Each of these cases raises ethical issues of concern to businesspeople today. They illustrate the central importance of ethics. Almost all important business decisions contain an ethical component. One purpose of this chapter is to better equip us to make effective ethical judgments.

## FACTS, VALUES, AND ACTS

Ethics provides the tools for making ethical judgments, and helps develop the habits that result in morally good behavior. Good behavior requires the ability to make moral decisions, so we present norms, methods, and models that enable an individual to make ethically good decisions. Making ethical judgments involves three steps: (1) gathering relevant factual information, (2) selecting the moral norm(s) that are most applicable, and (3) making the ethical judgment on the rightness or wrongness of the act or policy (see Figure 3-1).

Ethical judgments are not always easy to make. The facts of the case are often not clear-cut, and the ethical criteria or principles to be used are not always agreed on, even by the experts. Hence, to many businesspeople, ethics seems to be ill-defined, subjective, and thus not very useful. Just as in the cases of politics

---

[2]"For Many Executives, Ethics Appear to Be a Write-Off," *Wall Street Journal,* March 26, 1996, pp. C1, C13; for teenagers, *Business Week,* September 20, 2004, p. 16.
[3]"The Ethics of American Youth: 2004 Report Card," polling done by and reported by the Josephson Institute of Ethics, at www.josephsoninstitute.org/Survey2004/, accessed December 31, 2004.

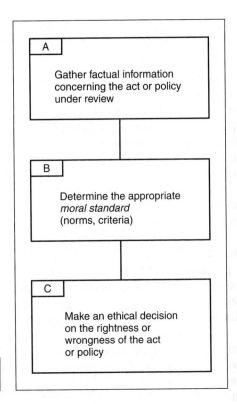

**FIGURE 3-1** Steps in Ethical Decision Making

A

Gather factual information concerning the act or policy under review

B

Determine the appropriate *moral standard* (norms, criteria)

C

Make an ethical decision on the rightness or wrongness of the act or policy

and religion, there is often more heat than light generated by ethical discussions. This lack of knowledge of and confidence in ethics is unfortunate, since without ethical principles, it is everyone for him- or herself. As a result, trust, which is essential to any business transaction and to all commerce, is lost.[4]

## Dilemmas to Decisions

Let us begin our examination of ethical decision making by assessing a case that was first judged by 1,700 business executive readers of the *Harvard Business Review*. This case was part of an early large-scale study of business ethics by Raymond C. Baumhart, S.J.[5]

---

[4]For an overview of the importance of trust in organizations, see LaRue Tone Hosmer, "Trust: The Connecting Link Between Organizational Theory and Philosophical Ethics," *Academy of Management Review,* 20 (April 1995): pp. 379–403; see also Roger C. Mayer, James H. Davis, and F. David Schoorman, "An Integrative Model of Organizational Trust," *Academy of Management Review,* 20 (July 1995): 709–734.

[5]Raymond C. Baumhart, S.J., *Ethics in Business* (New York: Holt, Rinehart and Winston, 1968), p. 21. For later views using the original instruments, see Steven Brenner and Earl Molander, "Is the Ethics of Business Changing?" *Harvard Business Review* 55 (January–February 1977): 57–71. The dollar figures in this case have been adjusted for inflation. Also, S. T. Vitell and T. A. Festervand, "Business Ethics: Conflicts, Practices, and Beliefs of Industrial Executives," *Journal of Business Ethics,* 5 (1987): 111–122; Chiake Nakano, "A Survey Study on Japanese Managers' Views of Business Ethics," paper presented at the Society for Business Ethics, Vancouver, B.C., 1995.

An executive earning $150,000 a year has been padding her expense account by about $7,500 a year.[6]

Is it ethical to pad one's expense account? On numerous occasions over the decades hundreds of managers have been asked to judge this case, and the results have been substantially the same. Replying to an anonymous questionnaire and speaking for themselves, 85 percent of executives both in the United States and in Japan think that this sort of behavior is simply unacceptable. Perhaps more telling, almost two-thirds of them think their business colleagues would also see such behavior as unacceptable under any circumstances.

Why would padding an expense account be considered wrong by these executives? An expense account is not a simple addition to one's salary. It is designed to cover the actual expenses required to do one's work.

Pocketing a company pencil or making a personal long-distance phone call from the office may seem relatively trivial. Perhaps, but fabricating expenses up to 5 percent of one's salary is not trivial; it is a substantial violation of justice. The executive in the case is stealing money not owed to her. Presumably the executive's salary is ample compensation for her work, and the extra $7,500 is not intended as direct compensation, nor is it recognized by law as such.

Circumstances are often cited that might seem to mitigate the injustice. Some might say, "Many others are also doing it" or "My superior knows about it and says nothing." In the cited study, only about a quarter of the executives thought that their peers would justify such actions on these counts. A mere handful (about 10%) said that they themselves thought that it would be acceptable in such circumstances. Let us further examine these mitigating circumstances.

## But Others Are Doing It; My Superior Knows About It and Says Nothing

The fact that many people are performing certain actions, or that certain actions are condoned, or even ordered, by one's superiors never in itself makes those actions ethically acceptable. For example, the fact that superiors ordered actions is not a legal or moral defense for the unethical managers at Enron. It is not a defense for the military guards who tortured Iraqi prisoners at Abu Ghraib prison outside Baghdad. Nor was it a defense for concentration camp officers being tried at the post–World War II Nuremberg war crime trials. Even though these Nazi officers were under orders, and even though many of their peers felt that killing "undesirables" was alright, it was not accepted as either a moral or a legal defense. Although ethics is influenced by conditions, a moral principle is not established by voting.

Let us go back to the case of the expense account. It would be to the executive's benefit if she could increase her salary by 5 percent. To have that extra $7,500 would be in her self-interest. Focusing primarily on her self-interest could easily lead her to

---

[6]An expense account is to be prepared for expenses that are incurred in the course of one's work. It is not fair to ask an employee to use personal funds, without reimbursement, for legitimate business expenses.

be less objective in her search for the right action and would make her more prone to look for excuses to do that which would benefit her.

Justice calls for a fair distribution of the benefits and burdens of society. In this case, we are concerned with benefits. Is it ever ethical to claim funds from an expense account that were not expenses? The executive's family is not starving because she has an abnormally low salary, so justice tells us that the expense account should not be used as a salary supplement. Ignorance and coercion can lessen responsibility. However, in this case, the executive could hardly claim that she did not know what an expense account was or that she was forced into taking the money.

But if she is not likely to be caught, why shouldn't she pad her expense account? Practically all businesspeople agree that a businessperson should be ethical. That is, individuals should try to do good and avoid evil, not only on the job but in all aspects of life. An essential foundation for business transactions is confidence that most businesspeople are trustworthy, truthful, and ethical. If most businesspeople were not ethical, it would be extremely difficult to purchase goods, sell property or securities, or do most of the exchange that we are accustomed to doing in modern society.

Admittedly there can be a short-term financial benefit for an embezzler or a supplier who charges $10 million and delivers defective goods. It is because of individuals like this that we have laws, courts, and jails. Yet we also know that not all activities can be regulated, nor can all unethical acts be fully punished (in this life, anyway). If a large percentage of businesspeople did not pay their bills and cheated their business partners, the business system would collapse.[7]

## ETHICAL PRINCIPLES FOR BUSINESS ACTIONS

How to help people make better ethical decisions has been the subject of much reflection over the centuries. The theory of rights and duties is founded on the human dignity of individual people and results in personal entitlements. Immanuel Kant[8] (personal rights) and John Locke[9] (property rights) were the first to fully develop the theory of rights and duties. The theory of justice is also based on the dignity of each person and has a longer tradition, going back to Plato and Aristotle in the fourth century BC.[10]

Businesspeople feel most at home using the ethical norm of utilitarianism. This is not surprising, because this norm examines consequences of actions, and traces its origins to Adam Smith, the father of modern economics. The main proponents

---

[7]See Nobel Prize–winning economist Amartya Sen, "Economics, Business Principles and Moral Sentiments," *Business Ethics Quarterly,* 7 (July 1997): 5–15; James H. Davis and John A. Ruhe, "Perceptions of Corruption: Antecedents and Outcomes," *Journal of Business Ethics,* 43 (April 2003): 275–288.

[8]Immanuel Kant, *The Metaphysical Elements of Justice,* trans. J. Ladd (New York: Library of Liberal Arts, 1965).

[9]John Locke, *The Second Treatise of Government* (New York: Liberal Arts Press, 1952).

[10]Aristotle, *Ethics,* trans. J. A. K. Thomson (London: Penguin, 1953).

of utilitarianism are Jeremy Bentham[11] and John Stuart Mill,[12] both of whom helped to formulate the theory. Utilitarianism evaluates actions on the basis of their outcomes. In any given situation, the action which would result in the greatest net gain for all concerned parties is considered to be the right, or morally obligatory, action.

The ethical norm of caring was developed more recently from feminist ethics.[13] At the current time, theoretical work in each of these four ethical norms—rights and duties, justice, utilitarianism, and caring—continues.[14] For an overview of these four ethical norms—their history, strengths, weaknesses, and areas of application—see Table 3-1.

## The Norm of Individual Rights and Duties

A moral right is an important, normative, justifiable claim or entitlement to something.[15] Moral rights and duties flow from every person's human dignity and ultimately from the Creator, and are often supported by law, such as our constitutional rights of freedom of conscience or freedom of speech. Moral rights enable individuals to pursue their own interests, and they also impose duties or correlative requirements or prohibitions on others.[16]

Legal rights are stated in rules, laws, or a constitutional system. The U.S. Bill of Rights and the United Nations Universal Declaration of Human Rights are examples of documents that spell out individual rights in detail. Most legal rights stem from moral rights; but not all moral rights are enacted into law, and some bad laws can even attempt to abrogate human rights (e.g., the rights of blacks in the United States pre-1960s, Jews in Nazi Germany, and women in Saudi Arabia.)

Every right has a corresponding obligation or duty. Your rights place an obligation on others to respect your rights. In addition, your right to freedom of conscience demands that you may not unnecessarily limit that freedom for others. In business, my right to be paid for my work corresponds to my duty to perform that work. In the latter case, both the right and duty stem from the right to private property, which is a traditional pillar of American life and law. However, the right to private property is not absolute. A factory owner may be forced by morality, as well as by law, to spend money on pollution control or safety equipment. For a listing of selected rights and other ethical norms, see Figure 3-2.

People also have the right not to be lied to or deceived, especially on matters about which they have a right to know. Hence, a supervisor has a duty to be truthful in giving feedback on work performance even if it is time consuming and difficult

---

[11]Jeremy Bentham, *An Introduction to the Principles of Morals and Legislation* (New York: Hafner, 1948).
[12]John Stuart Mill, *Utilitarianism* (Indianapolis: Bobbs-Merrill, 1957).
[13]See Carol Gilligan, *In a Different Voice* (Cambridge, MA: Harvard University Press, 1982); Nel Noddings, *Caring* (Berkeley: University of California Press, 1984).
[14]For example, John Rawls, *A Theory of Justice* (Cambridge, MA: Harvard University Press, 1971). See the book of readings from Thomas Donaldson and Patricia Werhane, *Ethical Issues in Business: A Philosophical Approach,* 5th ed. (Englewood Cliffs, NJ: Prentice Hall, 1996).
[15]Richard T. De George, *Business Ethics,* 5th ed. (Upper Saddle River, NJ: Prentice Hall, 2006), p. 94–95.
[16]Manuel Velasquez, *Business Ethics: Concepts and Cases,* 6th ed. (Upper Saddle River, NJ: Prentice Hall, 2002), p. 90.

**TABLE 3-1** Models for Business Decisions

| Definition and Origin | Strengths | Weaknesses | Example | When Used / Summary |
|---|---|---|---|---|
| 1. *Norm of Rights and Duties* Individual's freedom is not to be violated: Locke (1635–1701)—property Kant (1724–1804)—personal rights | 1. Ensures respect for individual's personal freedom and property 2. Parallels political Bill of Rights | 1. Emphasis on rights can encourage individualistic, selfish behavior | 1. Unsafe workplace 2. Flammable children's toys 3. Lying to superior or subordinate | 1. Where individual's personal rights or property are in question 2. Use with, for example, employee privacy; job tenure, work dangerous to person's health |
| 2. *Norm of Justice* Equitable distribution of society's benefits and burdens: Aristotle (384–322 BC) Rawls (1921–2002) | 1. The "democratic" principle 2. Does not allow a society to become status- or class-dominated 3. Ensures that minorities, poor, handicapped receive opportunities and a fair share of the output | 1. Can result in less risk, incentive, and innovation 2. Encourages sense of entitlement | 1. Bribes, kickbacks, fraud 2. Delivery of shoddy goods 3. Low wages to Hispanic, African, American, or women workers 4. Sweatshops | 1. Fairness, equal opportunity for poor and unemployed 2. Setting salaries for workers vs. executives 3. Public policy decisions: to maintain a floor of living standards for all 4. Use with, for example, performance appraisal, due process, distribution of rewards and punishment |

**TABLE 3-1** Models for Business Decisions (continued)

| Definition and Origin | Strengths | Weaknesses | When Used | | |
| --- | --- | --- | --- | --- | --- |
| | | | Example | Summary |

| Definition and Origin | Strengths | Weaknesses | Example | Summary |
| --- | --- | --- | --- | --- |
| **3. Utilitarianism**<br><br>"The greatest good for the greatest number":<br>Bentham (1748–1832)<br>Adam Smith (1723–1790)<br>David Ricardo (1772–1823) | 1. Concepts, terminology, methods are easiest for business people to use<br>2. Promotes view of entire system of exchange beyond "this firm"<br>3. Encourages entrepreneurship, innovation, productivity | 1. Impossible to measure or quantify all important elements<br>2. "Greatest good" can degenerate into self-interest<br>3. Can result in abridging another's rights<br>4. Can result in neglecting less powerful segments of society | 1. Plant closing<br>2. Pollution<br>3. Condemnation of land or buildings for "development" | 1. Use in all business decisions, and will be dominant criteria in most<br>2. Version of model is implicitly used already, although scope is generally limited to "this firm" |
| **4. Caring**<br>Responsibility to a person because of relationship:<br>Gilligan (1936–)<br>Noddings (1929–) | 1. Emphasizes care and responsibility for people<br>2. Builds trust, healthy communications, and teamwork<br>3. Supports community and good for group | 1. Poor at discriminating various responsibilities and equities<br>2. Without personal relationship there are no obligations | 1. Mentoring colleagues and subordinates<br>2. Flexible hours and flexible leave policy for sake of family duties<br>3. At time of delivery of poor performance report or layoffs | 1. Emphasizes interpersonal relationships<br>2. Care for employees and members of work group<br>3. Concern for those with personal or family needs |

83

**FIGURE 3-2** Selected Ethical Norms

### Rights and Duties

1. *Life and Safety:* Each person has the right not to have her or his life or safety unknowingly and unnecessarily endangered.
2. *Truthfulness:* The individual has the right not to be intentionally deceived by another, especially on matters about which the individual has the right to know.
3. *Privacy:* The individual has the right to do whatever he or she chooses to do outside working hours and to control information about his or her private life.
4. *Freedom of conscience:* The individual has the right to refrain from carrying out any order that violates those commonly accepted moral or religious norms to which the person adheres.
5. *Free speech:* The individual has the right to criticize conscientiously and truthfully the ethics or legality of corporate actions so long as the criticism does not violate the rights of other individuals within the organization.
6. *Private property:* The individual has the right to hold private property, especially insofar as this right enables the individual and his or her family to be sheltered and to have the basic necessities of life.

### Justice

1. *Fair treatment:* People who are similar to each other in the relevant respects should be treated similarly; people who differ in some respect relevant to the job they perform should be treated differently in proportion to the difference between them.
2. *Fair administration of rules:* Rules should be administered consistently, fairly, and impartially.
3. *Fair compensation:* A person should be compensated for the cost of their injuries by the party that is responsible for those injuries.
4. *Fair blame:* Individuals should not be held responsible for matters over which they have no control.
5. *Due process:* A person has a right to a fair and impartial hearing when he or she believes that personal rights are being violated.

### Utilitarianism

1. *Organizational Goals* should aim at *maximizing the satisfactions* of the organization's constituencies.
2. The members of an organization should attempt to attain its goals as *efficiently* as possible by consuming as few inputs as possible and minimizing external costs which organizational activities impose on others.
3. The employee should use *every effective means* to achieve the goals of the organization and should neither jeopardize those goals nor enter situations in which personal interests conflict significantly with the goals.

### Caring

1. Each person has responsibility for the well-being of those people with whom one has a relation.
2. The responsibility to care increases as the dependency of the other person increases.
3. One cannot be obligated to provide care that one is incapable of providing.

for the supervisor to do so. Each of us has the right not to be lied to by salespeople or advertisements, even though this right is often violated. Perjury under oath is a serious crime; lying on matters where another has a right to accurate information is also seriously unethical. Truthfulness and honesty are basic ethical norms, and they are essential for business.

Rights and duties express the requirements of morality from the standpoint of the individual. Rights and duties protect the individual from the encroachment and demands of society or the state, while utilitarian standards promote the group's interests and are relatively insensitive regarding a single individual except insofar as the individual's welfare affects the good of the group.

A business contract establishes rights and duties that did not exist before: the right of the purchaser to receive what was agreed upon and the right of the seller to be paid what was agreed upon. Formal written contracts and informal verbal agreements are essential to business transactions.

Immanuel Kant recognized that an emphasis on rights can lead people to focus largely on what is due them. Kant sought to broaden this perspective, so he emphasized what he called the *categorical imperative*. The first formulation is: *I ought never to act except in such a way that I can also will that my principle should become a universal law.* An equivalent statement is this: *An action is morally right for a person in a certain situation if and only if the person's reason for carrying out the action is a reason that he or she would be willing to have every person act on, in any similar situation.*[17]

Kant's second formulation of the categorical imperative cautions us against using other people as a means to our own ends: *Never treat humanity simply as a means, but always also as an end.* In effect, an action is morally right for a person if and only if in performing the action the person does not use others merely as a means for advancing his or her own interests, but also both respects and develops their capacity to choose for themselves. This principle, often called The Golden Rule, "Do unto others as you would have them do unto you," is a reflection of a principle found in the Old Testament (Leviticus 19:18) and restated by Jesus in the New Testament (Matthew 22:19): "Love your neighbor as yourself."

Capital, businesses, and networks are means, and are thus to be used to serve the purposes of people. A person, on the other hand, is not to be used merely as an instrument for achieving another's goals. Thus, respect for human dignity demands that I not deceive, manipulate, or exploit other people.

## The Norm of Justice

Justice requires that all people be guided by fairness, equity, and impartiality. Justice calls for evenhanded treatment of groups and individuals (1) in the distribution of the benefits and burdens of society, (2) in the administration of laws and regulations, and (3) in the imposition of sanctions and the awarding of compensation for wrongs suffered.

---

[17]Immanuel Kant, *Groundwork of the Metaphysics of Morals,* trans. H. J. Paton (New York: Harper & Row, 1964), pp. 62–90.

Standards of justice are generally considered to be more important than the utilitarian consideration of consequences. If a society is unjust to a group (e.g., segregation, job discrimination), we generally consider that society to be unjust and we condemn it, even if the injustices bring about greater economic productivity. On the other hand, we are willing to trade off some equality if the results will bring about greater benefits for all. For example, differences in income and wealth are justified when they bring greater prosperity *for all.*

Standards of justice are not as often in conflict with individual rights as are utilitarian norms.[18] This is not surprising, because justice, like moral rights, is based on the recognition of the dignity of human beings. The moral right to be treated as a free and equal person, for example, undergirds the notion that benefits and burdens should be distributed equitably. Personal moral rights (e.g., right to life, freedom of conscience, the right to free consent) are so basic that generally they may not be taken away to bring about a better distribution of benefits within a society. On the other hand, property rights may be sacrificed for the sake of a fairer distribution of benefits and burdens (e.g., graduated income tax, limits on pollution).

Distributive justice becomes important when a society has sufficient goods but everyone's basic needs are not satisfied. The question then becomes: What is a just distribution? The fundamental principle is that equals should be treated equally and that non-equals should be treated according to their inequality. For example, few would argue that a new person hired for a job should receive the same pay as a senior worker who has 20 years of experience. People who perform work of greater responsibility or who work longer hours should also receive greater pay. Hence, pay differentials should be based on the work itself, not on some arbitrary bias of the employer.

Even knowing all of the previously-mentioned facts, we still wouldn't always be able to determine a fair distribution of society's benefits and burdens. In fact, quite different notions of equity are proposed. For example, the capitalist model (benefits based on contribution) is radically different from the socialist (from each according to abilities, to each according to needs). An important contribution to the theory of justice has been made by John Rawls.[19] Rawls would have us construct a system of rules and laws for society as if we did not know what roles we were to play in that society. We do not know if we would be rich or poor, female or male, African or European, manager or slave, physically and mentally fit or handicapped. Rawls calls this the *veil of ignorance.* Constructing a system of rules under the veil of ignorance allows us to rid ourselves of the biases we have as a result of our own status. Rawls proposes that in such circumstances, each of us would try to construct a system that would be of the greatest benefit to all and that would not undermine the position of any group. According to Rawls, people under the veil of ignorance would agree to two principles:

---

[18]Jerald Greenberg, "A Taxonomy of Organizational Justice Theories," *Academy of Management Review,* 12 (January 1987): 9–22.
[19]Rawls, *A Theory of Justice* (Cambridge, MA: Harvard Press, 1971).

1. Each person would have an equal right to the most extensive liberty compatible with similar liberty for others.
2. Social and economic inequalities would be arranged so that they are both reasonably expected to be to everyone's advantage and attached to positions and offices open to all.

The first principle is parallel to the American sense of liberty and thus is not controversial in the United States. The second principle is more egalitarian and also more controversial. However, Rawls maintains that if people honestly choose as if they were under the veil of ignorance, they would opt for a system of justice that is most fair to all members of society.[20] We now turn to a norm that observes the *consequences* of actions on the entire group.

## The Norm of Utilitarianism

Utilitarianism examines the consequences of an act. It judges that an action is right if it produces the greatest utility, "the greatest good for the greatest number." The decision process is much like a cost-benefit analysis applied to all parties who would be affected by the decision. That action is right which produces the greatest net benefit when all the costs and benefits to all the affected parties are taken into account. Although it would be convenient if these costs and benefits could be measured in some comparable unit, this is rarely possible. Many important values (e.g., human life and liberty) cannot be quantified. Thus, the best we can do is to list the effects and estimate the magnitude of their costs and benefits as accurately as possible.

The utilitarian norm says that the right action is that which produces the greatest net benefit over any other possible action. This does not mean that the right action produces the greatest good for the person performing the action. Rather, it is the action that produces the greatest net good for all those who are affected by the action. The utilitarian norm works best for cases that are complex and affect many parties. Although the model and the methodology are clear in theory, carrying out the calculations is often difficult. Taking into account so many affected parties, and the extent to which the action affects them, can be a tallying nightmare.

Several shortcuts have been proposed that can reduce the complexity of utilitarian calculations. Each shortcut involves a sacrifice of accuracy for ease of decision. Among these shortcuts are (1) calculation of costs and benefits in dollar terms for ease of comparison, and (2) restriction of consideration to those directly affected by the action, putting aside indirect effects. In using these shortcuts, an individual should be aware that they result in over-simplification and that some interests may not be sufficiently taken into consideration.

In the popular mind, the term *utilitarianism* sometimes suggests selfishness and exploitation. We do not intend this meaning. However, a noteworthy weakness of utilitarianism as an ethical norm is that it can advocate, for example, abridging an

---

[20]An organization that treats its employees justly reaps many rewards. See Blair H. Shepard, Roy J. Lewicki, and John W. Minton, *Organizational Justice: The Search for Fairness in the Workplace* (New York: Lexington, 1992).

individual's right to a job or even life for the sake of the greater good of a large number of people. This and other difficulties are discussed elsewhere.[21] One additional caution in using utilitarian rules is in order: It is considered unethical to choose narrower benefits (e.g., personal goals of career, or money) at the expense of the good of a larger number, such as a firm, neighborhood, or a nation. Utilitarian norms emphasize the good of the *group*. As a result, an individual and what is due to that individual may be overlooked. Hence the norm of utilitarianism must be balanced by the use of the norms of justice, rights, and duties, and the norm we will discuss next, caring.

## The Norm of Caring

Over the centuries ethicists, who were almost all male, developed the norms of rights and duties, justice, and utilitarianism. These norms emphasize impartiality and abstract principles. A norm of *caring* has been recognized in the past few decades.[22] Caring is built upon relations between people and is an extension of family life. Rather than autonomous individuals making objective, impartial ethical judgments, in reality we experience numerous relationships, and each of these relationships influences our ethical obligations. We care for each other, and we have responsibilities to each other.

Ethicists who use caring as their norm demonstrate how women's moral experience up to this time has been neglected. When facing moral dilemmas, women tend to focus on the relationships of people rather than on impartial, theoretical principles.[23] As we saw in Chapter 2, Carol Gilligan amended the existing descriptions of the levels of moral development in light of the experience of women. The male matures by developing autonomy and sees himself in opposition to the other, and thus typically is characterized by an insistence on personal rights. However, a businessperson who is excessively influenced by rights and competition can develop paranoid tendencies which can cause him or her to have difficulty relating to others or to relate to others only by contract.

The female matures by developing relationship-based morality. Although feminist ethicists are reluctant to analyze caring in too much detail, we can note some qualifications of the norm of caring. First, the obligation to care is proportional to one's relationship. In extended relationships, caring does not require action if that action is very costly. Second, one's roles and obligations influence the responsibility to care. Caring for one's child has greater priority than caring for someone in one's work group. Third, one cannot be obligated to provide care that one is incapable of providing.[24] For the manager, caring is a relevant norm for

---

[21]Gerald F. Cavanagh, Dennis J. Moberg, and Manuel Velasquez, "The Ethics of Organizational Politics," *Academy of Management Review,* 6 (July 1981): 363–374. For a more complete treatment, see Velasquez, *Business Ethics,* pp. 73–88.
[22]See Rosemarie Tong, *Feminine and Feminist Ethics* (Belmont, CA: Wadsworth, 1993), esp. Chapters 3 and 4.
[23]Gilligan, *In a Different Voice* (Cambridge, MA: Harvard University Press, 1992).
[24]Gerald F. Cavanagh, Dennis J. Moberg, and Manuel Velasquez, "Making Business Ethics Practical," *Business Ethics Quarterly,* 5 (July 1995): 399–418.

many current business challenges. Trust, teamwork, good personal relationships, and communications build upon caring, and must be achieved, if the firm is to be successful.[25]

Caring engages our emotions, but it is also true that in order to do *any* ethical reasoning, our emotions must be involved. While ethics is not just feeling, or even primarily feeling, Ethical decision making is a sterile intellectual exercise if one's feelings are not engaged. In making ethical judgments it is essential to consider the interests of others. In order to incorporate the interests of others into one's decision-making processes, one must be able to feel and to empathize with those that are affected by one's decisions. In Kohlberg's terms, one must at least have achieved Level II moral development (see Chapter 2). Ethical decision makers must learn how to regularly and habitually put themselves in the position of other people. They must learn how others perceive a situation and sense what others feel and suffer. Without this ability to care for others on a sensible level, it is impossible to examine the moral dimensions of life in any significant way.

## Ethical Norms for Global Business

Some claim that the varying business customs and practices in countries around the world demand new norms in international business ethics. They propose a variety of different models, based upon rights, social contract, and negative and modified utilitarianism.[26] Other scholars, however, have found common basic ethical values in business in different cultures. Although global business norms do not yet exist, the various attempts to achieve norms and the codes of ethics that we will examine in Chapter 9 may indeed be developing into an international policy regime.[27] These attempts seem to be gradually providing a convergence of moral expectations for the global firm.

Manuel Velasquez applied the new proposed models to several cases in global business ethics.[28] He demonstrated the limitations of each of these new proposals. On the other hand, he found that a comprehensive model containing the norms of rights and duties, justice, utilitarianism, and caring as presented in this chapter is more flexible and more effective for the global business manager. Let us now apply these norms to the solution of some ethical problems.

[25]Jeanne M. Liedtka, "Feminist Morality and Competitive Reality: A Role for the Ethic of Care?" *Business Ethics Quarterly,* 6 (April 1996): 179–200.
[26]Thomas Donaldson and Thomas W. Dunfee, *Ties That Bind: A Social Contracts Approach to Business Ethics* (Boston: Harvard Business School Press, 1999); Andrew Spicer, Thomas Dunfee, and Wendy J. Bailey, "Does National Context Matter in Ethical Decision Making? An Empirical Test of Integrative Social Contracts Theory," *Academy of Management Journal,* 47 (August 2004): 610–620.
[27]Duane Windsor, "The Development of International Business Norms," *Business Ethics Quarterly,* 14 (October 2004): 729–754; see the business ethics text in both Chinese and English, Stephan Rothlin, *Eighteen Rules of International Business Ethics* (Beijing, 2004); Japanese business managers have roughly the same values as do Americans, according to Chaiki Nakano, "A Survey Study."
[28]Manuel Velasquez, "International Business Ethics: The Aluminum Companies in Jamaica," *Business Ethics Quarterly,* 5 (October 1995): 865–882; for a supporting position, see Hans Kung, "A Global Ethic in an Age of Globalization," *Business Ethics Quarterly,* 7 (July 1997): 17–31.

## SOLVING ETHICAL PROBLEMS

A good human judgment is preceded by three steps: accurately articulating the issue, gathering the facts, and determining the appropriate criteria for judgment (see Figure 3-3). Before any ethically sensitive situation can be assessed, it is essential that all the relevant data be considered. Failure to gather all the data, an inadequate understanding of ethical norms, and/or trying to make an important decision too quickly can result in a poor judgment.[29] As an aid to determining the appropriate criteria, we have presented four norms—rights and duties, justice, utility, and caring. Figure 3-3 is a schematic diagram of how ethical decision making can best proceed. Although it contains greater detail than Figure 3-1, it includes the same three steps: (1) data gathering, (2) analysis, and (3) judgment. Even Figure 3-3 is simplified, but nevertheless it can aid in solving ethical problems.

Note that each of the four ethical norms is listed in Figure 3-3. In making ethical decisions, we must keep in mind how the norms relate to one another, and determine which norm has priority in a particular case. For example, basic moral rights, such as the right to life, cannot be negated by other norms, even if negation of these rights might result in "greater good." The norm of caring can outweigh the norm of justice when the case involves close relationships and privately held resources.

Let us apply our scheme to the case presented earlier of the executive who padded her expense account. We will accept the limited data provided in the case. The rights norm is not so useful here: The executive has no right to the extra money, although we might argue that the shareholders' and customers' right to private property is being violated. Using the justice norm, we note that salary and commissions constitute ordinary compensation for individuals. Expense accounts have a quite different purpose. Most managers responding to the case held that it was unethical for the executive to pad her expense account. John Rawls would maintain that all of us would set the rules to prohibit such padding of expenses if we did not know what roles we ourselves would have in society. Using the utility criterion, we judge that although padding her expense account is in the interest of the executive, it does not benefit others. Her actions hurt shareholders, customers, and more honest executives. Moreover, padding one's expense account adds to the cost of business and in this way also violates utility. Claiming nonexistent expenses does not indicate care for others in the firm. Hence, we conclude that padding one's expense account is judged unethical on all four ethical norms, and is therefore morally wrong. Note that 73 percent of the executives who were asked came to the same judgment.

Let us consider the case from the beginning of the chapter of students cheating. Are our ethical norms violated by students cheating? If a student looks at another student's paper or takes a "cheat sheet" into an exam, that student's finished exam does not represent what the student actually knows. The student has

---

[29]Paul C. Nutt, *Why Decisions Fail: Avoiding the Blunders and Traps That Lead to Debacles* (San Francisco: Berrett-Koehler, 2002).

**FIGURE 3-3** Flow Diagram of Ethical Decision Making

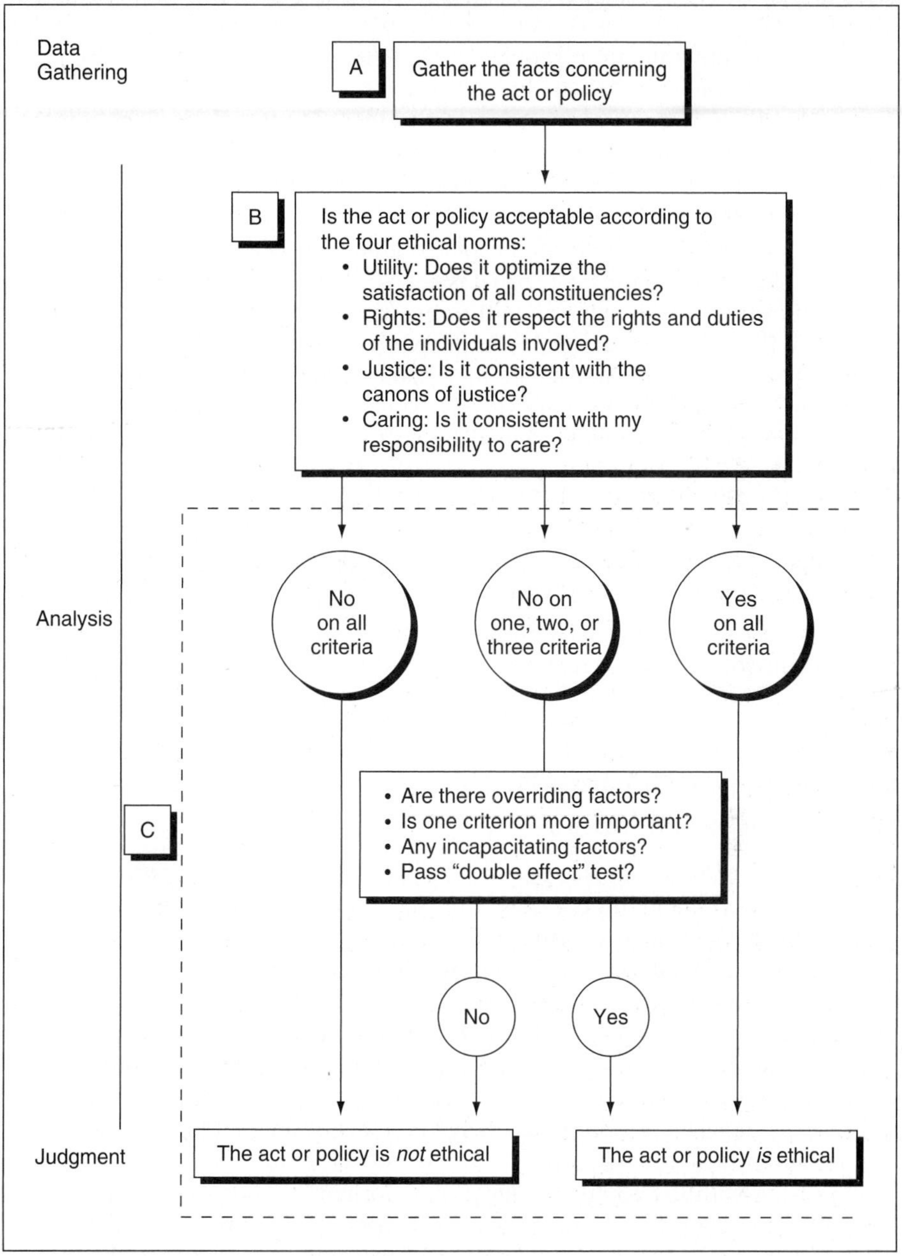

**Data Gathering**

**A** — Gather the facts concerning the act or policy

**B** — Is the act or policy acceptable according to the four ethical norms:
- Utility: Does it optimize the satisfaction of all constituencies?
- Rights: Does it respect the rights and duties of the individuals involved?
- Justice: Is it consistent with the canons of justice?
- Caring: Is it consistent with my responsibility to care?

**Analysis**

- No on all criteria
- No on one, two, or three criteria
- Yes on all criteria

**C**
- Are there overriding factors?
- Is one criterion more important?
- Any incapacitating factors?
- Pass "double effect" test?

- No
- Yes

**Judgment**

The act or policy is *not* ethical

The act or policy *is* ethical

*Source: Adapted from Gerald F. Cavanagh, Dennis J. Moberg, and Manuel Velasquez, "Making Business Ethics Practical,"* Business Ethics Quarterly *(July 1995); Manuel Velasquez, Gerald F. Cavanagh, and Dennis Moberg, "Organizational Statesmenship and Dirty Politics,"* Organizational Dynamics *(Fall 1983).*

"stolen" answers from another source, and thus violates justice. That is, the student seeks to obtain credit for material that the student does not know. Other students, who are playing by the rules, do not have that extra access to answers. So the cheating student is taking unfair advantage of his fellow students. From the utilitarian perspective, the only person who benefits is the student cheater. All the other students suffer because their performance is considered to be relatively poorer than the student who cheated. It is true that cheating may eventually hurt the cheater, since that student will not have the knowledge that a future employer may expect him to have. Moreover, cheating may become a habit, and that could lead to the person being fired for cheating on the job. So, although cheating may benefit a person in the short term, in the long term it is not a benefit even to the cheater himself.

What of the case in which an entrepreneur advertised official-looking blank receipts of fictitious restaurants? Salespeople and managers could falsely fill out the receipts and submit them for reimbursement. The receipts would document the purchase of meals that never existed. Using our model, what would we say of the ethics of the person selling such receipts? Or of the person purchasing them and using them? Respond to this case using the flow chart in Figure 3-3. Examine Andrew Fastow's case (above) using the same norms.

A short-cut test of one's own decisions may be helpful in making correct moral judgments: Could my decision and behavior bear the sharp scrutiny of a probing reporter? Would I do it if I knew that the decision was going to be featured on this evening's TV news? Or from another perspective: Could I freely acknowledge this decision to my mother or to another for whom I have respect?

## Decision Making Using the Model

Let us examine another case:

> Brian Curry, financial vice president of Digital Robotics Corporation, is about to retire and has been asked to recommend one of his two associates for promotion to vice president. Curry knows that his recommendation will be acted on. He also knows that because both associates are approximately the same age, the one not chosen will have difficulty getting future promotions. Debra Butler is bright, outgoing, and has better leadership skills. She is the most qualified for the position. Moreover, her father is president of the largest customer of Digital, and Curry reasons that Digital will more likely keep this business if his president's daughter is made an officer. On the other hand, John McNichols has been with the company longer, has worked 70-hour weeks, and has pulled the company through some very difficult situations. He has continued putting in extra effort because he was told some time ago that he was in line for the vice presidency. Nevertheless, Curry recommends Butler for the job.

Let us again use our norms and Figure 3-3 to decide this case. Neither Butler nor McNichols has a right to the position. As for justice, we conclude that because

the promotional decision was made on the basis of relevant abilities, it did constitute fair treatment. On the other hand, McNichols worked extra hours because of
the promised promotion. Much of his work effort was based on a false promise.
McNichols had a right to know the truth and to be treated fairly. Utility tells us
that the selection of Debra Butler optimally benefits shareholders, customers,
management, and most of the workers, because she is a better leader.[30] Caring is
not a primary norm to use in a promotion case.

Thus, according to the criteria of overall justice and utility, the appointment
of Butler is morally acceptable. However, because of the promise made earlier to
McNichols, which resulted in extended work weeks, he is being treated wrongly.
We can then ask if there are any "overriding factors" that ought to be taken into
consideration.

## Overriding Factors

Overriding factors are factors that may, in a given case, justify overriding one or
two of the four ethical norms: rights and duties, justice, utility, and caring (see
Figure 3-3). Overriding factors can be examined when conflict exists in the conclusions drawn from the ethical norms. For example, there might be *incapacitating*
factors. If any elements coerce an individual into doing a certain action, then that
individual is not fully responsible. Let us take the example of Bausch & Lomb.
CEO Daniel Gill expected division managers to show double-digit earnings each
quarter. Under this unrelenting pressure, the managers faked sales of sunglasses,
forced distributors to accept unneeded products, and probably laundered drug
money at a profit. This eventually resulted in a collapse of revenues and an SEC
investigation. Even though what they did was unethical, the fact that these managers were coerced means that they are not as guilty as they otherwise would be,
because the pressure by their CEO is an incapacitating factor.[31]

Also, someone might not be able to utilize the norm owing to a *lack of information.* A manager might suspect that another manager is embezzling from the
firm. However, to report her to superiors might ruin that person's reputation.
Therefore, even though stealing is a violation of justice, in this instance there is
not yet sufficient information to act. In addition, the manager may be sincerely
uncertain of the norm or its applicability in this particular case.[32]

Consider again our case of appointing a financial vice president. Utility calls
for recommending Debra Butler for the position. The right to full information
and perhaps justice supports McNichols' claim. McNichols has worked harder
and more hours because of a promised reward. Because the position was
promised to him, fair treatment requires giving him special consideration. On the

---

[30]A manager can score him- or herself as being predominantly a user of the utility, justice, or rights
norm by using a set of questions developed by Marshall Sashkin. See his *Managerial Values Profile*
(Bryn Mawr, PA: Organizational Design and Development, 1986).
[31]"Blind Ambition: How Pursuit of Results Got Out of Hand at Bausch and Lomb," *Business Week,*
October 23, 1995, pp. 78–92, 146.
[32]For how incapacitating factors lessen a moral agent's responsibility, see Oswald A. J. Mascarenhas,
"Exonerating Unethical Marketing Executive Behaviors: A Diagnostic Framework," *Journal of
Marketing,* 59 (April 1995): 43–57.

basis of the importance of a verbal promise and of justice, we might conclude that McNichols should get the position.

A conflict now exists between these two norms. Is one norm more important? The effective operation of the firm is an important ethical goal, because many jobs and family incomes depend upon it. How much better a manager is Butler and how would her selection affect the firm's performance and the jobs of others at Digital?

In examining incapacitating factors, *coercion* does not seem to be involved. That Debra Butler's father is president of Digital's largest customer might constitute psychological pressure. However, Curry seems to have made his decision freely.

Another factor to consider is exactly what sort of promise was made to McNichols. Was it clear and unequivocal? If the "promise" was in fact a mere statement that McNichols had a good chance at the promotion and if Butler's performance in the VP job is expected to be significantly better than McNichols', then Curry could ethically recommend Butler. However, some sort of compensation should then be made to McNichols.

When different norms provide opposing conclusions in the same case, another kind of overriding factor helps us judge. It is the *principle of double effect*. Let us take an example of firing a worker who is not a good performer but who is the sole provider of a family. Using the utility norm, we could say the firing was ethical. But using the justice norm, we might call it unethical, because an entire family would be deprived of income. There is a conflict between the conclusions reached using the different norms, so the principle of double effect is appropriate. The principle is applicable when an act has both a good effect (bringing greater efficiency to the firm and providing honest feedback to the worker) and a bad effect (eliminating the principal support for the family). One may ethically perform such an act under three conditions: (1) One does not directly intend the bad effect (depriving the family of income); (2) the bad effect is not a means to the good end but is simply a side effect (depriving the family of income is not a means of making the firm more efficient); and (3) the good effect sufficiently outweighs the bad (the benefits of greater firm efficiency are sufficiently greater than the difficulties the family will face). Some ethicists reduce the principle of double effect to utilitarianism; it is much the same. It might be instructive to go back to the preceding case and ask if the appointment of Butler would pass the double effect test.

## Case of Selling Cigarettes

Let us assess the ethics of the following case:

> Philip Morris and RJR Nabisco hold about two-thirds of the market for cigarettes in the United States. Approximately 430,000 Americans and 3 million people worldwide die prematurely each year of tobacco related causes. Medical scientists estimate that 30 to 40 percent of all who smoke will die of cancer, cardiovascular disease, or chronic obstructive lung disease caused by their smoking. The number of

people in the United States who smoke has declined to 25 percent. Nevertheless, through successful marketing, the tobacco firms are still quite profitable.

Tobacco executives initiated strategies to market cigarettes to: (1) teenagers and minorities, and (2) people in other countries. They employ "image" advertising and widespread distribution. Cigarette advertising pictures members of the dominant social or racial group smoking cigarettes in attractive surroundings. In addition, U.S. trade negotiators have opened Asian markets for U.S. cigarettes. Market share of U.S. firms in four Asian countries rose 600 percent because of this, and cigarette smoking was found to be about 10 percent higher than it would be if it were not for the U.S. cigarettes.[33]

Smoking is thus increasing in Asia, South America, and Africa. More than two-thirds of men in Korea, Cambodia, Indonesia, China, and Japan now smoke. Advertising now also targets women, whose use of tobacco is rapidly rising. Experts predict the death rate due to tobacco worldwide will reach 10 million annually by the year 2020. And total exports of American cigarettes have increased by more than 300 percent in the past decade. In 2004 the tobacco firms paid hundreds of millions of dollars to settle a charge that they sold cigarettes in huge quantities, deliberately trying to avoid the tax on cigarettes.[34]

Let us apply our norms in deciding the ethics of the above case. Cigarette executives claim that they are not violating anyone's right to life in selling cigarettes to them, since information is available on the health hazards. However, some people, especially youth and those overseas, may not be aware of the likelihood of serious disease and death that follow use of tobacco. Both justice and rights call for cigarette sellers to be truthful in advertising products with such dangerous consequences.

Applying the utilitarian norm, we can calculate that those who benefit are the cigarette companies and the users who in the short term are able to feed their nicotine addiction. On the other hand, the users' health is often seriously impaired. This can result in large health and dollar costs to the cigarette smokers and their dependents and employers. Society as a whole pays, since income is lost and costs rise because of the many serious tobacco-related illnesses. Justice calls for tobacco firms, which reap large profits from cigarette sales, to share in the burdens of paying the additional health costs.

Genuine caring would lead tobacco executives to stop trying to attract new smokers and possibly even to withdraw tobacco products from the market

---

[33]"Big Tobacco's Backlash in Asia: Health Critics Decry U.S. Invasion," *Business Week,* June 17, 1996, p. 30.
[34]David Kessler, *A Question of Intent: A Great American Battle with a Deadly Industry* (New York: Public Affairs, 2001); "RJR's New Ad Campaign: It's Hip to Smoke," *Wall Street Journal,* April 16, 1996, pp. B1, B6; see also Philip Hilts, *Smokescreen: The Truth Behind the Tobacco Industry Cover-up* Reading, MA: (Addison Wesley, 1996); Richard Kluber, *Ashes to Ashes: America's Hundred-Year Cigarette War, the Public Health, and the Unabashed Triumph of Philip Morris* New York: (Knopf, 1996).

altogether. We do not seem to see any overriding factors in this case—no inca-pacitating factors, lack of information, or coercion. Have we been too harsh on cigarette firm executives and their supporters? How would you analyze the case?

The ethical principles and the model described and used in this chapter are also presented in many management books. They enable the manager to integrate ethical analysis with business decisions, and to thus complement and correct traditional financial analyses. Yet problems of conscience can still some-times face a member of an organization.

## Loyalty and Whistle-Blowing

In addition to making ethical decisions, members of organizations sometimes face situations in which superiors seem to ignore or be blind to unethical acts. Sherron Watkins of Enron, Cynthia Cooper of WorldCom, and Coleen Rowley of the FBI were named as *Time* magazine's 2003 "persons of the year" for blowing the whistle internally at their organizations.[35] In each case they found that infor-mation was being falsified, thus misleading important stakeholders of their orga-nization. Blowing the whistle presents a difficult dilemma and ultimately demands courage. Let us examine the following case, where the stakes were high:

> An engineer in the design section of an airplane manufacturing firm is convinced that the latch mechanism on a plane's cargo door does not provide sufficient security and that the door needs to be redesigned in order to insure against the possibility of a crash. She goes to her supervi-sor and presents the information, and is told that the Federal Aviation Administration (FAA) has given the required approval and that she should not "rock the boat." She goes to the president of the firm and gets the same answer.

Would that engineer be justified in making this information public, perhaps taking it to the news media? The answer to this question is extremely important. The danger to the lives of hundreds of passengers might argue for going public.[36] On the other hand, the reputation and perhaps the financial viability of the air-craft manufacturing firm are also to be weighed. A mistake in either direction could be disastrous. So it is important to do the ethical analysis very carefully.

The right to life and safety is at issue. If the designer is correct that the faulty latch mechanism puts the plane in danger of a crash, then the lives of the passengers would assume paramount importance in the calculations. Although the designer owes loyalty to her employer, nevertheless justice requires that future passengers should not unknowingly be in danger of their lives due to the faulty design.

---

[35]Richard Lacayo and Amanda Ripley, "Persons of the Year," *Time,* January 6, 2003, pp. 30–60.
[36]Janet P. Near, Michael Rehg, James Van Scotter, and Marcia Miceli, "Does the Type of Wrongdoing Affect the Whistle-blowing Process?" *Business Ethics Quarterly,* 14, no. 2 (2004): 219–242.

Applying the norm of utilitarianism would involve totaling up the costs and benefits to all parties affected. Redesigning the aircraft and recalling planes already in service would cost the firm tens of millions of dollars. More immediately, taking the issue to the scandal-oriented and poorly educated media would result in a serious erosion in reputation for the firm. On the other hand, assuming that 300 people would be aboard a plane that crashed, how much are 300 lives worth? Applying the norm of utilitarianism would lead to the conclusion that the designer would be justified in taking the issue outside the firm. Caring would cause the engineer to opt for the safety of the passengers also. Even 69 percent of the corporate executives who examined the case thought that the designer was justified in breaching loyalty and taking the issue to the media.[37]

## When to Blow the Whistle

Because opportunities for whistle-blowing seem to be more pervasive, and because the stakes are often very high, it is important to give some attention to the special conditions that would allow and sometimes require whistle-blowing. *Whistle-blowing* has been defined as "the disclosure by organization members (former or current) of illegal, immoral, or illegitimate practices under the control of their employers, to persons or organizations that may be able to affect action."[38] Note that this definition covers both blowing the whistle internally to upper management (as the three *Time* women-of-the-year did), and also to external parties (e.g., government agencies or the media). According to Sissela Bok, to be ethical, whistle-blowing should meet several criteria:[39]

1. The purpose should be moral: to benefit the public interest.
2. What is protested should be of major importance and should be specific.
3. The facts of the case must be certain; they should be checked and rechecked.
4. All avenues for change within the organization must be exhausted before resorting to external whistle-blowing.
5. The whistle-blower's motive should be altruistic. In particular, the whistle-blower should not gain anything through revealing the information. Ideally the individual should openly accept responsibility for the whistle-blowing.

Let us examine these criteria. The first demands that the purpose of whistle-blowing should not be to attract attention, to seek revenge, or to achieve some personal goal. In some cases, whistle-blowers are seeking vengeance on a supervisor or a company that they believe has been unfair to them. Perceptions

---

[37]"Business Executives and Moral Dilemmas," *Business and Society Review,* Spring 1975, p. 52.
[38]Janet P. Near and Marcia P. Miceli, "Effective Whistle-blowing," *Academy of Management Review,* 20 (July 1995): 680.
[39]Sissela Bok, "Whistleblowing and Professional Responsibilities," in *Ethics Teaching in Higher Education,* ed. Daniel Callahan and Sissela Bok (New York: Plenum Press, 1980).

regarding one's own grievances can be biased and do not provide a solid basis for whistle-blowing. Instead, the revelation of wrongdoing should be for the common good.

Second, whistle-blowing requires that the wrongdoing be a serious breach of ethics. Much is at stake, and the action should not be taken lightly. The unethical act protested should be a specific act, not a vague attitude which is hard to document.

Third, the facts of the case must be ascertained, and the evidence must be double-checked. The fourth criterion demands that higher officials in the organization, officials who could rectify the situation, have been informed, but that they refuse to take action. This means that a whistle-blower must go to the president and the board before going to an outside party. Further, by extension, this criterion means that if there is a federal (or other) regulatory agency involved, then, assuming all internal avenues have been tried, the agency is to be preferred to the news media.

The fifth criterion is that the whistle-blower should not benefit from the revelation. The motives of a whistle-blower whose career is benefited or who makes money from exposing the situation are suspect. Considerations of self-interest can unconsciously enter into one's deliberations. To compensate for possible personal bias, a person should seek competent objective advice so as not to blow the whistle on the basis of poor or partial information. The potential whistle-blower should also be aware of all the arguments for and against whistle-blowing before going to an outside party. Ideally, the whistle-blower should be willing to accept responsibility for providing the information. This takes courage, since the person's job may be on the line. It is also a test of one's motives. Moreover, anonymous informers are justifiably not as trusted.

Let us apply the criteria to the case of the aircraft designer. Her purpose in blowing the whistle is to serve the public interest by preventing an airplane crash and saving hundreds of lives. The facts of the situation should be checked. In this case, let us presume that the engineer is mentally stable, has checked her data with competent peers, and has nothing to gain from the revelations. The whistle-blower has already gone to her own supervisor and to the president of the organization. The FAA does not seem to recognize the design problem. However, before going to the media, the designer should check to make sure the FAA is aware of it. If not, telling the FAA of the design flaw could achieve the safety goal without a public splash, and thus prevent severe loss to the manufacturer and to the airlines that use the plane. Because the whistle-blower has not yet acted, we do not know whether she will identify herself. We also know nothing of her character, but let us presume that no personal advantage will be gained by the whistle-blowing.

In conclusion, the whistle-blower, assuming she has the correct facts, would be justified in going to an external agency. This case is not fictitious. Had someone recognized and protested the cargo door latch problem on the DC-10, a Turkish airliner taking off from Paris would not have crashed and taken more than 300 lives.[40]

---

[40]Paul Eddy, Elaine Potter, and Bruce Page, *Destination Disaster* (New York: New York Times Book Co., 1976), esp. pp. 33–63.

Wrongdoing within the firm can "damage a company's profitability, tarnish its reputation, demoralize its employees, and result in substantial fines or costly lawsuits."[41] Hence, in order for management to obtain information on such potentially damaging actions or products, it should provide a vehicle for an employee to report wrongdoing internally.[42]

A serious deterrent to whistle-blowing is the well-known fact that most whistle-blowers are penalized by being demoted, frozen out, or fired. They are labeled as "stool pigeons" and "squealers." Legislation and court decisions have provided some protection for whistle-blowers. People cannot be fired for whistle-blowing, at least in certain restricted circumstances.

On the other hand, as any experienced manager knows, only when there is bad management, poor communication, and managers do not want to hear bad news does whistle-blowing become necessary. The moral problem does not arise, for example, when a firm possesses accurate and honest financial reporting, good product design, and open communications. Whistle-blowing becomes necessary when supervisors do not listen to subordinates and their legitimate concerns. These concerns are sometimes not well-founded, but it is essential that they be heard. Ambitious managers can encourage shoddy practices and then blind themselves to them while they attempt to show higher quarterly profits. In short, blowing the whistle is more likely to occur when an organization is not performing well, has poor management, or both.

## GOOD HABITS BUILD CHARACTER AND VIRTUE

Given recent business scandals, executives increasingly ask how good character can be developed within the organization. Character development includes the good habits of integrity, trust, and loyalty.[43] Because of the greater cooperation and loyalty that is required in the global marketplace, many suggest that the character development of its employees must be an important priority for a firm. Moreover, a firm cannot build trust, commitment, and effort among the stakeholders of the firm without giving attention to character development within the firm. And, time and again, organizations that are virtuous have been shown to be more effective and more profitable.[44] Many conclude that since there are fewer middle managers today, subordinate members of organizations must evidence greater personal responsibility in order to perform their ordinary

---

[41]Marcia P. Miceli and Janet P. Near, "Whistleblowing: Reaping the Benefits," *Academy of Management Executive,* 8 (August 1994): 65–72.
[42]Michael Gundlach, Scott Douglas, and Mark Martinko, "The Decision to Blow the Whistle: A Social Information Processing Framework," *Academy of Management Review,* 28 (January 2003): 107–123.
[43]See Alan Wolfe, *Moral Freedom: The Search for Virtue in a World of Choice* (New York: W. W. Norton, 2002).
[44]Kim S. Cameron, "Organizational Virtuousness and Performance," in *Positive Organizational Scholarship: Foundations of a New Discipline*, eds. Kim S. Cameron, Jane E. Dutton, and Robert E. Quinn (San Francisco: Berrett-Koehler, 2003).

tasks. Such personal responsibility has been described and measured, and is called "organizational citizenship."[45]

Some argue that trust and a healthy community life is essential for prosperity. Francis Fukuyama maintains that some societies currently have low trust (e.g., China, Italy, and France), and others possess high trust (e.g., Germany, the United States, and Japan). He warns that individualism is a threat to trust and that some non-rational factors, such as religion, tradition, honor, and loyalty, are essential in building trust.[46]

The development of character and virtue (for definitions, see Figure 3-4) is now receiving attention in firms. We often speak of honesty, trust, justice, and integrity as if people are born with those virtues. This is not the case. Such virtues are achieved only by specific effort. Note also that high intelligence does not necessarily bring ethical behavior. Intelligent and sophisticated people who supported Hitler (Martin Heidegger, Carl Jung, Ezra Pound), and the straight "A" student who sexually exploits others demonstrate that intelligence and a good education do not necessarily result in good character.[47]

The Aristotelian description of a virtuous person, which for centuries has helped us understand virtue, can be of help to the manager and the business firm.

---

**FIGURE 3-4** Moral Habits Terms

| | |
|---|---|
| *Altruism* | Unselfish concern for the welfare of others |
| *Character* | A stable, organized personality with a composite of good and bad moral habits within a person |
| *Ethics* | The principles of conduct governing an individual or a group, and the methods for applying them |
| *Habit* | An acquired behavior pattern followed until it becomes almost automatic |
| *Moral* | Dealing with or capable of distinguishing right from wrong |
| *Moral habit* | A morally good or bad behavior pattern |
| *Value* | A lasting belief that a certain goal or mode of conduct is better than the opposite goal or conduct |
| *Vice* | A bad moral habit |
| *Virtue* | A good moral habit that has been acquired by choosing the good |

---

[45]Robert H. Moorman, Gerald Blakely, and Brian Niehoff, "Does Perceived Organizational Support Mediate the Relationship Between Procedural Justice and Organizational Citizenship Behavior?" *Academy of Management Journal,* 41, no. 3 (1998): 351–357; see also Linn Van Dyne, Jill Graham, and Richard Dienesch, "Organizational Citizenship Behavior: Construct Redefinition, Measurement, and Validation," *Academy of Management Journal,* 37 (1994): 765–802; Rabindra N. Kanungo and Jay A. Conger, "Promoting Altruism as a Corporate Goal," *Academy of Management Executive,* 3 (1993): 37–48.

[46]Francis Fukuyama, *Trust: The Social Virtues and the Creation of Prosperity* (New York: Free Press, 1995).

[47]Robert Coles, "The Disparity Between Intellect and Character," *Chronicle of Higher Education,* September 22, 1995, p. A68.

Aristotle (384–322 BC) shows how the virtuous person avoids extremes, and claims that "what we call selfishness is guaranteed to be self-destructive as well."[48] A morally mature person is able to and will develop good habits, commonly called virtues; "the ultimate aim of the Aristotelian approach to business is to cultivate whole human beings, not jungle fighters, efficiency automatons, or 'good soldiers.'" Certain virtues are important for business: honesty, fairness, trust, and toughness; friendliness, honor, loyalty, caring (developed from using the ethical norm of caring), compassion, and justice (developed from using the ethical norm of justice). Each of these virtues is strengthened by repeated actions. Envy and resentment are vices for the businessperson; they poison the firm. Vices are bad habits that develop in the same fashion as good habits, through repeated acts.

A person who wishes to develop a good habit does so by consciously and repeatedly performing the desired act.[49] As Aristotle put it: "We are what we repeatedly do." Developing a habit takes time and effort, but once a good habit is in place, through the active effort of the person, later similar actions come easily and naturally. Thus a person who intentionally develops good habits through good acts makes additional good acts easier to perform. In fact, the development of good moral habits is also a good test of the basic spiritual values of the individual person.[50] Moreover, people who possess virtue will be more reliable colleagues and they will build a more effective firm in the long term.

Ethical decisions are generally the core of moral acts, and these good acts then provide the building blocks for good habits. Once a person has developed a good moral habit, say courage or prudence, that person is able to act with courage or prudence much more easily in each new instance. This ability we identify as *virtue.* Before we proceed further, let us provide two examples of good and bad moral habits:

> When a demented individual placed cyanide in Tylenol capsules, and seven people in Chicago died, James Burke, CEO at manufacturer Johnson & Johnson, spent hundreds of millions of dollars to recall all existing capsules rather than endanger additional lives. Although consultants and the FBI advised against it (it might encourage others), the recall decision was made quickly. By the account of Burke himself, this was because they based their decisions upon the mission and basic values of Johnson & Johnson, and the good moral habits that had been developed over the years.[51]

---

[48]Robert C. Solomon, "Victims of Circumstances: A Defense of Virtue Ethics in Business," *Business Ethics Quarterly,* 13, no. 1 (2003): 46–62; see also Solomon, *Ethics and Excellence: Cooperation and Integrity in Business* (New York: Oxford University Press, 1993), p. 106.
[49]Rushworth M. Kidder makes this same point with excellent examples in his chapter "Ethical Fitness" in *How Good People Make Tough Choices* (New York: William Morrow, 1995); see also George P. Klubertanz, S.J., *Habits and Virtues,* "How Is Virtue Acquired?" (New York: Appleton-Century-Crofts, 1965), pp. 171–177. For excellent references, see Klubertanz and Alasdair MacIntyre, *After Virtue* (Notre Dame: University of Notre Dame Press, 1981).
[50]Gerald F. Cavanagh and Mark R. Bandsuch, "Virtue as a Benchmark for Spirituality in Business," *Journal of Business Ethics,* 38 (June 2002): 109–117.
[51]See Laura L. Nash, "Johnson & Johnson's Credo," in *Corporate Ethics: A Prime Business Asset* (New York: The Business Roundtable, 1988), pp. 80–82.

The New York Stock Exchange (NYSE) is a non-profit, self-regulatory body that oversees the exchange of equity stock in the largest U.S. firms. Its chairman, Richard Grasso, was awarded $188 million in pay in 2003. The CEOs of some of the largest Wall Street firms that he was regulating, Goldman Sachs, Lehman Brothers, and Bear Stearns, sat on the compensation committee of NYSE that awarded the pay. These and other executives have been criticized by shareholders for their excessive pay. Grasso was fired and sued by his successor after his pay was revealed.[52]

Why did these two men act so differently? Why did Burke of J & J almost instinctively look to the benefit of the company's customers, while Grasso of NYSE ignored the conflict of interest and seemed to be more concerned with his own compensation? Grasso sought primarily his own self-interest at the expense of those for whom he had responsibilities, the firm's stakeholders. We will show that moral habits; that is, virtue or vice, account for most of the difference. Moreover, we maintain that the presence or the absence of such moral habits is the foundation for and an accurate predictor of good or bad behavior in the future. Let us examine these moral habits in greater detail.

### Self-Discipline, Courage, Justice, and Prudence

A moral virtue is a facet of character which is manifested in personal excellence in that area of human activity. Virtue is a stable, good moral habit that moves one toward the middle ground or between extremes in acting. Four basic moral virtues were identified by Aristotle and examined in detail by Thomas Aquinas. These four virtues are sometimes called the cardinal, principal, or chief virtues: self-discipline (temperance), courage (fortitude), justice (fairness) and prudence.[53]

*Self-discipline* is the developed ability of not pursuing a good excessively. Whether in regard to the appetites of our senses (e.g., eating, drinking, sex), or in wanting to possess or control things, we often experience a temptation to obtain or consume too much of these goods. A temperate person is not avaricious or greedy. Our senses do not incline us to be self-disciplined, yet we understand that there is a need to stop at a suitable, harmonious mean before we destroy ourselves from gluttony, sclerosis of the liver, or sexually transmitted diseases. Richard Grasso appears to have lacked the virtues of self-discipline when he arranged for his $188 million compensation. Rather, he displayed the vice of greed. Unfortunately, we witness avarice and greed among many people today. Many businesspeople try to rationalize this vice by explaining that the market system directs them to make as much money as possible.

---

[52]Michael Useem, "Behind Closed Doors," *Wall Street Journal,* September 23, 2003, p. B2; Landon Thomas, "Big Board Said to Want Legal Action in Grasso Pay Case," *New York Times,* January 8, 2004, pp. 1, 11.
[53]Thomas Aquinas, *Summa Theologia,* I–II, Questions 49–67; Aristotle, *Ethics.* See Edwin M. Hartman's discussion of virtue, "The Good Life and the Good Community," in *Organizational Ethics and the Good Life* (New York: Oxford University Press, 1996), pp. 182–185; Robert G. Kennedy, "Virtue and Corporate Culture: The Ethical Formation of Baby Wolverines," *Review of Business,* 17 (Winter 1995–1996): 10–15.

Providing the necessary capital for business is important and generally demands virtue to achieve it. However, Aristotle maintains that to own significantly more than is required for one's family or more than is ultimately a benefit to others is a vice. This traditional limit on the possession of wealth challenges contemporary attitudes on the accumulation of money and goods and the inviolability of private property.

*Courage* enables one to overcome obstacles to do what is necessary to achieve a good goal. An entrepreneur must have courage in order to take the necessary risks to begin and maintain a business. Courage enables one to overcome the temptations of both cowardice and rashness. The virtues of patience and perseverance are necessary for courage. For example, James Burke of J & J had courage to order the $100 million recall of Tylenol. On the other hand, given its non-profit status and the conflicts of interest, the members of the NYSE board of directors probably lacked courage when they agreed to the large compensation package for Grasso. In our everyday work, it is often easy to dodge difficult issues; we need courage to overcome those challenges.[54]

The virtue of *justice* is the regular and constant disposition to give another her or his due. The virtue of justice is related to, but is not the same as, the ethical norm of justice. The norm enables one to make an ethical judgment. The virtue disposes one to choose to do the just thing *because it is just*. The virtue of justice would lead a manager to pay an equitable wage and to avoid race and gender discrimination. When Bausch & Lomb CEO Daniel Gill forced unrealistic sales goals on his division executives and distributors, he violated the virtue of justice. Rather than provide a corporate climate that supported justice, Gill's policies pushed his subordinates into unjust behavior.

*Prudence* is the concrete judgment that a person makes to recognize a good goal and to determine the means or strategy to be used in order to obtain that goal. The other virtues also require the judgment of prudence in order to be exercised. Although the virtues are independent, they are nevertheless intertwined in each person. For example, without self-discipline greed will lead us to unjust actions. In strategy classes business students learn the techniques of marketing *any* product, or financing *any* endeavor, and some might call this prudence. However, the ability to develop strategies to obtain goals that are not good is not prudence. For example, to develop strategies to sell a product that kills, such as tobacco; or to take over a firm in a hostile fashion, loot its retirement plan, and fire its employees, as has been done too often, is an act we might call *shrewdness*, but it does not manifest the virtue of prudence.[55]

A manager cannot develop virtue in people by making them do things. The motivation must come from within; they must *intend* the good act. So developing virtue requires a good intention and perseverance, and it is difficult because of our own instinctive self-interest. As one expert puts it: "If people cared as much about the rights of others as they care about their own rights no virtue of justice would

[54]See Gerald F. Cavanagh and Dennis J. Moberg, "The Virtue of Courage Within the Organization," *Research in Ethical Issues in Organizations,* vol. 1 (Stamford, CT: JAI Press, 1999), pp. 1–25.

[55]Klubertanz, *Habits and Virtues;* see also Charles M. Horvath, "Excellence v. Effectiveness: MacIntyre's Critique of Business," *Business Ethics Quarterly,* 5 (July 1995): 499–532.

be needed to look after the matter, and rules about such things as contracts and promises would only need to be made public, like the rules of a game that everyone was eager to play."[56]

Good moral behavior is influenced by mentoring, modeling, executive vision, and the particular corporate culture that this creates. Just as individuals must choose to be virtuous and must repeatedly act to bring that about, so, too, managers must choose a specific style of managing if they seek to encourage a moral corporate culture. However, the contrary is also true. Managers who themselves engage in morally selfish acts thus model and encourage bad behavior and unjust habits for their colleagues and subordinates.[57]

Founders and leaders of organizations would like their organizations to be successful over the long term. To accomplish long-term results requires the moral habits of trust, fairness, and courage. Good moral habits, like moral principles, enable one to achieve moral goals. Most managers also would like to encourage ethically good behavior and good moral habits for the people in the work group they lead. Such basic ethical characteristics as honesty, trust, respect for other people, and an ability to cooperate and work with others help make an effective organization.

A good moral habit develops when one repeats morally good actions. Hence, when a person regularly makes ethical decisions and performs ethical acts, it will develop that person's good moral habits or virtues. Good moral acts performed by the members of the work group will also encourage good moral habits in other members of the work group.[58]

## The Virtuous Organization

To develop a habit of a particular good moral act requires that the individual *choose* that moral act. Virtue will grow to the extent that the person performs the act because she chooses the behavior for its own sake. However, good moral acts that are motivated largely by fear, peer pressure, a control-oriented supervisor, or purely extrinsic rewards like compensation, will not develop virtue. Nevertheless, motives are seldom pure.

Virtue in organizations has become of considerable recent concern for both managers and scholars.[59] Leaders of organizations regularly attempt to communicate the values of the organization through socialization processes to new hires and to those who are already colleagues.[60] Leaders attempt to select people

---

[56]Philippa Foot, *Virtues and Vices and Other Essays in Moral Philosophy* (Berkeley: University of California Press, 1978), p. 9. The virtue of loyalty was featured in several articles in a special issue of *Business Ethics Quarterly,* 11, no. 1 (2001). See, for example, Daniel R. Gilbert, Jr., "An Extraordinary Concept in the Ordinary Service of Management."

[57]Valerie S. Folkes and Ykun-Oh Whang, "Account-Giving for a Corporate Transgression Influences Moral Judgment: When Those Who 'Spin' Condone Harm-Doing," *Journal of Applied Psychology,* 88, no. 1 (2003): 79–86.

[58]Helen J. Alford, O.P. and Michael J. Naughton, *Managing as If Faith Mattered* (Notre Dame: University of Notre Dame Press, 2002), pp. 70–96; MacIntyre, *After Virtue.*

[59]See Kim S. Cameron, Jane E. Dutton, and Robert E. Quinn, eds., *Positive Organizational Scholarship: Foundations of a New Discipline* (San Francisco: Berrett-Koehler, 2003).

[60]H. M. Trice and J. M. Beyer, *The Cultures of Work Organizations* (Englewood Cliffs, NJ: Prentice Hall, 1993).

appropriate for the firm and for the job, and then socialize them to be people who will work well within that organization. Formal and informal socialization are discussed in Chapter 7. Nevertheless we here mention the importance of performing acts of, for example, trust, honesty, justice, and courage, because they are morally *good* acts. When the modeling behavior of leaders support this, it can be effective in developing good moral habits, which then change behavior and thus form a person's character.

A leader must have a vision of how she wishes to operate and must be proactive, if she wishes to affect the behavior of members.[61] Stories of managers who model the values that are described in the mission statement of the firm support that vision. The compensation system of the organization must also support the kind of behavior that is to be encouraged. We tend to build reward systems around measurable standards of performance, but trust, honesty, and courage are not easily measurable. A "colleague-of-the-week" program, bonuses, and other rewards can identify people who have done something of benefit for the firm or for others.[62]

A reward system that relies on narrowly defined and easily measurable financial returns may encourage vice rather than virtue. Bausch & Lomb managers inflated profits, coerced distributors, and engaged in other immoral activities.

The development of good moral habits is diagramed in Figure 3-5. Each person has his own unique package of good moral habits. Practice in making ethical decisions and performing good acts develop those moral habits. Examining the diagram, person number one possesses better–developed moral habits (virtue), so the ethical issues that require judgment and action will be easier to identify, decide, and act on for that person. Moreover, each additional act of that virtue will come more

**FIGURE 3-5** **Development of Good Moral Habits**

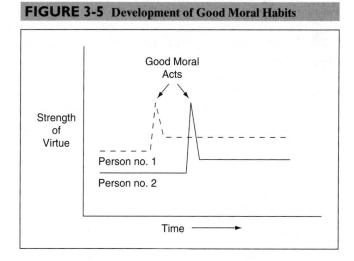

[61]Linda Klebe Trevino and Michael E. Brown, "Managing to Be Ethical: Debunking Five Business Ethics Myths," *Academy of Management Executive,* 18 (May 2004): 69–80.
[62]Bruno Dyck and Rob Kleysen, "Aristotle's Virtues and Management Thought," *Business Ethics Quarterly,* 11, no. 4 (2002): 561–574.

easily. That is, each individual act strengthens the virtue, so that the act is easier to perform the next time. Person number 2 has lesser development of good habits, so it will be harder for that person to identify the issues, and more difficult (i.e., a greater stretch) to make an ethical judgment. But notice that in this case, also, the level of virtue is increased, even if slightly, after each individual good moral act.

A person's *character* is formed by the aggregate of that person's moral habits. Every group or organization of which a person is a part influences that person's attitudes and actions, builds good and bad habits, and ultimately forms that person's character. Moreover, an organization made up of people with mostly good habits and hence good character, will possess a good ethical climate and thus a good corporate culture.

The *goal* of a business is to increase the well-being of women and men, which includes the development of virtue in colleagues of the working group. Virtue will not develop if a business meets only its goals of profit and growth. Profit, return on investment, and increasing market share are important measurable *means* to achieve the *ultimate goals* of the firm.

In the process of becoming a manager, a good manager generally develops many good habits, many virtues. For example, a manager who regularly trusts subordinates develops the virtue of trust and eventually trusts almost automatically, and encourages the trust of others. A manager who does not trust will sow distrust throughout his unit. Such a manager finds that it takes far more time and energy to be a good manager—if indeed that person ever becomes a good manager.

One method of affecting attitudes and behavior and in that way developing virtue, is to help the disadvantaged.[63] Ford Motor Company encourages its people to help in soup kitchens and homeless shelters, tutor inner-city youth, deliver food to the elderly and handicapped, and engage in other projects for those in need. Ford will provide time off from work at full pay for up to 20 hours a year for these service projects. Other firms encourage their people to volunteer to help the poor overseas.[64] Service projects are also common in colleges and universities; one's motivation is almost always positively affected by personal contact with those in need. The virtue and good character that is thus engendered also increases the social capital of the firm; that is, the trust, cooperation, and honesty. Moreover, research by health care professionals shows that helping other people is often good for your heart, your immune system, and your longevity.[65]

---

[63]S. D. Papamarcos, "The Next Wave in Service-learning: Integrative, Team-based Engagements with Structural Objectives," *Review of Business,* 23, no. 2 (2002): 31–38; P. C. Godfrey, "Service Learning and Management Education: A Call to Action," *Journal of Management Inquiry,* 8, no. 4 (1999): 363–378.

[64]Kerry Capell, "A Volunteer's Mexican Diary: One Week of Building Homes for the Poor," *Business Week,* March 31, 1997, pp. 94–98; William Honan, "President of Harvard Cites Need for Commitment to Social Service," *New York Times,* November 1, 1993, p. 16.

[65]Paul S. Adler and Seok-Woo Kwon, "Social Capital: Prospects for a New Concept," *Academy of Management Review,* 27, no. 1 (2002): 17–40; Eileen Rockefeller Growald and Allan Luks, "Beyond Self: The Immunity of Samaritans," *American Health,* March 1988, pp. 51–53.

For those interested in character education, the organization *Character Education Partnership* provides a Web site that offers resources, conferences, and news.[66] Unfortunately, building character is not a priority in most U.S. colleges and universities. Arthur Schwartz, director of character-education programs at the John Templeton Foundation, says:

> Only relatively few institutions—usually small liberal arts colleges or those that are religiously affiliated or faith-inspired—have a comprehensive commitment to character development in all dimensions of college life.[67]

This leads us into the next subject: how ethics and character education are taught in business schools.

## ETHICS IN BUSINESS EDUCATION

After the financial and ethical bankruptcies of Enron and Arthur Andersen and the ethical debacles at NASDAQ, Solomon Brothers, Merrill Lynch, ImClone, and Tyco, the accusation has been made that business education is at fault. To that point, a former Harvard Business School teacher criticized business schools in a widely quoted article, "When It Comes to Ethics, B-Schools Get a F." An Aspen Institute study of business school students' attitudes found that at the beginning of their MBA program most students felt that the purpose of business was to produce quality goods and services. By the end of their MBA education, only one-third continued to see producing goods and services as the purpose, and 75 percent felt that the purpose of business was to increase shareholder value.

Just before the recent business debacles, an empirical study of ethics teaching in business schools found that ethics was not taken seriously at the majority of business schools, and this was especially true at large state universities. As an illustration he related how students tried for many decades unsuccessfully to have a required business ethics course in the undergraduate and MBA curriculum. He found that ethics at his university, University of Michigan, is treated by his peers with an attitude that is somewhere between "ambivalence and disdain." Surprisingly, in the last few years and even since the public scandals, many business schools have dropped or downgraded their business ethics courses.[68]

A consensus has emerged that the ethical debacles of Tyco, ImClone, Qwest and Computer Associates were the result of an "overemphasis American corporations have been forced to give in recent years to maximizing shareholder value without regard for the effects of their actions on other stakeholders." Yet most

[66]See www.character.org.
[67]Arthur J. Schwartz, "It's Not Too Late to Teach College Students About Values," *Chronicle of Higher Education,* 46 (June 9, 2000).
[68]LaRue T. Hosmer, "Somebody Out There Doesn't Like Us," *Journal of Business Ethics,* 22 (November 1999): 91–106; Amitai Etzioni, "When It Comes to Ethics, B-Schools Get an F," *Washington Post,* August 4, 2002, p. B4; see also Marjorie Kelly, "It's a Heckuva Time to Be Dropping Business Ethics Courses: MBA Programs Are Downsizing Ethics Requirements at Precisely the Wrong Time," *Business Ethics,* Fall 2002, pp. 17–18.

business school faculty teach "running the numbers" and take little account of the effect that these decisions have on employees, customers, or the local community. Ethics and social responsibility courses "are considered 'soft' subjects . . . and are given short shrift in favor of applied analytical tools and techniques, conceptual models, and measures of profitability."[69] A comprehensive business education, as well as the study of each business discipline, requires a consideration of the social and ethical consequences of any major decision and policy. Supporting this effort are 85 percent of firm recruiters who say that personal ethics and integrity is "very important" in any person that they seek to hire for their firm.[70]

Recognizing that ethics is as important as finance, marketing, and other professional business content areas, hundreds of business school faculty members petitioned the business school accrediting association to include an ethics course in the required curriculum. The accrediting body refused to require ethics, but did urge that ethics be an integral part of any graduate or undergraduate program and has provided materials for teaching ethics.[71] It remains to be seen if ethics and social responsibility will be taught and/or learned at most business schools.

The concern for ethics in business education is not new. Executives and citizens have agreed for many years that there is a need for ethics in business and in schools. In a survey more than a decade ago of corporate CEOs, business school deans, and members of Congress, 94 percent said that the business community is troubled by ethical problems. Further, 63 percent of these leaders believe that a business firm actually strengthens its competitive position by maintaining high ethical standards. Perhaps surprisingly, these leaders also said that a difference in the quality of ethics can be observed in various parts of the United States. Areas of the country they ranked from most ethical to least are as follows: Midwest, Northwest, New England, South, Southwest, West, and East.[72]

Difficulties in arriving at an ethical judgment stem largely from our lack of knowledge of ethical norms and the classical ethical traditions. Most managers are not immoral, but many are amoral. They simply fail to adequately consider the morality of their actions.[73] They are hampered by the fact that ethics and the importance of good character generally are not taught in American schools, from grade schools to universities. On the contrary, the tradition of competitive, individualistic methods of learning and grading

---

[69]Sandra Waddock, "Hollow Men at the Helm: Until Business Schools Teach Future Managers How Deep the Connections Are Between Business, Society, Nature, and the World, Corporations Will Continue to Be Run by Hollow Leaders with No Sense of Ethics or Responsibility," *BusEd,* July/August 2004, pp. 24–29. *BusEd* is published by AACSB, the international business school accrediting agency.

[70]Ronald Alsop, "Business Schools Recruiters' Top Picks," *Wall Street Journal,* September 22, 2004, p. R8.

[71]See "Ethics Education in Business Schools," *Report of the Ethics Education Task Force to AACSB International's Board of Governors* (St. Louis: AACSB International, 2004). This report is also available at www.aacsb.edu/metf.

[72]*Ethics in American Business: An Opinion Survey of Key Business Leaders on Ethical Standards and Behavior* (New York: Touche Ross, 1988), pp. 1, 10; see also "Why Ethics Is Also B-School Business," *Business Week,* January 27, 2003, p. 105.

[73]Archie B. Carroll, "In Search of the Moral Manager," *Business Horizons,* March–April 1987, pp. 7–15.

retards the development of a sense of community and obligations to others. Hence, in universities the environment often obstructs the development of moral maturity and ethics. Managers often are constrained by their own lack of moral imagination; that is, their options are narrowed because they often fail to consider the more ethical act.[74]

Ethics was not always so unknown. Ethics, or moral philosophy as it was then called, was the center of the curriculum of American colleges and universities throughout the nineteenth century. An ethics course was required of all seniors and, because of its importance, was often taught by the college president himself.[75] This course was designed as an integration of all that students had learned, and prepared them for the working world. It sharpened their ethical sensitivity and enabled them to better address the ethical problems they were about to face.

Educators during this period judged that no nation could survive and prosper without common social and moral values. For a society such as the United States, which is fragmented because of differences in ethnic backgrounds, allegiances, interests, and expertise, it seemed important to provide a structure whereby students could unify their learning. "The entire college experience was meant above all to be an experience in character development and the moral life, as epitomized, secured, and brought to focus in the moral philosophy course."[76] Is this need still present today?

Business education has been criticized for being too narrow, analytic, and technical by business executives and also by a committee set up by the business school accrediting association.[77] An early authoritative report by the accrediting association concluded that MBA curricula lacked vision and integration. Among other omissions, insufficient attention was given to ethics and the social and political environment of business.

Practical reasons exist for including ethics in the business program. We find that making ethical judgments before one is exposed to real business pressures to act unethically can result in behavior that is more ethical. In an experiment, college students were given a case involving an ethical dilemma and asked to judge a course of action. The experimenters then presented the actual situation to these same students two weeks later. The students acted more ethically than did a control group that had not earlier discussed the case. On the job, the pressures of "efficiencies" and time push one to compromise.[78]

---

[74]Patricia C. Werhane, *Moral Imagination and Management Decision Making* (New York: Oxford University Press, 1999).

[75]Douglas Sloan, "The Teaching of Ethics in American Undergraduate Curriculum, 1876–1976," in *Ethics Teaching in Higher Education,* ed. Daniel Callahan and Sissela Bok (New York: Plenum Press, 1980), p. 2.

[76]*Ibid.,* p. 7.

[77]Lyman Porter and Lawrence McKibbin, *Management Education and Development: Drift or Thrust into the 21st Century?* (New York: McGraw-Hill, 1988).

[78]Steven J. Sherman, "On the Self-erasing Nature of Errors of Prediction," *Journal of Personality and Social Psychology,* 39 (March 1980): 211–219.

When considering a dilemma away from the pressures of the actual situation, a person tends to consider the ethical issues in a more objective and balanced way. Moral reasoning ability is also improved when ethics is taught in courses.[79] The conclusion: An informed discussion of ethical cases and making ethical judgments will have a significant positive effect on ethical behavior, and it may even help to develop good moral habits.

American executives and their firms have developed policies and training to help their workers understand ethical issues. A survey of firms showed ethics policies and codes are distributed to almost all workers, especially people at the higher level of the organization. Moreover, more than 85 percent of firms require that people receiving the ethics policy indicate in writing that they have received it and are in compliance with it. Going beyond distributing ethics policies, 55 percent of workers say that their employers provide ethics training; this number goes to 68 percent if restricted to firms of 500 or more workers. Ethics training programs are more effective when they are integrated into other training at the firm. The goals of ethics programs are, on the one hand, to provide information and policies on what is acceptable and what is not, and on the other hand, to lessen penalties on the firm if an errant worker is charged with a crime. General Electric, IBM, Johnson & Johnson, Boeing, Merck, and many other firms provide ethics training and have done so for at least two decades.[80] We will discuss ethics codes and training in greater detail in Chapters 8 and 9.

## SUMMARY AND CONCLUSIONS

We examined moral development in the last chapter and found that selfish (Kohlberg's Level I) behavior is more typical of adolescents and the immature than of mature women and men. Most businesspeople want to be ethical; they have many good moral habits. Nevertheless, inflating revenues, hiding expenses, not revealing important information to customers, fraud, bribery, and stealing trade secrets remain major ethical problems for business. In many cases, managers who have committed ethical blunders say that they could not distinguish the right action from the wrong action. Those in the generations now growing up have fewer moral skills. The media and advertising teach us that ethics is relative. Many people have not learned how to make ethical judgments and do not have the moral imagination to do so.

The ethical principles, models, and cases presented in this chapter are intended to aid businesspeople in the development of their ethical skills and even their character. The decision norms and models are not perfect; they will not solve all ethical problems easily. Ethical decisions affect behavior, enabling people to be more honest and trustworthy, and ultimately possess greater integrity and virtue.

---

[79]Elinar Marnburg, "Educational Impacts on Academic Business Practitioner's Moral Reasoning and Behavior: Effects of Short Courses in Ethics or Philosophy," *Business Ethics: A European Review,* 12 (October 2003): 403–413.

[80]Linda Klebe Trevino and Gary Weaver, *Managing Ethics in Business Organizations* (Stanford, CA: Stanford University Press, 2003), pp. 79–80; see also Susan J. Harrington, "What Corporate America Is Teaching About Ethics," *Academy of Management Executive,* 5 (February 1991): 21–30.

Businesspeople lament the lack of ethical skills among new workers and the lack of formal ethics classes in college curricula. In earlier centuries ethics had a central place in the education of college students. It is a paradox that businesspeople have learned precise decision rules for inventory, finance, and brand marketing, but have so few models for moral decisions and actions. If businesspeople are not moral, business will become a jungle, both hostile to people and highly inefficient.

These ethical norms and models can be learned and used, and thus become an aid to businesspeople. The decision rules can be expanded to handle more difficult cases, including cases in which the norms conflict. Moreover, the evidence shows that making ethical judgments in the classroom helps to bring about more ethical behavior in business.

The intentional repetition of good moral acts develops desirable moral habits or virtues. Good moral habits among colleagues can make a working environment more humane and more effective. Few business schools have been thorough and consistent in presenting ethics and providing ethical tools for future businesspeople. Graduates who have learned ethics and developed character with the help of their business school are more likely to be trusted and are less likely to cost their firm its reputation.

## DISCUSSION QUESTIONS

1. What is the principal difference between rights and duties and utilitarian norms? Do an individual's intentions have any role in utilitarianism? Do intentions have a role in the theory of rights? Explain.
2. What does John Rawls add to the traditional theory of justice? Compare Rawls's theory and the traditional theory of justice with utilitarianism.
3. Upon what is the norm of caring built? How does it compare with rights and duties, justice and utilitarianism?
4. Indicate the strengths and weaknesses of using the norms of (a) utility, (b) justice, (c) rights, and (d) caring.
5. Is anything always morally right or always morally wrong (e.g., murder)? Is lying or stealing always or generally wrong, or is it relative, a matter of social expectations and the law?
6. Outline the criteria for whistle-blowing. If you knew of payments by your firm to a manager in a competing firm for insider information, should you blow the whistle? Apply the criteria in deciding this question.
7. How can the four principle virtues—self-discipline, courage, justice, and prudence—help an individual succeed?
8. Do many college students take a course in ethics? What is the advantage of such a course? What is the disadvantage of ethics not being learned? Have you had such a course?
9. Is the purpose of studying ethics to develop ethical decision-making skills or to influence good behavior? Does the former affect the latter? How?
10. Describe how a person can develop good habits. What is the relation of virtue and character?
11. Give an example of when you have exercised a virtue. What virtues do you see in others?

12. As a manager would you prefer that the members of your work group have good character? As a peer in a firm, would you prefer colleagues have good character? Why?
13. What is the purpose of business, according to graduate business students at the beginning of their program? How does that attitude shift by the end of their program?
14. In the fragmented, pluralistic society of the nineteenth century, colleges and universities saw the need for integration of education with a capstone ethics course for all students. Is this need still present today?
15. Do business schools have a responsibility to help students learn ethics and develop good character? Why or why not?

# CASES

## Case 3-1      Double Expense Account

Frank Waldron is a second-year MBA student at Eastern State University. Although he has had many job offers, he continues to have the university placement office arrange interviews. He reasons that the interview experience is good for him and a better offer may even come along. Frank has also discovered a way to make money from job interviews.

Two firms invited Waldron to Los Angeles for visits to their home offices. He scheduled both visits on the same day and billed each for his full travel expenses. In this way he was able to pocket $1,000. When a friend objected that this was dishonest, Frank replied that each firm had told him to submit his expenses and that therefore he was not taking something to which he had no right. One firm had not asked for receipts, which he interpreted to mean that it intended to make him a gift of the money.

1. Is what Frank is doing unethical?
2. Which norms help most in deciding the question?
3. What advice would you give Frank? ■

## Case 3-2      PETA vs. Pfizer

People for the Ethical Treatment of Animals (PETA) wants all drug companies to stop or do less testing on animals. PETA filed a shareholder resolution with Pfizer, asking the firm to reduce the amount of animal testing that it does. The occasion of the resolution was that Pfizer lost a dog which was left in a cage that was sent through scalding water to be cleaned. The U.S. Department of Agriculture's investigation labeled the death as an accident. Nevertheless, PETA pressed its case against Pfizer with a shareholder resolution. Pfizer's Board voted unanimously against the resolution. In Britain activists have slashed researchers' tires and have placed pipe bombs at laboratories. Additional security costs British pharmaceutical firms $128 million per year, and some estimate that Britain, with more stringent regulations on animal testing than the United States, is losing $2 billion a year in new investment.[81]

1. What are the ethical issues involved in Pfizer's use of animals when testing pharmaceuticals?

---

[81]"Animal-Rights Activism Turns Rabid: Attacks on Drug Companies and University Labs Are Chilling Research," *Business Week,* August 30, 2004, p. 54.

2. Should Pfizer curtail or stop the use of animals in its testing?
3. Should it do so if such testing does not provide full information on the safety of the pharmaceutical?

4. What are the ethics of the protesters' tactics?
5. What ethical norm(s) are most helpful here? ■

---

## Case 3-3     Tax Assessment Kickback

You own a large building in a major city. The real estate assessor offers, for a fee, to underestimate the value of your property and save you a substantial amount in real estate taxes.

Assume that this is a common practice in this city.
1. Do you pay the fee?
2. Which norm is most helpful here? ■

---

## EXERCISE

### Memo to the Chief Executive

You are a manager in a firm in a very competitive industry. A competitor has made an important scientific discovery that could give it an advantage that would substantially reduce, but not eliminate, the profits of your company for approximately a year. A scientist who knows the details of the discovery applies for a job at your firm. There are no legal barriers to hiring the scientist.

The CEO knows that you studied ethics in your MBA program and so asks you to give her your advice. In a single page memo to the CEO, indicate the major issues and ethical norms to be used, and make a recommendation.

## EXERCISE (2 ALTERNATIVE EXERCISES: A & B)

### A. Ethical Climate of an Organization

*The goals, values, and ethics of an organization are vitally important yet often do not receive the attention they deserve. The purpose of this exercise is to enable you to examine and articulate the values, ethics, and commitments of an organization of your choice.*

To complete the project, do the following:

1. Choose an organization that you wish to study. A firm where you work would be best; in any case, choose a firm for which you have access to information.
2. On a single sheet of paper indicate (a) your choice of firm, and (b) sources of information. Turn this in at the beginning of the next class.
3. Determine the *proclaimed* goals, values, and ethics of the organization and its proclaimed commitments to its key stakeholders—customers, employees, suppliers, the

local community, the larger community (including the physical environment), and shareholders. For this purpose, study the mission or goal statement of the organization, its code(s) of ethics, the speeches of top managers, and relevant materials from Web sites, annual report, or training manuals. Indicate any values missing from those proclaimed. Be explicit and comprehensive.

4. Determine the *real* goals, values, ethics, and commitments of the organization. Consult individuals who have direct contact (employees, customers, others), use personal observation, and study written materials evaluating the company.

5. Prepare a 12–15 page double-spaced typed report of your findings. This may include an appendix with supporting materials. Spell out the (a) *proclaimed* values and (b) *real* values of the firm. Determine if the organization is doing what it claims. Specify what it is doing to meet obligations to stakeholders. Indicate if it is meeting these obligations very well, satisfactorily, or not well and give suggestions for improvement. Be explicit and specific.

This report could also be done with a team of diverse students. In that case, decide at the beginning exactly what each member of the team will contribute to the project. At the end, evaluate your own and each team member's contributions to the project and give feedback to each team member. This written evaluation is due with the report.

## B. Ethical Climate of a Business Compared to Caux Round Table Principles for Business

*The purpose of this assignment is to familiarize you with the Caux Round Table's (CRT) Principles for Business and how they might be used as a benchmark for a firm's ethics code. You will compare one firm's (if possible, the one for which you work) Mission, Vision, and Code of Conduct with the Caux Round Table's Principles for Business (See Appendix A).*

Specifically, the assignment is to:

1. Obtain a copy of the firm's Mission, Vision, and Code of Conduct.

2. Compare (a) the firm's statements with (b) CRT's *Principles for Business.* In your comparison, note the major issues that are covered by both documents. Compare the content of both codes and evaluate the adequacy and comprehensiveness of your firm's code.

3. Write a paper to summarize your comparison of the firm's Mission, Vision, and Code of Conduct with the CRT's *Principles for Business.*

The following questions may help you to examine and compare:

### General Principles

Does your firm's Code, Mission, or Vision have any statements like Caux's *General Principles?*

Briefly describe them. Does the firm's code cover the material of the seven *Principles?* Answer for each. If so, briefly describe how it is covered.

### Stakeholder Principles

Does your firm's code have a section on responsibilities to customers?

If so, briefly compare the two codes.

Does it have a section on responsibilities to employees? If so, briefly compare the two codes.

Does it have a section on responsibilities to owners/investors? If so, briefly compare the two codes.

Does it have a section on responsibilities to suppliers? If so, briefly compare the two codes.

Does it have a section on responsibilities to competitors? If so, briefly compare the two codes.

Does it have a section on responsibilities to the community? If so, briefly compare the two codes.

Finally and most important, is your firm's code designed to protect only the company? Or is it designed to protect customers, employees, and outside stakeholders, also? Does it give proportionate coverage to both the firm and the various stakeholders?

Summarize your comparison of the firm's Mission, Vision and Code of Conduct with the CRT's *Principles for Business*. The paper should be no more than 10 double-spaced pages. Use any format that is useful for your comparison. Include a copy of the relevant Mission, Values, and Code of Conduct of the firm you use in an appendix. Organization, spelling, punctuation, and grammar will be included in the evaluation.

# CHAPTER 4

# Historical Roots of Business Values

Those who do not study history are doomed to repeat it.

GEORGES SANTAYANA (1863–1952), PHILOSOPHER, POET

Probe the earth and see where your main roots are.

HENRY DAVID THOREAU (1817–1862), AMERICAN PHILOSOPHER

Knowing history benefits the businessperson and the student of business. The manager who understands history is able to recognize problems that were faced and solved earlier by others, and is better able to recognize situations that are new and hence demand new solutions. History reveals the details behind such diverse elements as the growth of business and cities and the energetic, entrepreneurial attitudes of earlier generations.[1]

We are products of our past. No matter how rapidly society changes, current attitudes have their roots in history. What we do and how we think are influenced by past values and attitudes.[2] Whether we view the present as part of an organic development from earlier events or as breaking new ground, the past influences us. For example, an historical faith in progress undergirds the conviction of many that global markets are good for all. On the other hand, concern for work satisfaction and a sustainable environment stems partly from disenchantment with attitudes of earlier generations that were short-sighted and wasteful. It is impossible to understand fully our current values and what the future might bring without understanding the path that has led us to where we are.

---

[1]"Why History Matters to Managers," a roundtable discussion with Alfred D. Chandler et al., Alan M. Kantrow, ed., *Harvard Business Review,* January–February 1986, pp. 81–88. On the importance of history, ethics, and social responsibility in business, see Steven P. Feldman, *Memory As a Moral Decision: The Role of Ethics in Organizational Culture* (New Brunswick, NJ: Transaction Press, 2002).
[2]*Ibid.*, p. 84.

## QUESTIONING THE PAST

People, especially those in developed societies, need to assess their goals and values for several reasons. First, if we are to make the best decisions concerning the many choices that we face—choosing a career, a lifestyle, whether to marry, when to have children, and so on—we must know our goals and values.

Second, change is now taking place so rapidly that we need a firm, considered foundation for our goals and activities. Some goals are basic, provide a sense of stability, and endure through major changes; other goals are no longer helpful. It is essential to examine our values so as to determine which of them remain relevant.

Third, as we have more education, we become more questioning and reflective, and thus more conscious of our goals and values.

Fourth, an examination of basic goals and values is necessary because actions, goals, and rights often conflict. For example, the goal of loyalty to a firm conflicts with downsizing. The goal of producing at lowest cost conflicts with the goal of avoiding sweatshops and reducing pollution. The resolution of these conflicts requires clarification of personal and group goals.

Some ask the fundamental question: Why work? What is the value of work? Further, what is the value of business? Granted, if I want a car or a PC, someone must design and manufacture it and I must have money to obtain it. But if I can obtain it in a lawful fashion without working, why not? If I can get rich speculating or gambling without working, why not do so? Does work have any value to a person or to society beyond the dollar rewards? Citizens around the world ask about the intrinsic value of work and the goals of free enterprise. A reasonable response is essential for mature people and a successful society.

These questions are not new; however, now they are being asked by more people. In earlier centuries, they were asked only by a few educated people, not by ordinary citizens. These few educated people were the only ones who had leisure to ask such questions. The ordinary worker's life was largely determined at birth. If a man's father was a shoemaker or a baker, he would become a shoemaker or a baker, and would use the workshop, tools, and home that had belonged to the family for generations. Rarely was the question raised of whether a person *would* work, or at what occupation. There was little choice. Heredity, geography, and custom determined most of a person's life. To ask a person in an economically less developed, traditional society why he works is like asking him why he tries to stay alive. He has little reason to question the value of work.

Attitudes toward work are the foundation blocks for business success. The early American Puritan ethic supported tireless work and economic growth. However, this is but one strand of our history. Let us examine other strands.

## LISTENING TO OUR FOREBEARS

Change took place rapidly in the United States from its beginning. Most of its people emigrated from other lands, largely from Europe. The Founding Fathers were influenced by European thinkers such as John Locke, Jean-Jacques

Rousseau, and Adam Smith, on the value of work, business, and private property. Although there were alternate strands of thought in the Eastern Hemisphere, those values have had less impact on American business values. Hence in the United States we draw largely on Western history and philosophies as they affect business.

Throughout history, work has been an integrating activity for most people. It was a binding cord for the fabric of the family, the city, and the social system. It gave stability and meaning to people and their relationships. However, work changed as societies industrialized; mass production, division of labor, and "scientific management" were introduced. From the individual's standpoint, the worker had more choice as to the type and location of the work he or she performed. It is ironic that just when individuals were able to choose their work and thus hope for greater satisfaction from their jobs, more people worked in large organizations and the work itself became more fragmented, repetitive, and less able to provide pride of workmanship.

## The Ancient Greek Attitude Toward Business and Work

History seems to reflect that the ancient Greeks thought of work and commerce as demeaning to a citizen. At best, it was a burden required for survival. The meager legitimacy and value Greeks accorded to work was not because it had any value in itself, but because it was a necessary evil. We must remember, however, that what we know about ancient attitudes toward work is colored by two limitations to our knowledge of ancient history. First, most of our information comes from written sources whose authors were generally citizens and hence people of leisure, a minority; they were not from the working class. Second, slaves did most of the work under dirty, grueling, and often unsafe conditions. These slaves were uneducated and often prisoners of war from conquered nations.

Plato speaks of work as if it were a temptation to be avoided because it hinders a person's ability to live, to think, and to contemplate. In his *Laws,* Plato speaks for his fellow citizens when he urges, "If a native stray from the pursuit of goodness into some trade or craft, they shall correct him by reproach and degradation until he be brought back again into the straight course."[3] Citizens of ancient Athens thought of work as something not worthy of a citizen. Plato, however, reveals the extent to which his contemporaries' attitudes were based on the conditions under which work was done, as he cuts to the heart of their disenchantment and even revulsion with work:

> Suppose the very best of men could be compelled—the fancy will sound ludicrous, I know, but I must give it utterance—suppose they could be compelled to take for a time to inn-keeping, or retail trade or some such calling; or suppose, for that matter, that some unavoidable destiny were to drive the best women into such professions: then we should discover that all are humane and beneficent occupations; if they were only conducted

---

[3]Plato, *The Laws of Plato,* trans. A. E. Taylor (London: Dent, 1934), p. 847B.

on the principles of strict integrity, we should respect them as we do the vocation of mother and nurse.[4]

Thus, Plato recognizes that most of the objections to work are not inherent in work itself. In fact, these occupations are in themselves "humane and beneficent."

Plato's pupil Aristotle is more severe in his condemnation of the life of the worker or tradesperson. To him, such a life is irksome and beneath the dignity of a citizen:

> Citizens must not lead the life of mechanics or tradesmen, for such a life is ignoble, and inimical to virtue. Neither must they be husbandmen, since leisure is necessary both for the development of virtue and the performance of political duties.[5]

From his observations, Aristotle found crafts, trade, and business detrimental to health and character. Much of the work was done in cramped and unhealthy surroundings, and it was necessary to have daily dealings with rude, unprincipled, and unethical people. So industrial and commercial life was thought to rob the body of its health and to degrade the character. This sort of work was generally done by slaves, and many contemporary states did not admit even the most skilled worker and or laborer to citizenship. "Even in states which admitted the industrial and commercial classes to power, popular sentiment held trade and industry cheap."[6]

Aristotle speaks of two types of business and trade activity, and his distinction goes to the root of a difficulty that perplexes many to the present day: the difference between the careful management of goods and what often appears to be a merely selfish profit orientation. He approves of the first but disapproves of the second. *Oeconomia,* from which our word economics derives, is literally "household management." It includes careful, prudent use not only of the household but of all one's property and resources. On the other hand, *chrematistike* means the use of skill and goods to achieve a profit. This term described the city traders, who were few in number compared to the farmers and skilled workers. These traders often resorted to deceptive practices; and it seemed to Aristotle, and scores of generations that followed him, that they contributed little or nothing to society. Aristotle's objections are not unlike those of Karl Marx: The trader's service as a middleman adds no value to the good. Hence, Aristotle approved of *oeconomia* but disapproved of *chrematistike.*

Plato and Aristotle generally agree in their objections to the pursuit of a career in trade or a craft, although Aristotle raises these objections more strongly: (1) The practice of business or a craft deprives a person of the leisure necessary to contemplate the good, the true, and the beautiful. (2) It hinders

---

[4]*Ibid.,* p. 918B–E.
[5]Aristotle, "Politics," in *Basic Works of Aristotle,* ed. Richard McKeon (New York: Random House, 1941), p. 1141.
[6]W. L. Newman, *Politics of Aristotle,* vol. 1 (Oxford: Clarendon Press, 1887), p. 98.

proper physical, intellectual, and moral development. (3) It is "illiberal" because it is done for pay. (4) It is less perfect because its end is outside of itself.

## Work in Biblical Times

Unlike the Greeks, who had slaves, the ancient Hebrews, who at times in their history were slaves themselves, could not remain aloof from work. They saw work as an essential part of their lives but also as a hardship. Even the painful aspect of work had its self-inflicted cause in original sin. Stemming from their strong sense of God and community, the Jews pointed to the commands of God in Genesis that men and women were to cultivate the world and subdue it (Gen. 2:15).[7] This gave reason, integrity, and even verve to what for most other cultures was only something to be endured. Craftsmen like Bezalel, who built the ark of the covenant, were honored in the Jewish tradition (Exodus, 35:30–33).[8] Thus work was integrated into the lives of the Hebrews people, and had meaning for them. The God of the Hebrews is close to them. God is often pictured as one who labors: a vine dresser (Ezek. 15:6), a pottery maker (Gen. 2:7), a soldier (Is. 27:1). Today contributions to the ethics of commerce continue to come from Jewish scholars and the Jewish tradition.[9]

Christianity built on the Jewish tradition regarding work, trade, and commerce. The members of the new religion were from the working class. Jesus was a carpenter (Mark 6:3) and Paul, a tentmaker (Acts 18:2). The apostles were all working people; many were fishermen. They were not from the priestly class. Jesus in the Gospels cautions against an excessive concern about work and the things of this world (Matt. 6:24–34), but he also makes clear that work is a serious responsibility for the Christian (Luke 12:41–49). Furthermore, in the often-quoted parable of the talents (Matt. 25:14–30), the servant who has intelligently and profitably invested his money and his efforts is the one who is given additional rewards.

But the unique contribution of Christianity on the value of work is its view that work is done also out of love and concern for one's brothers and sisters. Work is necessary not only to earn one's living, asking alms of no one, but above all so that the goods of fortune may be shared with one's needy sisters and brothers.[10] The foundations of industrial civilization rest on a new concept of love preached by Jesus Christ and presented in the New Testament. It is "a peculiarly generous concept of charity, of the opportunity we have to give ourselves to others here and now, insofar as we love our neighbors for God."[11] Throughout the ages, including our own time, Christians often have fallen short of these ideals. Nevertheless, as a foundation for

---

[7]Moses L. Pava, *Business Ethics: A Jewish Perspective* (Hoboken, NJ: KTAV Publishing, 1997), p. 84.
[8]Thanks to Daniel H. Kruger for this insight; and Rabbi Jeffery Salkin, *Being God's Partner: How to Find the Hidden Link Between Spirituality and Your Work* (Woodstock, VT: Jewish Lights Publishing, 1994).
[9]Edwin Epstein, "Contemporary Jewish Perspectives on Business Ethics: The Contributions of Meir Tamari and Moses L. Pava," *Business Ethics Quarterly,* 10, no. 2 (2000): 523–541; see also three additional articles on Jewish contributions in *Business Ethics Quarterly,* 7 (March 1997).
[10]Adriano Tilgher, "Work Through the Ages," in ed. Sigmund Nosow and William Form, Man, Work and Society (New York: Basic Books, 1962), p. 13.
[11]John U. Nef, *Cultural Foundations of Industrial Civilization* (Cambridge, MA: Cambridge University Press, 1958), p. 89.

work and business values, especially in its emphasis on love of neighbor, Christianity was an important step toward regarding work in a positive light.

In the early centuries of the Christian era, the most important commentator was Augustine. He approved of handicraft, farming, and commerce on a small scale. But when selling, no more than a "just price" can be asked; charging interest on the use of money is immoral. Those who have wealth should prize it as a trust from God. After their own modest needs are met, they should give the rest to the poor.[12] Let us now examine the principles of several other great world religions—Islam, Hinduism, and Buddhism—and how they have influenced work and business values.

## Work in Islam, Hinduism, and Buddhism

Muslims take the Qur'an as the verbatim word of Allah, as revealed to the prophet Mohammad and dictated by the Archangel Gabriel in the period 610–632. The Muslim view of life is holistic. All aspects of life are regulated by the Qur'an, including family, worship, politics, and work. Although 1.3 billion Muslims live in varying cultures and hence have different views, there is consensus that the teaching of the prophet in the Qur'an defines Islam.[13]

According to the Qur'an, labor has the potential of worship, and so is sacred. Hence all forms of exploitation of labor are condemned. Moreover, the Qur'an teaches that methods of production should not cause undue and excessive harm to Allah-given resources. Any buying and selling must be done honestly (Qur'an 83:1–3). However, some products, such as wines and other intoxicants, and some activities, such as gambling, prostitution, and other indecent occupations, are forbidden.[14] The Qur'an supports private property, commercial honesty, and competition tempered by concern for the disadvantaged. It rejects the free market doctrine that "personal actions, motivated entirely by selfishness and self-interest, can produce socially desirable outcomes." If guided by Islamic Law, "people will be consistently altruistic and principled and avoid waste and extravagance,"[15] a position we recognize from Aristotle.

Unlike Medieval Western Europe, the Islamic world at that time was remarkably unified—sharing the same language and many of the same religious and secular customs:

> In the high Middle Ages the commerce of the Islamic Middle East was in every way ahead of that of Europe—richer, larger, and better organized, with more commodities to sell and more money to buy, and a vastly more

---

[12]Tilgher, "Work Through the Ages," pp. 14–15.

[13]Jamal A. Badawi, "Islamic Teaching and Business," in *Business, Religion and Spirituality*, ed. Oliver F. Williams, CSC (Notre Dame: University of Notre Dame Press, 2003), pp. 139–167; see also Tanri Abeng, "Business Ethics in Islamic Context: Perspectives of a Muslim Business Leader," *Business Ethics Quarterly*, 7 (July 1997): 47–54.

[14]*Ibid.*, p. 151.

[15]John L. Esposito, ed., *The Oxford Encyclopedia of the Modern Islamic World.* See articles "Capitalism and Islam" and "Economic Theory" (New York: Oxford University Press, 1995).

sophisticated network of trading relations. By the end of the Middle Ages, these roles were reversed.[16]

In most Muslim countries, commerce and trade are more highly valued than is agriculture. Although Muslim societies excelled in irrigation techniques, they developed few innovations in farming. Industrial innovations in Muslim societies were and remain rudimentary.

Muslim business attitudes differ from those of Western nations at several major points. First, for Muslims money must not be lent at interest (Qur'an 2:275). Second, in conservative Muslim societies, such as those in the Middle East, women are not allowed in business. Third, the belief that all laws come directly from Allah and are inviolable causes rigidity, and stifles innovation. Deviants are often branded as "apostates" or "infidels." This belief also causes divisiveness in nations where not all people are Muslim. Some Muslim nations, for example Indonesia, attempt to provide basic rights for people of all faiths. However, in many of the conservative Arab states of the Middle East strict Muslim rules (*Shariah*) are imposed on non-Muslims also.[17]

Hindu and Buddhist spirituality and religion are neither as cohesive nor coercive as is Muslim spirituality; they tend to be more open and tolerant. Hinduism focuses on the interior peace of the individual, according to the Vedic scriptures. The notion of *dharma,* one of four major goals of human life, includes the virtue and good character of the individual.[18] Good *dharma* brings peace, emancipation, and liberation to the person. For Hinduism, among the differences from Western attitudes that pertain to business are that women must be subject to men. Although the caste system is outlawed in India, the largest Hindu nation, the effects of caste are still present. Depending upon heredity, the caste system requires the placing of a person in a work role of their "lower" or "higher" caste, which can cause discrimination at work.

Buddhism gives prominence to practices, and does not include the worship of a creator God. It seeks to bring about personal serenity, largely through the practice of meditation. Among the Buddhist basic elements is "right livelihood"—to be achieved by those who transform their experience so as to be fully responsible for their lives, and thus develop wisdom and compassion. Buddhism is characterized by non-violence, tolerance of differences, the practice of meditation, and a lack of dogma. Among the hindrances to the wise life are selfishness and laziness. Buddhist values can be useful in countering the individualism, selfishness, and deception sometimes found in Western business managers.

---

[16]Bernard Lewis, *The Middle East: A Brief History of the Last 2000 Years* (New York: Scribner, 1995), p. 169.

[17]Sayyid Abul A'la Maududi, *Toward Understanding Islam* (Lahore: Idara Tarjumank-ul-Quran, 2000).

[18]Krishna S. Dhir, "The Corporate Executive's Dharma: Insights from the Indian Epic Mahabharata," in *Business, Religion and Spirituality,* pp. 122–138; see also Arvind Sharma, "A Hindu Perspective on Spirituality and Management," in *Spiritual Intelligence at Work: Meaning, Metaphor, and Morals,* ed. Moses L. Pava and Patrick Primeau (Amsterdam: Elsevier, 2004).

The above is a brief overview of some of the elements and differences in Muslim, Hindu, and Buddhist attitudes that affect work.[19] Let us now return to the early Christian era, and examine the Benedictine monasteries where new work values developed.

## Monks as Capitalists

Christian Benedictine monasteries have been credited as being "perhaps the original founders of capitalism."[20] The Benedictine Rule, as embodied in tens of thousands of monasteries throughout Europe, brought a much more positive attitude toward work. For the monks, manual work was not a curse or a degradation. They looked on work as an opportunity to build, and to grow and develop personally and as a community. They chose to work together, and they were among the first to cooperate voluntarily in all tasks. Because the monks often worked in groups and varied their occupations, they found it helpful to work by the clock. They would begin and end their work together. They standardized tasks so that almost anyone could handle most jobs.

Living and working as a cooperative community stimulated the use of various labor-saving devices. When, in 1115, Bernard of Clairvaux led a band of monks to found a new monastery, one of his prime requisites for a new site was that it have a rapidly moving stream that could be harnessed by the monks to help them do their work. Bernard himself gives us a description of his famous abbey at Clairvaux, and he provides considerable detail on the mechanical devices that are geared to waterwheels to make the work of the brothers easier.[21]

The monastery, Bernard explains, is situated at the base of a mountain and extends over a fast-moving stream to make best use of the waterpower. The river is guided by "works laboriously constructed" by the monks so that the water may be of the greatest help to their efforts. The water thus "passes and repasses the many workshops of the abbey." The water is channeled so that it "passes on at once to drive the wheels of a mill." In moving these wheels, "it grinds the meal under the weight of the mill-stones, and separates the fine from the coarse by a sieve." The river's waters are also harnessed to raise and drop hammers for the fulling of cloth and to help the shoemaker in his chores. The water is then split into smaller streams where it helps "to cook the food, sift the grain, to drive the wheels and hammers, to damp, wash, soak and so to soften, objects; everywhere it stands ready to offer its help." The monks also constructed an elaborate irrigation apparatus to water the fields. Recall that all this happened in the twelfth century, six centuries before the Industrial Revolution.

A century later the great Christian theologian of the Middle Ages, Thomas Aquinas, provided a rationale for work. He spelled out clearly and in some detail

---

[19]For additional material on Islam, Judaism, Buddhism, and Christianity, see Steward W. Herman, ed., *Spiritual Goods: Faith Traditions and the Practice of Business* (Bowling Green: Philosophy Documentation Center, 2001).

[20]Lewis Mumford, *Techniques and Civilizations* (New York: Harcourt, Brace, 1934), p. 14.

[21]Bernard of Clairvaux, *Patrologiae Latinae*, ed. Migne, vol. 185 (Paris: Garnier, 1879), pp. 570–574. A translation of much of this is in Samuel J. Eales, *Life and Works of St. Bernard,* vol. 2 (London: Burns & Oakes, n.d.), pp. 460–467. The quoted words are those of Bernard himself.

the reasons why it seemed to him that manual labor was necessary for all: to obtain food, to remove idleness, to curb concupiscence, and to provide for alms-giving.[22] Although Aquinas saw that work was not only necessary but also of great value, a remnant of the view that work was a burden, something to endure for the sake of later leisure, still remained.

Work, however, was not a burden for the monks; it was a means of love and service. When setting up a new monastery, the monks would deliberately choose a site far from existing towns. They did this both because it would be a better locale for prayer and because they deliberately set out to communicate their new view of the value of work as rooted in charity. Benedict and Bernard expected their monks to work in the fields and the shops, whether they were sons of aristocrats or of serfs. According to Lynn White, Jr., historian of technology and industry, this provision:

> Marks a revolutionary reversal of the traditional attitude toward labor; it is a high peak along the watershed separating the modern from the ancient world. The Benedictine monks regarded manual labor not as a mere regrettable necessity of their corporate life but rather as an integral and spiritually valuable part of their discipline. During the Middle Ages the general reverence for the laboring monks did much to increase the prestige of labor and the self-respect of the laborer. Moreover, since the days of St. Benedict every major form of Western asceticism has held that "to labor is to pray," until in its final development under the Puritans, work in one's "calling" became not only the prime moral necessity but also the chief means of serving and praising God.[23]

The monks lived together thriftily, and that enabled them to invest in productive machinery, like that described by Bernard, to aid them in their work. This is why some call monks the first capitalists. Their cooperation and inventiveness resulted in division of labor, interchangeable work, a clock-regulated workday, and ingenious labor-saving equipment—all of which contributed to greater productivity. They used the additional time that was then available for their prayer and community life together. A few hundred years later, this same love-centered ethic was brought to the cities and marketplaces of seventeenth-century France by an eminent group of artists, poets, theologians, and saints. John Nef maintains that it was this unique emphasis on the centrality of love for one's sisters and brothers, especially as embodied in women, along with its requirement of cooperation and hard work, that made industrial society possible.[24]

By 1700, Christianity, and its central love ethic, had helped to provide many of the elements necessary for the development of business and commerce as we know it today. Work was looked upon as something of value; it provided

---

[22]Thomas Aquinas, *Summa Theologica,* II-II, qu. 87, art. 3.

[23]Lynn White, Jr., "Dynamo and Virgin Reconsidered," *American Scholar,* 27 (Spring 1958): 188. Quoted by permission.

[24]See Nef, *Cultural Foundations;* see also his briefer *Civilization, Industrial Society and Love* (Santa Barbara, Fund for the Republic, 1961).

self-discipline and an integrating force in a person's life. Christianity helped the individual to focus on the value of the product of work; if the same thing could be produced more easily, this was good—especially when it enabled one to help one's family and neighbors. The importance of producing a greater quantity of goods and a new consciousness of time developed first in the monasteries and then spread to the larger society. Furthermore, the Catholic Church urged all to attend mass side by side: rich and poor, worker and artisan, peasant, scholar, and duke. This fostered communication and cooperation.

In its otherworldly theology, however, Catholicism thwarted the coming of capitalism. Material goods, wealth, and success were not the measures of holiness. According to Jesus, the purpose of life on earth was not merely to build up material goods. This attitude led to suspicion of those who would lend money to others and charge them for the use of it. Even as late as the sixteenth century, theologians condemned the opening of state banks. In the Christian and Muslim traditions, the sin of usury was described as lending money at interest. In Christian society, work and industry were much more respected than they had been in aristocratic Greece or Rome. The average citizen had many reasons to do tasks well, and there were no slaves to do them instead. In addition, a person's trade or craft gave meaning and integrity to life. But it was the Protestant Reformation that provided the impetus for the development of attitudes that would propel Western society toward rapid economic growth.

## From Luther and Calvin to the Protestant Ethic

It was Protestantism that eventually established hard work and the making of profits as central to a Christian life. Ironically, Martin Luther (1483–1546), who began this new movement, disapproved of the commerce and economic individualism of his day. Luther was appalled at the regal high living of merchants, princes, and popes. The contrast between the ideals of Christianity and what Luther actually found around him motivated him to push for reform. He called for a return to a simple, hardworking peasant life; this would bring sufficient prosperity for all. A person should earn a living and not make an excessive profit.

Luther thought a number of Christian customs encouraged idleness: the many religious holidays, the mendicant friars glorifying begging, and the monasteries' support of some who did not work. Idleness is unnatural, according to Luther, and charity should be given only to those who cannot work. His original contribution was in emphasizing the importance of one's profession. The best way to serve God was to do the work of one's profession as well as one could. Thus Luther healed what had been a breach between worship and work. As long as work was done in obedience to God and in service to one's sisters and brothers, every type of work had equal value in God's eyes.

Luther held that a person's salvation is achieved solely through faith in God; good works do not affect salvation. Moreover, all legitimate human activities are acts of worship, no one more than another. Since formal prayer and worship, and especially the monastic life of prayer, are no more valuable than tilling the fields, Protestantism released all human energies for the world of work. The farmer, the smith, and the baker all do work that is as honorable as that of the monk or priest. Although the life of the simple worker is better, Luther concedes that:

> Trade is permissible, provided that it is confined to the exchange of necessaries, and that the seller demands no more than will compensate him for his labor and risk. The unforgivable sins are idleness and covetousness, for they destroy the unity of the body of which Christians are members.[25]

Luther was vehement in preaching against lending at interest, yet paradoxically his denial of religious authority eventually set economic life free from strictures on usury. This denial left business and commerce to develop their own life and laws independent of existing moral authorities. Capitalism thus set up its own norms of right and wrong, and capitalist activity was carried on beyond the influence of the church.

Luther's insistence on giving everyday life the same value as worship and on breaking the system of canon law and religious authority eventually resulted in profound changes in economic and social life. The elaborate prescribed relationships with neighbor, family, and church were swept away. This seems to be a loss to society as a whole, for, although these laws were encumbering and limiting, they also provided roots, personal relationships, and meaning for life. Secular interests, work, and business now formed a separate world removed from the religious and moral values that had until this time governed all aspects of life.

The most important influence on what we now call the Protestant ethic was the theology of John Calvin (1509–1564), who followed Luther as a reformer of Christianity. Calvin and his followers did not idealize the peasant, as did Luther, but accepted urban life as they found it. "Like early Christianity and modern socialism, Calvinism was largely an urban movement."[26] Calvin's central theological notion, which distinguishes his position from that of Luther and of Catholicism, is predestination. According to Calvin, God is infinite, absolute, supreme, and totally above and beyond human beings. It is impossible for us to fully understand God and God's ways. Moreover, God because of infinite wisdom knows all people who were and *will be saved* in the world. In God's power and wisdom, he has determined that it is fitting for his glory if only a small number of men and women are saved. Moreover, Calvin maintains that there is absolutely nothing a person can do to influence his or her own salvation; from all eternity God has freely predetermined it. A person lives to glorify God, and the major way a person glorifies God is in his or her life. If a person bends every talent and expends every energy in work, and achieves success, this may be an indication that he or she is one of the saved. Although these individual efforts cannot directly effect salvation, if successful they do glorify God, and may thus be a sign that the person is numbered among the elect. Perhaps even more motivating is the conviction that if a person is idle, dislikes work, or is not successful, these are most likely signs that person is not among the saved.

Calvin taught that all must work and must never cease working. Profits earned must not be hoarded but must be invested in new works. Investment and

---

[25]R. H. Tawney, *Religion and the Rise of Capitalism* (New York: Mentor, 1947), p. 83.
[26]*Ibid.*, p. 92.

the resulting profit and wealth were thus encouraged: "With the new creed comes a new man, strong-willed, active, austere, hard-working from religious conviction. Idleness, luxury, prodigality, everything which softens the soul, is shunned as a deadly sin."[27] Calvin proposed a unique paradox: Deny the world; live as an ascetic in the world, because it cannot guarantee your salvation. Yet remember that your one duty is to glorify God, and the best way of doing that is by being a success at your chosen work, your calling. It is a precarious balance, difficult to achieve and even more difficult to maintain.

The Protestant ethic, therefore, stems directly from Calvin's teachings. He stressed the importance of hard work and the necessity to reinvest one's earnings in new works. Moreover, Calvin did not condemn interest and urban trade, as did Luther and Catholic leaders. Calvin not only urged working hard at one's occupation but also held that successful trade and commerce was but another way of glorifying God.

## Weber's Analysis of the Protestant Ethic

Before leaving the influence of the Reformation on business ideology, let us look at the analysis of that influence more than three hundred years later in 1905 by the sociologist Max Weber in *The Protestant Ethic and the Spirit of Capitalism.* It is ironic that Weber, a German, cites no other person more often as an example of the Protestant ethic than Benjamin Franklin, an American. We will examine Franklin's contributions later in this chapter.

Weber began his analysis by noting that "business leaders and owners of Capital, as well as the higher grades of skilled labor, and even more the higher technically and commercially trained personnel of modern enterprises, are overwhelmingly Protestant." He went on to compare the Catholic and the Protestant: "The Catholic is quieter, having less of the acquisitive impulse; he prefers a life of the greatest possible security, even with a smaller income, to a life of risk and excitement, even though it may bring the chance of gaining honor and riches."[28] In trying to determine the reason why Protestants seemed to be more successful in business, Weber examined the roots of the theology of Luther and Calvin, as we have done above. He noted that Reformation theology encouraged individuals to look on their work more seriously. Life demanded sobriety, self-discipline, diligence, and, above all, planning ahead and saving. A person's attention to the life of this world was serious in the extreme. In addition to having its own rewards, success was a reflection of God's glory and hence a hint as to whether a person was saved or not. It was therefore incumbent on all to be successful. Moreover, the individual had the means to achieve that success. "In practice this means that God helps those who help themselves. Thus the Calvinist himself creates his own salvation, or, as would be more correct, the conviction of it."[29]

---

[27]Tilgher, "Work Through the Ages," p. 19.
[28]Max Weber, *The Protestant Ethic and the Spirit of Capitalism,* trans. Talcott Parsons (New York: Scribner, 1958), pp. 35–41. Quoted with permission.
[29]*Ibid.,* p. 145.

An asceticism to achieve the goal flowed from the Calvinistic ethic: "Waste of time is thus the first and in principle the deadliest of sins." On the same theme, the Calvinist asceticism "turned with all its force against one thing: the spontaneous enjoyment of life and all it had to offer." On the positive side, in the Calvinist and Puritan churches Weber found "the continually repeated, often almost passionate preaching of hard, continuous bodily or mental labor." But Weber observed that "the people filled with the spirit of capitalism today tend to be indifferent, if not hostile, to the Church." In that climate, the pursuit of business and a career often take on the vehemence and all-embracing aspects of active religion: "Business with its necessary work becomes a necessary part of their lives." But this is what is "so irrational about this sort of life, where a man exists for the sake of his business, instead of the reverse." The Protestant ethic changed history. Contrary to the ethical convictions of centuries, "money-making became an end in itself to which people were bound, as a calling."[30]

In his last chapter Weber quoted founding Protestants John Wesley and John Calvin when they point out a paradox. It is religion that makes people careful, hardworking, frugal; and this, in turn, enables them to build up wealth. "But as riches increase, so will pride, anger, and love of the world," in Wesley's words. Speaking of those on the lower end of that same economic ladder, Weber quoted Calvin: "Only when the people, i.e., the mass of laborers and craftsmen, were poor did they remain obedient to God."[31] Therein lies a paradox; the men who themselves are most responsible for the Protestant ethic foresee its collapse. Their religion demands hard work and saving, and this provides wealth. But wealth brings pride, luxury, and lack of will. It is therefore an unstable ethic, in part because its religious foundations tend to dissolve. Protestant ethic has become a term descriptive of this careful, hardworking, frugal lifestyle, which is often called the *Puritan Ethic*. As we will see when we examine Benjamin Franklin, this ethic took on a secular life of its own.

The Protestant ethic (see Figure 4-1) derives from the Calvinist vision of how people should act in order to be successful in this life and also in the next. Following its tenets, many have achieved success and developed the values that will be described in the next chapter in the section "Values in Modern Life."

The Protestant ethic urges planning ahead, sobriety, diligence, and self-control on the part of the individual. It promises a material reward and, in its religious strand, a good chance of salvation. Moreover, the Protestant ethic serves an additional and psychologically perhaps more important purpose. It assures the

---

[30]*Ibid.*, pp. 70–73, 157–166.
[31]*Ibid.*, pp. 175–177. Some reject the attempt to show a relationship between economic success and religious faith. They maintain that there are more plausible explanations for commercial success, such as "special education, family relationships and alien status." See Kurt Samuelson, *Religion and Economic Action*, trans. E. G. French (New York: Basic Books, 1961), p. 154. Nevertheless, the fact that Weber's theses are so widely accepted makes it a theory to be taken seriously. Whatever the causal relationships, religious values and economic development are there to be observed, and they have had a marked influence on one another.

> **THE PROTESTANT ETHIC URGES:**
>
> - Hard work.
> - Self-control and sobriety (that is, humorlessness).
> - Self-reliance.
> - Perseverance.
> - Saving and planning ahead.
> - Honesty and "observing the rules of the game."

**FIGURE 4-1** The Protestant Ethic.

successful and wealthy that their wealth is deserved. They have property because they have worked for it and so have a right to it. As Weber observed, the wealthy man is not satisfied in knowing that he is fortunate:

> Beyond this, he needs to know that he has a right to his good fortune. He wants to be convinced that he "deserves" it, and above all, that he deserves it in comparison with others. He wishes to be allowed the belief that the less fortunate also merely experience their due.[32]

Thus the Protestant ethic not only provided a set of directions on how to succeed and a motivation for doing so but also attempted to legitimatize the wealth that was acquired. The successful person can say, "Anyone who was willing to work as hard as I did could have done as well, so it is clear that I deserve the wealth I have." This attitude laid the foundation for social Darwinism and the doctrine of the survival of the fittest, which we will examine later in this chapter.

### John Locke and the Right to Private Property

John Locke (1632–1704) had a considerable influence on the American Founding Fathers and through them on the American Constitution. He and Jean-Jacques Rousseau also influenced the French Revolution and most of the subsequent efforts to move toward more democratic governments. The Oxford-educated Locke was both a philosopher and a politician. He was a practical man, having served various government figures of his day, so he wrote about political and social questions.

Locke focused on natural rights, but the right to which he devoted most of his energy was the right to private property.[33] Locke held that an individual has a right to self-preservation and so has a right to those things that are required for this purpose. Individuals require property so that they may feed and clothe their families and themselves. A person's labor is what confers primary title to property. If individuals settle on land and work it, they therefore deserve title to it.

---

[32]Max Weber, "The Social Psychology of World Religions," in *Max Weber: Essays in Sociology,* ed. H. H. Gerth and C. Wright Mills (New York: Oxford University Press, 1946), p. 271.
[33]John Locke, *An Essay Concerning the True Original Extent and End of Civil Government,* especially Chapter 5, "Of Property," and Chapter 9, "Of the Ends of Political Society and Government." See also the summary in Frederick Copleston, *A History of Philosophy,* vol. 5 (London: Burns and Oates, 1964), pp. 129–131.

Locke's ideal was America, which offered unlimited property to anyone who was willing to clear and work it.

Locke has been criticized for overemphasizing the rights of private property and thus catering to the interests of his landowning patrons, and this criticism may be justified. However, he did not allow for a person's amassing wealth without limit. Whatever is beyond what the individual can use is not by right his or hers.[34] It belongs to others and should be allotted to them.

### Rousseau's Social Contract

Jean-Jacques Rousseau (1712–1778) distrusted contemporary society and its institutions, as did other members of the French Enlightenment. He believed that society, and even Enlightenment ideals such as reason, culture, and progress, had created unhealthy competition, self-interest, pseudo sophistication, and a destruction of the "simple society" he valued. He believed society was unjust, effete, and dominated by the rich and by civil and church authorities. According to Rousseau, "Man was born free and everywhere he is in chains." Men's and women's original state in nature is free, and although some form of society is necessary, freedom, reverence, family life, and the ordinary person must be central to it.

The *Social Contract* was an attempt to achieve the necessary activities, associations, and governments required in a civilized society without losing basic individual rights. A citizen's duty of obedience could not be founded simply on the possession of power by those in authority. To be legitimate, it must rest on some sort of freely-given consensus.[35] Among the institutions of society that Rousseau distrusted was private property. According to him, when private property was introduced into a society, equality disappeared. Private property marks a departure from primitive simplicity and leads to numerous injustices and evils such as selfishness, domination, and servitude. In the state he proposes, Rousseau supports a sharply increased tax on any property that is not necessary for people to modestly support themselves and their family. For property that is necessary for support, there should be no tax at all. Rousseau and Locke agreed on the illegitimacy of excessive wealth.

### Adam Smith and Free Enterprise

The Scot Adam Smith (1723–1790) is the grandfather of capitalism and of free enterprise economics. As a political economist and moral philosopher, he was among the first to emphasize free exchange and to present economics as an independent branch of knowledge. His best known and classic work, The *Wealth of Nations,* supported independence for economics and business in 1776, the same year that the American colonies declared their political independence from England. In an earlier book that is often ignored, Smith provided

---

[34]Matthew Kramer, *John Locke and the Origins of Private Property: Philosophical Explorations of Individualism, Community, and Equality* (Cambridge, MA: Cambridge University Press, 1997).
[35]Jean-Jacques Rousseau, *The Social Contract and Discourse on the Origin and Foundation of Inequality Among Mankind* (New York: Washington Square Press, 1967); see also the summary of Rousseau in Copleston, *History of Philosophy,* vol. 6, especially pp. 68–69 and 80–100.

a humane foundation for the economic system with his emphasis on virtue, sympathy, and justice.[36]

In explaining economics Smith said, "Nobody ever saw a dog make a fair and deliberate exchange of one bone for another with another dog." Later he spelled out the implications of this inability to exchange by showing that each animal was obliged "to support and defend itself, separately and independently, and derives no sort of advantage from that variety of talents with which nature has distinguished its fellows." Human beings, said Smith, are quite different in that they can take advantage of one another's unique genius. What one is good at he does in abundance, sells to others, and thus "may purchase whatever part of the produce of other men's talents he has occasion for." Smith's first and most familiar example is of the division of labor in making pins. One man, working alone and forming the entire pin, might "make one pin in a day, and certainly not make twenty." But when the operation is divided up into a number of separate operations so that "one man draws out the wire, another straights it, a third cuts it, a fourth points it, a fifth grinds it at the top for receiving the head," and so on, a group of pin makers are able to make pins at a daily average of 4,800 pins per pin maker.[37]

In addition to the value of exchange and the division of labor, Smith also examined the value of the free market, competition, and profit maximization. Smith was among the first to make a clear and plausible case that when morally conscientious individuals follow their own self-interest, it works to the benefit of society as a whole. As individual competitors pursue their own maximum profit, they are all thus forced to be more efficient. This results in cheaper goods in the long run. Free competition in all markets and for all goods and services is thus to be encouraged; government intervention serves only to make operations less efficient and is thus to be avoided. The same principles apply to international trade. There should be a minimum of government interference in the form of duties, quotas, and tariffs. Smith's is the classical argument in support of free trade.

Smith took some of his insights from the English philosopher Thomas Hobbes (1588–1679). Hobbes maintained that individuals act simply to gain that which gives them pleasure or to avoid that which causes displeasure. Because this may differ for each individual, there is no objective good or value in reality itself. Hobbes's view of human motivation is that of "egoistic hedonism." Since Hobbes's view was that human nature is largely self-seeking and that there is no objective morality, it is not surprising that he held that might makes right. It is important to have power to protect one's person and goods. Whatever a person has the power to take, belongs to that person. Hobbes acknowledged that this leads to insecurity and even war but maintained that insecurity and war are an inescapable part of the human condition. On the theme of trade and economic activity, Smith quoted

---

[36]Adam Smith, *The Wealth of Nations*, ed. J. C. Bullock (New York: Collier, 1909), pp. 19–23. On comparing the two works and on Smith's influence, see Patricia Werhane, *Adam Smith and His Legacy for Modern Capitalism* (New York: Oxford University Press, 1991).
[37]*Ibid.*, pp. 9–10.

Hobbes' claim that "wealth is power." Wealth enables its possessor to purchase what he or she wants, and this in itself gives that person considerable control over others. So it is in the interest of individuals to increase their wealth.

To explain profit maximization, Smith used the example of rent. Even though the owner of the land contributes nothing to production beyond the fact of ownership, nevertheless the owner will strive for a contract stipulating the highest rent the tenant can possibly afford to pay. Contrary to the earlier principle of a "just price," the landlord will try to leave the tenant as little as possible of what he or she earns. Smith contends that this is as it should be. On some occasions the landlord may leave the tenant a bit more for him- or herself, but this is and should be exceptional; it is due to "the liberality, more frequently the ignorance, of the landlord."[38]

As the grandfather of modern economics, Smith spelled out clearly and graphically most of the current major principles operating in economic and business theory. He illustrated the advantages of the division of labor, the free competitive market, and profit maximization, and how they contribute to more efficient production. As individuals pursue self-interested goals, Smith's famous "invisible hand" guides economic and business activities so that they are more productive and cheaper and thus benefit society as a whole.

Industry and commerce in the two centuries following Adam Smith have been extraordinarily successful. Moreover, business activities closely followed the model Smith described. The free market encouraged rapid economic growth. Economic motivation for most people up to Smith's time had been based more on obligations to a lord, proprietor, or one's family and on threats, fears, and sanctions. The free market and potentially unlimited monetary rewards shifted the entire basis of economic activity.

The free market and the possibility of unlimited profits are at the heart of the system's greatest strength: It taps positive motivation and rewards. It draws a person into greater activity and creativity and rewards those efforts. Furthermore, the rewards are tangible and measurable; there is little doubt as to who is a success. On the other hand, this new model for economic activity also includes its greatest weakness. It can insulate a person from obligations to friends, family, fellow citizens, and the larger community, and replace these obligations with an easily broken contract whose purpose is to obtain individual profit. Hence, individuals can much more readily come to feel that they are alone, isolated, and easily replaceable. Literature on the attitudes of managers and blue-collar workers alike show that most have experienced this feeling of isolation and alienation.[39] Adam Smith recognized that free markets can encourage selfishness and isolation. As a moral philosopher himself, he emphasized that a free market required a moral and ethical foundation for it to be efficient. He pointed out that the free market system could only work effectively when its participants understood and practiced moral principles.

---

[38]*Ibid.*, pp. 153–171; see also William Keep, "Adam Smith's Imperfect Invisible Hand: Motivations to Mislead," *Business Ethics: A European Review,* 12 (October 2003): 343–353.

[39]See evidence of this dissatisfaction, for example, in Theodore V. Purcell and Gerald F. Cavanagh, *Blacks in the Industrial World* (New York: Free Press, 1972), pp. 72–75, 236–238.

Using an analogy, Adam Smith and the Industrial Revolution that followed shifted people's view such that they tended to compare society to a machine instead of to an organism, as they had formerly. In earlier times, men and women knew they were part of something larger than themselves. Families worked together, and they cared for their neighbors. They were dependent upon one another—like parts of an organism. They had a stake in their community and they belonged. This was replaced by a market in which one's own work was sold. One no longer belonged, and one's very self became just another commodity in the market. Every individual can and will be replaced when he or she becomes obsolete, old, and inefficient, just as is true for the parts of a machine.[40]

Adam Smith provided an accurate and integrated picture of developing business activities. He detailed the advantages of free exchange. As such, he is the father of free market economics. Smith is still widely quoted and remains to this day a principal spokesperson for capitalism and free enterprise. European thinkers and leaders formed many of the foundation values for the "New World"—America. Let us now turn our attention to the activities of that new people across the Atlantic Ocean.

## ENTERPRISE VALUES IN THE NEW WORLD

The Europeans who crossed the ocean to the "New World" came as immigrants to a land they thought of as open and free. Yet Native Americans had been on the continent for scores of centuries before the Europeans arrived. Because they were few, they were ignored unless they provided aid or got in the way of the newly arrived. Often the settlers made peace with the natives. As more immigrants arrived, conflict arose between the farmers, the exploiters of minerals, and the hunter-gatherers who revered the mountains. The newcomers treated the native people in a practical, entrepreneurial, self-centered fashion.

Like immigrants today, these earlier settlers came to the New World risking their lives and their fortunes in the hope of finding freedom and new opportunities. They came to a land that seemed to them to have limitless natural resources—timber, coal, and much good farming land. Clearing the land was backbreaking, but the result was good, fertile acreage that could be handed on to one's children. The changing climate encouraged work—it was brisk and invigorating—and the winters, when there would be no fruits or crops, demanded that settlers plan ahead and save something from the harvest. Two wide oceans provided natural defenses that allowed the New World to focus on its own needs and development without much fear of foreign intrusions.

These natural characteristics affected the values and ideology of the people. But when the settlers came, they also brought their own values and ideals which heavily influenced their attitudes. Many of the early American immigrants came to the colonies for religious reasons—some because of religious persecution in their

---

[40]For this and other insights, the author thanks Otto Bremmer. Concerning Smith anticipating and providing suggestions on the major moral failures of capitalism, see James Q. Wilson, "Adam Smith on Business Ethics," *California Management Review,* Fall 1989, pp. 59–72.

native countries. They sought a land where they could live and pray as conscience dictated. The men and women who settled the new continent came from Europe and so also brought the religion that predominated there—Christianity. The Catholic Spanish came first to Mexico and Peru, and founded cities, colleges, and businesses. But the English Puritans, who came a century later to the northern New World, had a more lasting influence on business values and ideology.

The Puritans fled Europe so that they might freely follow their anti-hierarchical religious faith and practices. To these men and women, who came before the American Revolution, their work or their "calling" was an essential part of their total world view. To us today, the Puritan ideal is a delicate, even mysterious, paradox. Puritan preacher John Cotton (1584–1652) described it thus:

> There is another combination of virtues strangely mixed in every lively, holy Christian: and that is, diligence in worldly business, and yet deadness to the world. Such a mystery as none can read but they that know it.[41]

Puritans plunged into their work with a dedication that could come only because it was their calling. Worship of God was not shown in hymn singing, colorful religious services, or sterile monasticism; worship was a simple, reverent prayer. Moreover, the Puritans' prayer was not separated from work, for work was their most effective means of giving glory to God. So work was disciplined and clear-eyed, because "when he serves man, he serves the Lord; he doth the work set before him and he doth it sincerely and faithfully so as he may give account for it."[42] This early Puritan ideology strengthened the emerging social order by giving importance to every type of work. Again, in John Cotton's words, "[Faith] encourageth a man in his calling to the most homeliest and difficultest and most dangerous things his calling can lead and expose himself to."[43] Self-discipline was also important. They were ascetics in the world; although in it, they were detached from it.

Two generations later, Cotton Mather (1663–1728) was born into the same lineage of learning and clerical leadership. Like his grandfather, Mather held that:

> A Christian has two callings: (1) a general calling to serve the Lord Jesus Christ, and (2) a particular calling which was his work or his business. Both of these callings are essential if the Christian is to achieve salvation. Contemplation of the good means nothing without accomplishment of the good. A man must not only be pious; he must be useful.[44]

The Puritan businessman fully integrated his work and his worship. Often he would mention God in his invoices, thanking God for a profit or accepting losses

---

[41]Perry Miller, *The American Puritans* (Garden City, NY: Doubleday, 1956), p. 171.
[42]*Ibid.,* p. 173.
[43]John Cotton, quoted in Miller, *The American Puritans,* pp. 176–177.
[44]A. Whitney Griswold, "Two Puritans on Prosperity," in *Benjamin Franklin and the American Character,* ed. Charles L. Sanford (Boston: D. C. Heath, 1955), p. 41.

for God's greater glory. Moreover, each individual determined his or her calling, and work was generally done individually. In the same fashion, people achieved salvation individually.

American Puritans did not invent this position; they took the theology of John Calvin and spelled out in detail the implications for the businessperson. The businessperson, in turn, eager for some justification of the efforts to which he devoted most of his waking hours, happily received the Puritan preacher's words. So there began a mutual understanding and support between preacher and businessperson that became a hallmark of New World society.

## Benjamin Franklin's Way to Wealth

In the period before the American Revolution, Benjamin Franklin (1706–1790) accepted the work values of the Puritans, shifted them from a religious to a secular foundation, and restated them for Americans. Franklin, especially in *Poor Richard's Almanac,* was incisive, mundane, prolific, and influential. Many of his homely bits of advice have become common sayings in our speech today. Franklin brought together 25 years of his *Almanac* writings on work and business and published them in 1758 as the essay "The Way to Wealth."

> God helps them that help themselves. Diligence is the mother of good luck, as Poor Richard says, and God gives all things to industry. Then plough deep, while sluggards sleep, and you shall have corn to sell and to keep, says Poor Dick. Work while it is called today, for you know not how much you may be hindered tomorrow. Be ashamed to catch yourself idle. When there is so much to be done for yourself, your family, your country, and your gracious king, be up at peep of day; 'Tis true that much is to be done, and perhaps you are weak handed, but stick to it steadily, and you will see great effects, for constant dropping wears away stones and little strokes fell great Oaks.[45]

In his own graphic way, Franklin focuses on the importance of saving and the need for capital when he notes that "a man may, if he knows not how to save as he gets, keep his nose all his life to the grindstone. If you would be wealthy, think of saving as well as of getting."[46] It was satisfying to Franklin's early American contemporaries to see him supporting the same values and justification for their work as did their Puritan ministers. He provided a rationale for work and a purpose for life; at the same time, he buttressed the existing social order.

Franklin's writings were best sellers in his day and have exerted a significant influence up to the present. In his *Almanac,* his *Autobiography,* and his own life, Franklin embodied the Puritan virtues. He was successful as an inventor, printer,

---

[45]Benjamin Franklin, *The Autobiography and Other Writings* (New York: New American Library, 1961), p. 190.
[46]*Ibid.,* p. 192.

statesman, diplomat, and businessman. Although some aristocrats of his day, such as John Adams, resented Franklin's popular wisdom, he was held in esteem by the people. Harvard-educated John Adams, second president of the United States, was a New England patrician: brilliant and courageous but also haughty and stubborn. Adams conceded that Franklin was a genius, a wit, a politician, and a humorist, but he questioned his greatness as a philosopher, a moralist, or a statesman.[47] In spite of Adams's petty quarrels with Franklin, history shows Franklin to have had a greater influence on values. Even today his vision is cited in calling for exercising restraint in the pursuit of work and money because of moral commitments ingrained by character. If such restraint is not exercised, chasing the American dream will bring more discontent than happiness.[48]

Thomas Jefferson agreed with the hard-working, individualistic ideals of Franklin, although Jefferson, who wrote the *Declaration of Independence,* was convinced that these virtues could best be fostered in, and the new nation grow best as, an agricultural society.[49] Jefferson felt that as long as one had one's own land to till and crops to care for, the economy would thrive and people would be happier. At this time more than 80 percent of American workers were farmers, and if Jefferson had his way, that is how it would have remained. Jefferson was opposed to the industrialization he had seen in England. He would rather import finished manufactured goods than undergo the undesirable changes manufacturing inevitably brings: urbanization, landless workers, banking. In an agricultural society, where work and initiative immediately pay off for the individual and for the society as a whole, government intervention could be kept to an absolute minimum. Government would only retard the natural forces of growth through regulations and bureaucracy. In Jefferson's own oft-quoted words, "That government is best which governs least." His ambivalent feelings toward and even fear of business appear early, for business spawns cities. An agrarian society is simpler; duties and rewards are more easily seen and measured. So early Americans were not always favorably disposed toward business or cities, or the increasing government both require.

## Slavery and Productivity

Slavery was early practiced in the United States; four of the first five presidents were slave holders.[50] Slaves constituted one-fifth of the new nation's population in 1776, and slavery continued in the southern states until the U.S. Civil War. Slavery gave the slave holder an economic advantage over his competitors. The work of slaves cost their master only food and shelter for the slave, and thus slavery

---

[47]For this essay, see John Adams, "An Exaggerated Reputation," in Sanford, *Benjamin Franklin,* pp. 22–26; see also David McCullough, John Adams (New York: Simon & Schuster, 2001).
[48]Robert Wuthnow, *Poor Richard's Principle: Recovering the American Dream Through the Moral Dimension of Work, Business and Money* (Princeton: Princeton University Press, 1996).
[49]Arthur M. Schlesinger, "Ideas and Economic Development," in *Paths of American Thought,* ed. Arthur M. Schlesinger, Jr., and Morton White (Boston: Houghton Mifflin, 1963), pp. 108–109.
[50]See Henry Wienek, *An Imperfect God: George Washington, His Slaves, and the Creation of America* (New York: Farrar, Straus & Giroux, 2003); Gary Wills, *Negro President: Jefferson and the Slave Power* (Boston: Houghton Mifflin, 2003).

increased productivity in the southern slave states by an estimated 9 percent over the free states.[51]

Forced labor continues to exist in various forms in many countries—especially in Asia, Africa, and Latin America. Because slavery is part of the illicit economy, there are no exact figures on its extent. Researchers estimate that today 27 million people worldwide live in slavery. Traditional forms of slavery, such as chattel slavery and bonded labor, are still widespread.[52] Trafficking in human beings is today's fastest growing form of forced labor, and it affects 4 million people. Slavery or bonded labor is known to exist in many nations, such as Sudan, Brazil, Liberia, India, Pakistan, and Bangladesh. For centuries slaves have been the reward of victory in war, because slaves bring lower labor costs for the winners. In Sudan, a civil war raged for decades between the northern Arabic Muslim rulers and the poor southern black Christians and animists. In this civil war, tens of thousands of men have been killed, and perhaps 90,000 women and children have been abducted and put into slavery. As another example, there are now probably some 90,000 young rural women in India who were forced into prostitution in the city of Mumbai (formerly Bombay).[53]

Virtually all people in all cultures agree that slavery is both unethical and illegal. Slavery denies the human dignity and the most basic personal rights of the person enslaved. In addition, it is unjust, since the slave master obtains the economic benefit of the slave's work, and the slaves receive little or no wage for their work. Nevertheless, slavery supported and helped develop the economy of the United States, especially southern agriculture. Moreover, even today millions of poor and defenseless people are enslaved in many nations. Let us bring this issue closer to each of us. We in wealthy nations benefit from low price apparel, shoes, sports gear, jewelry, and toys. Their costs are kept low because of people working at slave-like wages and working conditions in mines and manufacturing facilities.

## The American Frontier

The continuing westward expansion on the "new" continent kept alive the simpler, measurable agrarian values. This westward movement and the frontier affected the American character. Successive waves of hunters, traders, ranchers, and, finally, farmers always found new lands to conquer. It seemed to be a world without limits. Most of the Native Americans were nomadic, and there were fewer of them to offer resistance. For the brave and hearty immigrant, it was worth taking great risks, whether in moving or in building. Success brought wealth; failure allowed one to try again somewhere else.

The new territories demanded strenuous labor to clear the land. The first farmers faced the difficult task of pulling out trees and building their homes and

---

[51]Robert Fogel, "Three Phases of Cliometric Research on Slavery and Its Aftermath," *American Economic Review,* 65, no. 2 (May 1975): pp. 37–46; see also Fogel and Stanley Engerman, *Time on the Cross: The Economics of American Negro Slavery* (New York: W. W. Norton, 1989).
[52]Matthias Busse and Sebastian Braun, "Trade and Investment Effects of Forced Labor: An Empirical Assessment," *International Labour Review,* 142, no. 1 (2003): pp. 49–71.
[53]Richard Re, "A Persisting Evil: The Global Problem of Slavery," *Harvard International Review,* 23, no. 4 (Winter 2002): 32–35.

barns. Nevertheless, the rewards were great: They would have homes and farms, and could pass them on to their children. The rewards were clear, tangible, and permanent, and they gave settlers incentive and zest. The land was open to human effort; if one worked harder, one would be able to produce more.

Frederick Jackson Turner summed up how the frontier has given the American intellect its striking characteristics:

> That coarseness and strength combined with acuteness and inquisitiveness; that practical, inventive turn of mind, quick to find expedients; that master- ful grasp of material things, lacking in the artistic but powerful to affect great ends; that restless, nervous energy; that dominant individualism, working for good and for evil, and withal that buoyancy and exuberance which comes with freedom—these are traits of the frontier or traits called out elsewhere because of the existence of the frontier.[54]

Turner's thesis has been widely quoted and has had a great influence on thinkers and leaders. Do current challenges to all people demand the same kind of imagination, creativity, energy, risk taking, and sense of purpose?

## Tocqueville's View of Americans

As anyone who has lived in another culture knows, the characteristics of that culture stand out in bold relief to the foreigner. In that same process, of course, the "foreigner" is better able to recognize the unique qualities of his or her own culture. A people's characteristic values and ideology can best be understood by comparing them to those of another culture. Thus a perceptive foreign visitor often is able to describe the values and characteristics of the host people with penetrating insight. Alexis de Tocqueville was such a person. He is one of the most incisive commentators on the American character.

A young French lawyer, Alexis de Tocqueville came to the United States in 1831 to observe and learn from the people. His reflections, in his book *Democracy in America,* attained instant success not only in France but also in England and the United States. Published in an English translation in 1838, the book was immediately praised for its insight and lack of bias, and 170 years later it is still regarded as one of the finest commentaries on American life. Tocqueville tried to understand Americans on their own terms.

On arriving, Tocqueville noted the physical expanse of the new country: "The inhabitants of the U.S. constitute a great civilized people, which fortune has placed in the midst of an uncivilized country."[55] It was this same combination, of course, which was to help give rise to the independence, resourcefulness, and frontier spirit of which Frederick Jackson Turner was later to write. Tocqueville noticed that, preoccupied by the great task to be accomplished, Americans tended to value facts more than consistent ideals; to value that which worked more than the

---

[54]Frederick Jackson Turner, *The Frontier in American History* (New York: Holt, 1920), p. 37.
[55]Alexis de Tocqueville, *Democracy in America,* trans. Henry Reeve, vol. 1 (New York: Knopf, 1946), p. 422.

beauty of a comprehensive ideological system. He characterized the American "philosophical method," the American method of reflection and learning, as "to evade the bondage of system and habit, of family maxims, class opinions, and, in some degree, of national prejudices." Americans accepted tradition only as a starting point; the existing situation only "as a lesson to be used in doing otherwise and in doing better." Each person sought to understand for him- or herself. All these characteristics Tocqueville summed up as an individualism of thought: "Each American appeals only to the individual effort of his own understanding." This mentality shows that a generation gap is not new: "Every man there readily loses all traces of the ideas of his forefathers or takes no care about them."[56]

Tocqueville saw Americans as hardworking and individualistic. The only rationale they might have for their actions and attitudes, he said, is enlightened self-interest. According to Tocqueville, Americans are not inclined to reverence tradition, to philosophize, or even to engage in much reflection. He focused on the same favorable attitude toward work that has been attributed to the Puritan, the immigrant, and the frontier settler. Americans see work, he noted, "as the necessary, natural, and honest condition of human existence." Labor is not only not dishonorable, it is held in honor among the people. Even the rich person feels the obligation to take up some sort of worthwhile work, whether this work be private or public.

When Americans were asked why they work, act, and think as they do, Tocqueville reported that they gave a rather consistent response:

> The Americans are fond of explaining almost all the actions of their lives by the principle of self-interest rightly understood; they show with complacency how an enlightened regard for themselves constantly prompts them to assist one another and inclines them willingly to sacrifice a portion of their time and property to the welfare of the state.[57]

Although not unique to America, by the time of Tocqueville's visit enlightened self-interest had taken firm root in the United States. In the generation following the publication of *Democracy in America,* social Darwinism was to make even more popular the doctrine that acting in one's own self-interest contributes to the common good, as we shall see later.

Tocqueville underscored both the strengths and the weaknesses of this philosophy. The principle of self-interest does not entail lofty goals, but it is clear and certain. It does not demand much of a person, yet acting according to it does produce results. It is not difficult to understand for all classes of people. As a principle of human life, self-interest builds on people's infirmities:

> By its admirable conformity to human weaknesses it easily obtains great dominion; nor is that dominion precarious, since the principle checks one

---

[56]*Ibid.,* vol. 2, pp. 3–4.
[57]*Ibid.,* pp. 152, 122.

personal interest by another, and uses, to direct the passions, the very same instrument that excites them.[58]

The principle of enlightened self-interest produces no great acts of self-sacrifice, but it encourages a daily discipline of self denial. By itself self interest cannot make people good and virtuous, and hence can hardly serve as a cornerstone of morality. Nevertheless, said Tocqueville, "it disciplines large numbers of people in habits of regularity, temperance, moderation, foresight, self-command."

Enlightened self-interest is closely related to individualism (for definitions, see Figure 2-2). Tocqueville was the first person to discuss individualism and, in fact, he brought the word into the English language. It is characteristic of Americans that individualism was not a common word among them, even though it so well described some of their salient attitudes and values. People develop a vocabulary for those things of concern to them and what they want to discuss. Tocqueville suggested that there was probably no other civilized country in which less attention was paid to reflection and philosophy than the United States. Americans were not then, nor are they now, a very reflective people.

Tocqueville described individualism as a mature and calm feeling which disposes each member of the community "to sever himself from the mass of his fellows and to draw apart with his family and his friends." Each individual retreats to his or her own familiar turf and thus "leaves society at large to itself." The Frenchman compared individualism and selfishness, and he found both deficient:

Selfishness originates in blind instinct; individualism proceeds from erroneous judgment more than from depraved feelings; it originates as much in deficiencies of the mind as in perversity of heart.

Selfishness blights the germ of all virtue; individualism, at first, only saps the virtues of public life; but in the long run it attacks and destroys all others and is at length absorbed in downright selfishness.[59]

Tocqueville pinpointed probably the most serious weakness of the American character. Enlightened self-interest and individualism narrow one's perspective. They encourage one to think less of public responsibilities, and they lead eventually to selfishness. When we read Tocqueville now, he sounds like a contemporary critic reflecting on the mistakes of the unethical corporate executive or politician. Tocqueville's sensitive assessment of the American character—task-orientation and individualism; impatience with tradition, reflection, and abstract ideals; self-interest leading to selfishness—still stands as one of the great social commentaries. Later

---

[58]*Ibid.*, pp. 122–123.

[59]*Ibid.*, p. 98. For a comparison of contemporary U.S. individualistic culture and more collective cultures, see Harry C. Triandis, "The Many Dimensions of Culture," *Academy of Management Executive,* 18, no. 1 (2004): 88–93.

observers often use Tocqueville as a starting point, but few have done a better over-all appraisal than he.[60]

## Social Darwinism and Herbert Spencer

Events of the latter half of the nineteenth century had a profound impact on attitudes and values. The Industrial Revolution, the growth of cities, and the concept of evolution shook the foundations of life and thought. Herbert Spencer's theories of "social Darwinism" were based on the newly discovered theories of evolution.

Spencer (1820–1903) proposed a grim "survival of the fittest" philosophy. His thesis was that the bright and able contribute most to society and so are to be encouraged and rewarded. The poor, the weak, and the handicapped require more than they contribute and so should not be supported but rather should be allowed to die a natural death. Harsh and demanding reality provides a maturing experience that should not be diluted by well-intentioned but actually destructive charities and handouts. If "natural" principles are followed, evolution and the survival of the fittest in the competition of human life would be the result. Spencer did not set out to examine any particular society and its values; rather, his critique was proposed as "culture-free." According to Spencer, it applied to all people, for it was derived from basic, organic principles of growth and develop-ment. Spencer applied to society the same principles that Charles Darwin saw in biological life—hence the name *social Darwinism*.

Spencer and other proponents of the new evolutionary social ideology were impressed by the suffering of the poor, but they nevertheless felt that progress in an industrial society could come only by means of long hours of work, saving, self-discipline, and even the death of the less able. Rather than considering this a tragedy, they were convinced that through this process of natural selection, those of greater talent, intelligence, and ability would survive and be successful. The physically and mentally handicapped, unable to compete successfully, are less apt to survive. It would be a mistake for a government to provide assistance to these handicapped and deficient people. That would allow them to stay alive, and worse, to reproduce and so transmit their deficiencies to future generations.

Any attempt to minister to the needs of the poor or needy is misguided on several counts. It keeps alive those who are less able. It diverts the attention and abilities of able people who would be better off pursuing more fruitful careers. And, finally, it insulates the less able from a sobering harsh reality and poverty, an opportunity that might jar them from their complacency and encourage them to work harder to better themselves. Although it is painful to all in the short run, the overall good of society in the long run demands that it not support these less fit individuals. Society improves because of the survival of the fittest.

---

[60]See, for example, Michael A. Ledeen, *Tocqueville on American Character: Why Tocqueville's Brilliant Exploration of the American Spirit Is as Vital and Important Today as it Was Nearly Two Hundred Years Ago* (New York: St. Martin's Press, 2000).

The poverty of the incapable, the distresses that come upon the imprudent, the starvation of the idle, and those shoulderings aside of the weak by the strong, which leave so many "in shallows and in miseries," are the decrees of a large, farseeing benevolence. Under the natural order of things society is constantly excreting its unhealthy, imbecile, slow, vacillating, faithless members.[61]

It is especially clear in primitive societies that the strongest and cleverest survive. But this is a natural process, and so it occurs in civilized societies, too. People would be wise to prepare themselves and their children for this struggle.

Society as a whole will benefit from this struggle for survival. Since the most intellectually and physically fit survive, the race will improve. Given a difficult and demanding environment, over several generations the ideal man and woman will develop. There should therefore be little state interference in this natural selection process. The state must not regulate industry, impose tariffs, give subsidies, establish a church, regulate entry into the professions, operate schools, or run the mail service. Most especially, the government must not provide for the poor, improve sanitation, or look to the health needs of the less able.[62]

An example of applying Spencer's views to social issues occurred in 1845–1850. Ireland then experienced a blight of the potato—its staple food, which caused widespread famine, disease, and death. England had invaded and occupied Ireland for several hundred years, and the English took the most fertile land to grow grain to send back to England. At the time of the famine, grain was available from these fields in the Irish midlands. Members of British Parliament were advocates of free markets and they used Spencer's arguments in debating whether to continue to send the grain to England or to allow some grain to go to the Irish. Members of Parliament in London argued that the Irish race would be stronger and better if the weaker and less able did not survive. It would be harmful in the long run for the government to intervene. So Parliament voted not to provide grain to those who were starving. More than one million people out of a pre-famine population of eight million in Ireland died.[63]

Herbert Spencer's philosophy was, and still is, even more popular in the United States than in his native England. His praise of the strong, clever, and aggressive individual reflected the values of the American spirit. Further, his theory of inevitable progress was received enthusiastically in a country already marked by general optimism. Spencer's thinking provided both a rational foundation for existing attitudes and a justification for many public and private practices. In the last third of the nineteenth century, Spencer was an influential leader of thought and a hero to many in the United States.

---

[61]Herbert Spencer, *Social Statics* (London: Appleton, 1850), pp. 323–326, 353.

[62]See Donald Fleming, "Social Darwinism," in Schlesinger and White, eds., *Paths of American Thought,* pp. 124–125.

[63]R. Dudley Edwards and Desmond Williams, *The Great Famine* (Dublin: Browne and Nolan, 1956), pp. 177–186, 243–246; see also, E. R. R. Green, "The Great Famine (1845–50)," in *The Course of Irish History,* ed. T. W. Moody and F. X. Martin (New York: Weybright and Talley, 1967), pp. 268–274.

The personal attributes that Spencer extolled are those that many hold to be necessary for a free enterprise system: an intelligent, hearty, adaptable individual in a hostile climate. Survival requires careful advance planning, hard work, loyalty and responsibility to family, and individual self-sufficiency. Spencer's theories are conservative; he saw great good in the way things were. He saw no need to change or to plan ahead on a local or national level. Because natural processes will inevitably produce the best people and thus the best society, any sort of government or private intervention will hurt society in the long run. Citizens must repress their feelings of pity for the poor and allow natural processes to work themselves out. Spencer's theories challenged the mainstream religious views of the time and were therefore opposed by many. But to others his position seemed a natural extension of the traditional Puritan ethic, especially its secularized counterpart as expressed by Benjamin Franklin. It is no surprise that Spencer's theories were so enthusiastically received by the business community of his day.

## Struggle for Survival

The businessperson, and especially the entrepreneur, has always found the world to be nothing less than a struggle for survival. One may want to be humane and conscientious, but cannot afford to be. Herbert Spencer's theories of the survival of the fittest and what has come to be known as social Darwinism had an immense influence on America in the late nineteenth century.

William Graham Sumner (1840–1910), a social science professor at Yale, was an advocate of Spencerism. Sumner's father was an immigrant English workingman who taught his children the Puritan virtues of thrift, self-reliance, hard work, and discipline.[64] His son was convinced that egalitarianism, made fashionable by the French Revolution and the freeing of slaves, would undermine the initiative and independent spirit that encourage the best people to develop their talents fully. According to Sumner, the less able and adept are jealous of the successes of the more talented and through the political process they will require the latter to support them. This perversion undermines the creativity and motivation of the better and more talented people. Sumner clashed with Yale president Noah Porter when the latter objected to Sumner's assigning Herbert Spencer's book to students. Nevertheless, Sumner won the long-term battle and also thus won probably the first clear statement of academic freedom within the university.

Sumner and Spencer urged a tight-fisted, unemotional aloofness. Both one's self and one's wealth must be saved and not spent without chance of a good return on investment. Following the Puritans, free emotions and spontaneity were suspect; a person could lose all in a lighthearted or thoughtless moment. In the same vein, Sumner urged that government should not intervene in social and economic affairs. The environment should be kept clear of restrictions, taxes, restraints, and other needless and even harmful laws and regulations.

The opposition to social Darwinism was led by Lester F. Ward (1841–1913). Ward's view, expressed in his *Dynamic Sociology,* is that people should control

---

[64]Fleming, "Social Darwinism," p. 128.

their environment and not allow it to control them. Evolution and natural selection as outlined by Darwin led to change without direction and without goals. According to Ward, the great value of evolution and natural selection was that they had brought people to the position in which they found themselves now. Moreover, it was precisely in the current era that individuals became able to control their own future and not leave it to blind chance. For Ward, it would be the supreme paradox for men and women, now that they had discovered these natural laws and forces, to retreat and allow themselves to become victims of them. Ward labeled Spencerism a do-nothing philosophy.

## SUMMARY AND CONCLUSIONS

From ancient times to the Middle Ages, Western attitudes toward work became progressively more positive. Biblical injunctions and monastic practices helped to integrate work, labor-saving devices, and a planned day into the average person's life. Then, in the sixteenth century, the Protestant Reformation made the successful performance of an individual's "calling" or occupation one of the primary duties of life. Although a joyless vision, it encouraged a focusing of energies that made possible rapid economic growth. The central importance given to private property and the freedom of the individual further supported this growth.

In this chapter, we also examined the geography, inherited values, and personal characteristics that contributed to the major values and ideals in American life. The vast expanse of virgin land was a challenge to the righteous, task-oriented Puritans. Their moral theology supported their work ethic: early rising, self-denial, hard work, and thrift. Furthermore, the favorable results of working hard showed that the individual was saved. Though not a Puritan, Benjamin Franklin approved of this work ethic, and he presented a secularized version of it.

The values of American Puritans—hard work, saving, regular habits, diligence, self-control, and sobriety—still characterize the American work ethic for some. These values constitute what is known as the Protestant ethic, which will be discussed in greater detail in the next chapter.

## DISCUSSION QUESTIONS

1. How does a knowledge of history help the manager? How does it help in understanding the development of business values?
2. What were the attitudes of Plato and Aristotle toward work?
3. How would the ancient Greeks view work in the United States today?
4. What influence did Jesus and the Gospels have on peoples' attitudes toward work?
5. What is the "love ethic" that was encouraged by Christianity? Describe its origins.
6. Describe Muslim, Hindu, and Buddhist views on work. Do they differ from Western values? How so?
7. What views of work did the early Benedictine monasteries contribute? What meaning might these attitudes have for work today?
8. Did Martin Luther have a favorable view of business and commerce?

9. Describe John Calvin's attitude toward work. How did his notion of predestination contribute to the Puritan ethic?

10. What is the Protestant ethic? Is it the same as the Puritan ethic? What are its elements?

11. Describe how John Locke's position on private property influenced the Protestant ethic and early American attitudes. How does it influence current business values?

12. Did Locke and Rousseau advocate a high tax on property that is not necessary to support a family? Why or why not?

13. Why is Adam Smith called the grandfather of economics?

14. Compare Adam Smith's position on work and efficiency with that of Benjamin Franklin.

15. How did Adam Smith's theories shift the model of society from the earlier view of society as an organism to that of a machine?

16. According to the Puritans, what constitutes a person's calling?

17. How did Benjamin Franklin alter the Puritan ethic?

18. Compare and contrast Benjamin Franklin's attitudes toward work and efficiency and those of Thomas Jefferson.

19. Did slavery give the southern states of the United States an economic advantage? Is slavery still practiced? How so? What are the ethical arguments against slavery?

20. Describe the effect of the frontier on American values.

21. Outline Alexis de Tocqueville's appraisal of enlightened self-interest.

22. According to Tocqueville, what are the strengths and weaknesses of enlightened self-interest as a basic motive for people? To what extent are his assessments still valid today?

23. What is social Darwinism?

24. Why did Herbert Spencer argue that evolution and the "survival of the fittest" are not to be thwarted? Does this ideology exist today?

25. Compare the effect of the frontier and the effect of social Darwinism on American values.

26. Of the various historical business values illustrated in this chapter, which most closely reflect your own views? Explain.

# CHAPTER 5

# Factories, Immigrants, and Ideology

In the past the man has been first; in the future the system must be first.
FREDERICK WINSLOW TAYLOR (1865–1915), FOUNDER OF SCIENTIFIC MANAGEMENT

To continue much longer overwhelmed by business cares and with most of my thoughts wholly upon the way to make money in the shortest time must degrade me beyond hope of permanent recovery.
ANDREW CARNEGIE (1835–1918), FOUNDER OF U.S. STEEL, PHILANTHROPIST

The lives of people are strongly influenced by their history, as we saw in Chapter 4. Our ancestors' experiences in business and in life help us understand current business values. In this chapter we continue to examine the people and events that have affected us. We then investigate the origin and content of business values and ideology.

Values and ideologies are statements of purpose, but they are more than that. They also are motivators to action. A personal ideology gives a rationale for life and action, and answers questions such as: What goals and activities are most important to me? How do I explain my life, my values, and my actions when they are questioned by others?

Both a person and a group can possess an ideology. An ideology embodies accepted ideals (for terms, see Figures 1-1, 2-1, 2-2), the ultimate goals possessed by an individual or a society. Ideals can influence values, but ideals are sometimes distant, whereas values affect actions. Unless ideals are integrated by a person into an ideology, they do not have much influence on values, choices, and actions. We can better understand our goals and values by examining how history has influenced us. Let us continue to learn from our forebears.

## CAPITALISM AND INDIVIDUALISM STEER BUSINESS PRACTICES

We continue our examination of the business values of a new nation. In Chapter 4 we surveyed the work values of Western civilization, and continued by viewing the Puritans and the writings of Benjamin Franklin. After the nation became independent, those values had an unprecedented opportunity to be realized. The new nation provided an ideal testing ground for enterprising farmers, traders, prospectors, and entrepreneurs. Business and commerce grew very rapidly. We shall briefly examine that growth and the values that provided the foundation for it.

The early days of the new republic were dominated by the farmer. The colonial merchant provided the link between early Americans, trading and transporting food and goods. From 1800 to 1850, wholesalers took the place of merchants. They "were responsible for directing the flow of cotton, wheat and lumber from the West to the East and to Europe."[1]

The rapid growth of the American industrial system, which was to make the United States the most productive nation in the world, had begun by the middle of the nineteenth century. "In 1849 the United States had only 6,000 miles of railroad and even fewer miles of canals, but by 1884 its railroad corporations operated 202,000 miles of track, or 43 percent of the total mileage in the world." The number of those working in factories also grew very rapidly during this period. In terms of manufactured goods, "By 1894 the value of the output of American industry equaled that of the combined output of the United Kingdom, France and Germany."[2] Growth continued to accelerate, until within 20 years the United States was producing more than a third of the industrial goods of the world.

The mining of the mountains of the far West provides a paradigm of the strengths—energetic, flexible, enterprising—and weaknesses—self-centered, with little concern for long-term consequences—of the American character. Tales of silver, gold, and other minerals in the mountains thrilled the imagination of people across the continent. Mining called for strong, resourceful people. Hundreds of thousands took the challenge, risking their lives, their fortunes, and often their families to try to find the ore. Vast amounts of capital and superhuman energies were expended. The "get rich quick" spirit of these prospectors was a prelude to that of the entrepreneurs who came later. Virginia City, Nevada, was built over the Comstock Lode of silver ore. What had been bare desert and mountains in 1860 became within 5 years one of the most rapidly growing and thriving cities in the western United States. The energies and genius of thousands sank dozens of shafts into the rock, supported them with timbers, built flumes—and an entire city. Between 1859 and 1880 more than $306 million worth of silver was taken from the

---

[1] Alfred D. Chandler, "The Role of Business in the United States: A Historical Survey," *Daedelus,* 98, no. 1 (1969): 26.
[2] *Ibid.,* p. 27.

mountains.[3] The magnitude of the effort and the accomplishment can be gathered from this description:

> In the winter of 1866 the towns and mills along the Comstock Lode were using two hundred thousand cords of wood for fuel, while the time soon came when eighty million feet of lumber a year went down into the chambers and drifts. Since the mountains were naked rock, flumes (channels for carrying water) had to be built from the forested slopes of the Sierras, and by 1880, there were ten of them with an aggregate length of eighty miles.[4]

Adolph Sutro owned a quartz mill on the opposite side of the mountains on the Carlson River, and he envisioned an easier way to get the ore out of the mountains. He planned a three-mile-long tunnel that would extend through the mountain from the river valley and intersect the Comstock mines 1,600 feet below the surface. The tunnel would drain the series of mines to that level and also enable the ore to be taken out through the tunnel for processing where fuel and water were plentiful. By 1866, Sutro had obtained contracts from 23 of the largest mining companies to use the tunnel when it was completed.

> After incessant effort, in which any man of less marvelous pluck and energy would have failed, he raised sufficient capital to begin the project. In 1869 he broke ground for the tunnel and set a corps of drillers upon the task that was to occupy them for eight weary years.[5]

Sutro finished his tunnel and put it into use in 1877. But within 3 years, the boom collapsed. The value of the silver mining stock sank from a high of $393 million in 1875 to less than $7 million in 1880. People slowly began to leave Virginia City, and today it is a ghost town; only remnants of roads, homes, an opera house, and some saloons are left to remind us of its place in history.

Virginia City illustrates how the talents and wealth of a people can be quickly channeled to accomplish tremendous feats; it also shows how such accomplishments are often short-lived and not designed to encourage stability. This sort of activity attracts energetic and fast-moving entrepreneurs; it does not appeal to people who desire family and neighborhood relationships. The gold rush a decade earlier in California left a more permanent mark, because the new inhabitants did not leave when the gold ran out. The prospectors, miners, and fortune seekers converged from all parts of the country, disrupting families and communities. Before their coming, California had a unique style. "To these

---

[3]Allan Nevins, *The Emergence of Modern America,* vol. 8 (New York: Macmillan, 1927), p. 137; see also Daniel T. Rodgers, *The Work Ethic in Industrial America, 1850–1920* (Chicago: University of Chicago Press, 1978).
[4]Nevins, *Emergence of Modern America,* p. 136.
[5]*Ibid.,* p. 137.

California imperatives of simple, gracious, and abundant living, Americans had come in disrespect and violence." Exploitation of the land kept people moving and leaving problems in their wake.

> Leaving the mountains of the Mother Lode gashed and scarred like a deserted battlefield, Californians sought easy strikes elsewhere. Most noticeably in the areas of hydraulic mining, logging, the destruction of wildlife, and the depletion of the soil Americans continued to rifle California all through the nineteenth century.
>
> The state remained, after all, a land of adventuring strangers, a land characterized by an essential selfishness and an underlying instability, a fixation upon the quick acquisition of wealth, an impatience with the more subtle premises of human happiness. These were American traits, to be sure, but the Gold Rush intensified and consolidated them as part of a regional experience.[6]

Throughout these years of rapid economic change, the role of entrepreneurs was central. Their brains, ingenuity, and willingness to risk gave us most of our economic success and growth. At the same time, their myopic desire for short-term gain caused many failures and much personal anguish. Given this background, let us return to the leaders of thought who have had a profound influence on American business values.

## American Individualism and Ralph Waldo Emerson

To this day, the American businessperson is characterized as an individualist. One articulate and influential champion of freedom and the importance of the individual was Ralph Waldo Emerson (1803–1882). Coming soon after the French Enlightenment and Rousseau, Emerson is the best-known American proponent of individualism. He sees human nature as having natural resources within itself. Societal structures and supports tend only to limit the immense potential of the individual. Given freedom, individuals can act, grow, and benefit themselves and others. But they require an absence of restraints imposed by people, cultures, and governments. Emerson's friend Henry David Thoreau acted on this ideology and built a hut outside Boston at Walden Pond, where he reflected and wrote alone in the unimpeded, open atmosphere of trees, grass, and pond.

In Emerson's book of essays *The Conduct of Life*, there is one entitled "Wealth."[7] Here Emerson applied his philosophy of individualism to economics and the marketplace. A person should contribute and not just receive. If an individual follows his or her own nature, he or she will not only become a producer but will also become wealthy in the process. Individuals contribute little if they only pay their

---

[6]Kevin Starr, *Americans and the California Dream* (New York: Oxford University Press, 1973), pp. 33, 63–66. Starr is the California State Librarian Emeritus.
[7]Ralph W. Emerson, *The Conduct of Life and Other Essays* (London: Dent, 1908), pp. 190–213.

debts and do not add to the wealth available. Meeting only one's own needs is inefficient; it is better to be rich and thus be able to meet one's needs and add to wealth as well. And doing both builds upon one's own natural inclinations. Emerson insisted that getting rich is something any person can achieve given a little ingenuity. It depends on factors the person has totally under his or her own control.

> Wealth is in applications of mind to nature, and the art of getting rich consists not in industry, much less in saving, but in a better order, in time-liness, in being at the right spot. One man has stronger arms, or longer legs; another sees by the course of streams, and growth of markets, where land will be wanted, makes a clearing to the river, goes to sleep, and wakes up rich.[8]

Emerson's heroes were the independent Anglo-Saxons. They are a strong race who, by means of their personal independence, have become the merchants of the world. They do not look to government "for bread and games." They do not look to clans, relatives, friends, or aristocracy to take care of them or to help them get ahead; they rely on their own initiative and abilities. Emerson's optimistic view of the potential of the free and strong individual released from the fetters of government and custom remains an important support of American values. While many values related to the Protestant ethic have changed, Emerson's view of the individual remains.

## Children and Immigrants in Nineteenth-Century U.S. Factories

Before 1840, factory workers in the United States labored 12–14 hours a day, six or seven days a week. An 84-hour work week was common. By 1860, the average workday dropped to 10.6 hours, six days a week; but the 12–14 hour workday was still typical in many industries, including the textile mills of New England.[9]

In 1890, steel workers worked 12 hours a day, seven days a week; most made $1.25 a day. Those wages went for rent, and there was little left to buy even food. Even if a steel worker worked 12 hours a day every day of the year, it was still not sufficient to support a family.[10] Therefore, many of these poor immigrants were single, and others left their families in Europe.

When the immigrants came, they knew that the work would be difficult and dangerous. They were at the bottom of the status ladder and therefore had to accept the hardest and most poorly paid work. A Hungarian churchman examined the conditions in Pittsburgh steel mills and said, "Wherever the heat is most insupportable, the flames most scorching, the smoke and soot most choking, there we are certain to find compatriots bent and wasted with toil."[11]

---

[8]*Ibid.*, p. 192.
[9]Gary M. Walton and Ross Robertson, *History of the American Economy* (New York: Harcourt Brace Jovanovich, 1983), pp. 280, 437.
[10]David Brody, *Steelworkers in America: The Nonunion Era* (Cambridge, MA: Harvard University Press, 1980), p. 98.
[11]*Ibid.*, p. 99.

Many young children also worked under some of these same conditions. In 1910 two million boys and girls, one-fifth of all American children 10 to 15 years old, worked 10 to 14 hours a day. In Syracuse, New York, factories would not hire children unless they were at least eight years old.[12] Those who worked were the children of the immigrants and the poor, since their families needed the additional income. Child labor was a bargain for employers, since children's wages were less than those for adults. Further underscoring contemporary values and the acceptance of such factory conditions is the fact that before 1920 two laws passed by the U.S. Congress to restrict child labor were declared unconstitutional by the Supreme Court. Child labor still exists in the United States; more children illegally work in the United States than in any other developed country.[13]

Working conditions were often miserable and dangerous. Textile workers suffered brown lung disease, quarry workers breathed stone dust, coal miners suffered black lung disease and many deaths due to cave-ins, and many other workers inhaled toxic chemical fumes. The annual toll of those killed or injured in industry was almost one million at the turn of the century.

At U.S. Steel's South Works in the Pittsburgh area in 1910, "Almost one-quarter of the recent immigrants in the works each year—3,273 in five years—were injured or killed."[14] Working on the railroads was also very dangerous. In 1890, 2,451 railroad workers were killed, and this does not include many more civilians killed by trains. Some 30,000 workers were killed and 5 million injured each year.[15]

Companies often provided housing for their workers. Steel companies built good housing for managers and what the companies called "shanties" for the unskilled. Four men slept, ate, and washed in a 10-by-14-foot shanty. The annual rent charged was more than twice the cost of building the pine board shanty.[16] Steel owners and executives had ready responses to criticisms: The immigrants were eager for work, they made much more than they would have made in Europe, and their living conditions were poor because they used their salaries on beer and whiskey.

Given such low wages and poor treatment, it is not surprising that in the United States during this period the rich became richer and the poor became poorer. One percent of the population owned as much as the remaining 99 percent combined.[17]

## Churches and Their Influence

Churches have two roles to play in society: (1) to help people worship God and (2) to help them understand and handle the moral issues of their everyday lives. These roles sometimes are in conflict. The second role involves sensitizing people

---

[12]Walton and Robertson, *History of the American Economy*, p. 439.

[13]Marvin J. Levine, *Children for Hire: The Perils of Child Labor in the United States* (Westport, CT: Praeger, 2003).

[14]Brody, *Steelworkers in America*, p. 101.

[15]Otto L. Bettmann, *The Good Old Days: They Were Terrible!* (New York: Random House, 1974), p. 70; see also Harold Evans, "The Grim Face of Labor: America's Working Stiffs Included Men, Women and Children," *U.S. News & World Report*, October 12, 1998, p. 32.

[16]Brody, *Steelworkers in America*, p. 110.

[17]Donald T. Phillips, *Lincoln on Leadership: Executive Strategies for Tough Times* (New York: Warner Books, 1992).

to the moral problems that exist. Before 1920 this required calling attention to the abuses indicated above: child labor, dangerous working conditions, and working hours so long that decent family life was impossible. Yet as a church and its leaders become respected in society, they are easily lulled into blindness concerning the evils of the society that gives them support and status; they are thus deterred from acting as prophets who prod the public conscience.

A church has the responsibility to help all people. Because of this mission most churches make special attempts to help the poor, since often the poor have desperate needs and lack a voice in society. Nonetheless, a church can be so influenced by its affluent members that it becomes part of the Establishment, and its leaders oppose change, social justice, and what they called "rabble rousers." Such a church and its members risk losing too much if change occurs. We can learn a lesson for today by examining the actions of some of the more respected churches in the United States in the previous century.

The dominant American Protestant churches in the nineteenth century, while preaching charity and concern for the poor, nevertheless defended the economic system that the Protestant ethic had produced. In this period, churches and schools had more influence over American life and morals than they do today. The prestigious private colleges in the eastern United States taught the values of private property, free trade, and individualism. These religiously-oriented schools (both Harvard and Yale were Protestant at the time) generally taught conservative economic and business values alongside their moral philosophy.

Many clergy believed that God had established the existing economic laws, so it would be dangerous to challenge them. Francis Wayland, president of Brown University and author of the most popular economics text then used, intertwined economics and theology in stating his basic position: "God has made labor necessary to our well being. We must work both because idleness brings punishment and because work brings great riches; these are two essential, powerful, and immutable motives for work."[18] Wayland concluded from this simple principle that all property should be private and held by individuals. Charity should not be given except to those who absolutely cannot work, and the government should not impose tariffs or quotas or otherwise interfere.

In the last 25 years of the nineteenth century, the major Protestant churches went through an agonizing reexamination. Up to this time, the churches had wholeheartedly accepted Adam Smith's economics and canonized it as part of the "divine plan." They defended private property, business, the need to work, and even wealth. Then two severe, bloody labor disturbances occurred that forced the churches to reconsider their traditional survival-of-the-fittest theories.

The first of these conflicts followed a severe economic depression in 1877. Wages of train workers were cut by 10 percent, and they protested. They picketed and halted trains. Army troops were called to defend railroad property, and they fought desperate mobs of workers. In the confusion, scores of workers were shot.

---

[18]Henry F. May, *Protestant Churches and Industrial America* (New York: Harper & Row, 1949), p. 15.

The churches generally supported the Establishment and self-righteously preached to the workers on the divine wisdom of the American economy. Hear the newspaper *Christian Union*:

> If the trainmen knew a little more of political economy they would not fall so easy a prey to men who never earn a dollar of wages by good solid work. What a sorry set of ignoramuses they must be who imagine that they are fighting for the rights of labor in combining together to prevent other men from working for low wages because, forsooth, they are discontented with them.[19]

The religious press, reflecting the attitudes of its patrons, took a hard line against what it saw as anarchy, riots, and support of weak and lazy men.

A decade later another serious confrontation occurred. On the occasion of a labor meeting at the Haymarket in Chicago, the police shot several in a group of strikers. A few days later, a bomb was thrown at the police. As is often the case in such situations, facts and circumstances were forgotten as near hysteria swept the press. The journal *Protestant Independent* was typical: "A mob should be crushed by knocking down or shooting down the men engaged in it; and the more promptly this is done the better."[20] Only when these strikingly un-Christian outbursts had ended did the clergy have the opportunity to reflect on what had happened and how they themselves had reacted. It then became clear how inflexible, biased, and even violent had been their attitude—hardly what one would expect of churches. During this period, the clergy had been anxious to accommodate their churches' position with regard to the new industrial movements. They had not changed creeds or confessions, but had "progressively identified [themselves] with competitive individualism at the expense of community."[21] From the rubble of these mistakes and later reflection came the impetus toward a new social consciousness, specifically in the form of the Social Gospel.

## Praise of Wealth

During this period the Baptist preacher Russell Conwell traveled the country giving his famous "Acres of Diamonds" speech. He delivered it more than five thousand times around the turn of the century to enraptured audiences eager to hear that to gather wealth was God's will.

Conwell's speech tells of a man who goes out to seek wealth; in the meantime his successor on the farm finds diamonds in the yard he had left behind. His message: Any man has it within his grasp to make himself wealthy if he is willing to work at it.

> I say that you ought to get rich, and it is your duty to get rich. How many of my pious brethren say to me, "Do you, a Christian minister, spend your time going up and down the country advising young people to get

---

[19]*Ibid.*, p. 93.
[20]*Ibid.*, p. 101.
[21]Martin Marty, *Righteous Empire: The Protestant Experience in America* (New York: Dial, 1970), p. 110.

rich, to get money?" "Yes of course I do." They say, "Isn't that awful. Why don't you preach the gospel instead of preaching about man's making money?" "Because to make money honestly is to preach the gospel." That is the reason. The men who get rich may be the most honest men you will find in the community.[22]

Conwell here cites what to him was the happy confluence of deeply felt religious convictions and the life of the marketplace. Because of the traditional religious values of poverty and humility, riches often brought qualms of conscience to believers. Conwell tried to wed faith and fortune: There can be no better demonstration of faith in God than to use one's abilities to their fullest, to be a success, and to accumulate the goods of the earth (to be used responsibly, of course). Conwell himself made a fortune from his lectures and, following his own advice on investment, used the money to found Temple University. Conwell is much like contemporary Christian preachers who gain thousands of followers by lecturing on how Jesus supports material success. Critics point out that the message is eagerly received, but that it disregards the essential Christian elements of human suffering, sin, death, redemption, and resurrection.

## Andrew Carnegie and John D. Rockefeller

Praise of wealth also came from those who became wealthy. A handful of industrialists—called "the robber barons"—had an immense, enduring influence on America and American industry around the turn of the century. Among them, the immigrant Scot Andrew Carnegie (1835–1919) enjoyed his role as industrial and "moral" leader. Financier J. P. Morgan helped Carnegie put together U.S. Steel in 1901. Carnegie accumulated immense wealth in the process and loved to tell all who would listen why he deserved it. He established 2,509 libraries in cities and towns throughout the United States, each proudly bearing the Carnegie name.

Carnegie amassed a huge personal fortune, even though he was well aware that his own steelworkers were very poorly paid. He maintained that God gave him his wealth. Carnegie made no apology for the inequality and in fact defended it as the survival of the fittest. The rich man's money would do no good if it were paid to the workers.

Much of this sum, if distributed in small quantities among the people, would have been wasted in the indulgence of appetite, some of it in excess, and it may be doubted whether even the part put to the best use, that of adding to the comforts of the home, would have yielded results for the race at all comparable.[23]

---

[22]Russell Conwell, *Acres of Diamonds* (New York: Harper, 1915), p. 18.
[23]Andrew Carnegie, "Wealth," in *Democracy and the Gospel of Wealth*, ed. Gail Kennedy (Boston: D. C. Heath, 1949), p. 6.

According to Carnegie, it is only the wealthy who can endow libraries and universities and who can best look after the long-term good of society as a whole. The money is much better spent when the wealthy accumulate it in large amounts so that they can use it to accomplish great things.

For this reason, Carnegie felt that the wealthy person should "set an example of modest, unostentatious living, shunning display or extravagance." He should hold his money in trust for society and be "strictly bound as a matter of duty to administer [it] in the manner which, in his judgment, is best calculated to produce the most beneficial results for the community."[24] The accumulation of great fortunes is good for society, as is "the concentration of business, industrial and commercial, in the hands of a few." He believed that this concentration of wealth enabled the most able to use the funds for the best interest of society. During his lifetime, Carnegie gave away $350 million.

Carnegie defended his fortune and his right to have it and dispose of it as he saw fit. Thus he was able to overlook the injustices he and his company supported. Of course, he was not entirely objective in his examination of the socioeconomic system; he profited much from it.

During the same period, John D. Rockefeller formed the Standard Oil Company. To build his firm, he sold his product at below cost until competitors were forced out of business; then, as the sole seller, he doubled his prices. He also received then legal secret rebates and kickbacks from the railroads on his large shipments. The Standard Oil Company monopoly was later broken up by new U.S. antitrust legislation.

On the other hand, during his lifetime Rockefeller gave away $530 million, most of it to medical research. As a devout Baptist, Rockefeller believed that God gave him his money. In a "complex amalgam of godliness and greed, passion and fiendish cunning," he lived by the Protestant ethic.[25] During the Microsoft antitrust trial, many compared the monopoly, business activities, resulting wealth, and civic-mindedness of Bill Gates to that of Rockefeller. Both Carnegie and Rockefeller were convinced that a rich man should wisely contribute to society most of their wealth, and they both did so before they died. Carnegie favored a steep inheritance tax, if it was necessary to force the rich to give their money to society rather than leave it to pampered heirs. Given their immense fortunes, contemporary U.S. business executives seem not to be as caring of their fellow citizens.

## Manufacturing and Scientific Management

The growth of manufacturing did, in fact, provide a new and much faster means of attaining wealth and economic growth. As productivity increased, higher wages could be paid and greater profits obtained for the owner at the same time. This was

---

[24]*Ibid.*, p. 7. David M. Potter, in *People of Plenty: Economic Abundance and the American Character* (Chicago: University of Chicago Press, 1954), maintains that in an even more fundamental sense, a democratic system depends on economic surplus (p. 111f).

[25]Ron Chernow, *Titan: The Life of John D. Rockefeller, Sr.* (New York: Random House, 1998); see also Chermow's "Philanthropy the Smart Way: Today's Rich Can Learn from the Robber Barons," *New York Times,* September 27, 1999, p. 23.

a considerable departure from past eras, when fortunes had been made by trade, transport, or lending (and, of course, wars and plunder). Thus, in the past, wealth had been considered more of a fixed quantity: What one person gained, another lost. The advent of manufacturing demonstrated that the economy was not a zero-sum game—it was possible for each party in the exchange to benefit financially. Increases in productivity enabled this to take place.

Frederick W. Taylor (1865–1915), founder of scientific management, focused on better methods in manufacturing as a way to increase productivity. Productivity is, of course, the amount of a product that is produced per given input of resource—generally per worker. Mechanization and careful planning enable workers to produce more than they could without planning. Taylor's insight was that worker and management experience plus intuitive judgment are not enough. To achieve greater productivity, which benefits all, the work setting and the motions of the job itself ought to be carefully planned, so to result in the most efficient tools, techniques, and methods.

As factory work became more complex, Taylor gained greater support for his view. No single person, worker, or supervisor could be aware of all the mechanical, psychological, and technological factors involved in planning even one job. Efficiency required careful planning by a team which possessed various competencies. Intuition, experience, and seat-of-the-pants judgments would no longer do. Scientific management undermined Spencer's notions of survival of the fittest, since, as Taylor pointed out, allowing the "best person" to surface naturally was inefficient. In this new complex world, few people had the ability to achieve maximum productivity by themselves. Greater efficiency and productivity demanded the intervention of planners.[26]

Taylor was in favor of higher wages and shorter hours for workers, but he saw no need for unions. If scientific management is implemented and the best and most efficient means of production is achieved, he claimed, there would be no grounds for petty quarrels and grievances. Policies and procedures would be set by scientific inquiry into what objectively is most efficient, and that which is most efficient will benefit both workers and managers, since both will share in the results of this greater productivity: greater profits. In Taylor's scheme, the personal exercise of authority would be eliminated. Managers would be subject to the same policies, rules, and methods as the workers themselves.

Although Taylor followed the traditional managerial ideology that workers pursue their own self-interest and try to maximize their own return, he challenged the notion that each person could work out this struggle in isolation, apart from and competing with other human beings. In an industrial organization, greater productivity can be achieved only when each worker, alongside management, cooperates to find the best means of production. Taylor pointed out how the returns to all were diminished if a single worker is not working at his or her most efficient job and pace. Taylor set out to help both worker and manager achieve

---

[26]Frederick Winslow Taylor, *Scientific Management* (New York: Harper & Brothers, 1947), pp. 36, 98, 99; see also Daniel Nelson, *Frederick W. Taylor and the Rise of Scientific Management* (Madison, WI: University of Wisconsin Press, 1980).

maximum efficiency, which can be done only in cooperation. Up to Taylor's time a lazy man or woman had been penalized. But Taylor proposed to reward workers by enabling them to work to their greatest capacity and receive greater financial return.

Scientific management was not greeted happily by either workers or managers, because it deprived each of some freedom and judgment. Scientific management chronicled the shift from craft to industrial work. In the long run, Taylor's methodology, and perhaps even more his ideology, has had an immense impact on industrial life.[27] In a sharp break from earlier American individualism, Taylor demonstrated that productivity and the system, in this case manufacturing, were more important than the lone individual. The emerging corporation itself bore additional testimony to the new importance of expertise, planning, and cooperation. In subsequent decades, generally under pressure from labor unions, the business firm provided more benefits to individuals: vacations, retirement, and medical care. Soon the majority of people worked and cooperated within a larger group to achieve greater productivity, and this still characterizes American business.

## Biased Management

The world and the ideals we have discussed in this chapter are those of the business*man*. For centuries, business, commerce, and trade were all largely "for men only." Women did not even obtain the right to vote until the twentieth century. Hence half of the potential technical and managerial talent was lost. Although women currently have a better chance of being promoted, it is still the androgynous woman—the one who is most like a man—who is more likely to be chosen.[28]

In addition, a glance at any firm's list of its employees by rank, and also by race and ethnic group, places a spotlight on the results of centuries of racial prejudice. Even today, relatively few blacks, Hispanics, and women are in top management. Moreover, it has been only within the past two generations that religious prejudice in the executive suites of the largest corporations has broken down so that the WASP (White Anglo-Saxon Protestant) clique has cracked, allowing an increasing number of Blacks, Jews, Catholics, and women to climb the managerial ladder into the executive suites.

## Americans as Seen from Abroad

As was stated before when Alexis de Tocqueville was discussed, an outsider viewing a culture is sensitive to elements to which members of that culture are often blind. Tocqueville was one foreigner who had superb insights about America; other visitors also expressed important insights.

Another French observer, the Jesuit paleontologist Pierre Teilhard de Chardin (1881–1955), lived and worked in the United States in his later years and noted

---

[27]See Martha Banta, *Taylored Lives: Narrative Productions in the Age of Taylor, Veblen, and Ford* (Chicago: University of Chicago Press, 1993).
[28]Russell I. Kent and Sherry E. Moss, "Effects of Sex and Gender Role on Leader Emergence," *Academy of Management Journal,* 37, no. 5 (1994): 1335–1346.

many of the same qualities as did Tocqueville. Teilhard had a sympathetic view of the American character, in spite of his own personal inclination for reflection and asceticism. Writing while on an expedition alongside some Americans in the Gobi desert Teilhard said:

> People here are inclined to treat the Americans as a joke, but the more I see of them the more I admire their ability to work and get things done, and the kinder and more approachable I find them. In my own branch of science it's the Americans who are showing us how we must set to work on the earth if we are to read its secret and make ourselves its masters.[29]

While it is true that Americans have the ability to get a job done, their orientation to action is also the source of criticism. Many foreign observers see Americans as individualistic, shallow, and materialistic—more wedded to things than to people, more inclined to do than to reflect. Let us examine some comments on Americans made by other foreign observers.

Albert Einstein (1879–1955), the brilliant mathematician and physicist who came to live in the United States in the 1920s, admired the country. But in a caution that sounds contemporary, he said:

> The cult of individuals is always, in my view, unjustified. To be sure, nature distributes her gifts unevenly among her children . . . It strikes me as unfair, and even in bad taste, to select a few for boundless admiration, attributing superhuman powers of mind and character to them. This has been my fate, and the contrast between the popular estimate of my powers and achievements and the reality is simply grotesque.[30]

Einstein's comments might be applied today to the superstars in sports and entertainment, and to Bill Gates and Donald Trump in business.

Israeli writer Amos Oz adds that this individualistic view is spreading throughout the world:

> America has promoted and spread all over the world the simple ideal of individual happiness. Various religions, civilizations and ideologies throughout history regarded happiness as a collective rather than an individual experience. Almost all of them are losing ground to that triumphant American vision of private happiness. Hundreds of millions of people, from Tokyo to Leningrad, from Cairo to Buenos Aires, dream of being happy in the American way. But is the new global America, this international happiness-oriented village, a happy place?

---

[29]Pierre Teilhard de Chardin, *Letters from a Traveler,* trans. Rene Hague et al. (New York: Harper & Row, 1962), p. 106.
[30]Albert Einstein, *Ideas and Opinions,* ed. Carl Seelig (New York: Modern Library, 1994), p. 4.

The popular American dream of living happily ever after, while dazzling the world, reminds me of the American landscape itself: plentiful, elusive, and forlorn.[31]

Businesspeople are more positive about American values. Hear Akio Morita, the founder and former chairperson of Sony Corporation of Japan:

What I like about the Americans is their frankness, their openness. In America, I feel I can openly express whatever opinion I have, and it is welcomed, even if it conflicts with other opinions. In Japan, even among friends we can't have a difference of opinion—disagreement destroys friendship. But in America, a difference of opinion can make friends, bring people closer together. That open-mindedness and frontier spirit is why I am so comfortable in the U.S.[32]

Foreign social commentators have felt the pulse of America and pointed to the strengths and weaknesses of the American character. They underscore the openness, flexibility, pragmatism, and respect for individuals. But they also see parochialism, lack of interest in other languages and cultures, materialism, and self-centeredness. It is essential that each of us be aware of our own national character lest we uncritically be victims of our own biases. Such awareness is even more important as we attempt to have some influence on our own values and the values of our nation. The changes that we must undergo if we are to live and compete in the global marketplace make this task more urgent.

Historical events and social commentators provide insight into our origins and character. Examining these foundation values helps us get a better grasp of current business values. In the past, the geography of the United States and the attitudes and values of the people who settled it gave the country a unique world position. It had rich and abundant farmland, protected east and west borders, a slowly retreating frontier, and people who worked by the Puritan ethic. The geography and history of a land and the personality of its people contribute to values that are shared by all.

## IDEOLOGY AND VALUES

An ideology is a system of values that provides life goals and personal values. An ideology is a coherent, systematic, and moving statement of basic values and purpose. It is a constellation of values generally held by a group, and members of the group tend to support one another in that ideology. An ideology answers questions such as: What is most important to us? Why are we doing this? How can I explain my life and my society to myself and to others? A corporate or group mission statement attempts to articulate an ideology, as does a personal mission statement (for additional terms, see Figure 1-1).

---

[31]Quoted in "To See Ourselves as Others See Us," *Time,* June 16, 1986, pp. 52–53. Quoted by permission.
[32]*Ibid.*

Without an explicit ideology, a group or nation is left without clearly stated purposes and hence without a consensus or the drive that comes from purpose. When an ideology is spelled out, it can be examined, challenged, and altered as conditions change and new needs arise. It is then open for all to accept or reject as they see fit. When an ideology is not explicit, it is sometimes claimed that there is no ideology; but this is hardly true. The ideology exists; it is merely implicit, unspoken, and hence unexamined. Having only an implicit ideology places any group in an unstable position, because difficult questions which arise can cause confusion and chaos.

Ideologies possess certain common features. They are selective in the issues they treat and in the supporting evidence and arguments they use. Ideologies are largely straightforward and uncomplicated, even when the issues are complex. Their content is limited to what is publicly acceptable. Finally, although ideologies are answers to questions and hence address the intellect, they nevertheless do so in a manner that also engages the emotions. They can inspire and motivate men and women to cooperate and even undergo great hardship for the sake of a compelling goal.

The positive effect of an ideology is that it gives people direction, coherence, norms, and motivation. It can bring clarity and assurance to the mind and hence vigor and enthusiasm to life and work. These are advantages, especially to people troubled by doubts, inadequate leadership, and little confidence in institutions, as is often the case in contemporary societies. A group possessing an ideology is thus given meaning, direction, and drive. Nations and peoples have left their mark on history, whether for good or ill, to the extent to which they possessed a comprehensive and compelling ideology—consider, for example, ancient Rome (Pax Romana), Victorian England (Mother England), and Nazi Germany (master race). Currently the ideologies of Christian and Islamic fundamentalists have a strong impact.

Most of the important things we do stem from an often implicit ideology, from raising children to going to work, from conducting foreign policy to meeting neighbors. Even a position that ideologies are unnecessary or oppressive is itself an ideology. Subgroups within a society, such as the Rotary Club, also possess an ideology. Generally the more embracing a group, movement, or state, the more comprehensive will be its ideology.

On the other hand, ideologies have some disadvantages. They can rigidify. They may lock people and systems into classes, roles, and expectations. A doctrinaire ideology can cause fanaticism, intransigence, and uncompromising attitudes (e.g., white supremacy). It can impede progress and cause problems for those in the group who oppose elements of the ideology, often those who are the most creative and talented. The group then may expend much effort defending its position instead of looking to the future.

Leaders of a nation should examine their place in history and spell out national values and the ideology in which they are embedded, thus clarifying them for themselves and for their followers. Demands for a clarification of one's ideology come from a variety of sources:

**1.** Many are asking themselves, their peers, and their national leaders: What are we about? What are our goals? What is worth living for? Why?

**2.** Less restrictive government regulation requires that individuals and organizations have their own internalized goals, ethics, and self-discipline—which take into account the public interest and the common good.

**3.** As the population increases and we live closer together, we find that what one person does often affects others. Many actions place burdens on *other* people—for example, building a Wal-Mart on farmland, driving a pollution-producing SUV, or moving a business to a water-scarce area. As government officials, managers, or citizens, we need criteria for making decisions that impinge upon others.

**4.** Disagreements over public policy—for example, taxes, support for the poor, and pollution control—force us back to more basic questions about what kind of society we want, what our priorities are, and what tradeoffs we are willing to make. Special interest groups plead their own causes, but do not address the common good. Under such conditions, people often find it easier to know what they dislike than what they like—their positive goals, values, and policies—even though the latter are more important.

We all need to face such questions in order to clarify personal and corporate values and goals. Each person is challenged to work out her or his own answers to such basic questions, to formulate her or his own constellation of values. Moreover, some consensus is necessary on these values in order to articulate consistent national policies. Without an agreed-upon ideology, major policy decisions are made based on unexamined and short-term criteria; popular myth; and the most recent, vocal, and powerful special-interest groups. The agreed-upon values, especially those that touch upon the issues of public life, are an ideology. As such, they provide direction and verve. A firm's ideology provides a clearer psychological contract and potentially greater satisfaction in the workplace for the individual.[33] And an awareness of the dangers of any ideology—for example, that it may mask privilege or that it may rigidify—should better enable us to avoid those dangers. There is a parallel need for a mission statement for business firms, and this will be discussed in Chapter 8.

## Origin and Impact of Ideology

An ideology that is a rationalization of the existing order defends the status quo. An ideology based on ideals that aim to change the status quo into something that is viewed as better can be called utopian. To Americans, *utopian* has an idealistic, pie-in-the-sky, pejorative connotation. Here we will use it as a descriptive term only: An ideology is utopian if it has ideals that transcend reality. Utopian ideologies provide the motivation for groups to act to challenge the existing order. Such utopian ideals "tend to shatter, either partially or wholly, the order of things prevailing at the time."[34]

---

[33]Jeffery A. Thompson and J. Stuart Bunderson, "Violations of Principle: Ideological Currency in the Psychological Contract" *Academy of Management Review,* 28, no. 4 (March 2003).
[34]Karl Mannheim, *Ideology and Utopia,* trans. Louis Wirth and Edward Shils (New York: Harcourt, Brace & World, 1936), p. 192. Quoted by permission.

Many utopias of today become the realities of tomorrow. The principles of freedom and democracy were utopian in the minds of Jefferson, Adams, Washington, and the others who founded the United States. Their notions of individual rights and representation were ideals which, when they were written into the Declaration of Independence and the U.S. Constitution and acted upon, challenged the status quo, shattered the existing order, and caused a revolution. A utopian ideology of freedom for all races in the United States became translated into the civil rights movement of the 1960s. Looking back over the history of rising aspirations, especially in the Western world, the prevailing ideology of freedom was a utopia. Freedom meant freedom of thought and political freedom, which were unheard of and utopian in earlier societies.[35]

Any nation or group that wants to translate its ideals into reality must formulate an ideology that builds on the existing needs, values, and aspirations of the people. This utopian ideology may then catch the imagination and be the inspiration for change. The New Deal (unemployment insurance, minimum wage, etc.), the civil rights movement, the environmental movement, and other social movements all possess an ideology; and each has left a positive imprint on society. For every utopian ideology that eventually becomes reality, however, there are many others that never get beyond the state of ideas. Such ideologies may cause discord in society, and their adherents may be considered fanatical.

It is true that dangers are inherent in any ideology; for example, the dangers of being closed to facts and of fanaticism. Nothing is more removed from actual events than the closed rational system. Under certain circumstances, nothing contains more irrational drive than a fully self-contained intellectualistic world view. Al Qaeda, Nazis, skinheads, survivalists, and the rural militia are examples of groups that get their direction and enthusiasm from an ideology. The lack of meaningful goals and ideology among the majority encourages such fringe groups. Moreover, an absence of a consensus ideology results because many feel themselves perfectly content with the current state of affairs, and thus have little incentive to reflect. These people are comfortable in their condition, and so they defend the status quo.

As long as people are content, they do little reflecting about situations in which they find themselves. They tend to regard their current situation as part of the natural order of things; the way things are is the way they ought to be. An emphasis then evolves that focuses on practical "how to do it" concerns—the means of coping within existing structures. It is only in the face of challenges to the status quo that most people do much reflecting. So the reflection and therefore the ideology of the majority of people is generally not as profound or comprehensive as that of the persons who challenge the status quo. Thus the "most recent antagonist dictates the tempo and the form of the battle."[36]

---

[35]*Ibid.,* p. 203. A presentation of empirical work on ideologies and some synthesis can be found in Chapter 2 of Harrison M. Trice and Janice M. Beyer, *The Cultures of Work Organizations* (Englewood Cliffs, NJ: Prentice Hall, 1993), pp. 35–76. However, Trice and Beyer neglected the empirical work on these subjects from the social issues in management literature.
[36]*Ideology and Utopia,* pp. 219, 229, 231.

## Challenge and Fundamentalism

A valuable by-product of challenge to goals and ideologies is that people are compelled to examine themselves. Making ideology explicit can clarify goals for individuals and society as a whole. A society that has a weak ideology, or one in which ideology seems unimportant, is generally stable, complacent, and at ease in its inherited laws, customs, and ideals. Mannheim presents an impersonal, alienating, and frightening prospect of a nation or group without utopias; a sad, even desperate picture of a society or a people without ideals or engaging goals:

> The disappearance of utopia brings about a static state of affairs in which man himself becomes no more than a thing. We would be faced then with the greatest paradox imaginable, namely, that man, who has achieved the highest degree of rational mastery of existence, left without any ideals, becomes a mere creature of impulses. Thus, after a long, tortuous, but heroic development, just at the highest stage of awareness, when history is ceasing to be blind fate, and is becoming more and more man's own creation, with the relinquishment of utopias, man would lose his will to shape history and therewith his ability to understand it.[37]

On the other hand, injustices can also be perpetrated in the name of an irrational but compelling ideology. Any strong, moving ideology risks being gross, oversimplified, and unjust. Mannheim's own Germany a few years later was to undergo a tragic revolution in the name of "Aryan superiority" and the "master race." "Ethnic cleansers" in Bosnia, Rwanda, and Sudan; neo-fascists; and armed citizen militias are examples of groups that are confident, closed, and paranoid. Each of these ideologies fills a vacuum.

## Suspicion of Ideology

Many people in industrialized nations share a distrust of ideology. In an attempt to outline what has caused the rapid economic development of the United States, Arthur Schlesinger, Jr., acknowledges the physical assets of the continent. But he points out that Native Americans, too, had fertile lands and natural resources, but these original inhabitants never exploited the riches of the land.[38] Schlesinger maintains that the most important element in the economic success story of the United States is the spirit of the settlers. He contends that this spirit manifested itself in three important ways. The first was a faith in education—investment in people through education results in increases in productivity. A second factor encouraging development was the commitment to self-government and representative institutions—democracy is important for releasing people's talents and energies.

---

[37]*Ibid.,* pp. 262–263.
[38]See "Epilogue: The One Against the Many," in Schlesinger and White, *Paths of American Thought* (Boston: Houghton Mifflin, 1963), pp. 531–538.

The third uniquely favorable element in the American spirit, said Schlesinger, was a rejection of ideology—"America has had the good fortune not to be an ideological society." Schlesinger defines ideology as "a body of systematic and rigid dogma by which people seek to understand the world—and to preserve or transform it." Many agree that ideology narrows perspective and distracts one from reality. They would not allow ideology to "falsify reality, imprison experience, or narrow the spectrum of choice."[39] This attitude encourages innovation and experimentation, part of the dominant empirical and pragmatic American approach.

Many in the United States hold the ideology that if each person or group uses its talents, intelligence, and resources to pursue its own long-term self-interest, it will work out most favorably for all. However, the long-run effectiveness of this ideology is questioned by many around the world, especially those whose own freedom and best interests have not been well served.

In sum, without an ideology people lose direction and enthusiasm for life. People cease questioning themselves and their goals, so little new is accomplished on any significant scale, and society does not improve. An ideology is required for a healthy, stable society. An ideology has ideals that are as yet not attained and questions the status quo. Some elements of a *utopian* ideology are needed for a society to improve itself.

## Values in Modern Life

We will now attempt to outline some basic human values, and then give special attention to those values that characterize industrial societies. Focusing on business and the society it serves, veteran business scholar William C. Frederick has identified two basic values of business, "economizing values" and "power-aggrandizing values." He finds that these values are in tension with the third and more important value of society, which he calls "ecologizing values." Economizing is the root of the efficient use of resources and the profit orientation. It is essential to any organization, especially business. "Power aggrandizing" is also common in organizations; it operates when executives, managers, or others wish to accumulate power and status. Not surprisingly, power aggrandizing often thwarts efforts to economize. Although economizing and power aggrandizing are found to varying extent in all business organizations, these values are not sufficient, says Frederick.

The basic value of society is that of ecologizing. Ecologizing is preserving life and what is necessary for life, and it is thus more basic than the two business values that Frederick proposes. Often, ecologizing goals are opposed and hindered by those pursuing economizing and power-aggrandizing values. Nevertheless, ecologizing values must be supported by business leaders if business is to aid, and not injure, people in the long-term.[40]

---

[39]*Ibid.,* pp. 532, 533.
[40]William C. Frederick, *Values, Nature and Culture in the American Corporation* (New York: Oxford University Press, 1995).

There are other values that are more a part of our direct experience and hence our vocabulary. Individualism and enlightened self-interest remain basic values. Moreover, these values affect entire lifestyles, not merely work attitudes. Whenever predominant American values are listed, it is no accident that so many of them support attitudes that are directly related to individualism and enlightened self-interest. The current serious challenge to some of these values will be discussed in later chapters. Here, let us attempt to indicate what these values are.[41]

### Achievement and success

American culture has been and still is characterized by a stress on individual achievement. Sam Walton, who rose from poverty to riches, is a legend. The American myth says that anyone who works hard enough can succeed in what he or she sets out to do. Moreover, when we meet a successful person, we are more impressed if he or she did not inherit wealth. Someone who was born poor and then worked hard to obtain what he or she has is a model. For some, it is embarrassing to be reminded that several of our recent presidents were born into wealthy families.

Money and wealth are valued for the comforts they bring, but even more because they are symbols of success. Income is a signal to the owner and to the world of our own personal worth. People desire growing businesses, large homes, and luxury automobiles; these things indicate success. This achievement and success ideal is manifested most extensively in business. The drive to achieve is especially strong among business managers; this will be discussed in greater detail in Chapter 7.

### Activity and work

A devotion to work on the part of both the unskilled worker and the executive has provided most of the wealth we now enjoy in the United States. Work is respected not only because it results in wealth but also for its own sake—"The devil finds idle hands." A person's self-respect is damaged when he or she is without work. Americans have traditionally not valued leisure for its own sake; it is recreation, and its purpose is that afterward a person can work better. Task orientation has become a compulsion for which Americans are frequently criticized.[42]

Unskilled workers know that even when they are ahead of schedule on their job, they had better appear busy. To call a person lazy is a serious criticism, especially because the amount of activity that a person engages in is something over which he or she seems to have control. Americans set out to shape and control their own lives and their world. They heed the biblical injunction "to subdue the world."

### Efficiency and practicality

Closely related to the foregoing cultural values are efficiency and practicality, which describe methods of working and acting. We have seen how Tocqueville

---

[41]For a basic work to which the author is indebted, see the chapter "Values in American Life" in Robin M. Williams, Jr., *American Society: A Sociological Interpretation*, 3rd ed. (New York: Knopf, 1970), pp. 438–504.

[42]Edward C. Stewart and Milton J. Bennett, *American Cultural Patterns* (Yarmouth, ME: Intercultural Press, 1991), pp. 69–76.

was much impressed by American ingenuity and ability to "get the job done." Americans are often criticized for placing an overemphasis on technique, and having less concern for goals. Critics say that engineers and accountants run American society, and that their values are instrumental and thus only means. These professionals know how to accomplish a specific task but rarely consider whether it is good to do so. A practical person, focusing on efficiency, assumes the basic worth of the task and of the economic and social order itself. A practical orientation requires only short-range adjustments to immediate situations.

Americans are known as people who can quickly and effectively find the best way to accomplish a task. They are active in the search for solutions and are rarely reflective or contemplative. To call an American a "dreamer" or "impractical" is a severe criticism. Characteristically, the best-known American philosophers, such as Dewey, Peirce, and William James, are not idealists but rather pragmatists.

### Equality

The American emphasis on equality is found in early constitutional ideals: All people are created equal. Citizens of the "New World" witnessed the eventual elimination of indentured servitude, imprisonment for debt, primogeniture, slavery, and property requirements for voting and public office. New immigrants were able to acquire land and a free public education, and minorities and women have gained important civil rights.

Observers remark on the unusual informality, frankness, and lack of status consciousness in American interpersonal relations. Such open and direct relations can endure only if they are supported by the values of the equality among all people and the importance of each person. But the value of equality can run counter to that of freedom. When people pursue freedom in the rugged individualist climate in which the fittest survive, it results in a few becoming very rich and many remaining poor. Varying opportunities, talents, and effort will influence what a person can achieve.

Of all the government and corporate policies to bring about better equality of opportunity in the workplace, none meets more opposition than "affirmative action." Those proposing affirmative action hold that, in order to compensate for past discrimination, when an equally qualified minority person or woman is a candidate for a position, the minority person or woman should be chosen. Ironically, both the reason for the practice (to compensate for past discrimination) and the major objections to it (reverse discrimination) stem from the American ideal of equality of opportunity—and more basically, justice.[43]

---

[43]See Theodore V. Purcell and Gerald F. Cavanagh, *Blacks in the Industrial World: Issues for the Manager* (New York: Free Press, 1972), especially Chapter 10, "Equal Versus Preferential Treatment," pp. 275–293.

### External conformity

Visitors find a uniformity in speech, housing, dress, recreation, and attitudes in the United States. Observers point to a certain flatness, to homogeneity, to a lack of serious dissent and challenge. Witness the "uniform" of blue jeans on young people, the desire to own an SUV, and books written on dressing for success.

To individualists, these comments may seem unfair. Yet, on closer examination, American individualism for many consists largely in the rejection of government restrictions on personal and business activity.

### Freedom

Freedom is a prime and most discussed value in American life. The individual has freedom to operate in the social Darwinian world in which the fittest survive best, as we have seen earlier. He or she may freely choose a marriage partner, friends, a home; change jobs; or move. Freedom is the bedrock value not only of our laissez-faire, free enterprise economic system but for most of the rest of American life. Freedom was touted by the Founding Fathers and is touted by the members of the local neighborhood group. American individualism is possible only when freedom is the foundation value.

The value of freedom inspired the women's and civil rights movements. Cultural norms that bind people to expected roles can be oppressive. Freedom urges the elimination of these one-sided and unjust bonds. Defense of freedom is a foundation of American foreign policy, and freedom is the cornerstone of the business system—*free* enterprise. As pointed out earlier, this freedom is primarily for me and mine. Freedom so permeates business ideology that it is discussed in almost every chapter of this book.

### Material comfort

Americans place a high value on a luxurious automobile, a spacious home in the suburbs, and a good meal. The fact that these things are material comforts and that they are highly valued does not tell us why they are valued. For each item, the underlying reasons may range from its being a symbol of achievement to its providing hedonistic gratification in its own right. Younger people are more likely to spend their income on items that bring them comfort than to save for some future need.

The rise in popularity of television, rock concerts, spectator sports, packaged tours, film, and alcohol indicates a greater passivity on the part of people. There seems to be less active participation and more passive desire to be entertained. The drug culture and chemically induced pleasure take this tendency to its limit. Seeking pleasure follows a decline in the Puritan values of self-denial and asceticism.

### Moral orientation and humanitarianism

Although Americans are eminently practical, they still see the world in moral terms. Conduct of self and of others is constantly judged. Someone may be gauged as honest and trustworthy: "a winner," or as lazy: "a loser." Basic honesty and frankness are also part of our moral and humanitarian value orientation. The effectiveness of President Bill Clinton's presidency was limited by his personal moral failings and lack of honesty. Foreign commentators are often surprised at how open and straightforward they find Americans to be. American charities and social legislation since the 1930s showcase Americans' humanitarian attitudes. Social Security, the minimum wage, and medical care for the poor are examples of our attempt to take care of the less fortunate. However, a moral person can become cynical if that person finds his or her moral code to be superficial, inapplicable, or too idealistic.

### Patriotism

Every society has a sense of the greater value of its own people. Anthropologists tell us how in tribal societies the rules of respect for another's person and property do not apply to "outsiders"; rather, they apply only to the members of one's own tribe. Racism and sexism stem from these same parochial values.

In the United States loyalties in the early days of the republic were more to local cities (e.g., Boston, Philadelphia) than to the states. For business and defense, our loyalties go to the nation. Individual patriotism is often considered a moral issue.

### Rationality and measurement

This value is probably best exemplified when approaching a problem. A person is expected to be objective, to gather the facts first, and not to be unduly influenced by bias or emotions. The scientific method, which embodies this approach, is the model for problem solving. If data for a solution can be measured, that will make the solution more objective and therefore acceptable.

The value of science is demonstrated in its intelligent use in mastering our external environment. This orientation is compatible with a culture that does not value emotion, and looks on the world as open to eventual control.

### Optimism and the inevitability of progress

The combination of an immigrant people willing to work hard and what seemed like unlimited natural resources and the existence of the frontier created an optimistic atmosphere in the United States during the nineteenth and much of the twentieth centuries. Anything could be accomplished if only one put one's mind to it. The result was a growth of jobs, products, and cities.

We define progress largely in economic terms. As long as sales and the gross national product are increasing, progress is occurring. Figure 5-1 charts the growth or decrease of each of the values we have discussed previously. The problems stemming from global competition, stagnating wages, wasteful use of finite resources, the necessity of rethinking what "progress" is, and the impact these issues are having on business and business values will be discussed in greater detail in Chapters 8, 9, and 10.

|                                              | Increase or Decrease*<br>1945–2005 |
|----------------------------------------------|:----------------------------------:|
| Achievement and success                      | + –                                |
| Activity and work                            | –                                  |
| Efficiency and practicality                  | + –                                |
| Equality                                     | +                                  |
| External conformity                          | +                                  |
| Freedom                                       | + –                                |
| Material comfort                             | +                                  |
| Moral orientation and humanitarianism        | –                                  |
| Patriotism                                   | –                                  |
| Rationality and measurement                  | + –                                |
| Optimism and the inevitability of progress   | –                                  |

+ = increase          – = decrease
+ – = indicates evidence of both

**FIGURE 5-1**  Changing Importance of Basic American Values

*Adapted from Robin M. Williams, *American Society; Harrison Trice and Janice Beyer, The Cultures of Work Organizations.*

# THE NECESSITY OF AN IDEOLOGY FOR BUSINESS

An ideology is essential for business, as it is for any social system.[44] For people in a business firm an ideology (or a mission statement) supports shared values, decisions, operations, and cooperation.[45]

An ideology is important for a business that has global operations, because it can provide a useful response to several problems:

1. Global operations require a firm to be clear about its goals and objectives, because many managers are operating in different continents and cultures. Yet markets demand that a firm be flexible and able to quickly meet new needs. An ideology provides goals but not a straitjacket.

[44]Richard M. Weiss, in *Managerial Ideology and the Social Control of Deviance in Organizations* (New York: Praeger, 1986), presents ideology as a social control mechanism in the rehabilitation of alcoholics and other "troubled" employees.
[45]Janice M. Beyer, "Ideologies, Values, and Decision Making in Organizations," in *Handbook of Organizational Design,* ed. Paul C. Nystrom and William H. Starbuck, vol. 2 (New York: Oxford University Press, 1981), pp. 166–202. This provides an overview of social science research on values and ideologies in organizations. See also Richard M. Weiss and Lynn E. Miller, "The Concept of Ideology in Organizational Analysis," *Academy of Management Review,* 12 (January 1987): 104–116.

**2.** Executives sometimes manage for short-term results and neglect long-term planning and needed investment for the firm. An ideology and a mission statement help managers to focus on the long-range goals of the firm.

**3.** Some have long questioned the legitimacy of the corporation. Since the corporation was originally chartered to serve a public purpose, does its present form retain any legitimacy? An acceptable and even inspiring ideology helps to provide legitimacy.

Managers and scholars alike know the importance of organizational legitimacy.[46] They know that without a mission statement, it is difficult for businesspeople to move swiftly to make decisions, establish new policies, rectify abuses, and defend themselves against unfair attacks. More basically, without an ideology, the corporation risks losing its privileged position in the United States, perhaps even its legitimacy. Adolph A. Berle expressed his now classic position on the corporation:

> Whenever there is a question of power there is also a question of legitimacy. These instrumentalities of tremendous power have the slenderest claim of legitimacy. . . . Legitimacy, responsibility and accountability are essential to any power system if it is to endure.[47]

Notice how Berle links legitimacy, responsibility, and accountability. In clarifying these basic issues, the corporation is on weak ground. Without reviewing the classic position of Berle and Means,[48] suffice it to say that the corporation is responsible to no one. Management often has little ownership, yet makes decisions. Shareholders generally have little input into major corporate decisions, although various fund managers have recently exercised some influence. The board of directors is elected from a slate chosen by the board itself.[49] If three directors are to be elected, only three candidates are on the ballot. This is hardly a democratic process.

Questioning the corporation's power and legitimacy goes to the heart of its purpose and responsibilities. The role and responsibilities of the chief executive officer and the board of directors will be discussed in more detail in Chapter 8. As we will see, assessment of these issues requires understanding the purpose and responsibilities of the corporation, its very reason for existence — its ideology.

An ideology for the individual firm and for business in general will enable executives and others to answer the questions of purpose and legitimacy. Without accountability and a clear statement of purpose, business risks losing its respected

---

[46]See Mark C. Suchman, "Managing Legitimacy: Strategic and Institutional Approaches," *Academy of Management Review,* 20 (July 1995): 571–610.

[47]Adolph A. Berle, *Economic Power and the Free Society* (New York: Fund for the Republic, 1958), p. 16.

[48]Adolph A. Berle and Gardiner C. Means, *The Modern Corporation and Private Property* (New York: Macmillan, 1932). David Cowan Bayne, a disciple of Berle, maintains that trust is the essential controlling element of corporate power. See his *Philosophy of Corporate Control* (Chicago: Loyola University Press, 1986).

[49]Harold S. Geneen, "Why Directors Can't Protect the Shareholders," *Fortune,* September 17, 1984, pp. 28–32.

position in American society. A firm's statement of purpose must be understandable to its many stakeholders and the firm must be held accountable to act according to it; otherwise, the rebuilding of trust in business will not happen. The following chapters are intended to aid that rebuilding.

## SUMMARY AND CONCLUSIONS

The business values described in this chapter supported a period of expansion, rapid growth, and exploitation of land and resources. They exploited the immigrant's eagerness for work and gave the poor an opportunity to advance. They also gave a new nation its railroads, mines, banks, manufacturing firms, and cities.

Visitors to America note an honesty, frankness, and directness. They find a pragmatic people who do not spend time on unproductive theorizing. Freedom is a bedrock value that has been institutionalized in our Constitution, laws, and attitudes.

Several elements contributed to this new American business ideology:

1. The **frontier** provided opportunities to the immigrants who had come to the New World looking for new opportunities in farming, mining, or manufacturing, where potential rewards were immense.
2. The **Protestant ethic**, which underscored the value of hard work, was carried to the New World by the Puritans and translated into a secular vision by people like Benjamin Franklin.
3. Faith in **free enterprise** gave a person motivation and confidence. The system encouraged economic growth, and was shown to be intellectually and practically sound by the classical economists.
4. **Competition** became more explicit because of the theory of evolution and the principles of natural selection and the survival of the fittest. Natural forces, operating without constraint, would identify the efficient firm.
5. The **role of government** was to apply as few constraints as possible to business activity; its central purpose was to protect the private property of its citizens. Thomas Jefferson is often quoted: "That government is best which governs least."

It is an irony of history that emphasis on the rugged individualist peaked during the latter half of the nineteenth century, just at the time the business scene was dominated by oligopolies and trusts. One or a few firms in each industry (e.g., U.S. Steel and Standard Oil) virtually controlled production, prices, and even wages. It was difficult for an individual, no matter how rugged, to raise the capital necessary to compete. Since that time, it has become apparent that this American business ideology, although it provides a motivation and a vision for the entrepreneur, is not an entirely accurate description of the marketplace. For the market is not totally free.

The values of American Puritans—hard work, competition, regular habits, diligence, self-control, sobriety, saving, and planning ahead—constitute what is called the Protestant ethic. These values were preached in church, school, and town meetings.

Given this historical background, this chapter assessed the current major values and ideologies of Americans. Business and business values exist in society, yet people have considerable suspicion of business, especially big business. An adequate response to this lack of trust is possible only by spelling out an ideology for business firms that better meets their needs and the expectations of citizens.

The goal of the traditional American business ideology is expansion and growth; the goal of business is material reward for the individual. But the assumption that an individual always seeks more material goods leads to further questions. Is the goal of more material goods sufficient to motivate the morally mature person to give most of her or his physical and psychic energy to the business enterprise? Are there other personal values in an affluent society that must be tapped if we are to continue to be economically successful and a healthy society? To what extent will one's "calling" continue to be central in one's life? Is a goal of material growth necessary for a business creed for the future? If so, what sort of growth? These and other, similar questions will be addressed in the following chapters.

## DISCUSSION QUESTIONS

1. Citing historic events and attitudes, indicate what characteristic American values were illustrated during the silver-mining days at Virginia City, Nevada. How does the Sutro Tunnel demonstrate both the positive and negative values?
2. According to Ralph Waldo Emerson, how does one achieve success and wealth?
3. Describe the hours, wages, and working conditions of poor people, immigrants, and children before 1920.
4. Describe the attitude of people in the Establishment churches to the new immigrant laborers in the United States in the late 1800s.
5. Compare the values shown by the factory owners with those of the Establishment churches during roughly 1860–1890.
6. What are the similarities and dissimilarities between the Protestant ethic and American individualism?
7. Outline how the Protestant ethic aided in the economic development of the New World.
8. What are the two conflicting responsibilities of churches? How does your church meet each of these responsibilities?
9. Outline the arguments of Conwell and Carnegie on the goodness of acquisitiveness and wealth.
10. What was Andrew Carnegie's position on wages? What was his justification for the wealth of the rich? Is this position held today? If so, by whom?
11. According to Carnegie, how should a wealthy person use one's wealth? For self? Or for society? Why?
12. Compare Carnegie's attitudes on work with those of Frederick W. Taylor (scientific management). What do they have in common? How do they differ?
13. What are the insights of Teilhard de Chardin, Albert Einstein, Amos Oz, and Akio Morita on the American character? Describe common themes that run through their observations.

14. Distinguish between values, goals, ideals, and ideologies.
15. What is an ideology? What does a utopian ideology do for a society?
16. How do values relate to an ideology?
17. What sort of an ideology do people in the United States possess? Is it utopian?
18. What are the advantages and disadvantages to a society of having a well-articulated ideology? What happens to a society without such an ideology?
19. Do Americans possess a utopian ideology? Describe the American ideology as you see it.
20. Are the American values outlined in this chapter predominant for the average American? For people in your environment? For you?
21. Do businesses today possess a consistent and motivating ideology? What are the disadvantages of not having such a business ideology?
22. What is the ultimate purpose of a business? Is it to make a profit? Or is it to provide jobs and family income, while also providing quality goods and/or service at a low price? What is the difference?
23. To repeat the questions in the summary of the chapter: Are there other personal values in our affluent society that must be tapped if we are to continue to be an economically successful and healthy people? To what extent will one's "calling" continue to be central in one's life? Is a goal of material growth necessary for a business creed for the future? If so, what sort of growth?
24. Does your firm have a mission and goal statement? Is it comprehensive and motivating?

## CASES

## Case 5-1  Educational Reimbursement

Rob Stewart, an assistant professor of marketing, is teaching the introductory marketing course for the fall term at Southwestern State University; there will be about 600 in the course. Stewart can select from among six basic marketing texts, and he negotiates with various publishers to determine which will provide the best "educational reimbursement" (that is, gifts to a person or department of computers, teaching software, or dollars). The publishing house of Smith and Luster agrees to $600 worth of reimbursement, and Stewart decides on its text even though it is not as good as another text.

1. How do you judge the ethics of Stewart's decision?
2. Is there a conflict of interest here? Explain.
3. Who benefits? Make any necessary distinctions. ■

## Case 5-2  Safe Drug

Your firm has developed a prescription drug that cures the flu. The Food and Drug Administration (FDA) has delayed giving it clearance. Your own scientists think that the drug is safe, and that the FDA is overly cautious. Other governments, which also have high standards for safety, have approved the drug for sale in their countries.

1. Should your firm market the drug overseas?
2. Or should you wait for U.S. approval? ■

## EXERCISE

### International Management Consultant

Business today is global. To be successful, businesspeople must understand other *cultures* and other peoples. A fellow student from another country is a resource for learning about that person's country and its people. The purpose of this project is to learn about the climate for living and doing business in a country that has different customs, expectations, laws, and language. Consult someone from another country who has been in her or his home country within the previous 6 months for information and help.

## *Procedure*

1. Find a student from another country who will help you. Try not to overburden the same consultant.
2. Examine a social issue that faces business. For example:
   a. Equal employment opportunities (minorities or women)
   b. Air or water pollution
   c. Marketing or advertising practices
   d. Safety of products or workplace
   e. Corruption: bribery, kickbacks, tax evasion, or other practices
   f. Operation of foreign firms within the country
   g. Host government regulations
   h. Other (consult instructor)
3. Prepare a summary report on a single sheet of paper outlining the following:
   a. Country chosen
   b. Name of international student consultant
   c. The issue or problem examined, and provide some background
   d. Any special industry or firm involved

## EXERCISE

### An American Ideology

A utopian vision or ideology that is intelligent, consistent, and inspiring is necessary for any society to advance. The Declaration of Independence was such an ideology; it motivated early citizens to risk their lives and fortunes for the country. Commentators have noted that in recent federal election campaigns little utopian vision of society is presented to citizens by candidates of either party. Sound bites, 30-second TV ads, negative attacks, and appealing to special interests, crowd out and make it difficult to outline a vision that will appeal to most U.S. citizens.

For this exercise, outline in a few paragraphs (maximum one page) an ideology for U.S. citizens that is cohesive, motivating, and inspiring. You might choose to use as a beginning some of the values outlined in this chapter. Moreover, you may include any additional values or ideals that you think appropriate.

# CHAPTER 6

# Critics of Capitalism

> Seven blunders of the world that lead to violence:
> politics without principle,
> wealth without work,
> commerce without morality,
> pleasure without conscience,
> education without character,
> science without humanity,
> worship without sacrifice.
>
> MAHATMA GANDHI (1869–1948)

Free enterprise, or capitalism, is the socioeconomic system of most of the countries of the world. Free enterprise has come to be taken for granted almost as much as the air we breathe. We have seen in earlier chapters the great strengths and also the severe weaknesses of free markets. Hence free enterprise has many critics; and no critique has proven as perceptive or as comprehensive as that of Karl Marx. Marx raises serious questions about the moral and social consequences of capitalism. He had an extraordinary ability to pinpoint and articulate the deficiencies of the free market system. On the other hand, Marx and his followers have not been successful in providing a workable alternative to capitalism.[1]

For much of the twentieth century, the Soviet Union, Eastern Europe, and other nations had collectivist economies and Marxist governments. These nations equitably improved their economies and provided jobs. Marxism became the banner around the world for many who sought to support the plight of the poor. Nevertheless, because of inefficiencies, favoritism, trampling on individual rights, and persecution of critics, these governments fell in the early 1990s.

Nevertheless, Marxism and the attempts to organize people and production cooperatively are important movements in world history, and deserve our attention. Their ideology stands in contrast to the ideology of free markets and self-interest.

---

[1]Arthur F. McGovern authored this chapter in the first three editions of this book. I remain indebted for his friendship, wisdom, insights, and competence.

There is much that is admirable in their practices of shared living and working. Moreover, we can learn from their valid criticisms of free enterprise, and the alternative values that they espouse.[2]

Throughout history most communities worldwide and many still today are built on cooperative, rather than competitive, ideals. Medieval European communities were more cooperative than their contemporary counterparts. Stable populations, extended families, and guilds, living within walking distance of one another, gave these early communities cohesion. On the other hand, these communities also had a rigid hierarchical social system. If your father was a carpenter, so too were you. This remains true today of many communities in Africa and Asia, and among Native Americans. We will discuss examples of cooperative economic communities later in this chapter.

American free markets are only one version of a market economy. The European Union is close to the American model, but European governments provide greater guidance for their economies; for example, they provide health care for all. China now has a free market economy, although it still has a repressive Communist government. Russia and Eastern Europe also have "free" markets, although the state has a stronger role. Since the fall of Communism, some countries, including Russia, are dominated by unscrupulous captains of the market system, with predictable results: a few huge fortunes; many unemployed; products, contracts, and advertisements that cannot be trusted; pollution, bribery, favoritism, and organized crime. Some of these problems characterize China today, also.

Before examining the criticisms of capitalism, let us step back for a moment to probe some of our *own beliefs*. To obtain additional clarity on your own goals, beliefs, and value system, ponder these questions. What do *you* believe regarding the following:

1. Is competition the most effective motivator for you? Is cooperation more effective, or do you respond to some combination?
2. Are human beings essentially good, needing only support and encouragement for their development, or are they essentially self-seeking, such that an economic system is wise to build on this selfishness and make the best use of it?
3. Are human beings headed for progress and a better life or for overcrowded cities, depleted resources, and a decline of civilization?
4. If neither progress nor decline is inevitable, do we have it in our power to influence our society and the world 10 years hence? If so, in what way?
5. Does life end at death? Is there an afterlife? How does your response influence your life, work, and attitudes?
6. Have you ever thought about the above questions or do you put them aside—either because you do not understand their relevance or because you judge that you do not have time to consider them?

---

[2]Jerry Z. Muller, *The Mind and the Market: Capitalism in Modern European Thought* (New York: Knopf, 2002); "Marx After Communism: As a System of Government, Communism Is Dead or Dying; As a System of Ideas, Its Future Looks Secure," *Economist,* December 21, 2002.

Your answers to these questions can expose the framework you use in making daily and long-term decisions. It is possible that you have not thought much about these questions. Perhaps your goals, values, and ethics have been taken from other people: parents, peers, neighbors, media, or superiors at work. In that case, you are making decisions, some everyday and others having immense implications, without examining the assumptions beneath your decisions. Problems which stem from this posture, and how people cope or fail to cope, will be discussed in Chapter 7.

Each of the above questions can be asked of any of the major leaders we have examined in this book. If we asked these questions of Bernard of Clairvaux, John Calvin, Benjamin Franklin, Adam Smith, Karl Marx, or Mahatma Gandhi, how would they respond? With that background, let us now continue our examination of Marx's critique of capitalism.

# THE MARXIST CRITIQUE

Karl Marx's (1818–1883) criticisms of capitalism were incisive and based on empirical studies. His language was intentionally polemic; he and his followers used terms like *exploitation, imperialism,* and *alienation.*[3] These criticisms come from a viewpoint that is foreign to most Americans. Despite the differences in language, values, and attitudes, the Marxist critique helps us to examine national priorities and the values that govern our economic, political, and social policies. If we seek an objective examination of the goals and values of free enterprise, we must not neglect its critics.

A man of real genius, Marx had both analytic power and an ability to weld his ideas into an overall theory of history. According to his theory, economic forces are the primary determinant of history. Economic structures give rise to class differences; class conflicts provoke social and political struggles. Marx thought class conflict between workers and owners would inevitably erupt in revolution and usher in a new socialist system of production.

Marx pointed out that economists view the factors of production (money, raw material, and labor) as things. Marx insisted that economics does not deal only in things; it involves social relations. Every commodity produced and sold and every wage paid involves very definite relationships between human beings. In failing to recognize these social relations, capitalist theory ignores the real effects of the system on human beings and society.

This basic critique can be divided into several accusations made by critics of the capitalist system. Some may find these accusations exaggerated and one-sided. But we present them in the conviction that intelligent criticism leads to a more just and effective socioeconomic system.

## Exploitation of the Worker

Free enterprise, following Adam Smith, is based on the theory that when people work for their own self-interest, they will simultaneously contribute to the

---

[3]John E. Elliott, "On the Possibility of Marx's Moral Critique of Capitalism," *Review of Social Economy,* 44 (October 1986): 130–144.

welfare of all. Everyone profits from economic growth, and each person receives monetary rewards in proportion to his or her efforts and skill. Marxists challenge these assumptions. For Marx, who knew the Industrial Revolution during its grimmest stage, it was difficult to see how workers benefited proportionate to their labors. As we saw in Chapter 5, factory workers lived in hovels, worked exhausting 12-hour workdays 6 days a week, and died prematurely. Marx's classic work, *Capital,* describes the price paid in human suffering for industrial growth: workers suffering from pulmonary diseases caused by the dust and heat of factories, small children working 15-hour days, a young girl dying of exhaustion after 26 consecutive hours of work.[4] Workers were forced to live on subsistence wages while owners acquired fortunes and lived in luxury.

In capitalist countries the gap that existed a century ago between the poor and the wealthy remains today. In some developed countries labor unions and government legislation have brought higher wages and better working conditions. But in order to provide lower cost consumer goods, globalization forces slimmer margins on producers, and the "outsourcing" of work takes many formerly well-paid jobs, both skilled and unskilled, to countries where wages are much less. The less-skilled jobs left in the United States are low wage, and most often without medical or retirement benefits.[5] Globalization and its effects are a result of free markets and capitalism.

If one looks to the *distribution* of wealth and income, very large inequalities are present, and those gaps are increasing. In a study of incomes in 16 industrialized countries during two recent decades, the United States had the *greatest inequality* of all. The income gap between the rich and the poor was wider in the United States than in any other industrialized country. Next in income disparity were Ireland, Italy, Canada, Australia, and Britain, in that order. Finland had the least disparity, followed by Sweden, Belgium, Netherlands, Norway, and West Germany. By another measure, the top fifth of income earners' share of national income rose from 44 percent in 1973 to 50 percent in 2000. Even more skewed, we find that the wealthiest 1 percent of all households control 38 percent of national wealth, while the bottom 80 percent control only 17 percent. However, note that in an opinion poll, 19 percent of all Americans believe themselves to be in that top 1 percent. In another measure of growing inequality, in 2000 the richest 20 percent of the global population received 60 times the income of the poorest 20 percent, whereas in 1960 it was 30 times.[6]

For a Marxist, the reason for this gap is clear. At best, workers can only bargain for higher wages. Managers determine compensation both for workers and for themselves. The manager controls the system, and inequalities are a result. Workers

---

[4]Karl Marx, "The Working Day," *Capital,* vol. 1 (New York: International Publishers, 1967), pp. 244–254.
[5]Aaron Bernstein, "Waking Up from the American Dream: Dead-end Jobs and the High Cost of College Could Be Choking off Upward Mobility," *Business Week,* December 1, 2003, pp. 54–58.
[6]Richard J. Ward, "Worsening Income Gaps and a Sustainable Future," *International Journal of Social Economics,* 29, no. 6 (2002): 480–490; "Inequality: Would You Like Your Class War Shaken or Stirred?" *Economist,* September 5, 2003, p. 28; Edward N. Wolff, *Top Heavy: The Increasing Inequality of Wealth in American and What Can Be Done About It* (New York: The New Press, 2002).

are not paid the full value of their work contribution, according to Marx. The difference, the surplus value, between the value workers add to the product and their actual wage, is the source of profit.

Marx argued that profit is the surplus after all costs have been paid. Marxists recognize the need for investment in new equipment and research; their only quarrel is when it is privately possessed and controlled. If workers are a prime source of production, then they, not managers and owners, should be prime beneficiaries, and they should also have a significant voice in the production process. For a Marxist, the fact that labor unions have reduced inequities for workers does not alter the basic fact of exploitation. The manager still seeks to pay as little as possible for workers' services. The resulting profits or "surplus" are not the rewards of the capitalist's hard work or enterprising spirit, but simply result from ownership of property and control over the work of others.

Sweatshops are common in Asia and Latin America, and exist even in the United States. Workers labor 12 hours a day, 6 days a week for less than minimum wage, and are often kept in virtual slavery. Adolescent girls sew and assemble shoes, sportswear, toys, and name-brand garments. The purchasing policies of firms like Wal-Mart and Nike almost demand that clothes and shoes be manufactured under such low-cost conditions. The garments and shoes are often sold at premium prices, and the profit goes to owners.

Marx challenged the contention that wealth is the product of "free" enterprise. In the past, could the wealthy be said to have "earned" their total income without acknowledging the takeover of native lands, slavery, or the minimal wages paid immigrant workers, as we saw in the previous chapter? Or today, do low-paid service workers receive a wage proportionate to their work when top executives of the same company earn 450 times their salary? The problem of the poor falling further behind will probably become worse, since well-paying careers require a college education and often the right connections. The odds are not in favor of a young person growing up in a poor, single-parent family and attending an inner-city school.

The income gap between top managers and others in their firms continues to increase. In the United States, excessive chief executive officer (CEO) pay is of concern to workers, shareholders, and the public. The pay of CEOs has risen to 531 times that of the average employee in the United States. Compare this to other countries: Brazil: 57; Mexico: 46; U.K.: 25; Canada: 21; France: 16; Germany: 11; and Japan: 10. J. P. Morgan once said that CEOs should receive no more than 20 times the average salary in their firm. At the 100 largest firms in the United States, median CEO compensation in 2002 rose 14 percent, in spite of the fact that average return to these firms was down 22 percent. This is hardly pay for performance. Because of excessive CEO compensation, shareholders have rebelled and are threatening to try to replace company directors if they do not exercise more effective oversight.[7]

---

[7]Gretchen Morgenson, "Explaining Why the Boss Is Paid So Much," *New York Times,* January 25, 2004, p. BU1; Jerry Useem, "Have They No Shame," *Fortune,* April 28, 2003, p. 57; "Executive Pay: Labor Strikes Back," *Business Week,* May 26, 2003, p. 46. For current data on the pay of hundreds of CEOs, see www.paywatch.org. This site is maintained by the AFL-CIO.

These large salary increases were granted at a time when many of these same executives were cutting jobs and asking others to accept pay reductions. Two examples illustrate different approaches. Ronald W. Allen, CEO of Delta Airlines, announced the reduction of 15,000 jobs, about 20 percent of the workforce; Allen did not take a bonus and actually took a pay reduction himself. He said that if flight attendants, reservation clerks, and others were taking pay cuts, he should do the same. Allen has worked for Delta all his life, and he wants to maintain solidarity with the rest of the workforce and support their loyalty. On the other hand, Donald Carty, CEO of American Airlines, negotiated sweeping wage concessions from the major unions, because the airline was facing serious financial difficulties—perhaps even bankruptcy. However, just weeks before these negotiations a $41 million pension fund was set up for 45 top executives, and they were granted bonuses worth twice their salaries. When this became public, the bonuses were canceled and Carty was forced to resign. Carty was more concerned with the welfare of the executives than the loyalty of the workers. In another case, Albert J. "chainsaw Al" Dunlap, CEO of Scott Paper, announced cuts in the Scott workforce of about one-third or 11,200 jobs. He then received $3.5 million in salary and bonus, while his predecessor the previous year had received but $618,000. He argues that he added much to shareholder value. Concern for solidarity and loyalty of the workforce were not considerations for Dunlap; he left Scott shortly thereafter and again cut thousands of jobs and gave himself immense pay at Sunbeam. The SEC later charged Dunlap with accounting fraud of $60 million during his tenure at Sunbeam. Edward Brennan of Sears Roebuck announced job cuts of 50,000 and then received a 198 percent increase, to $3 million, the following year. George David, CEO of United Technologies, cut 10,600 jobs, and then received a 115 percent increase in pay. Most CEOs take pay increases in spite of cutting jobs and asking for sacrifice on the part of others in order to cut costs. As a result of the above, 68 percent of Americans think that the top executives of large U.S. companies make too much money.[8]

Critics of free enterprise argue that investments produce more income than does work itself. A study of people who reported incomes of $1 million or more showed that only 4 percent of their income came from salaries; the rest came from dividends and capital gains.[9] Estate or inheritance taxes attempt to give everyone a more equitable advantage in beginning a career and life. For this reason William H. Gates, Sr., the father of Microsoft founder Bill Gates, despite both his and his son's considerable wealth, advocates a steep inheritance tax. Both Andrew Carnegie and John D. Rockefeller used their wealth to fund libraries and education. Gates, Sr. cites U.S. Supreme Court Justice Oliver Wendell Homes: "Taxes are the price we pay for civilization."[10] As important as these issues are,

[8]Hugh M. O'Neill and D. Jeffery Lenn, "Voices of Survivors: Words that Downsizing CEOs Should Hear," *Academy of Management Executive,* 9 (November 1995): 23–34; "Too Much Corporate Power?" *Business Week,* September 11, 2000, p. 149.

[9]Richard C. Edwards, Michael Reich, and Thomas E. Weisskopf, eds., *The Capitalist System* (Englewood Cliffs, NJ: Prentice Hall, 1986), pp. 223–224; Ferdinand Lundberg, *The Rich and the Super-Rich* (New York: Bantam Books, 1968), pp. 43, 935–936.

[10]William H. Gates, Sr. and Chuck Collins, *Wealth and Our Commonwealth: Why America Should Tax Accumulated Fortunes* (Boston: Beacon Press, 2003).

Marx was concerned about more than the distribution of wealth and a fair wage for work done.

## Alienation of the Worker

Job dissatisfaction and a lack of commitment and loyalty are common among working people today. Marx saw the roots of this when he charged that work was forced and dehumanizing. The work is forced because jobs are scarce and the average worker, though theoretically free to accept a job or not, has little choice but to take the job. Nor do workers have much freedom in the way they do their work. Most do their job in the way and at the pace designated. The work is thus dehumanizing because it does not enable workers to make decisions, to be inventive, or to develop different skills. Few jobs challenge one's real skills, imagination, or spirit. The worker is often simply an appendage to a machine. He "does not affirm himself in his work but denies himself, feels miserable and unhappy, develops no free physical and mental energy but mortifies his flesh and ruins his mind." The capitalist works him as he would "a horse that he has hired for a day."[11]

Free enterprise emphasizes the goals of efficiency and increasing share-holder value more than humanizing work. In most traditional societies one's work was one's life. Work, play, and social life flowed into each other. Work meant simply tasks to be done, and there was no division of life into work and non-work. For most moderns, in contrast, work has unpleasant connotations. Note the number of people who take early retirement. Because of increasing specialization, a worker is assigned to a small portion of a task. The work is finished by another, out of sight and out of mind. Thus there is little sense of satisfaction from work. Many jobs simply call for a capacity to follow exact routines in an orderly way, such as fast-food work. As a result, work does not mean much to most of those people and they do not enjoy it.[12]

Workers are not asked to use their minds or to be creative. Frederick Taylor proposed scientific management in the late nineteenth century (see Chapter 5), and it influenced the U.S. system of production by deliberately divorcing mental and physical labor. Taylor wrote:

> The managers assume the burden of gathering together all of the traditional knowledge which in the past has been possessed by the workmen and then of classifying, tabulating, and reducing this knowledge to rules, laws, and formula. All possible brain work should be removed from the shop and centered in the planning or laying-out department.[13]

[11]Marx, *Capital,* vol. 1, p. 185; Loyd D. Easton and Kurt H. Guddat, trans. and eds., *Writings of the Young Marx* (Garden City, NY: Anchor, 1967), p. 292.
[12]Kenneth Keniston, "The Alienating Consequences of Capitalist Technology," in Edwards, Reich, and Weisskopf, *The Capitalist System,* pp. 269–273; see also Herbert Gintis's essay on alienation, which follows Keniston's.
[13]Harry Braverman, *Labor and Monopoly Capital: The Degradation of Work in the Twentieth Century* (New York: Monthly Review, 1974), pp. 31–39, 112–118.

Assembly lines carried this concept of mechanized labor to its fullest expression. Henry Ford's decision in 1914 to raise workers' pay to $5 a day was hailed as an enlightened, progressive move done to enable workers to become better customers. Critics maintain that this view overlooks the fact that Ford faced an angry revolt by workers against his new assembly lines. The turnover rate in 1913 at Ford Motor Company was 963 percent.[14] Such work does not allow for creativity on the job, and this is true not only in manual work but in clerical work as well. The drive for speed and efficiency reduces work to simplified, routinized, and measured tasks.

Although work is sometimes inhumane, unemployment proves still far more degrading. To speak of *only* 5 percent unemployed does little to describe the frustration, powerlessness, and anxiety of millions of unemployed people. Unemployment benefits may permit an income on which to live for a short time, but it is dehumanizing. From a Marxist perspective, worker exploitation and alienation are among the most serious failures of the free enterprise system. More on the effect of the work environment on workers will be reviewed in the next chapter.

## Big Business Dominates National Goals

Americans take pride in their democracy: "Whatever its faults, it's the best in the world." Every citizen has a voice in the government. All can vote; all can aspire to political office. The two-party system offers choices in policies and candidates. The division of the government into executive, legislative, and judiciary branches is a model of balance of power.

Critics challenge this faith in U.S. democracy. These critics do not question the ideals of democracy but rather the claims that they have been realized in the United States or other free market nations. Marx argued that political freedoms created only an "illusion" of true human freedom, because political power reflects economic power. When John Locke, the seventeenth-century English philosopher, stated that the chief end of people uniting to form a government is "the preservation of property," he reflected the goals of his social class of wealthy people. The democratic state in market societies claims to represent the common good of all its citizens, and indeed sometimes it will pass legislation to legitimize that claim. But it serves primarily to further the interests of the wealthy and powerful.[15]

The government provides benefits to business and to the wealthy in many ways. Although some of the wealthy complain of excessive taxes and government regulation, they also benefit disproportionately from government's largess: a reduction of taxes on the wealthy, tax breaks for large firms, and subsidy of many industries and products. A recent study showed that 82 of the largest firms in the United States, including General Electric, Citigroup, SBC Communications, and IBM, paid no federal income tax for at least one of the first three years of the George W. Bush administration. General Electric had the largest saving and

---

[14]*Ibid.,* p. 149.
[15]"The Communist Manifesto," in *The Marx-Engels Reader,* ed. Robert C. Tucker (New York: Norton, 1972), p. 337.

a $9.5 billion tax break for the three-year period. The official U.S. corporate tax rate is 35 percent of profits, but in 2003 the actual corporate tax rate was 1.2 percent, the second lowest rate recorded since 1946.[16] The state also assists business by setting up structures that aid commerce (e.g., subsidizing exports, antitrust and bankruptcy legislation, and the Federal Reserve Bank) and by bearing much of the burden of social expenses (e.g., education, social security, and some health care). Government subsidy of business is illustrated in the automobile industry. Cars need roads, but business does not bear the cost of building them. The federal government pays 90 percent of the cost of interstate freeways and 50 percent of the cost of all other primary roads.

The state subsidizes business, and hence profits, in a variety of ways: subsidizing exports, helping to finance new housing and commercial building, providing tax abatements, funding research, and providing tax exemptions for building depreciation and oil exploration. The policies of the U.S. government have long subsidized "family farms." Yet over the previous two generations the number of small and medium-sized farms has declined dramatically; farming is now dominated by huge agribusinesses such ADM, Tyson, Perdue, Swift, and Cargill which receive most of the benefits of these subsidies. For example, the United States spends $1.7 billion to subsidize the purchase of U.S. cotton, while another $10 billion over 7 years was also given to U.S. cotton farmers.[17] By providing unemployment, welfare, and medical benefits, government tempers the discontent created by unemployment. It pays for much of the cost of cleaning up pollution caused by businesses. Moreover, government picks up most of the responsibility that business escapes through bankruptcy and negligence.

In addition, corporations know how to avoid paying taxes, as we saw above. As a result, average Americans today pay a larger portion of federal taxes than they did two generations ago. At that time roughly half of federal taxes were paid by corporations and half by individuals. However, businesses today pay only 13.7 percent and individuals pay 86.3 percent of federal taxes collected. KPMG and the other major accounting firms set up lucrative tax divisions which advertised that they could eliminate a firm's tax burden by exploiting provisions of the Internal Revenue Service Code.[18]

Because the role of government is to protect the common good of *all citizens,* one might ask how big business obtains such favorable policies. The short answer is influence on government or lobbying. And this lobbying worries many, especially when it is done by means of large financial contributions to help a candidate obtain public office. It is expensive to run for public office because of the cost of advertisements, staff, and polls. Nevertheless Sen. John McCain (R, AZ) has tried to get much of this money out of federal elections. McCain says that the federal campaign finance system is "an elaborate influence peddling scheme in

[16]"Some Top Companies Avoided Federal Income Tax Under Bush," *Wall Street Journal,* September 23, 2004, p. 2.
[17]Elizabeth Becker, "U.S. Subsidizes Companies to Buy Subsidized Cotton," *New York Times,* November 4, 2003, p. C1.
[18]Nanette Byrnes and Louis Lavelle, "The Corporate Tax Game," *Business Week,* March 24, 2003, pp. 79–87.

which both parties conspire to stay in office by selling the country to the highest bidder." In the 1920s the U.S. Congress made it illegal for a corporation to contribute to an American candidate or party, and in 1977 made it illegal for a U.S. corporation to contribute to (i.e., bribe) a foreign political leader. Yet the 2003 legislation to restrict corporate contributions is being sidestepped, because executives who can bundle hundreds of $2,000 personal contributions together are rewarded by the GOP and are called "pioneers" or "rangers."

Charles Lindbloom, in his classic *Politics and Markets,* examines the influence of big business on the state. Lindbloom defends the market economy, but he believes that giant corporations are inconsistent with democracy. Business executives and not government officials, he argues, make most of the public policy decisions that affect the economic life of the nation. Their decisions, in turn, affect almost every aspect of life—jobs, homes, consumer goods, leisure. These executives determine income distribution, allocation of resources, plant locations, the pattern of work, the technologies used, goods produced, the quality of goods and services, and of course executive compensation.[19] These major decisions which affect all citizens are turned over to business leaders and taken off the agenda of government. Thus citizens have no vote at all on policies that touch every sphere of their lives.

But these major decisions only begin to indicate the public role of business leaders. Their influence on government is much greater than that of any other group in society. Public functions in the market system are in their hands. For example, jobs, prices, production, outsourcing, the standard of living, and the economic security of everyone are under their influence. Business leaders are not just representatives of one or more special interest groups; the welfare of all people in a society depends on what they do. When business leaders ask for tax reductions to stimulate investment; subsidies for overseas exports, transportation, and research; for troops to protect investments in foreign countries; or for similar advantages, the state often responds favorably.

Public interest and citizen groups can lobby politicians, but they must use their members' volunteer resources and energies. Corporations can spend corporate funds, work on company time, and can use professional lobbyists to influence legislation. Business executives have myriad avenues by which to present their own point of view. Through lobbying, gifts, entertainment, and real or threatened litigation, business uses its resources to confirm its position and gain approval. Roughly $237 billion a year is spent on advertising and other sales promotion.[20] All of this promotes a firm and a brand, and some of this is corporate advertising with an overtly political content. The money spent on advertising and promotion matches all the funds spent on education and health in the United States. Dissenting voices do not have the resources to compete with dominant business views. It is for these reasons that Lindbloom concludes that the large private corporation is not consistent with democratic theory and

---

[19]Charles Lindbloom, *Politics and Markets: The World's Political-Economic Systems* (New York: Basic Books, 1977), p. 171.
[20]*Statistical Abstract of the United States—2002* (Washington, D.C.: U.S. Department of Commerce, 2002), p. 772.

vision.[21] Critics point out that this same pervasive business control today extends to the entire world.

## Corporations Exploit Other Countries

Much criticism of free enterprise has been directed against the influence of capitalism in poor countries. When people praise the achievements of free enterprise, they point to the overall affluence of Western Europe, Japan, and the United States and the political democracy that accompanies it. But in much of Latin America, the Middle East, Africa, and Asia, free enterprise often accompanies desperate poverty for the majority, corruption, right-wing rule, and exploitation by foreign companics. For example, in El Salvador free enterprise means 2 percent of the population owns 60 percent of the land, and 8 percent receive half of all personal income. The remaining 92 percent of the population live in poverty, and three-fourths of the children suffer from malnutrition. Yet for decades efforts at reform have been crushed by right-wing death squads, often trained in the United States by the U.S. Army at what was called the "School of the Americas" at Fort Benning, Georgia.

Critics argue that capitalist countries want to maintain the status quo in developing countries in order to exploit them. Exploitation has profit as its motive. Less developed countries of the world provide natural resources and cheap labor which make investment profitable, if the political regimes are stable and favorable. Economic development has brought jobs and income for some poor people, and also huge financial rewards to the wealthy elite in Brazil, Colombia, Indonesia, India, and other developing countries.

The very beginnings of capitalism in Europe, many contend, were made possible by the plunder of gold, silver, and other minerals from the American "colonies." Then specialized economies that were less flexible were developed by foreign investors. Today certain products bring to mind specific countries— coffee in Brazil, tin in Bolivia, copper in Chile, sugar in Cuba. But the specialization in such commodities did not result from initiatives within those countries. The economies of these countries were focused by European and U.S. firms to meet needs in the "developed world." The concentration on one or two products generally upset a natural balance of production and created "one-crop" economies dependent on the fluctuating prices in the world market for that one crop. For example, Brazil's northeast was once that country's richest area; now it is its poorest. Portugal granted lands to Brazil's first wealthy landlords, and sugar production flourished for a few generations. When depleted and eroded soil resulted, the landlords took their profits and left.[22] Barbados, in the West Indies, suffered the same fate. It once produced a variety of crops and livestock on small holdings: cotton, tobacco, oranges, cows, and pigs. Cane fields

---

[21]Lindbloom, *Politics and Markets,* pp. 172ff, 195, 214; see also the new criticism of the corporation's power in society in Ted Nace, *Gangs of America: The Rise of Corporate Power and the Disabling of Democracy* (San Francisco: Berrett-Koehler, 2003).

[22]Eduardo Galeano, *Open Veins of Latin America: Five Centuries of the Pillage of a Continent,* trans. Cedric Belfrage (New York: Monthly Review, 1973), pp. 72–75.

devoured all this; the soil was then exhausted and unable to feed the population. The story is similar in Africa and Asia. Gambia once grew its own rice on land now used to grow peanuts. Northern Ghana grew yams and other foodstuffs on land now devoted to cocoa. Much of Liberia and Vietnam were turned over to rubber plantations. Seizures of land, taxation, undercutting of domestic prices, and forced migrations were all employed by colonizers to gain control of the land.[23]

This has left a world divided between a very few who live in opulent affluence and the majority who live in "dehumanizing poverty, servitude, and economic insecurity." While chief executive officers, investment bankers, financial speculators, entertainers, and athletes bring in incomes of many millions of dollars each year, approximately 1 billion of the world's people "struggle in desperation to live on less than $1 a day."[24]

The countries and the people who are already wealthy control the priorities and determine what is to be made, financed, and traded. They have the power to make the rules, and they make these rules to suit their own interests. Consider the following data:

El Salvador and Costa Rica . . . grow export crops such as bananas, coffee and sugar on more than one-fifth of their crop land. Export cattle ranches in Latin America and southern Africa have replaced rain forest and wildlife range. At the consumer end of the production line, Japan imports 70 percent of its corn, wheat, and barley, 95 percent of its soybeans, and more than 50 percent of its wood, much of it from the rapidly vanishing rain forests of Borneo . . . [meanwhile] millions of pigs and cows are fattened on palm-kernel cake from deforested lands in Malaysia, cassava from deforested regions of Thailand, and soybeans from pesticide-doused expanses in the south of Brazil in order to provide European consumers with their high-fat diet of meat and milk.[25]

Does not the presence of foreign mining firms, manufacturers, fruit growers, and banks bring needed capital, technology, and know-how to poor countries? To some extent, yes. However, the income that comes back to the richer country from private investment in poor countries exceeds that going into initial investment by more than 80 percent.[26] In a typical year, only 30 percent of the earnings generated in developing countries is reinvested in those countries. The remainder is sent back to the wealthy country. Compare this to 63 percent of similar earnings

---

[23]Frances Moore Lappe and Joseph Collins, *Food First: Beyond the Myth of Scarcity* (Boston: Houghton Mifflin, 1977), p. 78ff.

[24]*World Development Report—2004* (Washington, D.C.: World Bank and Oxford University Press, 2003); see also David C. Korten, *When Corporations Rule the World* (San Francisco: Kumarian Press and Berrett-Koehler, 1995), p. 20. Korten provides a well-documented and reasoned critique of current global economic policies.

[25]Alan Durning, *How Much Is Enough? The Consumer Society and the Future of the Earth* (New York: W. W. Norton, 1992), p. 56. Quoted in Korten, p. 30.

[26]"U.S. Direct Investment Abroad," *Survey of Current Business,* August 1986, p. 70.

reinvested in developed countries.[27] Putting the situation graphically, for a box of bananas that retails at $13.45 in the United States, producers in Honduras receive roughly $1.49. This covers tending the bananas and cutting and packing them. Chain supermarkets in the United States gross $4.23 on that same box.[28]

The global economy has created a market in which competition among communities is as real as competition among firms. Moore Country, South Carolina won a bid in the 1970s to bring a Proctor Silex plant to their community. They later floated a $5.5 million bond to finance sewer and water for an expansion to the plant. Then in 1990, the firm moved to Mexico, leaving behind 800 unemployed Moore County residents.[29] This same sort of competition exists among cities, when they compete with one another to subsidize stadiums for professional athletic teams, in effect subsidizing the multimillionaire owners and players.

"The market will decide" and "consumer sovereignty" are bywords justifying such free enterprise and global markets. But the consumer who decides is the consumer who has money. The poor and hungry cannot pay enough for food to match the profits that can be made on exports. Therefore, Central America sends its vegetables to the United States, where large quantities are dumped or used as animal feed because their quality is not good enough or markets are oversupplied. Mexico grows strawberries, cantaloupes, and asparagus for Del Monte and other global firms to sell in the United States. Private Colombian landowners grow flowers for export because one hectare of flowers brings nine times the profit that wheat or corn could. Because the market in the United States and Europe demands it, cocaine in Colombia and opium in Afghanistan now bring far greater profits to farmers.[30]

Historically, when poorer people attempted to achieve a fairer democratic society, the United States often intervened and supported a military takeover. The United States sent Marines into Guatemala in 1954, supported the military overthrow of Goulart in Brazil in 1964, used the CIA to subvert and overthrow the elected Allende government in Chile in 1973, and supported the extreme right-wing dictatorship in El Salvador until 1988. In Cuba, before Castro's revolution, U.S. companies controlled 80 percent of Cuba's utilities, 90 percent of its mines, and almost 100 percent of its oil refineries. Firms headquartered in the United States received 40 percent of the profits on sugar, a crop that represented 89 percent of all Cuban exports. It was this argument that Castro made that garnered him the support of the people. When the United States invaded Panama it was to protect the Panama Canal, and the wars in Iraq aim to protect our supply of petroleum. The reason for many military interventions is the protection of U.S. business investments.

Finally, because foreign policy supported by military intervention is used to protect overseas business, the U.S. defense industry is essential to free enterprise.

---

[27]*Ibid.,* Table 4, p. 42.
[28]Lappe and Collins, *Food First,* pp. 194–198. The dollar figures have been adjusted for the rise in prices.
[29]Korten, *When Corporations Rule the World,* pp. 128–129.
[30]*Ibid.,* pp. 255–256.

It also sells planes, missiles, tanks, and guns to friendly poor countries, although they can barely afford them. Defense contracts, in turn, provide jobs, business, and reelection for government representatives. Hence we see that exploitation of other countries, military support of business interests, and a large arms industry are essential elements of contemporary "free markets."

## Social Consequences of Capitalism

Social problems abound around the world that are the consequence of subordinating social concerns to profit making. These problems are familiar. The United States has destroyed 85 percent of its wildlife and 80 percent of its forests; millions of acres of farmland have been misused, paved over, and lost. Pollution is rampant. Global temperatures and carbon emissions from the United States are increasing dangerously.[31] High infant mortality rates reflect the lack of medical care poor people receive. Crime, violence, and poor public schools undermine urban life. The incidence of armed robbery in Washington, D.C., is 20 times that of London. Unemployment, inadequate housing, broken families, racial prejudice, drugs, and great disparities in income are problems in most market economies.

The United States, Western and Eastern Europe, and Japan pride themselves on enjoying a high standard of living, but are now plagued by these serious social problems. Their citizens enjoy more material benefits than any other people in history. But many question even this achievement. How much of what we consume is a response to real needs? Our consumer-propelled economy demands the creation of mostly artificial "needs." Advertising and fashions encourage us to be dissatisfied with what we have and to buy what we do not need: the latest shirts, shoes, PCs, ever-drier deodorants, electric toothbrushes, larger and more luxurious autos, and automatic garbage compactors. Vacation advertisements try to convince us to go to ever more exotic and expensive places. Meanwhile, in Mexico, India, and Indonesia, the poor flock to the cities seeking work. Unable to find it, they subsist in shantytowns that have no water, electricity, or roads. Such shantytowns are hardly places to raise children.

The critics' charges about our economic and political system are many. The profit produced by business goes to owners and executives in far greater share than to workers. Return on investment multiplies the disproportionate distribution of wealth. Factory work often stunts the capacities of workers. Workers are seldom tapped for their initiative, self-determination, and voice in decision making. Competition and "survival of the fittest" self-interest characterize work at every level. Poverty and unemployment are considered to be one's own fault. A wealthy, powerful elite controls the highest public offices. Women are often still subservient. Laws favor the wealthy and protect their incomes by tax loopholes; large companies use their political influence to insulate themselves from competition. As a result, 74 percent of Americans say big companies have too

---

[31]For data, see *State of the World—2003,* ed. Linda Starke (New York: W.W. Norton, 2003); *Starke, Vital Signs—2003;* Lester R. Brown, *Eco-Economy* (New York: W.W: Norton, 2001).

much political influence.[32] Pollution, crime, drugs, racial discrimination, and false needs are by-products of an economy exclusively directed toward more and more production and profits.

Our legal system protects and provides freedom and immense privileges to the corporation. The corporation has been granted the status of a person under U.S. law. Yet if we do consider the corporation as a person, it now unfortunately manifests many of the signs of a pathological person. Arthur Andersen and Enron were not unique; they are accompanied by a multitude of other firms that are characterized by an obsession with profits accompanied by greed, a lack of concern for others, and an inclination for pushing the limits of or breaking legal restrictions. Thus if we consider such a firm to be a person, it acts like a psychopath: irresponsible, grandiose, lacking empathy, manipulating people and data to serve its own purposes, refusing to accept responsibility for its actions, and unable to feel remorse. From this perspective, the recent business scandals are less the result of unethical executives than they are the result of an economic and legal system that encourages this self-seeking behavior. Making these points, an award-winning documentary film, *The Corporation,* shows interviews with well-known economists, CEOs, and critics, and thus makes a surprisingly rational and coherent attack on capitalism's most important institution.[33]

Critics then ask why we have allowed ourselves to be duped into thinking that the corporation and the unneeded growth that it pursues present the best plan for the future. Why not instead "Concentrate on ending poverty, improving our quality of life, and achieving a balance with the earth. We can achieve these goals—if we can free ourselves from the illusion that *any* kind of growth is *the* path to better living."[34] The Critical Studies Interest Group of the Academy of Management consists of business faculty in universities around the world, and is newly dedicated to examining these questions.

Critics are often perceptive and eloquent in pointing out the flaws in the free market system, and they tell us much. If we ignore the critics, our weaknesses will not go away, but more likely will become worse. This could bring distress, instability, and potential breakdown of the system itself. We are wise to hear the critics, and try to repair the flaws in the system while they can still be repaired.[35] Giving priority to developing a sustainable economy that meets all peoples' needs, including the poor at home and in developing countries, is an important goal. There are tradeoff costs in this, but the costs are less than the potential disruption and chaos.

---

[32]See Raghuram G. Rajan and Luigi Zingales, *Saving Capitalism from the Capitalists* (New York: Crown, 2003); see also Charles Perrow, *Organizing America: Wealth, Power and the Origins of Corporate Capitalism* (Princeton, NJ: Princeton University Press, 2002); *Business Week,* September 11, 2000, p. 149.

[33]See the review of the film *Face Value: The Lunatic You Work For* in the *Economist,* May 8, 2004, p. 64. This argument is also made in the book by Joel Bakam, *The Corporation: The Pathological Pursuit of Profit and Power* (New York: Free Press, 2004).

[34]Korten, *When Corporations Rule the World,* p. 38. For a current, cogent statement of the case see also Roger Terry, *Economic Insanity: How Growth-Driven Capitalism Is Devouring the American Dream* (San Francisco: Berrett-Koehler, 1995).

[35]See, for example, the caution in Paul Hawken, "WTO Showdown," *Yes!: A Journal of Positive Futures,* Spring 2000, pp. 45–53.

## Cooperative Versus Competitive Market System

An economic system or specific programs designed to bring about a more just distribution of wealth and income generally results in a loss of efficiency and productivity. Government programs require planning and administrators. They are expensive, are influenced by political interests, and do not always achieve their intended goals. Moreover, such programs can have a negative effect on the incentive to work for both low- and high-income people. On the other hand, critics accuse capitalism not only of exploitation and alienation of the worker but also of encouraging selfishness. Excessive competition and selfishness among individuals can damage not only the health of a society, but also the efficiency of a firm.

Two ideals of a democratic society, justice and efficiency, are thus often placed in opposition to one another. That is, in the minds of many people, increasing one requires sacrificing some of the other.[36] The ideals of *justice* (or equity or fairness) are basic to any society, especially to a free, democratic one: All men and women have a right to the basics of food, shelter, and some education; all men and women should have an opportunity to work and should be treated fairly at work; all people should be treated equally before the law; and there should not be a huge disparity among families in income and wealth.

The ideal of *efficiency* is a pragmatic goal of industrialized societies. It includes the following convictions: A more efficient and productive society yields more jobs and income for all; all individuals should work hard according to their abilities; rewards should be in proportion to an individual's work and merits; and people, material, and capital should be able to move freely.

These two goals of justice and efficiency are basic. Although we fail in one or the other from time to time, it is also true that both remain explicit and real goals for Americans and those in other industrialized societies. Often achievement of one occurs at the expense of the other, yet we also know that it is unwise to undermine either justice or efficiency. Both are essential to any society. This follows from Kohlberg's Level III values, as we saw in Chapter 2.

Increasing productivity is a standard measure of efficiency. We often define productivity as output per person-hour. That is, productivity increases as the amount of labor expended to produce a good or service decreases. Less often do we define productivity as a function of energy or raw materials used. Energy and materials are becoming more scarce and valuable, yet are essential to a sustainable economy. Perhaps we need new terminology (perhaps *energy productivity* and/or *materials productivity*), and to describe labor productivity more broadly as the productivity of *all available* workers. This would better describe moving toward fuller employment and using less energy and materials in production.

The suggestion that a modern economy can be unregulated is mistaken. Government regulation provides protection that is necessary for business to operate. Regulation prohibits monopolies; limits toxic pollution; and ensures, for example, truthful advertising, accurate information on pharmaceuticals, and financial disclosure of publicly held firms. Bankruptcy legislation protects owners

---

[36]See Arthur Okun, *Equality and Efficiency: The Big Tradeoff* (Washington, D.C.: Brookings Institution, 1975).

from going to debtors' prison. Government legislation "levels the playing field" to assure fair business dealings for consumers, producers, and investors. Without such government regulation and monitoring the business environment would be a jungle. Business planning and growth would be impossible. We need only to examine pollution in China, Russia's business oligarchy, insider deals and corruption, or the few rich versus the vast majority of the poor in Latin America.

Every economy operates following certain priorities and a resulting set of rules. Thus, the important question is: On what priorities are the rules set? For example, every nation assesses taxes and ideally provides services in order to be of the greatest benefit to its people as a whole. That is, legislation, taxes, and other government activities are directed to the common good.

Rules or legislation directed to the common good often require that some individuals or groups must sacrifice some short-term benefits. For example, taxing people to pay for fire protection and parks is a cost to all, including those who may never use the fire department or the park. Thus, this demands a political decision that fire protection and parks are benefits for which all people should pay whether or not they use these services.

Governmental decisions require an objective and far-sighted approach to assessing the common good. Legislative resolutions in a democracy often are made that will infringe upon, and hence will not be popular among, certain groups of citizens. Such decisions are becoming harder to make, due to lobbyists, special interest groups, and contributors to a candidate's election campaign. It is difficult for a senator or representative to support legislation that would result in a long-term benefit for most people, if that law results in a short-term cost for a wealthy and powerful constituent. Good government is thus subverted by rich and influential special interests which skew government policy to their own narrow benefit.

For example, it would benefit most citizens of the United States if we could simultaneously lower both pollution and our excessive purchases of goods overseas. An energy plan that would encourage consumers to be more efficient in their use of petroleum would accomplish this. Such an energy plan could reduce pollution and the amount of petroleum we must import, aid city planning, slow urban sprawl, and preserve farmlands. The $73 billion or more that we spend annually for imported petroleum is a principal cause of our balance of payments deficit. Japan and the European nations have enacted a $2 to $3 per gallon gasoline tax for the above reasons. Such a tax would enable the United States to balance its budget and lower income taxes at the same time. In spite of all the benefits, the U.S. Congress does not have the will to tax petroleum to encourage more efficient consumption.[37] The United States stands apart from other nations and has earned their disapproval because of our voracious use of petroleum and our refusal to acknowledge our long-term common interests.

---

[37]For the same reasons, several well-respected national publications consistently have advocated a gradual but substantial tax increase on gasoline. See *Business Week,* March 1, 2004, p. 44; May 27, 2002, p. 28; August 23, 1993, p. 14; November 23, 1981, p.152; *U.S. News & World Report,* April 12, 2004, p. 80; August 27–September 3, 1990, p. 88; November 5, 1979, p. 92; *New York Times,* June 28, 1988, p. 29.

Enlightened self-interest can lead the businessperson to provide the products and services that people want—and to do so efficiently. But enlightened self-interest also encourages individuals to become more selfish. An infant is born self-oriented, but as it grows it comes to recognize the importance of other people. This realization comes gradually as one matures, as we have seen in Chapter 2. Excessive stress on self-interest can stunt a person so that he or she remains at the stage of early adolescence because of a focus on "me and mine." Hence enlightened self-interest must often be upgraded in order to achieve the common good, especially in contemporary society, where so many of our actions impact others (because of, e.g., noise, pollution, and the use of scarce resources). These issues are also discussed in Chapters 1, 5, and 7.

The case for private ownership of large firms is justified primarily in the name of efficiency. The large disparities in income and wealth that we witness in the United States and Europe are also defended on the basis of efficiency: Money motivates people to work and to work harder. The private sector is generally more efficient than the public sector. However, it is difficult to establish that large disparities in income and wealth also bring about greater efficiency. In fact, evidence exists that shows that such disparities within a firm bring discontent, jealously, and a lack of loyalty. We will discuss executive compensation in greater detail in Chapter 8. Here we find one of the most clear-cut conflicts among our basic values: justice versus efficiency. In this regard, recall that John Rawls (see Chapter 3) would require that, because of justice, we must demonstrate that disparities in income, wealth, and power must in some fashion contribute to the advantage of all. Do you agree with Rawls's assessment?

## FREE ENTERPRISE QUESTIONED FROM WITHIN

Rising median family income and increasing gross domestic product are generally considered indicators of a successful society. The United States has been successful in the production and consumption of material goods, so it is not surprising that we would like to make that the measure of success for all cultures. Frederick Winslow Taylor, the founder of scientific management, put it succinctly when he said, "In my judgment the best possible measure of the height in the scale of civilization to which any people has arisen is its productivity."[38]

An opposing point of view was presented a generation before Taylor, when England was at its height as an industrial and world power. Matthew Arnold objected to those who said that England's greatness was based on its railroads and steel. He went on:

---

[38]Frederick W. Taylor, *Hearings Before the Special Committee of the House of Representatives to Investigate the Taylor and Other Systems of Shop Management,* vol. 3 (Washington, D.C.: Government Printing Office, 1912), p. 1471.

> If England were swallowed up by the sea tomorrow, which, a hundred years hence, would most excite the love, interest, and admiration of mankind—and which would most, therefore, show the evidences of having possessed greatness?

Arnold asked whether it would be the England of the preceding two decades, a period of industrial triumph, or would it be an earlier period when culture was more valued? Arnold answered for his contemporaries:

> Never did people believe anything more firmly than nine Englishmen out of ten at the present day believe that our greatness and welfare are proved by our being so very rich.

And then he goes on to give his own response:

> The use of culture is that it helps us, by means of its spiritual standard of perfection, to regard wealth as but machinery, and not only to say as a matter of words that we regard wealth as but machinery, but really to perceive and feel that it is so.[39]

This same issue faces all of us as we move through the twenty-first century. How are we to judge the success of our civilization? What is our goal and what are our criteria for judging whether we are successful? Frederick Taylor says it is productivity; Matthew Arnold says productivity and wealth are merely tools to achieve something more. In this perennial debate, on which side do you stand? Or must we fashion some middle ground? A purpose of this book is to help each of us provide some answers to these questions.

## Prediction of the Decay of Capitalism

Fears of the decay of free enterprise and capitalism were voiced as long ago as the sixteenth century by religious reformers John Calvin and John Wesley. Those who fashioned the ideals underlying the Protestant ethic foresaw the ultimate collapse of that system (see Chapter 4). They predicted the collapse of the system once the goals of more material goods, greater financial rewards, and better efficiency in production were attained. One of the first economists to predict such a collapse was Joseph Schumpeter, who wrote more than two generations ago.

Schumpeter provided a detailed description of the decay of capitalism. He pointed out that the very success of the capitalist economic system in providing goods and income paradoxically lessens dependence on the system. As free enterprise is successful, human needs are satisfied and opportunities for

---

[39]Matthew Arnold, *Victorian Prose,* ed. Frederick William Roe (New York: Ronald Press, 1947), p. 399.

investment are fewer. That same success undermines the need for, and so the prestige of, the entrepreneur, who is no longer dominant or even highly respected in society.[40]

Contributing to the growing hostility to capitalism are the intellectuals. Academics and intellectuals are quick to see inequities and evils in any system.[41] The problems are there to see, and it is the vocation of the intellectual to point them out. Intellectuals and idealistic youth are the principal critics of totalitarian regimes worldwide. However, Schumpeter said that most intellectuals have had no experience in trying to manage an organization, so they do not possess the practical wisdom of those who have gotten their hands dirty. In addition, they have a captive audience in the universities and thus have a ready-made forum for their critical views. Schumpeter felt that intellectuals were undermining capitalism.

Another difficulty is that the professional manager does not have the same long-term vision as the owner he or she replaces.[42] A hired manager is likely to move on to another job that offers greater financial reward, and will not stay and fight for the integrity of a firm. Schumpeter's indictment is broad-gauged. He even went into some detail as to how capitalism and its attendant attitudes tend to undermine family life and child rearing. In his view, capitalism faces imminent death.

Schumpeter pointed to another weakness of capitalism: It has no compelling, motivating, all-embracing ideology and set of values. It is a pragmatic system, designed and pursued for a narrowly conceived end—economic growth. He then contrasted capitalism and Marxism. Marxism has a vision of the world and a systematic ideology; it calls on its followers to sacrifice for the sake of the poor and the oppressed and for a more just distribution of goods. This vision inspires people. In contrast, capitalism promises only a higher standard of living and is not directly concerned about the poor and disadvantaged. Capitalism is effective in production but crass and parochial in its view of people and their world. Schumpeter's critique has been widely quoted over the years. Is it still relevant today?

## Argument for Free Markets: A Rebuttal

An intelligent defense of capitalism and free markets provides a counter argument to critics. The most respected, articulate, and spirited contemporary spokesperson for free market ideology is Nobel Prize–winning economist Milton Friedman. He considers freedom the most important value in any economic or political system, and he sees economic freedom as absolutely essential to political freedom.

Friedman's position in defense of the free market and in opposition to government intervention goes back to Adam Smith. His is the now familiar position

---

[40]Joseph A. Schumpeter, *Capitalism, Socialism and Democracy* (London: Allen & Unwin, 1943), pp. 131–139.
[41]For a more recent statement of this, see Ernest van den Haag, "The Hostility of Intellectuals to Capitalism," *Intercollegiate Review,* Fall/Spring, 2000–2001, pp. 56–63.
[42]Schumpeter, *Capitalism, Socialism and Democracy,* pp. 143ff, 156.

that allowing every person the opportunity to buy and sell openly and without restriction will ensure that people will obtain the goods and services they need at the lowest possible price. Free competition in the marketplace will bring about the greatest efficiency in producing the goods for which people are willing to pay. The corporation, as the predominant economic institution, is a focus of Friedman's concern. He sees a corporation as solely economic, responsible primarily to its stockholders. The agents of the corporation, corporate management, have no right to dispose of stockholders' profits in any manner that does not directly benefit the corporation. Management has no right to spend to make the workplace safer, to install pollution-control equipment, or to give money to universities, unless in some way these actions benefit the corporation itself, at least in the long-term.

Friedman also argues that government has no role in central economic planning. He speaks disparagingly of the government exercising control over the market in the "public interest." In addition, he finds that citizen public interest groups generally have a negative influence.

> Whatever the announced objectives, all of the movements in the past two decades—the consumer movement, the ecology movement, the protect-the-wilderness movement, the zero-population-growth movement, the "small is beautiful" movement, the antinuclear movement—have had one thing in common. All have been antigrowth. They have been opposed to new developments, to industrial innovation, to the increased use of natural resources.[43]

Although the details of Friedman's indictment are not entirely accurate, it is clear that he believes these public interest movements have hurt rather than helped the operation of the market.

Problems such as worker safety, product reliability, and industrial pollution must be addressed. If government legislation and regulation are to be kept to a minimum, and if public interest groups do more harm than good, then the only alternative for solving such problems is management initiative. Yet Friedman is also convinced that management has no right to take the initiative on these issues out of a recognition of the common good. Friedman vehemently denies that corporations do have, or even *can* have, social responsibilities: "The only entities who can have responsibilities are individuals; a business cannot have responsibilities."[44] To presume that a corporation can have social responsibilities

> Shows a fundamental misconception of the character and nature of a free economy. In such an economy, there is one and only one social responsibility of business—to use its resources and engage in activities designed to increase its profits so long as it stays within the rules of the

---

[43]Friedman and Friedman, *Freedom to Choose: A Personal Statement* (New York: Harcourt, Brace, Jovanovich; 1980), pp. 54–56, 95, 191.

[44]Milton Friedman, "Milton Friedman Responds," *Business and Society Review,* 1 (Spring 1972): 6.

game, which is to say, engages in open and free competition, without deception or fraud.[45]

He is convinced that the growing sense of corporate social responsibility undermines basic freedoms.

> Few trends could so thoroughly undermine the very foundations of our free society as the acceptance by corporate officials of a social responsibility other than to make as much money for their stockholders as possible. This is a fundamentally subversive doctrine. If businessmen do have a social responsibility other than making maximum profits for stockholders, how are they to know what it is?[46]

He then points out the difficulty in making such a determination, citing the fact that some German business executives contributed to the Nazi party in the early 1930s. Managers thus wrongly presumed an authority and a wisdom they did not possess.

Friedman argues for the abolition of all corporate taxes and for ensuring that corporate profits are returned to the stockholders, who can then decide how they will spend their money. It is their money, so it should be their decision whether to use it for community purposes. His position is simple, straightforward, and consistent: The interests of stockholders, consumers, and citizens as a whole are best served if the corporation sticks to its traditional role of producing goods and services and does that as efficiently as possible. This is the best long-run service that the business firm can provide for society. He does, however, recognize the problem of unemployment and disability, and proposes a guaranteed minimum income (or "negative income tax") for all those of wage-earning age in the economy. He would substitute a minimum income for the variety of welfare, disability, and unemployment programs that have proliferated, all of which now require separate, expensive, and inefficient administrative apparatuses.

The same principles also apply to such diverse areas as schooling and medical care. Friedman does not think the government should be in the business of education, for government funded public education becomes a monopoly insulated from the challenges to excellence and efficiency that come from free competition. Rather, the government should provide redeemable tuition certificates for parents and children to use at the school of their choice. As is true in the production of goods and services, he is convinced that better and more effective education will result when free competition is present.[47] He has a parallel position on medical doctors and the monopoly that certification gives to the American Medical Association. Better, more efficient, and cheaper medical service would result if no monopoly existed. If anyone who

---

[45]Milton Friedman, *Capitalism and Freedom* (Chicago: University of Chicago Press, 1962), p. 133.
[46]*Ibid.*
[47]Friedman and Friedman, *Freedom to Choose*, pp. 150–188.

has some medical knowledge could hang out a sign, the public would eventually find out who was giving better service and who should not be patronized. Friedman says this would better enable us to find the most effective and efficient treatment.

Milton Friedman acknowledges that his views on the corporation and the free market system do not possess the depth, insight, or balance of his Nobel Prize–winning work in economics. He fails to respond to basic criticisms of free enterprise, such as costs to third parties, inequities, and the encouragement of selfishness. Furthermore, Friedman has little patience for any of the major alternative solutions: public interest group pressures, voluntary actions by management, or government regulation. He is even less interested in cooperative methods of organizing an economy, which were popular in the nineteenth century and continue at present.

## ALTERNATIVES TO INDIVIDUALISM AND CAPITALISM: COOPERATIVES

Some people who came to the United States from other countries organized their economic life cooperatively rather than competitively. In fact, many immigrants, after having experienced dangerous work, exploitative bosses, and child labor, came to the New World precisely to pioneer cooperative living. Hundreds of cooperative communities were formed in the United States during the previous two centuries.[48] Each of the following communities eventually counted their members in the hundreds and often thousands. The members shared work and income equally. They opposed the competition encouraged by capitalism and felt that only through cooperation could a truly human and Christian community develop.

One example of such a community was Brook Farm, which was located in West Roxbury, within the present-day city of Boston. Another is a well-known and still existing communal group called the Shakers. They are a religious group that began in the United States in 1774 and by the early 1800s had grown to 19 separate communities scattered throughout New England and the Midwest; their land holdings totaling nearly 100,000 acres. The suburb of Cleveland called Shaker Heights takes its name from the Shaker community that was there; its beautiful Shaker Lakes were built as millponds. Shaker men and women lived in separate communities; there was little contact between them at work or socially. There was no marriage; new members had to be converted. In the early days there were many converts, and the number of Shakers reached 6,000. They called themselves the Millennial Church. It was outsiders who, observing the long, loud, shaking movements in their prayer services, dubbed them Shakers. The Shakers were very innovative. They invented the flat brooms we use today, washing

---

[48]Rosabeth Moss Kanter, *Commitment and Community* (Cambridge, MA: Harvard University Press, 1972); see also David French and Elena French, *Working Communally* (New York: Russell Sage Foundation, 1975); William A. Hinds, *American Communities* (Chicago: Charles Kerr, 1902).

machines, packaged seeds, the rotary harrow, wrinkle-resistant fabric, and a machine for coring apples. They were also among the earliest to use photography, electricity, and automobiles.[49]

Most of the members of these communities farmed, but many other skills were present. Notable among communities where manufacturing began is the Oneida Community in the state of New York, which was founded by the minister John Humphrey Noyes in 1848. Although it is no longer a commune, it has paradoxically developed into a multimillion-dollar international company and is now the largest maker of stainless steel tableware in the United States.[50]

The communal experiment at New Harmony, Indiana, a community started by Robert Owen, was very well known at the time. Owen, a wealthy British factory owner, initiated work and social reforms; he was the first in England to limit the workday to 10 hours. Owen's dream was a community in which all work, life, and leisure would be shared. Unlike most other early commune organizers, Owen's vision was not religious in origin. In 1825, Owen purchased land and buildings from a religious community called the Rappites in southern Indiana and renamed it New Harmony. He advertised for members and accepted almost all comers; more than 900 arrived, among them some talented and well-known professional people. However, because of his other obligations, Owen himself found little time to be at New Harmony. Farming and other basic skills were scarce among the community members, and lack of a common vision and subsequent discord brought the community to an end in 1827, after only 2 years. It was a noble, highly publicized, and expensive experiment, but it was shorter lived than most cooperative communities.

## Communities to Aid Others

A much older example of cooperative life can be seen in the Benedictine monks, whom we discussed in Chapter 4. A very early tradition called for Christians to share their goods (Acts 2:44–47). Monastic living is an enduring model of sharing, living, and working together. However, Protestant and Catholic religious orders of women and men, which depend on shared Gospel values and a lifelong commitment, were never intended for everyone; they are voluntary associations for those who choose them.

In this spirit, there are today within the Christian and Buddhist communities tens of thousands of women and men in almost every country of the world who choose to live a life together in religious community. They choose to sacrifice in order to be of greater service to men, women, and God. The Christian ideal is generally a lifetime commitment, while the Buddhist tradition calls for people to spend a year of their life in a communal monastery.

These people are motivated to serve God, to try to make the world a better place, and to help other women and men, especially those who are poor and in

---

[49]Richard Wolkomir and Joyce Wolkomir, "Living a Tradition: At a Handful of Sites Shaker Communities Transport the Past into the Present," *Smithsonian,* April 2001, pp. 98–108; Marguerite F. Melcher, *The Shaker Adventure* (Princeton, NJ: Princeton University Press, 1941), p. 302.
[50]Hinds, *American Communities,* pp. 173–214.

need. They work in hospitals, schools, colleges, and social service agencies throughout the world. They live together and choose to hold income and property in common, such as salaries, savings, housing, autos, TV, and PCs. Thus, they seek to be a witness that one can live without being caught up in the vices of materialism, self-centeredness, and an overemphasis on sexuality.[51]

In summary, effective leadership characterizes all of these successful cooperative communities, and most are religious in origin. For a community to survive, it must continue to attract vigorous and talented people, not those who are looking for a refuge from the problems of the outside world. Self-discipline and order are necessary to resolve the multitude of differences that arise in a community, yet these communities are impossible to sustain without a shared vision. Many of the early American communes failed after the original leader was gone and the early goals and inspiration for the community faded. The older religious communities are more long lasting. Communes are not a new social phenomenon. They are a reflection of a deep-rooted desire that people have for humane relationships, cooperation, and communication based on shared values.[52]

## Working in Community

The need to encourage cooperation exists especially in free market societies, where enlightened self-interest pushes people toward individualism and selfishness. Religion is an aid in all societies in giving purpose in life, forming character, bringing people together, and helping them formulate long-range personal and group goals. However, because of fear of intolerance and secular bias, Western countries have kept religion at the periphery of society and of public policy. This has placed Western societies in a secular limbo, without strong religious values to support them. Nevertheless, the tide has turned, and in recent years religion is a newly respected force that is shaping public and political values.[53] Many contend that religion and moral values were determining factors in the 2004 U.S. elections. We will discuss the growing interest in spirituality in the workplace in Chapter 7.

Excessive individualism in Western countries has spawned problems of crime, the breakdown of the family, and a deserted central city, according to a group called Communitarians. This group calls for building upon shared values and mutual understandings in order to address our problems.[54] Communitarians contend that any society must limit some portion of what

---

[51]For additional information, see Patricia Wittberg, S.C., *Creating a Future for Religious Live: A Sociological Perspective* (New York: Paulist Press, 1989); Wade Clark Roof, *A Generation of Seekers: The Spiritual Journeys of the Baby Boom Generation* (San Francisco: Harper, 1993).

[52]See "Creating the Good Society: To Whom Is the Corporation Responsible?" *Business Horizons,* July–August 1991. The issue is devoted to the corporation as responsible to society. For a sociological analysis of American communes, see Benjamin Zablocki, *Alienation and Charism: A Study of American Communes* (New York: The Free Press, 1979).

[53]See Stephen Carter, *The Culture of Disbelief: How American Law and Politics Trivializes Religion* (New York: Basic Books, 1993).

[54]Amitai Etzioni, *The Spirit of Community* (New York: Touchstone Books, 1994). Etzioni's proposal for a less egoistic economic model is favorably reviewed by Bill Shaw and Frances E. Zollers, "Managers in the Moral Dimension: What Etzioni Might Mean to Corporate Managers," *Business Ethics Quarterly,* July 1993, pp. 153–168.

various people claim as "rights," in order to achieve the common good. For example, allowing everyone to claim as a right to do whatever they choose undermines both character formation for children, and also long-term public policy. This group of respected people in government, universities, and business is trying to build bridges between the feuding factions of Western society. The attention that Communitarians have received indicates that they are espousing values and goals that many people share.

Americans often do not realize that the United States is not the only standard for free enterprise. Other countries have different models, and even the U.S. pattern can be altered and improved. For example, there are cooperative models for organizing free markets. Two of these are: (1) European social democracy, and (2) the Mondragon model of cooperative work. The social democracy model is best known and practiced in Sweden, Norway, Holland, Germany, and Austria. These people see government as the conscience of the free market. Jobs are considered the bedrock essential of a society, so Sweden keeps unemployment at less than 2 percent. The Swedes elect to pay 50 percent of their taxes for education, health, housing, and other social security–type programs. They and other Europeans see taxes as a necessary price of civilization. However, two problems of this system are a growth of government bureaucracy and a decline in volunteerism and caring among ordinary citizens.

Mondragon is a group of more than 150 worker-owned and -managed firms in the Basque region of northern Spain. The cooperative businesses have been financially and socially successful for more than 70 years. Mondragon now includes manufacturing firms (household appliances, machine tools, automotive parts, engineering capital goods), banks, schools, universities, stores, hospitals, and more than 66,000 worker/owners. The group's annual sales in 2002 were 9.2 billion euros ($8.8 billion). Every major management decision has input from the owner/workers, and these firms have been run efficiently and effectively. For example, each position's salary is decided by a committee that consists of representatives of both management and worker/owners. Most of each cooperative firm's profits go back to the cooperative, but some is set aside for social projects in the community. When layoffs become necessary, the cooperative provides 80 percent of salary until that person returns to work. The Mondragon model requires that people have job skills, and it provides a world-renowned example of cooperative prosperity for both individuals and the community.[55]

An international cooperative business initiative, the Economy of Communion (EOC), also called the Economy of Sharing, began in Brazil in 1991. This group of more than 700 businesses voluntarily pledges to divide their profits in three ways: helping the poor, especially by providing jobs; investing to grow their business; and educating people in the Economy of Communion. According to founder Chiara Lubich, "Unlike the consumer economy which is based on the culture of having, the economy of communion is the economy of giving . . . " One

[55]Charles M. A. Clark, "The Mondragon Cooporacion Cooperativa," *Review of Business,* 25 (Winter 2004): 4–5. For another view of these two models, see Charles Derber, "Communitarian Economics: Criticisms and Suggestions from the Left," *Responsive Community,* Fall 1994, pp. 29–41.

EOC economist says they hope "to transform the field of economics from a place where apparently irreconcilable individual interests clash, into a place of encounter, of personal fulfillment." The EOC has spread to countries as varied as Italy, the United States, France, Israel, Cameroon, Germany, and Serbia, and meets regularly.[56]

## Cooperation in the Workplace

Many current programs that encourage greater cooperation and commitment among members of business firms are attempts to attain better product quality, create a more humane workplace, and achieve greater profitability. A producer cooperative is an entire firm built on cooperative ideals. Participative management, employee stock ownership plans, flexible work schedules, and profit sharing are all designed to build greater commitment and cooperation among workers in firms in the free market.[57]

Employee stock ownership plans (ESOPs) have a long history around the world. The largest 100 ESOPs in the United States range from 359,000 associates (United Parcel Service) to 200 people. They include firms in manufacturing, financial services, fast food, construction, and almost every other industry. Springfield Remanufacturing Corp. (SRC) in Missouri pushes responsibility down to the individual worker, and annual bonuses are often 18 percent of salary. The firm encourages new ideas and entrepreneurship by funding dozens of new cooperative enterprises; one of these is a spin-off that teaches other executives and firms how to operate a participative ESOP. Some of these new enterprises thrive, and this enables SRC to keep its number of employees at its intended size of approximately 450.[58] Linux software is cooperatively owned, and is constantly improved by volunteers. Both from the conviction that operating system software should be available to all, and to provide competition for Microsoft's Windows monopoly, Linux enthusiasts have contributed to its success. The software has been adopted by several computer hardware manufacturers such as IBM and Dell and other large corporations, and is used on a growing number of Web sites.[59] An organization that supports ESOPs boasts 1,200 firms and 750,000 employee-owners in the United States. Among those firms are Procter & Gamble, Anheuser-Busch, Amsted, and W.L. Gore Associates.[60]

An award-winning example of an ESOP is Chroma Technology Corp. of Rockingham, Vermont. It is 100 percent employee owned, and makes optical fibers for microscopes. With 68 workers and sales of $16 million, it is the major

---

[56]Michele Zanzucchi, "Economy of Communion: 10 Years from the Beginning," *Living City,* July 2001, pp. 6–10. See also the Web site www.focolare.org/en/.
[57]Richard Marens, Andrew Wicks, and Vandra Huber, "Cooperating with the Disempowered: Using ESOPs to Forge a Stakeholder Relationship by Anchoring Employee Trust in Workplace Participation Programs," *Business and Society,* March 1999, pp. 51–82. For a summary of these participation programs, see "Work and Job Satisfaction" in Gerald F. Cavanagh and Arthur F. McGovern, *Ethical Dilemmas in the Modern Corporation* (Englewood Cliffs, NJ: Prentice Hall, 1988).
[58]For the list of the 100 ESOPs, see Marjorie Kelly, "A Tale of Two Employee-Owned Companies: Moving Beyond Ownership to Governance," *Business Ethics,* September/October 2001, pp. 12–17.
[59]"The Wild and Woolly World of Linux," *Business Week,* November 15, 1999, pp. 130–134.
[60]Information from www.esopassociation.org/, accessed December 12, 2004.

supplier for microscope manufacturers in Germany, Japan, and China. Most major decisions are made on the shop floor by the people doing the work. No person at Chroma makes less than $37,500 and no one makes more than $75,000. A disadvantage of the flat pay structure is that it is more difficult to attract people with graduate degrees (although Chroma has three employees with doctorates in biology) or business experience. However, they find that the advantage "is the cooperative atmosphere, the self-direction, and the lack of a managerial class."[61]

Chroma's stakeholder theory provides a rationale for worker cooperation and partnering of other "factors of production." Employees, creditors, suppliers, customers, local communities, government, and other groups all have a "stake" in the business operation, and so deserve consideration. Some stakeholders then share in the decisions of the firm that affect them. Doing this successfully demands that executives possess listening and negotiating skills, but it also gives the firm a new legitimacy in society.[62]

Some people perform best when they work cooperatively, while others do better given individual incentives. Individualists are happier and work better when they are have specific, personal tasks to perform and are rewarded by separate incentives. On the other hand, others are more satisfied and operate better when they work cooperatively in a group and are rewarded by group incentives. Collectivists perform more poorly when working alone or in an out group than when working in an in group. Thus it is important to know what motivates a particular worker. These differences also influence managing, setting up incentive systems, and success in various cultures. Participation or organizational democracy is more appropriate in certain industries and with certain people.[63] Why people work, how work can be more satisfying, and the effect of the organization on motivation will all be discussed in the next chapter.

## SUMMARY AND CONCLUSIONS

Karl Marx pinpointed the weaknesses of capitalism and free markets. He and his followers have shown that free enterprise has some undesirable consequences and results in:

1. Exploitation of the worker
2. Alienation of the worker

---

[61]Peter Asmus, "Chroma Technology Corp: Living Economy Award," *Business Ethics,* Fall 2004, pp. 9–10.
[62]See R. Edward Freeman, *Strategic Management: A Stakeholder Approach* (Marshfield, MA: Pitman, 1984); see also Freeman, "A Stakeholder Theory of Modern Corporation," in Thomas Donaldson, Patricia Werhane, and Margaret Cording, *Ethical Issues in Business* (Upper Saddle River, NJ: Prentice Hall, 2002), pp. 38–48.
[63]Jeffrey S. Harrison and R. Edward Freeman, "Is Organizational Democracy Worth the Effort?" *Academy of Management Executive,* 18 (August 2004): 49–53; see also the articles on organizational democracy which follow in this special issue. See also R. Christopher Early, "East Meets West Meets Midwest: Further Explorations of Collectivistic and Individualistic Work Groups," *Academy of Management Journal,* April 1993, pp. 319–348. This research was done using Chinese, Israeli, and American subjects.

**3.** Big business dominating national policy

**4.** Corporations exploiting other countries

Marxists are at their best in criticizing capitalism. Negative economic and social consequences, such as unemployment, poverty, and corruption are certainly not advocated by the defenders of free enterprise. Nevertheless, a critique of capitalism and the market system does raise the important question of how priorities are formulated. Who decides what goals of a society are primary? Perhaps priorities are discussed in the political sphere, if at all. And government can regulate and tax, but it does not set specific economic goals. Free enterprise advocates defend this nonintervention as more efficient. Free enterprise recognizes only one priority: Will a given product, service, or action return a profit? The system does not ask how important the need is that is being fulfilled; it has no method of rating products or services on any scale of values other than dollars. Moreover, many goods, such as streetlights, police, parks, and public transportation have a market value that does not reflect their long-term value to society as a whole.

Perhaps profits should be the sole concern of business. If that is true, in free market countries who sets national priorities and implements them? Do individual consumers have the vision to look after their own long-term good and the long-term good of future generations? For example, how did we decide that private automobile travel was better than public rapid transit? How do we decide that we should spend more on advertising than on education, or on dog food and cosmetics than on helping hungry people feed themselves? As we will see in Chapter 8, in a market economy it is not clear where the responsibility for such decisions lies. Those advocating greater business responsibility point to the negative moral and social consequences of some business policies, such as those regarding toxic waste, product safety, plant closings, and energy and resource use. But the issue of national priorities goes beyond these policies.

Efficiency and justice are both important goals for any society. Competition encourages flexibility and efficiency. However, personal self-centeredness and competition often bring a decline in efficiency, and almost always lead to a decline in justice.

In short, it appears that some of the values that we cultivate in the name of efficiency and success make us less efficient and less successful. Moreover, in the process we can become blind to the importance of cooperation and justice. Considering critiques of free enterprise can give us an incentive to examine our own personal and national priorities. It helps us to see the inadequacies of our own ideology, so that we may amend this ideology, and thus improve our personal and collective ability to live a decent and happy life.

## DISCUSSION QUESTIONS

1. Explain what Mahatma Gandhi meant by each of the "seven blunders . . . that lead to violence."

2. How do you respond to each of the six questions posed at the beginning of the chapter?

3. What evidence does Karl Marx provide that capitalism exploits the worker? Is the argument valid? Does income tax rectify the inequality?

4. What evidence does Marx use to sustain his claim that capitalism alienates the worker? Evaluate this claim for the contemporary working person.

5. How does big business dominate the formulation of national goals? Provide evidence for your answer.

6. Why does Charles Lindbloom say that giant corporations and democracy cannot successfully coexist? Does the evidence support his claim?

7. How do large corporations exploit poor countries? Cite evidence and explain.

8. Do the four major problems of capitalism cited by Marx stem primarily from capitalism or industrialization? Why?

9. Marxism claims to be materialistic. Is it more materialistic than capitalism or free enterprise? In what way do the goals that Marxism holds out for the average worker transcend materialism?

10. Do you agree that a society that is wholly directed to efficiency is likely to be unjust and that a society that is wholly directed to equality is likely to be inefficient? Why?

11. How does one measure the success of a society? By its gross national product? By the average per capita income of its members? By its literature or art? By its care for the poor and disadvantaged? Which criteria would you use?

12. Why did Joseph Schumpeter say that capitalism would decay? How are his views on this subject the same or different from those of John Calvin?

13. Does Milton Friedman think that a corporation has social responsibilities? Why?

14. What is Friedman's free market prescription for education? For medical doctors? Do you agree?

15. Should profits and shareholder value be the sole and exclusive goal of a business firm?

16. Who has the responsibility to look to the long-term welfare of all citizens? What role does a business executive have in this?

17. Describe the origins and characteristics of early American communal societies.

18. How do Christian religious communities differ from the early American communal societies in their motivation? In their work ethic? In their ability to last?

19. What elements in a communal society support its continued existence?

20. Outline the comparative advantages and disadvantages of (a) cooperative and (b) competitive economic systems.

21. Examine: (a) European social democracies, (b) Mondragon cooperatives, and (c) the Economy of Communion. Are each of these legitimate free enterprise operations? What lessons could Americans learn from each model?

22. Does the current concern for teamwork and worker participation undermine competitive free enterprise?

# CASES

## Case 6-1    Nike and Sweatshops

Nike is the largest producer of athletic footwear in the world. Nike's founder Phil Knight has long cultivated a brash, arrogant style. In the late 1990s Nike faced charges of using 14-year-old girls in Indonesia and Vietnam as workers; they worked 65 hours a week and breathed carcinogens as they assembled Nike shoes, and were often fired when they reached the age of 30. At first Knight and Nike said they had no control; the girls worked for subcontractors. After popular protests and critical articles in the U.S. media, Knight decided to require subcontractors to raise the mandatory minimum hiring age from 14 to 18 and to provide better conditions in the factories.

1. Is this an example of exploitation of the worker? Why or why not?
2. What ethical norm is most helpful to us in dealing with these issues?
3. Do you think that Knight would have changed his position without the negative press reports?
4. Why is Nike especially vulnerable to such negative publicity? ■

## Case 6-2    California Sweatshop

In 1995 authorities raided an El Monte, California, sweatshop that employed 72 undocumented immigrants from Thailand. These men and women were often forced to work 17 hours a day, were closely guarded, and held against their will; if they refused to work, they were sent back to Thailand. The Thai workers were making clothing that was sold at retailers like B.U.M. and Mervyn's. Federal authorities had heard about the situation 3 years earlier, but failed to investigate.

After their release, lawyers defending the Thai immigrants obtained more than $1 million in back wages, largely because of the abuse they had undergone. Seven years later 71 of these Thais were granted permanent residency in the United States. Some government officials said that they thought that providing back pay and residency would encourage other illegal immigrants to come to the United States.

1. What ethical norms are involved in this case?
2. Discuss the ethical responsibilities of the: (a) owners of the sweatshop, (b) Thai illegal immigrants (c) government authorities, and (d) clothing retailers. ■

# Case 6-3 Superior's Expense Report

Sara McIntyre, a young management accountant at Tuloc, Inc., received an expense report for reimbursement from Elmer Cole, vice president of the division. The report requests $3,100 for a two-day trip to Boston, and most of the items have no receipts and seem to McIntyre to be inflated.

1. What should McIntyre do? What are her obligations and to whom?
2. What ethical norm is most helpful to McIntyre? ■

## EXERCISE

### Goals Notebook[64]

*This exercise builds on the findings of the Personal Goals and Values Inventory from Chapter 1. It will enable you to learn more about your goals, using both your left (logical) and right (creative) brain modes of thinking.*

1. Write a personal mission statement no longer than one page (a single paragraph is even better).
2. Record your goals in order of importance to you. Use the information from the Personal Goals and Values Inventory from Chapter 1.
3. List in detail five goal statements. At least two goals should be long term (attained in 3–5 years) and two should be short term (within 6 months). Each of the five goal statements should be one or two pages and should include:
   a. A statement of a goal that is specific, measurable, and attainable.
   b. The time frame in which you will attain this goal.
   c. Pictorial representation of the goal (e.g., drawings, photographs, cut-outs, clip art).
4. On the final page list at least three things you learned from this exercise.

## EXERCISE

### Debate Pros and Cons of Free Trade

The purpose of a debate is to enable two teams to research opposite sides of an issue, prepare and outline an oral presentation, and make their arguments to the class. Each team should be two to five people, and each member of the team should have something to contribute to the presentation(s). To enable the teams to do an appropriate preparation, the teams and the subject are assigned one week prior to the debate. A subject for debate that

---

[64]For this exercise, I thank Dr. Mary Ann Hazen, College of Business Administration, University of Detroit Mercy.

is suitable for this chapter is: Open markets (and free trade) are the best economic system for all countries of the world.

The order and time schedule of the debate could be:

Pro: Prepared presentation (7 min. max)
Con: Prepared presentation (7 min. max)
Preparation of rebuttals (3 min.)
Con: Rebuttal of the previous pro presentation and summary (3 min. max)
Pro: Rebuttal of the previous con presentation and summary (3 min. max)

The same format may be used to debate additional subjects. Another subject for a debate might be: The Global Reporting Initiative (GRI) is good for business. (See Chapter 8.)

# CHAPTER 7

## Personal Values and the Firm

If you would not be forgotten, as soon as you are dead and rotten, either write
things worth reading or do things worth the writing.
BENJAMIN FRANKLIN (1706–1790), AMERICAN INVENTOR, WRITER, STATESMAN


Money is my first, last, and only love.
ARMAND HAMMER (1898–1990), CEO, OCCIDENTAL PETROLEUM


In the medieval system capital was the servant of man, but in the modern system
it became his master.
ERICH FROMM (1900–1980), GERMAN/AMERICAN PSYCHOANALYST, WRITER


Ann Fudge was recruited in 2003 to be chair and CEO of Young &
Rubicam. This advertising, public relations, and consulting firm has
annual revenues of $2 billion, and several predecessors failed to turn it
around; the firm had "endured neglect, executive greed, and a messy merger."[1]
Two years prior, Fudge was the very successful head of a $5 billion division of
Kraft Foods; among her accomplishments she rejuvenated such brands as Kool-
Aid, Log Cabin syrup and Stove Top stuffing. She was listed as one of the most
powerful women in American business.[2] She loved her job and was slated for further promotions, but she felt she was missing something. Her parents and a friend
had died and her sister-in-law had contracted multiple sclerosis. She asked herself, "What are you really here for? What do you really want to accomplish?"
Most advised her not to quit; it would indicate that she didn't have the energy
and focus for an executive job and it would look bad on her résumé. Another

---

[1]Diane Brady, "Act II: Ann Fudge's Two Year Break from Work Changed Her Life: Will Those
Lessons Help Her Fix Young & Rubicam?" *Business Week,* March 29, 2004, pp. 72–82.
[2]"The 50 Most Powerful Women in American Business," *Fortune,* October 12, 1998.

commented, "Look at the damage to the economy to have all these talented 50-year-olds out." Nevertheless she quit her executive job at Kraft.

During her two years away from work, she reflected, wrote in her journal, and renewed friendships. She traveled to places she had dreamed about: Thailand, Bali, Morocco, and Cyprus. She loved "being around different cultures and being able to step back and absorb it all."[3] As a black woman, she has endured racism throughout her life, and has learned to deal with it. She is described by her peers as a well-rounded, solid business executive who nurtures her subordinates. It is unclear if she will be able to bring Y&R back to a successful level, but she has already visited most of the Y&R offices throughout the world, has good relations with the major directors and managers, and has landed a $250 million contract with Microsoft.

Ann Fudge recognizes the importance of both her work life and her personal life. She is one of a growing number of young managers who are unwilling to give unlimited priority to their work. In 1998, Brenda Barns, then 43, quit her job as head of PepsiCo North America to spend more time with her three children. In May 2004, Sara Lee named her president and chief operating officer. Both women have a strong influence on people at their work.

The work environment, in turn, has a strong influence upon Fudge and Barns, as it does on each of us. The groups and organizations of which we are members—from families to corporations—influence our personal values, goals, and ethics, although we are seldom explicitly aware of this influence. Personal values, which are among the basic components of personality, develop from exposure to others. Values are often received without conscious thought from parents, peers, teachers, and the media. A loving and listening parent encourages values that are quite different from those engendered by a parent who is annoyed, distracted, or absent. In a parallel fashion, an emotionally healthy executive or manager can have a great influence on a firm's culture and climate; such a firm is most likely a challenging and enjoyable place to work. On the other hand, emotionally ill executives can cause untold stress on people for whom they are responsible.[4]

During our working years, we often so identify with an organization that success within it becomes a primary measure of personal worth. Performing well at Merrill Lynch or Dow Chemical can influence our self-concept. Working in a firm that encourages pride in good work, autonomy, creativity, and risk-taking can give me self-confidence and joy in doing my work. On the other hand, personal values can be compromised by a business climate that condones unethical acts.[5] Moreover, an individual may identify so closely with work that success on the job is the total measure of self-worth. Realization of the inadequacy of that measure

---

[3]Interview: "Ann Fudge on Making Choices: The Y&R CEO Talks about the Benefits of Stepping Away from Work and How Her Priorities Changed Because of It," *Business Week,* March 29, 2004, pp. 72–82. For Brenda Barns, see *Business Week,* May 27, 2004, p. 48.

[4]James C. Quick, Joanne Gavin, Gary Cooper, and Jonathan Quick, "Executive Health: Building Strength, Managing Risks," *Academy of Management Executive,* 14, no. 2 (2000): 34–44; see also the more comprehensive, James Quick, Jonathan Quick, Debra Nelson, and Joseph Hurrell, *Preventive Stress Management in Organizations* (Washington, D.C.: American Psychological Association, 1997).

[5]William C. Frederick and James Weber, "The Values of Corporate Managers and Their Critics: An Empirical Description and Normative Implications," in *Research in Corporate Social Performance and Policy,* ed. William C. Frederick, vol. 9 (Greenwich, CT: JAI Press, 1987), pp. 131–151.

often does not come until midlife. When that realization comes, it can bring pro-found anxieties, frustrations, and even serious physical ailments. We discussed stress on the job and the midlife crisis in Chapter 2.[6]

A business firm can and should meet vital individual and social needs. It can enable an individual to achieve a sense of identity and "develop the skills and loyalties that are necessary to sustain the social structure of responsible and ethical organizational life."[7] If this relationship is to develop, trust must exist between the firm and the individual. The importance of such trust has received considerable attention.[8] Ford Motor Company encourages each person to develop his or her own spirituality. Levi Strauss promotes ethics in each worker's actions; it also seeks employee input on all work-related issues. Canon's former president, Ryuzaburo Kaku, ran the company on the principle of *kyosei*, working and living together with the people of the world for the common good. Avis began employee participation groups when it became 100 percent employee owned, and earnings and stock prices jumped immedi-ately. Domino's Pizza encourages its employees to use the Golden Rule in the workplace. These practices reinforce human values learned in the family and neighborhood, and encourage concern for people—whether neighbors, co-workers, suppliers, customers, or subordinates. Such firms thus help their people to maintain an integrated personality, not separating the values of family life from those of the workplace.

Some business firms, and even some universities and hospitals, show little social concern. As we will see later in this chapter, managers of such institutions tend to be more self-centered and show less concern about social conditions. They are less willing to make personal gain secondary to helping other people. The values of these managers contrast with the self-image most Americans have of themselves as generous. When people never question their personal values, those values contain the seeds of potential conflict and anxiety. Leaders of organizations who make decisions based on self-centered values often cause severe social disruption. Note some financial analysts who publicly urged their clients to buy shares of Enron and WorldCom while privately calling the firms "dogs," or recommended that their clients participate in the after-hours trading at many mutual funds. This is a paradox, because managers conceive of them-selves as objective, rational, and not led by personal prejudice. Managers should do a careful analysis of all the facts before coming to a judgment. The use of market surveys, outside consultants, product planning groups, and com-puter analyses indicates the high priority that rational decision making has

---

[6]For a more complete description of work and job satisfaction issues, see Cavanagh and McGovern, *Ethical Dilemmas in the Modern Corporation,* pp. 34–63.

[7]Timothy L. Fort, "Business as Mediating Institution," *Business Ethics Quarterly,* 6 (April 1996): 149–163.

[8]See, for example, Bennett J. Tepper and Edward C. Taylor, "Relationships Among Supervisors and Subordinates: Procedural Justice Perceptions and Organizational Citizenship Behaviors," in *Academy of Management Journal,* 46, no. 1 (2003): 97–105, and the entire issue dedicated to trust, "Special Topic Forum on Trust in and Between Organizations" in the *Academy of Management Review,* 23 (July 1998).

within firms. Yet these same managers are often unaware of how much their unexamined personal values bias their decisions; they thus hurt both themselves and their organizations.

Managers are often unaware that the decision-making process itself rests on unexamined assumptions. Beneath what appears to be a rational structure may lie presuppositions about the purpose of the firm—to maximize shareholder value and to increase market share. The ideological assumptions upon which rational decision making is based are often accepted unquestioningly, much as we accept traditional cultural norms.

Each organization develops a life and norms of its own. Schools provide values to children before they are in the workplace. Consider the values communicated when teachers in two different eras were asked what were the major problems in school (see Figure 7-1). In 1940 teachers said that major problems were such things as talking out of turn, cutting in line, chewing gum, and running in the halls. In 1992 teachers said that the major problems were alcohol abuse, pregnancy, suicide, and assault.[9]

Just as ethical norms and expectations within schools are affected by the problems listed, so too a business is affected by the problems that it faces. An organization's growth and/or struggle for survival can give apparent legitimacy to many activities that would not be undertaken if subjected to more careful scrutiny. These activities often conflict with the values of honesty, integrity, and concern for others that are possessed by members of the organization. This conflict may then cause members to reflect on the inconsistency of these personal and organizational values. The inadequacy of an exclusive reliance on market values often does not appear until the values of the firm come into conflict with the values of a person or of society; we will discuss this in greater detail in Chapter 8.

| Teachers' Listing of Discipline Problems in School* | |
| --- | --- |
| *1940* | *1992* |
| Talking out of turn | Drug abuse |
| Making noise | Alcohol abuse |
| Cutting in line | Pregnancy |
| Littering | Suicide |
| Chewing gum | Rape |
| Running in halls | Robbery |
| Dress Code infractions | Assault |

**FIGURE 7-1** Student Discipline Problems

* Congressional Quarterly Researcher, *September 11, 1992. Quoted in* The Responsive Community *(Summer, 1993): 56. Quoted with permission.*

---

[9]*Congressional Quarterly Researcher,* September 11, 1992. Quoted in *Responsive Community,* Summer 1993, p. 56.

This chapter will examine personal values in business, including the following topics:

1. The influence of *organizational values, climate, and expectations* on the values of individuals.
2. *Goals and motives of individuals* and how motives are affected by personal values and ethics.
3. *Workplace pressures,* and how these contribute to personal health or illness.
4. Achieving a *balance between work and the rest of life.*

## THE FIRM FORMS WORKERS: SOCIALIZATION

Any group of people working together must share goals and values; otherwise they suffer conflict and confusion. Hence to obtain cooperation in any human endeavor, socialization is essential. Formal socialization (see Figure 7-2) is the deliberate attempt by the organization to influence the attitudes of members. Informal socialization takes place among members through ordinary interaction. Many values are introduced in orientation and training programs, but others are formed by exposure to the expectations of superiors and peers during the work week. Socialization takes place through actions, stories, and myths that are passed down through the organization.[10] When coupled with the perceived importance of success in the firm, such socialization brings reinforcement or changes in values. Employee training provides payoffs for the firm; trained employees tend to perform better and show more citizenship and more commitment to the firm.[11] For example, Disney Productions, through both formal and informal socialization, ensures that new members know how to make "guests" feel welcome and comfortable.

Any organization has its own demands, which arise from the need to maintain the health of the organization. These demands are often determined by the market values of shareholder value, market share, and return on investment. Organizational maturity and stability, without profitability and growth, are not acceptable goals for the long term; chief executive officers are fired for having such unaggressive goals. Moreover, organizations affect almost every segment of our lives including our moral lives. Work climates have a strong influence on the ethical values and thus the actions of members of an organization.[12] "Because modern organizations have created and have largely defined the American value

---

[10]For research and theory on organizational culture and socialization, see Geert Hofstede, *Culture's Consequences: Comparing Values, Behaviors, Institutions and Organizations Across Nations,* 2nd ed. (Thousand Oaks, Sage, 2001); see also Joanne Martin, *Organizational Culture: Mapping the Terrain* (Thousand Oaks: Sage, 2002).

[11]Anne S. Tsui, Jone Pearce, Lyman Porter, Angela Tripoli, "Alternate Approaches to Employee Organization Relationship: Does Investment in Employees Pay Off?" *Academy of Management Journal,* 40, no. 5 (1997): 1089–1121.

[12]For an overview of this work, see James Weber, "Emphasizing the *Ethical* in Ethical Work Climates," Paper presented at National Academy of Management, 1993, Atlanta; see also Linda K. Trevino and G. Weaver, "Business ETHICS/BUSINESS Ethics," *Business Ethics Quarterly,* 4 (1994): 113–128; Bart Victor and John Cullen, "The Organizational Basis of Ethical Work Climates," *Administrative Science Quarterly* (March, 1988), pp. 101–125.

| TYPES OF SOCIALIZATION | METHODS OF SOCIALIZATION |
|---|---|
| FORMAL | 1. Orientation program |
| | 2. Job descriptions |
| | 3. Training programs |
| | 4. Codes of behavior |
| | 5. Performance appraisal and feedback |
| INFORMAL | 1. Expectations of superiors |
| | 2. Actions of and conversations with peers |
| | 3. Unwritten norms |
| | 4. Organizational culture |

**FIGURE 7-2** Socialization Within the Organization

system, they must be considered the most important socializing agencies in America."[13]

Organizations are generally effective in selecting individuals and then socializing them into people who "fit well" into the system. Moreover, people with traits similar to those of supervisors and peers tend to be picked for promotion in organizations.[14] Each organization has a subtle but potent influence on its members' attitudes, values, and ethics. Sociologist Robert Jackall paints an unflattering picture of American corporate bureaucracy. On the basis of extensive interviews with managers, he points out that managerial decisions are made on a short-term basis. Moreover, most firms reward this short-term perspective, and generally reward on the basis of political considerations rather than performance and merit. The most important things that are learned in the corporation are mastering expectations and fitting in.[15]

Large organizations offer many examples of such short-sighted and inflexible behavior. New products often come from startups, while firms like Nike and Microsoft become large and inflexible. A large organization develops a life of its own, protecting its own special interests and being jealous of its position, power, and prerogatives. The corporation's procedures, especially when they have been

---

[13]Deborah Vidaver Cohen, "Moral Climate in Business Firms: A Framework for Empirical Research," in *Academy of Management Proceedings*, 1995, ed. Dorothy P. Moore Vancouver, B.C., 1995. The original quote is from William G. Scott and David K. Hart, *Organizational America* (Boston, Houghton Mifflin, 1979), p. 36; see also John M Darley, "How Organizations Socialize Individuals into Evildoing," in *Codes of Conduct: Behavioral Research into Business Ethics* (New York, Russell Sage Foundation, 1996), pp. 13–43.
[14]John Schaubroeck and Simon S. K. Lam, "How Similarity to Peers and Supervisor Influences Organizational Advancement in Different Cultures," *Academy of Management Journal*, 45, no. 6 (2002): 1120–1136.
[15]Robert Jackall, *Moral Mazes: The World of Corporate Managers* (New York: Oxford University Press, 1988).

successful in the past, can become rigid and ossified. Each individual is expected to "learn Mitsubishi's way of doing things." Managers select for promotion subordinates who have values like their own. Although these managers pride themselves on making objective and rational decisions, personal likes and values play an important role in their decisions.

In large organizations, coordination between people and business units is essential. As various responsibilities are spelled out in writing, there is less room for individual judgment. Even in decentralized companies that are trying to be more flexible, standard practices and procedures limit new ideas and initiatives. Deviant values are eliminated, either in the selection process or through socialization.[16] It thus becomes clear which values are accepted and which are not; whether it is preferred behavior, for example, to come to work early and stay late, or to ask for overtime pay.

Compounding the problem, every organization has toxic employees: people who are rude, not civil, and sometimes unethical. These people take a large toll on their colleagues. Their fellow workers try to avoid them and withdraw from groups in which the toxic individuals are members. Because of uncivil and unethical co-workers, some colleagues report that they ceased voluntary efforts, stopped helping newcomers, or stopped offering assistance to colleagues. Often, managers do not address the difficulties that the toxic person causes. The toxic person may be judged too valuable or may be protected by regulations that make them impervious to sanctions, including firing. Often the toxic actions are triggered in reaction to toxic actions of the person's supervisor.[17]

In any organization, the competitive, achievement-oriented manager wants to be noticed quickly as a success. Such a manager tends to focus on short-term performance, as it is more easily measured and will provide early favorable notice to top management. Market values tend to crowd out personal and social values.

## Success and Loyalty at Work

Globalization demands that firms lower their costs. Downsizing and layoffs have been the result for the past decade. Partially as a result, productivity and profits have increased, yet wages are not increasing. The downsizing has had an immense human cost. As *Business Week* put it in 1994:

> Today's corporation is no longer a secure or stable place. It's an uncertain, turbulent environment where managers often find their compassion and humanity in conflict with pressures of competition and ambition.[18]

This statement remains true today.

---

[16]For a review of the role of deviants in the organization, see Danielle E. Warren, "Constructive and Destructive Deviance in Organizations," *Academy of Management Review,* 28, no. 4 (2003): 622–632.
[17]See Peter J. Frost, *Toxic Emotions at Work: How Compassionate Managers Handle Pain and Conflict* (Boston: Harvard Business School, 2003).
[18]"The Pain of Downsizing," *Business Week,* May 9, 1994, pp. 60–69. The harsh effect on supervisors of implementing layoffs is told in Lee Smith, "Burned-out Bosses" *Fortune,* July 25, 1994, pp. 44–52.

Acknowledging that much job security and loyalty have now evaporated, some maintain that an employer who is honest and provides satisfying work can expect a new form of commitment from workers.[19] Although a recent survey shows that 75 percent of workers find satisfaction in their jobs, only 30 percent can be considered truly loyal. Another 34 percent are looking for a job elsewhere and 31 percent feel trapped in their current job because of circumstances.[20] In spite of their insecurity, people still hope that their work will provide satisfaction and fulfillment. Satisfaction generally comes from doing a job well and contributing to the happiness of others. The conviction that one's life is worthwhile gives not only satisfaction but also energy and focus to one's work. Large organizations and efficiency demand specialization of tasks and interchangeability of personnel. As work is divided up and depersonalized, much of the joy of successfully accomplishing tasks is taken away. Whether providing services or manufacturing products, workers rarely produce a finished product by themselves; rather, they perform a portion of the entire job, because specialization of labor lowers costs. A large firm often further divides the labor, creating a greater physical distance between the individual worker and the finished product.

As a result, in industrial society, satisfaction, pride in work, and a sense of ownership—things essential for healthy human life—is neglected and repressed. The goals of a firm—production and growth—take precedence over the goals of individuals. When nonhuman objectives are valued over people, the result can be isolation, loneliness, and alienation. Even though there is more wealth and there are more conveniences, life is often less fulfilling.

One reason for a lack of satisfaction is that our work ethic no longer has a foundation. When the Protestant ethic was the basic value system for Americans (see Chapter 4), personal values supported work values. But for a generation this has not been the case. Daniel Bell wrote:

> What this abandonment of Puritanism and the Protestant Ethic does is to leave capitalism with no moral or transcendental ethic. It also emphasizes an extraordinary contradiction within the social structure itself. On the one hand, the business corporation wants an individual to work hard, pursue a career, accept delayed gratification—to be, in the crude sense, an organization man. And yet, in its products and its advertisements, the corporation promotes pleasure, instant joy, relaxing and letting go. One is to be "straight" by day and a "swinger" by night.[21]

This paradox continues today and is demonstrated in self-seeking individualism and materialism, which can tear apart families, neighborhoods, and business firms.

---

[19]See articles in a special issue of *Business Ethics Quarterly,* 11 (January 2001): 1–68; Domenec Mele, "Loyalty in Business: Subversive Doctrine or Real Need?"; George Randels, "Loyalty, Corporations, and Community"; Brian Schrag, "The Moral Significance of Employee Loyalty"; Daniel R. Gilbert, Jr., "An Extraordinary Concept in the Ordinary Service of Management."

[20]The figures are from "The Walker Loyalty Report for Loyalty in the Workplace—2003." Available from Walker Information at www.walkerinfo.com.

[21]Daniel Bell, *The Cultural Contradictions of Capitalism* (New York: Basic Books, 1976), pp. 71–72.

## Money as the Goal

Material values are central for many Americans. To foreign observers, it sometimes appears as if everything Americans do is directed toward providing and acquiring material goods. A few manifestations of this orientation are the centrality of work life, advertising, the latest PC software, and designer clothes. Americans act as if they believed that happiness consists of a larger SUV or a second home for vacations. We conceive of ourselves in terms of the goods we possess. For example, consider the attitudes of today's college students, who mirror our cultural values. More than 73 percent of college freshmen surveyed around the United States believe that being financially well off is a very important goal. This number has remained stable since it rose from 40 percent in 1970. Compare this with another goal. In 1970, 83 percent of college freshmen thought that developing a meaningful philosophy of life was very important; in 2003, the percentage was only 39 percent.[22] Are college students choosing the prospect of wealth over a good education? What does this tell us about our values?

The goals of college freshman reflect the goals of their elders. Consider the well-publicized salaries of entertainers, sports figures, and CEOs; their compensation is huge and disproportionate to their contribution. Derek Bok, former president of Harvard University, is troubled by the immense salaries of corporate CEOs.[23] We will discuss executive compensation further in the next chapter.

Economic goals and business values can have a profound influence on our social and political policies as well. Business lobbying often has a decisive influence on domestic legislation and foreign policy. For example, business considerations—to ensure a steady supply of petroleum—were important elements in our decisions to invade Kuwait and Iraq.

In the last chapter, we examined Karl Marx's position that an industrial society separates people from their work and alienates them. Is working in fact an attractive and rewarding activity for most people today? Repetitive work in fast-food restaurants and menial retail clerical jobs provide little job satisfaction. Lack of satisfaction occurs when work is cut into small segments, supervisors are distant and impersonal, and there is little pride in the final product. In many of these jobs, workers are used as single-purpose tools. Such jobs thus demand little intelligence or imagination, and the workers have little control over their work or their work setting. Productivity and efficiency are chosen over pride, responsibility, and the joy that can be gotten from work.

Another factor that has undermined respect for work is its presentation on TV. When did you last see a film or a TV program that showed a businessperson who worked hard, produced a valuable product, supported teamwork among her colleagues, and was satisfied with her work? A PBS documentary entitled "Hollywood's Favorite Heavy: Businessmen on Prime Time TV" was partially underwritten by Mobil Oil. Mobil cites the findings of this documentary: "By the age of 18, the average kid has seen businessmen on TV attempt over 10,000 murders."

---

[22]"Disengaged Freshman: Interest in Politics Among First-year Students Is at a 29-year Low," Obtained from www.gseis.ucla.edu/heri/darcu_pr.html on 7/10/2004.
[23]Derek Bok, *The Cost of Talent* (New York: Free Press, 1993); *Fortune* June 26, 1995, pp. 66–76.

Businesspeople on TV "seem to make an awful lot of money, without ever having to work hard or produce useful products. To succeed, all they seem to do is lie, steal, cheat, blackmail, even murder." The documentary then shows film clips of popular TV shows in which all of those took place. Moreover, in most TV shows, school and work are both treated as frustrating, boring, trivial, and/or a joke. One who works in TV and who is also a critic names many specific shows that place work in a poor light. He then asks why we cannot have some TV that shows work as a worthwhile human activity:

> People smart enough to make brilliant shows like "Cheers" or "The Wonder Years" or "Cosby" or "L.A. Law" easily have it in their power to do what Arthur Miller did in *Death of a Salesman*, what Norman Lear did in "All in the Family", and what many other writers have done before them: to show that discipline, work, and all the habits that make people and nations self-sufficient and proud of themselves are not for losers but for winners.[24]

Executives too often show a lack of concern for people. Managers sometimes acknowledge only the short-term, bottom-line goals of better productivity, higher return on investment, and a larger share of the market. The individuals who are attracted and make it to the corporate executive suite have a great need for success. To attain their goals, they must be able to make decisions unencumbered by emotional ties to people or groups. They must always be ready to move to a new location and leave old friends, associations, and neighborhoods behind. In fact, for many there is little point in making deep friendships or getting involved in local activities; it would only make parting more difficult. This is not new; it has been true for more than a generation.[25] Those attracted to corporate executive work are often people who do not depend on close personal relationships. They obtain their major satisfaction from completing a task. Their personal values set the tone for the organization and these values are communicated to others in the firm. It is clear to all that those who are promoted are more task-oriented than person-oriented.

## Winners and Self-Developers Among Managers

After interviewing managers in large, high-technology companies, Michael Maccoby concluded that such people were not primarily interested in skills, power, or loyalty but rather in "organizing winning teams."[26] Hence he characterized successful managers as "gamesmen." Gamesmen develop many positive intellectual characteristics to aid in "winning the game" (such as analysis, problem solving, and policy development), but at the same time they allow their emotional

---

[24]Benjamin Stein, "Work Gets No Respect on TV," *Responsive Community,* Fall 1993, pp. 32–37.
[25]William E. Henry, "Executive Personality and Large-scale Organizations," in *The Emergent American Society,* ed. W. Lloyd Warner et al., vol. 1 (New Haven, CT: Yale University Press, 1967), p. 275.
[26]Michael Maccoby, *The Gamesman: The New Corporate Leaders* (New York: Simon & Schuster, 1976), p. 34.

life to atrophy. They are more detached and emotionally inaccessible than others in the corporate hierarchy.

Gamesmen do not have a "developed heart." They lack compassion and appreciation for suffering—they cannot even bear to look at suffering. Maccoby calls them "weak hearted." Many younger managers are weak-hearted gamesmen. For Maccoby, a strong-hearted manager is able to understand and to empathize with the suffering that may come from a particular business decision. The strong hearted make the best executives, in Maccoby's judgment.

Gamesmen also have little sense of social responsibility. Unaware of and hence unconcerned about the social and human effects of their actions on others, they operate on the primitive notion that the success of their organization will automatically benefit all. They refuse to consider undesirable secondary effects.

Although most of the gamesmen that Maccoby interviewed indicated that they wanted friendship and help from their friends, fewer than 10 percent of them said that helping others was a personal goal. Compare this to more than half of a group of factory workers who mentioned helping others as a personal goal. Maccoby found managers in Mexico to be "more aware than Americans that their careers protect them from the poor, but even the Mexican executives are not aware that within their enclaves they are becoming more alienated from themselves." Around their houses they build walls, and on top of those walls they put broken glass or spikes to prevent the intrusion of "undesirables." In a similar way, many affluent neighborhoods in the United States and in other countries now have walls and guardhouses to separate the wealthy from others.

Gamesmen set out to be "winners." Their intelligent, aggressive behavior makes them successful in focused tasks at work. However, they trade off much of their emotional life. The fatal danger of gamesmen is to be trapped in perpetual adolescence, striving to be winners at the game throughout adulthood.[27]

Maccoby later identified a growing group among young managers: self-developers.[28] Self-developers value opportunities to learn, grow, and gain a sense of competence and independence in an egalitarian workplace. Wary of being swallowed up by work, they are less likely to become corporate chiefs than are gamesmen. More concerned with learning and cooperation, they are motivated to succeed in family life as well as in their careers and to balance work with play. In the future, with fewer layers of middle management and more moving from one firm to another, it will be important that people be able to manage themselves. The self-developers have those qualities, and seem better adapted to business in the coming decades than do gamesmen.

## Dissent in the Organization

The importance of independent judgment has always been recognized by Americans. But although we mouth our support of independent judgment, experience and research indicate that it does not hold the high priority we claim for it. In fact, the attitudes of the group have a profound influence on the

---

[27]*Ibid.,* pp. 109, 203.
[28]Michael Maccoby, *Why Work?* (New York: Simon & Schuster, 1988).

individual. Individuals are often willing to deny their own perceptions and judgments because of the stance of their group.[29]

One of the classic experiments in studying the influence of groups on the judgment of members was done by Solomon E. Asch.[30] Asch gathered groups of seven to nine engineering students at MIT for "psychological experiments in visual judgment." Members of each group were shown two cards simultaneously; one card bore a standard line and the other bore three lines, one of which was the same length as the one shown on the first card (see Figure 7-3).

They were asked which line is the same length as line X. Is it A, B, or C? In each group, all but one member were "confederates" (i.e., instructed ahead of time to pick the same incorrect line). The remaining member was "naive" and was the only real subject of the experiment. The question at issue was: How often would a group member pick the right line even in the face of unanimous agreement by the rest of the group that another was the right one? It was visually quite clear which line was the same length as X, and ordinarily only 1 percent of the subjects would pick the wrong line. The subject was seated near the end of the group so that most of the others had responded by the time it was the subject's turn to do so.

In our reputedly individualistic society, the findings are revealing: Faced with incorrect answers by the majority, 75 percent of real subjects erred as well. Only 25 percent braved conflict with the group and held to their own perceptions. As Asch points out, when a majority of reasonably intelligent and educated young students will call black "white" when faced with the opinions of the group, it is obvious that we lose much of the benefit of individuals' independent assessments of reality. The

**FIGURE 7-3** Line Perception Experiment

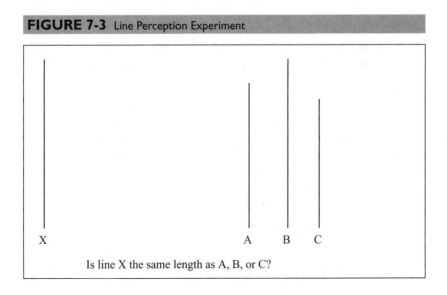

Is line X the same length as A, B, or C?

[29]Patricia Faison Hewlin, "Facades of Conformity in Organizational Settings," *Academy of Management Review,* 28, no. 4 (2003): 633–642.
[30]Solomon E. Asch, "Opinions and Social Pressure," in *Science, Conflict and Society* (San Francisco: Freeman, 1969), pp. 52–57.

opinions and values of the majority can become a tyranny. Americans can easily see this in Cuba, North Korea, or Iran, but we are less able to see it in our own society.

In spite of their positive contributions, people who exercise independent judgment are not always popular in an organization. This was shown in classic experiments involving problem-solving groups. A "deviant," a person whose values and attitudes were different from those of the group, was placed in half the groups. In every case, the groups that possessed a deviant had a better solution to the problem they were given than did the homogeneous groups. Each group was then asked to eliminate one member of the group before receiving the next problem. In every case, the deviant was thrown out, and this in spite of the fact that it was fairly clear the deviant had contributed significantly to the work they had done.[31]

Groups generally value harmony and unity more than new information and challenge. This behavior is sometimes called *groupthink*. It describes a deterioration of an individual's mental efficiency, reality testing, and moral judgment as a result of group pressures.[32] The suppression of dissent among those in working groups results in failure, often disastrous failure, as important information and options are not brought forward. Hence it is important to provide a vehicle for the expression of dissent. For example, the Challenger space shuttle accident in 1986, resulting in the loss of seven crew members, might have been avoided had not Morton Thiokol engineers' warnings about the danger of a launch at below freezing temperatures been ignored by NASA.[33] Even in the face of this disaster and its cause, NASA was unable to change, and the Colombia disaster in 2002 occurred for many of the same reasons. Even with human life at risk and in the glare of national publicity, NASA managers failed to take the necessary steps to change the culture and thus to safeguard those lives. NASA has an insular tradition; the kind that thinks it has all the answers.[34] In order to lessen the danger of such blockage of vital information and other problems, Northrop Grumman has established an ethics officer and an ethics training program at each facility; their ethics and human relations record has improved remarkably in the last two decades.

Other experiments have shown that in a group, individual competitive behavior (individuals looking exclusively to their own success and satisfaction) often leads to disruption and inefficiency in the group's effort. Competitive behavior may lead to greater efficiency when the job can be done entirely by an individual working alone. Although competitive behavior enhances speed, cooperative behavior enhances accuracy. So, in spite of the American myth, in most settings, including business, cooperative behavior leads to greater efficiency than does overly competitive behavior.[35]

---

[31]Elise Boulding, *Conflict: Management in Organizations* (Ann Arbor, MI: Foundation for Research on Human Behavior, 1964), p. 54.
[32]I. L. Janis, *Groupthink* (Boston: Houghton Mifflin, 1982); see also the discussion of groupthink in Stephen P. Robbins, *Organizational Psychology* (Englewood Cliffs: Prentice Hall, 1993), pp. 348–350.
[33]*Report of the Presidential Commission on the Space Shuttle Accident* (Washington, D.C.: U.S. Government Printing Office, 1986).
[34]William Langewiesche, "Colombia's Last Flight: The Inside Story of the Investigation and the Catastrophe It Laid Bare," *Atlantic Monthly*, 292 (November 2003): 58.
[35]Bianca Beersma et al., "Cooperation, Competition, and Team Performance: Toward a Contingency Approach," *Academy of Management Journal*, 46, no. 5 (2003): 572–590; Alfie Kohn, "How to Succeed Without Even Vying," *Psychology Today*, September 1986, pp. 22–28.

In sum, corporations tend to inculcate and thus perpetuate their own values. Like all organizations, corporations have the goals of survival and growth. These goals, plus the private enterprise goals of profit and shareholder value, have a profound influence on the attitudes and values of a firm's members. Members learn to accept the rules of the game that exist implicitly in their organization. Although creativity is of long-term benefit to the firm, it is not always tolerated. The material goals of the firm often force individuals into judging the success of their work in numerical terms: numbers of product and dollars of profit. This bias is widespread, because it is measurable and objective, but it can easily undermine long-range and human values, such as creativity, trust, and cooperation.

## WHY PEOPLE WORK: MOTIVATION AND IDEOLOGY

Why people work is no mere academic question. Executives regularly ask how to better motivate their associates and workers. There is, in fact, considerable evidence that there is a direct relationship between a company's financial performance and its commitment to a management style that considers its people as assets, not merely a cost of doing business. Yet much of our recent experience of downsizing, cutting benefits, and increasing responsibilities without increasing compensation does not seem to recognize the importance of people.[36]

One of the challenges for the concerned executive and the researcher is to determine how a firm can pursue its objectives effectively and at the same time encourage the development of its members as people. From the viewpoint of the person, social scientists have demonstrated that an individual can grow toward full maturity and achieve self-actualization only in an interpersonal atmosphere of complete trust and open communication.[37] Open, trusting, interpersonal relationships are essential to maturation. Working relationships can seldom attain total openness and trust. However, when managers are able to develop appropriate or optimal trust among stakeholders, it will improve firm performance.[38] On the other hand, if the working climate inhibits trust and personal growth, it will result in frustration and, eventually, a poor working environment. Managers are therefore especially concerned about the quality of working relationships within the organization. Management expert Charles Handy summarizes the issue this way: "The organization which treats people as assets, requiring maintenance, love, and investment, can behave quite differently from

---

[36]For the empirical evidence and the argument, see Frederick Reichheld, *Loyalty Rules!: How Today's Leaders Build Lasting Relationships* (Boston: Harvard University Press, 2001); see also Jeffrey Pfeffer and John F. Veiga, "Putting People First for Organizational Success," *Academy of Management Executive*, 13, no. 22 (1999); see also Pfeffer's *The Human Equation: Building Profits by Putting People First* (Boston: Harvard Business School Press, 1998).

[37]Herbert A. Shepard, "Changing Interpersonal and Intergroup Relationships in Organizations," in *Handbook of Organizations*, ed. James G. March (New York: Garland, 1987), pp. 1122–1137; see also Roger Mayer, James Davis, and David Schoorman, "An Integrative Model of Organizational Trust," *Academy of Management Review*, July, 1995, pp. 709–734.

[38]Andrew C. Wicks, Shawn Berman, and Thomas Jones, "The Structure of Optimal Trust: Moral and Strategic Implications," *Academy of Management Review,* 24, no. 1 (1999): 99–116.

the organization which looks upon them as costs, to be reduced wherever and whenever possible."[39]

Many business executives are dedicated to supporting the personal growth of their employees. At 3M and software designer SAS Institute, for example, executives know that the abilities of their employees can best be tapped by means of such support. It has even been shown that such support can indirectly improve flexibility, innovation, and product quality. The case for shared decision-making, which encourages individual initiative and creativity, has been building for decades. One indication of the concern firms have for these issues is the size of their training budgets and the amount of time and effort they spend encouraging shared decision-making and cooperation on the job. A variety of theories of motivation have been proposed over the years. Here we will examine a few that take account of the role of values and ideologies.

## Personal Growth Within the Organization

People in firms ask for more communication, participation, and opportunity for individual initiative. It is very important to provide challenging and satisfying work, encourage a sense of ownership, allow flexibility, and motivate employees to make their best effort. It is important to note that everyone benefits from the working environment that results from these policies. Such policies not only serve the individual need for self-development but also provide the foundation for improved product or service quality, new ideas, and greater efficiencies. Yet executives do not always perceive the importance of creating such an environment.[40]

When scholars ask why people work, they often look at values. What sort of values move the employee to work? Among the questions we might ask about popular theories and practices of motivation are these: To what extent do they imply values and goals? Do they presuppose goals or predispose one toward certain goals? Do these theories aid in a search for values and goals or do the theories mask their absence?

Businesspeople now know that there is an intimate relationship between personal values and motivation. Product quality and production efficiencies depend on the values and goals of the firm as articulated by the chief executive. Popular books and lectures of Peter Senge, Jim Collins, and Stephen Covey demonstrate that effective leadership is based on clear values and goals that are apparent in all managers in the firm.[41] These authors find that effective organizations where people are motivated are characterized by clear and articulated ideologies, values, ethics, and even spirituality. We now turn to several psychologists who have developed widely-held and influential theories of motivation.

---

[39]Charles Handy, *The Age of Unreason* (Boston: Harvard Business School Press, 1990), p. 24.
[40]Note the evidence in James E. Post, Lee E. Preston, and Sybille Sacks, *Redefining the Corporation: Stakeholder Management and Organizational Wealth* (Stanford, CA: Stanford University Press, 2002).
[41]Peter Senge, *The Fifth Discipline* (New York: Currency, 1995); Stephen R. Covey, *Principle Centered Leadership* (New York: Fireside, 1992); Covey, *Seven Habits of Highly Effective People* (New York: Fireside, 1990); see also James Collins, *Good to Great* (New York: HarperCollins, 2001).

## Self-Actualization

Abraham H. Maslow proposed the idea that motivation arises from a hierarchy of needs. Maslow based his theory of motivation on observations of healthy, mature people. For individuals to develop their own internalized philosophical and religious values, "lower needs" (food, water, safety, and security) must be somewhat satisfied. Maslow found that as lower needs were satisfied, they ceased to be motivators. The person then moved on to "higher needs" (belongingness, love, self-esteem, and self-actualization), so that healthy people are primarily motivated by their needs to develop their capacities and actualize their potentialities to the fullest.[42]

The higher needs are not dominant, according to Maslow. For all groups of people these needs are important for the individual, but they often do not emerge in people who do not have enough to eat or a roof over their heads. In Maslow's words, "The human needs for love, for knowledge or for philosophy, are weak and feeble rather than unequivocal and unmistakable; they whisper rather than shout. And the whisper is easily drowned out."

Maslow maintains that as individuals become more mature and accepting, they will establish their own values. He concludes that a firm foundation for a value system is furnished by open acceptance of one's own self, "of human nature, of much of social life, and of nature and physical reality." A society made up largely of self-actualizers is characterized by more free choice and nonintrusiveness. Under these conditions, "the deepest layers of human nature would show themselves with greater ease."[43]

Maslow goes on to describe the personal characteristics of the people he has examined—those whom he calls self-actualizers. They tend to be "strongly focused on problems outside themselves"; they are problem-centered rather than ego-centered. Most often these mature, self-actualized individuals have "some mission in life, some task to fulfill," a task outside themselves that enlists most of their energies. Such tasks are generally unselfish; they are directed primarily toward the good of others. Furthermore, self-actualizers have wide horizons; their major concerns are not ego-centered, tribal, or petty. They seem to have a stability that enables and encourages them to address large ethical and social issues.

Maslow describes in detail their ethical values. Self-actualizers "are strongly ethical, they have definite moral standards, they do right and do not do wrong." They are less confused about their basic values than others. It is easier for them to distinguish right from wrong, although their judgments do not always coincide with those of the accepted, conventional, surrounding culture.

Maslow holds that as people grow and mature, they will become less selfish and more concerned with other people and larger problems. Their values will

---

[42]Abraham H. Maslow, *Motivation and Personality* (New York: Harper & Row, 1954), pp. 35–58; *Eupsychian Management* (Homewood, IL: Irwin-Dorsey, 1965); see also Maslow's work in a larger context in Kathy Lund Dean, Charles J. Fornaciari, and James McGee, "Research in Spirituality, Religion, and Work: Walking the Line Between Relevance and Legitimacy," *Journal of Organizational Change Management,* 16, no. 4 (2003): 378–395.

[43]*Ibid.,* pp. 276–278.

become clearer, more explicit, and highly ethical. Indeed, although Maslow finds that these people are not always theists and that some have little loyalty to an institutional church, they are nevertheless the sort who could be described as godly or devout people.[44] We now turn to theories of motivation that explicitly concern the effect of the values of businesspeople.

## Need for Achievement and Need for Power

A need for achievement and a need for power are often strong motivations for businesspeople. Entrepreneurs generally have a high need for achievement; corporate executives often have both a high need for achievement and a high need for power. David C. McClelland has examined the need for achievement and the need for power. He finds that the success of an individual or a society is generally positively correlated with a high need for achievement. A person's need for achievement can be measured; it can even be increased, according to McClelland.

McClelland examines the long-range impact of a person's ideology on motivation. Just as we did in Chapter 4, McClelland cites Max Weber on the contribution of the Protestant ethic to attitudes that support modern capitalism.[45] Protestantism encouraged independence and self-reliance. Because the church was no longer the central agency for communicating values, individuals became independent.

Family upbringing has a great influence on the values and motivation, and ultimately the management style, of an adult. For example, a child whose achievements were never considered to be good enough may become a perfectionist and an approval seeker as an adult. A child whose parents exaggerate her importance may become overconfident and feel she is above the rules and can do no wrong as an adult. A workaholic more than likely assumed adult responsibilities as a child. A manager who is cowed by a boss, yet treats subordinates as children, likely had a domineering parent.[46] McClelland examined attitudes of independence, self-reliance, and a person's need for achievement, and showed how they are influenced by the manner in which parents bring up their children. From the content of children's stories, dreams, daydreams, and fantasies, McClelland determined whether there is a high or a low need for achievement. Because parents' own values and ideology influence which stories they tell their children and which books they give them, parents thus have a profound effect on their children's motivation. In experimental work, researchers found that boys who showed a high need for achievement had mothers who expected their sons to master a number of activities early in life—to know their way around the city, be active and energetic,

---

[44]*Ibid.*, pp. 168–169. Some empirical verification of Maslow's model is provided by Jean Davis-Sharts, "An Empirical Test of Maslow's Theory of Need Hierarchy Using Hologeistic Comparison by Statistical Sampling," *Advances in Nursing Science,* October 1986, pp. 58 72.
[45]Max Weber, *The Protestant Ethic and the Spirit of Capitalism,* trans. Talcott Parsons (New York: Scribner, 1958).
[46]For a review of recent research, see Michelle Conlin, "I'm a Bad Boss? Blame My Dad," *Business Week,* May 10, 2004, p. 61.

try hard to get things for themselves, do well in competition, and make their own friends.[47] On the other hand, the mothers of boys with a low need for achievement reported that they had restricted their sons more. These mothers did not want their children to make important decisions by themselves or to make friends with children not approved by their parents.

McClelland theorizes that the Protestant Reformation encouraged a new character type possessing a more vigorous and independent spirit. This spirit of self-reliance was then passed on through child rearing patterns, and McClelland holds that self-reliance forms the foundation for modern capitalism. He cites evidence that the need for achievement is increased following an ideological or religious conversion; for example, to Fundamentalism, Marxism, or Catholicism.[48] In the wake of this reflection, a challenge and a need for achievement emerge. According to McClelland, religion, ideology, and values are inextricably intertwined with motivation, especially the need for achievement. Their relationship is especially close when persons reassess and change their values.

McClelland cites Florence, Italy in the late Middle Ages as a society where the need for achievement was expressed in art. When one sees the cathedrals of Europe built in the Middle Ages, or the magnificent extant religious temples of the sun and moon built by the ancient civilizations in Mexico, it becomes clear that for many cultures religion was the major means of expressing achievement. However, in modern societies, business is the major outlet for the need for achievement. So McClelland's practical criterion for the success (and hence implicit goal) of the achiever today is economic growth. In using this criterion, McClelland accepts traditional business ideology and the prevailing social norms of industrial society—that economic growth is the final goal of a people.

McClelland acknowledges that achievement is measured in money, but he denies that the businessperson with a high need for achievement is motivated by money.[49] Money is a *symbol* of success. An increase in salary is a sign of success and is the reward to one who achieves; it is often demonstrated to friends and neighbors by a larger sport-utility vehicle, an Armani suit, or a home in Aspen. Some observations by Erich Fromm on money as a measure of personal success will be examined later in this chapter.

People who have a high need for achievement are more likely to achieve when they can be their own boss. Someone who begins a business—an entrepreneur—is motivated by a high need for achievement. Given that most new jobs are created in firms of less than 100 employees, business (and hence society as a whole) depends heavily on individuals who have a high need for achievement.

Most of McClelland's work was done examining males. More recent experimental work shows that males tend to have a high need for achievement and a high need for power, whereas females have a higher need for affiliation (relationships with others). Females tend to show achievement through nurturing and support. Women face a greater dilemma than do men in their

---

[47]David C. McClelland, *The Achieving Society* (Princeton, NJ: Van Nostrand, 1961), pp. 46–50.
[48]*Ibid.,* pp. 406–417.
[49]*Ibid.,* pp. 232–437.

business careers. Although a woman's career is quite important to her, marriage and having children increase in importance as a woman progresses in her career.[50] This calls for major decisions and often creates stress.

McClelland later turned his attention to the need for power and influence. The need for power is the desire to have an impact, to be strong or influential. McClelland found that top managers in large companies possess a need for power even greater than their need for achievement. This need for power must be "disciplined and controlled so that it is directed toward the benefit of the institution as a whole and not toward the manager's personal aggrandizement."[51] There is evidence that the Tyco, Hollinger International, WorldCom and other recent scandals resulted from the CEO's need for power; our earlier illustration of "Chainsaw Al" Dunlap warned us about that. Recall that most mergers are not profitable and that research shows that a primary motivation for mergers is the desire of the CEO for more power.[52] In addition, the huge salaries of top executives are probably less a reflection of merit and more a reflection of a need for power. We will discuss executive compensation in the next chapter.

Managers with a high need for power who do not exercise self-control can be very disruptive: "They are rude to other people, they drink too much, they try to exploit others sexually, and they collect symbols of personal prestige such as fancy cars or big offices."[53] People with a high need for affiliation are better liked by their subordinates and have a higher level of job performance. The work of the widely respected scholar-manager we examine next distinguishes two fundamental views of work.

## Work as Natural

Douglas McGregor was a business executive for several decades and later taught at MIT. He contrasts two sets of assumptions about individuals and their desire to work.[54] The first, which has heavily influenced management attitudes, he calls *Theory X:*

1. People do not like to work and will avoid it if they can do so.
2. People have little ambition, wish to avoid responsibility, prefer to be directed, and want security.
3. Therefore, in order to get them to do their work, they must be coerced, controlled, directed, and threatened by punishment.

---

[50]Janet T. Spence, "Achievement American Style," *American Psychologist,* December 1985, pp. 1285–1295. For limitations of McClelland's thesis, see R. Scott Frey, "Need for Achievement, Entrepreneurship, and Economic Growth: A Critique of the McClelland Thesis," *Social Science Journal,* 21 (April 1984): 125–134.

[51]David C. McClelland and David H. Burnham, "Power Is the Great Motivator," *Harvard Business Review,* 54, no. 2 (1976): 101.

[52]Mathew L. Hayward and Donald C. Hambrick of Colombia University Business School are quoted in "An Argument That Big Ego Is Behind a Lot of Mergers," *New York Times,* September 28, 1995, p. C2.

[53]McClelland and Burnham, p. 103.

[54]Douglas McGregor, *Human Side of Enterprise* (New York: McGraw-Hill, 1960), p. 33.

In contrast to this older, traditional view, McGregor presents his favored view, which he calls *Theory Y:*

**1.** Work is as natural to people as play or rest.
**2.** Individuals will exercise self-direction and self-control in the service of objectives to which they are committed.
**3.** Commitment to objectives is a function of the rewards associated with their achievement (especially satisfaction of ego and self-actualization).
**4.** People learn, under proper conditions, to accept and even ask for responsibility.

Each of these divergent views of the values and goals of people has a profound influence on the organizational culture, climate, and management style of any organization in which it predominates. Theory X leads to a formal, highly structured, control-oriented organization. One disadvantage that characterizes such organizations occurs when members turn procedures into goals. Mid-level managers can make adherence to the rules and preservation of their office the goal of their work—often at the expense of the people or processes they are serving. For example, an official is asked to process ten people per hour, and dutifully does so even on a day when the line is five times longer than normal. Recent strategies to increase motivation are based more on Theory Y. McGregor's approach continues to have a significant influence on managers' thinking and acting.[55]

These individual orientation–based motivation models consciously or unconsciously continue to influence managers and organizations. Meanwhile, other theories of motivation have been developed that take into account a wider variety of personality traits, attitudes, and needs as well as the situation, task, and organizational relationships. As an example, Equity Theory holds that a worker compares his tasks and compensation with peers. Negative equity comes when a worker perceives that she is receiving proportionately less than others. Positive equity comes when she perceives that she is receiving more than her peers. Expectancy theory holds that people's motivation will be determined when they perceive themselves to be receiving either positive or negative equity for their efforts.[56] Lists of salaries—which are now so easy to generate—whether of peers, CEOs, entertainers or sports figures, enable us to decide that we are not paid enough. This of course results in negative equity (and greater envy) for all.

Research shows that a person who is optimistic tends to attribute failures to temporary causes that can be overcome. Optimists therefore tend to be more resilient than pessimists. Salespeople who are optimists outsold pessimists by 20 to 40 percent. Perhaps surprisingly, optimism can be learned; we can change our view of our relationship to other people and the world.[57] On a related subject, people

---

[55]See Gary Heil, Warren Bennis, and Deborah Stephens, *Douglas McGregor, Revisited: Managing the Human Side of Enterprise* (New York: Wiley, 2000).
[56]For a summary of these theories, see Henry L. Tosi, John R. Rizzo, John Schermerhorn, James Hunt and Richard Osborn, *Managing Organizational Behavior* 5th ed. (New York: Wiley, 1994), pp. 179–185.
[57]Edwin A. Locke and Gary P. Latham, "What Should We Do About Motivation Theory: Six Recommendations for the Twenty-First Century," *Academy of Management Review,* 29 (July 2004): 394.

"in positive feeling states are more likely to behave generatively, focusing on exploring and obtaining anticipated positive outcomes." People who are "in negative affective states are more likely to focus on ... preventing negative outcomes, thus exhibiting a defensive behavioral orientation."[58] People can control their own positive and negative attitudes. Thus each of us can have a notable impact on our own attitudes, values and motivation.

It is noteworthy that a person's attitudes and values are acknowledged in these theories of motivation. The theories build upon the values of the individual. On the other hand, the values and goals of the organization in which the individual works are not overtly considered. Yet an organization's goals and values dramatically effect each participant's motivations. If the goals of an organization and an individual are in conflict, it will lead to frustration for the person and inefficiencies for the organization.

## Managing Blindly by Unexamined Assumptions

After his executive experience and working with Maslow, Douglas McGregor dug into the accepted ideology and the conventional assumptions that lie beneath thinking and literature on management and motivation. He shows that "it is not possible to reach a managerial decision or take a managerial action uninfluenced by assumptions, whether adequate or not." McGregor notes a resulting deficiency from such managerial blindness: "The common practice of proceeding without explicit examination of theoretical assumptions, leads, at times, to remarkable inconsistencies in managerial behavior."[59]

Management training and literature now emphasize the importance of reflection on our actions and goals.[60] It is not easy to cast a cool, clear eye on our own assumptions and values. We all engage in various shortcuts in considering our own and others' values. Rationalization, stereotyping, and other mechanisms block our ability to perceive what exactly these values are. Sometimes these barriers also block our ability to reflect on the goals and the values of the organization. Some convince themselves, for example, that the growth of the organization benefits some people and thus automatically compensates for damage done to others. Some think that businesspeople waste time when they reflect on abstract values and goals.

On the other hand, it is clear that there is no such thing as value-free management. Carrying out the goals of an organization without knowing what presuppositions undergird those goals is itself choosing to make decisions on the basis of a value. That value is the unquestioning faith that the goals of the organization are justifiable, and that in a conflict with another organization or with the

---

[58]Myeong-Gu Seo, Lisa F. Barrett, and Jean M. Bartunek, "The Role of Affective Experience in Work Motivation," *Academy of Management Review,* 29 (July 2004): 520. This issue of *AMR* has a special section on the future of work motivation theory.
[59]McGregor, *Human Side of Enterprise,* p. 7.
[60]See, for example, Jim Collins, Good to Great: *Why Some Companies Make the Leap and Others Don't* (New York: HarperBusiness, 2001); Peter Senge, *The Fifth Discipline* (New York: Currency, 1995); Stephen R. Covey, *Seven Habits of Highly Effective People.*

community, one should pursue the goals of one's own firm. The training program for traders at Wall Street's Salomon Brothers taught bullying, deception, and male chauvinist behavior toward customers. General Electric falsified overcharges to the government. Archer Daniels Midland conspired to fix artificially high prices for their products. Many people in each of these organizations were aware of the fraud and even contributed to it. Rationalizations and socialization of newcomers brought on continued corruption in these firms.[61] Such scandals encourage a lack of trust in management.

## PRESSURE FOR MORE WORK

Pressing for greater productivity, firms are increasing the work hours demanded each week in the United States, and this work week is now longer than in any other developed country. Workers in the United States now put in 1,800 hours a year on the job, 350 hours more than the Germans and slightly more than the Japanese, according to the International Labor Office. More than 30 percent of United States workers say they are always or often under stress at work. Perhaps as a result of this, only 25 percent of workers say they "are just showing up to collect a paycheck". And only 14 percent say they are very satisfied with their job. A major grievance is the continuing efforts of employers to squeeze more hours from their workers, thus lowering labor costs. In the United States, 62 percent of workers say that their job activities and responsibilities have increased during the past six months, and that they had not used all their allotted vacation time. Moreover, 60 percent said that they did not expect any lessening of pressure in the future. In addition, only 20 percent of United States workers feel their employer's promotion policies are fair.[62]

Americans not only work more hours, but also have less vacation time than people of any other industrialized nation; the American worker takes 10.2 vacation days per year while counterparts in France and Germany enjoy 30 or more vacation days per year.[63] In addition, the globalized economy operates 24 hours a day and 7 days a week, so that 40 percent of all employed Americans work during the evenings, nights, on rotating shifts or on weekends.[64] The work site for professionals is now more likely to be an open cubicle, which shows its air of impermanence, and is a reminder of a lack of stability and security in the corporate workplace.

Low-wage workers bear an increasing share of the work burden. Security guards, child-care workers, maids, tellers, cooks, home-health aids and hairdressers

---

[61]Vikas Anand, Black Ashforth, and Mahendra Joshi, "Business As Usual: The Acceptance and Perpetuation of Corruption in Organizations," *Academy of Management Executive,* 18 (May 2004): 39–53.
[62]See the figures in *Business Week,* March 28, 2005, p. 14; John Schwartz, "Sick of Work: Always on the Job: Employees Pay with Health," *New York Times,* Sept 5, 2004; and Mark Landler, "Europe Reluctantly Deciding It Has Less Time for Time Off," *New York Times,* July, 7, 2004, p. 1 and C2.
[63]Lou Dobbs, "The Perils of Productivity," *U.S. News & World Report,* November 10, 2003, p. 58; "Hate Your Job? Join the Club," *Business Week,* October 6, 2003, p. 40.
[64]"The 24-hour, Seven-Day Global Economy Is on Us," *Chemical and Engineering News,* June 28, 1999, p. 88.

earn less than the federal poverty level (about $9 an hour for a family of four in 2004). Minorities are over-represented in this group, but two thirds are white and about 60 percent are women.[65]

Some CEOs, such as Andy Grove of Intel and Steve Ballmer of Microsoft, rule by fear, which further increases stress. Moreover, e-mail and pagers enable a supervisor to give directions to subordinates, even while the subordinates are on vacation. Hence free time for many has all but disappeared. Some indict executives and corporations because they have betrayed us through longer hours, reductions in benefits, increased workloads, downsizing for workers, but immense executive compensation for themselves. If people expect meaningful work, most will not find it.[66] All of this places constant pressure and additional stress on workers and their families. This results in increased turnover, and that in turn is costly in morale, loyalty, and money.[67]

We have examined the increased demands that are placed on people in the workplace in the name of productivity, and how this results in less satisfaction at one's job and increasing stress in the workplace. Now let us examine the business manager and his impersonal values. A classic empirical study of the business executive characterizes him as a mobile person, able to leave and take up a new job in a new community rather easily: "The mobile [manager] must be able to depart; that is, to maintain a substantial emotional distance from people, and not become deeply involved with them or committed to them."[68]

These top managers are thus not always sensitive to the needs of other people. Even though their own success is often built on decisions that result in sometimes substantial loss for others, this does not seem to bother them. They are not "distracted into personal duels, for they do not allow themselves to become so involved with others." When Chevron cut 56,000 jobs and AT&T dropped 100,000 employees, executives could not allow that to overly affect them, even though more than a hundred thousand families were severely hurt. Yet evidence shows that if surviving managers do not understand the rationale for the downsizing effort, it is impossible to do it effectively. It is emotionally wrenching work, and such managers are ". . . often ill-prepared to make a full commitment, especially if they are confused about the reasons for the downsizing and their role in its implementation."[69]

---

[65]Beth Shulman, *The Betrayal of Work: How Low-Wage Jobs Fail 30 Million Americans* (New York: The New Press, 2003).

[66]Jill Andresky Fraser, *White Collar Sweatshop: The Deterioration of Work and Its Rewards in Corporate America* (New York: W.W. Norton, 2001); see also Joanne B. Ciulla, *The Working Life* (New York: Random House, 2000); Al Gini, *My Job My Self: Work in the Creation of the Modern Individual* (New York: Routledge, 2001).

[67]Arie C. Glebbeek and Erik H. Bax, "Is High Employee Turnover Really Harmful? An Empirical Test Using Company Records," *Academy of Management Journal*, 47, no. 2 (2004): 277–286. On stress in the workplace, see the two-day series of articles in *Wall Street Journal*, January 16, pp. B1, B4, and January 17, 2001, pp. B1, B4.

[68]W. Lloyd Warner and James Abegglen, *Big Business Leaders in America* (New York: Atheneum, 1963), pp. 81–82.

[69]Hugh M. O'Neill and D. Jeffery Lenn, "Voices of Survivors: Words that Downsizing CEOs Should Hear," *Academy of Management Executive*, 9 (August 1995): 23–34.

Mobility and lack of concern for others enable these executives to approach managerial decisions dispassionately. This objectivity contributes to their success. But that success does not allow them the satisfaction one might expect. There is rarely time to relax or to look back on their successes, "for an essential part of the system is the need for constant demonstration of one's adequacy, for reiterated proof of one's independence."[70] Also noteworthy is the fact that, when they began in the firm, most chief executives had a master's degree in business administration, and 60 percent did not have a specific career goal in mind.[71]

Even today chief executives are still most often white, male, married, and politically conservative. When chief executives were asked what they would look for in their successors, they replied that they would generally look for people who were much like themselves in background and attitudes. Organizations and their attitudes tend to be self-perpetuating. The ordinary struggle for survival and growth urges people and organizations to seek "their own kind." Although there are now some large black-owned and -managed firms and an increasing number of women are in executive positions, African-Americans, other minority groups, and women are still under-represented in chief executive positions.

Some people who can afford to do so are now retiring early. Eugene Bernosky, 38, sold the semiconductor equipment firm he co-founded, Applied Chemical Solutions Inc. After putting in 80-hour weeks for several years, he asked himself if this was really what he wanted to be doing. He says that there are only two things that money cannot buy you—time and friends. Lonnie Fogel, 41, worked as public relations director at Home Depot and had thousands of shares of company stock. He realized he had enough money to quit, if he lived frugally. He is now bicycling, writing a screen play, and doing volunteer work.[72] Another new social phenomenon is spouses who decide to remain behind when the working partner is transferred to another city. The home spouse decides that the move is too disruptive to children's schooling, family, friends, etc. The working spouse then commutes home on weekends to visit the family. One survey indicated that as many as 5 percent remain behind when the transfer is overseas and 7 percent stay behind when the transfer is within the United States.[73]

## Following Orders

Following orders within an organization is essential to any organization's success. However, to what extent should persons follow orders when those orders seriously violate their own moral values? Evidence of a person's willingness actually to do harm to another individual when instructed by authority to do so was provided by

---

[70]Warner and Abegglen, p. 83.
[71]"Profile of Leadership Emerges in Study of Top Corporate Executives," *Journal of Accountancy,* March 1987, pp. 36–38.
[72]"Retire at 40: Some Do, with a Small Fortune and a Dose of Frugality," *Wall Street Journal,* August 21, 1996, pp. 1, 4.
[73]"To Some Commuters, Going Home Means a Long Plane Ride," *Wall Street Journal,* March 7, 1996, p. 1.

a series of controversial laboratory experiments conducted by Stanley Milgram.[74] Subjects were told by an academic authority figure dressed in a white coat that they were to engage in experiments in memory and learning. Each subject was placed at a shock generator with 30 intervals marked, starting with 15 volts (labeled "Slight shock") and going up to 450 volts (labeled "Danger—severe shock"). Another person (the learner), who was strapped in a chair with electrodes on his or her wrists, could be seen in an adjoining room through a glass partition. The learners were in on the experiment and were not really subjected to shocks. The subject was then instructed to shock the learner, increasing the intensity for every wrong answer the learner gave. As the shock level rose, the learner cried out in seeming increasing pain, yet almost two-thirds of the subjects administered the highest level of shock.

Each subject would become nervous, agonize, and rationalize, but most nevertheless administered the highest level of shock under the auspices of authority. The experiment has been criticized as being unethical. Indeed, it did play on the subject's conscience. However, it also gave us frightening evidence of what one human being is willing to inflict on another when it seems to be called for by some authority.

Obedience in this experiment declines if the subject is in the same room as the learner or if the subject must actually touch the learner to administer the shock. The more impersonal the situation, the more willing the subject is to do harm to another. Ancient warfare involved face-to-face contact; some modern warfare is closer to the above experimental situation and easier to wage. A person can push a button and never witness the death and destruction caused by the exploding shell or missile.

In the workplace, lower-level managers are sometimes told to do something that violates their ethics and conscience. The aforementioned experiment shows that about 60 percent of us will perform actions at serious variance to what we know to be right if someone in authority instructs us. Yet this sort of obedience has its costs in tension, anxiety, stress, and attendant physical ailments.

Modern organizations are designed to produce results in an impersonal fashion. Downsizings, manipulative advertising, and pollution are all the result of decisions and policies made by executives. Such stressful and often unethical actions occur more often when executives do not see the victims of their actions. The manager does not have to face his victims; moreover, financial return on investment and preserving the jobs of others demand the downsizing. In the minds of some executives, the system demands that they act impersonally if their firm is to grow.

## Selling of Self: Careerism

Although the goals and values of a businessperson are influenced by background, education, and age, such goals and values are also influenced by the person's estimate of the profile that will "sell" in the marketplace. The market

---

[74]Stanley Milgram, *Obedience to Authority* (New York: Harper & Row, 1974).

value of a person—how much that person can obtain in the employment market—has a great influence on notions of self-worth.[75] We call selling oneself *careerism*.

For example, imagine the case of a business woman looking for a new position. She will be concerned about how she appears to prospective employers. Dressing for success and using proper grammar and vocabulary will be important. She might be less concerned about her own goals of achievement, satisfaction, and happiness. In short, her attention will be on pleasing someone else rather than on her own values and goals. The more her self-esteem depends on how much she perceives she is worth in the market, the less control she will have over her own life. She may think that she is not valued for the person she is and that her adequacy is determined by insensitive market forces—the price others put on her. When she receives an increase in salary, it will be less the money itself that delights her than the fact that someone has recognized that she has done a good job. Without a large salary increase, she might sink into depths of poor self-esteem and perhaps depression.

Furthermore, because the market is often the principal determinant of self-worth, and because value in the market is subject to many changing, unpredictable forces and fads, she must remain flexible. Her present value may collapse, simply because there are too many with the same talents on the market. She must be able then to shift to a new career. The phenomenon of glutted labor markets demands that businesspeople maintain flexibility and maximum exposure. No matter how much she may like her present work or locale, it is not to her advantage to sink deep roots. If she becomes known as a one-talent person, her value will be severely limited. This situation does not encourage developing loyalty to a firm or becoming involved in a community.[76]

This notion of self-worth makes a businessperson dependent on others for self-esteem. Self-worth stems not from accomplishments or the affection of others but rather from the impersonal forces of the employment market and from company superiors. The influence of a changing external environment on personal values forces Americans to be practical and pragmatic. They consider martyrdom to be folly, and will rarely dispute principles for their own sake. Thomas More's beheading by Henry VIII because he would not betray a principle makes superb drama in *Man for All Seasons*. Americans find the episode quaint but difficult to understand and smacking of fanaticism. Indeed, businesspeople find disputes over principles to be unproductive and time-consuming and will rarely allow themselves to be caught up in what seems to be impractical, and hence useless, battles.

---

[75]Erich Fromm, "Personality and the Market Place," in *Man, Work, and Society: A Reader in the Sociology of Occupations,* eds. Sigmund Nosow and William Form (New York: Basic Books, 1962), pp. 446–452.
[76]For more on these stresses, especially those on women in the workplace, see Arlie Russell Hochschild, *The Commercialization of Intimate Life: Notes from Home and Work* (Berkeley, CA: University of California Press, 2003).

## BALANCING WORK-LIFE CONFLICT

Being able to balance one's work and the rest of one's life is essential for personal happiness, but very often there is a conflict between them. A challenging job, long working hours, a distant commute, and young children are all conflicting demands. The stress they generate can result in physical and mental illness. Consider the fact that 58 percent of women with children under one year of age work, and the large portion of families in which both spouses work. The stress of work-family imbalance contributes to depression, hypertension, heart disease, heavy alcohol use, absenteeism, and loss of productivity.[77]

Women bear most of the burden of the work-family conflict. It is much more difficult for a woman to be both a successful executive and a successful mother than it is for a man to hold parallel successful roles. Note that of high-achieving women who are 40 years old and making $100,000 or more, only 57 percent are married, compared to 83 percent of men. Moreover, 49 percent of these women are childless compared to 19 percent of men in the same category. Perhaps more troubling, only 14 percent of these women said that they choose to be without children.[78] Promotions go to those who work 40–60 hour weeks and have no other demands on their time. This places working mothers at a disadvantage in the workplace. Over her career, a woman earns only about 44 percent of what a man in a similar job earns.[79] This is because women carry most of the burden of caregiving, which requires time and attention; thus women are often not viewed as being committed to their careers, so they do not receive the equivalent promotions.

In poor and lower-middle-income families, children are also the losers. The majority (70%) of American children come from homes where both parents work full-time. Although some firms provide child care, most do not. Paying for child care costs as much as tuition at a state university, and care is unavailable at night, when many parents must work. The school day is less than two-thirds the length of the work day, the school year is 30 percent shorter than the ordinary work year, and only 20 percent of schools offer after-school programs. The United States is behind 120 other countries in granting paid maternity leaves. France, Belgium, and Finland provide universal school or child care beginning at age two. Global competition pressures firms to cut costs, so business is unlikely to initiate new programs. Unlike other countries, the United States has no national program to aid families with child care issues that make life for working

---

[77]Marc Marchese, Gregory Bassham, and Jack Ryan, "Work Family Conflict: A Virtue Ethics Analysis," *Journal of Business Ethics*, 40 (October 2002): 145–154; also Philip Frame and Mary Hartog, "From Rhetoric to Reality: Into the Swamp of Ethical Practice: Implementing Work-Life Balance," *Business Ethics—A European Review*, 12 (October 2003): 358–368.

[78]Sylvia Ann Hewlett, *Creating A Life: Professional Women and the Quest for Children* (New York: Talk Miramax, 2002); see also "Mommy Is Really Home from Work: More Female High Achievers Are Stopping Out to Raise Kids—And Avoiding Corporate America When They Return," *Business Week*, November 25, 2002, p. 101–104.

[79]Aaron Bernstein, "Women's Pay: Why the Gap Remains a Chasm," *Business Week*, June 14, 2004, pp, 58–59.

people difficult. Moreover, the lack of care and supervision of children now will have a negative effect on the next generation.[80]

Many firms today do recognize the conflict between work and family and provide helpful work options for their people: flextime, telecommuting, a four 10-hour-day work week, help for child care, and advice and resources for employees on family problems they face. This can help to relieve the conflicting demands of work and home. However, increasing numbers of lower level, part-time, and contract workers do not qualify for these work-family options or even for pensions or medical insurance.

Motorola, Eli Lilly, Eddie Bauer, Unum Life Insurance, and DuPont get good marks from their employees for being family-friendly firms. Although workers at most firms feel that their work has a negative impact on their home life, this is not true in an increasing number of firms. Among other firms credited are American Home Products for child care programs, Bank One for expanded sick leave, adoption aid, and retirement savings plans, and Procter & Gamble for new training and internal communication plans for women. These firms and an increasing number of others recognize that work and family have a profound impact on each other. As a result, they encourage supervisors to be sensitive and they allow flexible hours to care for family needs, including children and elders.[81] Laura Nash recommends balancing one's primary spheres of life: happiness, achievement, significance, and legacy, and to recognize that having just enough in each sphere is far better than having too much or being the best in one. She maintains that it is more satisfying to maintain balance than to stress oneself over not being the best.[82]

On the individual level, businesspeople often experience a conflict between their personal attributes that are rewarded on the job and those that make for being a good spouse and parent. Consider an example: A typical manager is assertive, decisive, and fact-oriented, and makes decisions not on the basis of intuition or feelings, but on the basis of data and defensible reasoning. However, this talent of examining only the facts and using only reason does not work so well when the manager is at home with spouse and children. For example, when one's spouse asks to go to a movie, it is not necessarily because she wants to see a particular film; she may simply desire to be alone with her husband for a few hours away from the house and children. In fact, caring, sensitivity, and generosity to others, characteristics that make for being a good spouse and parent, have been found to have a positive value in the work organization as well, even increasing productivity. In a larger context, cooperation, trust, and good morale—fostered by the same qualities at work as at home—build social capital, which in turn

---

[80]The data in this section is from Jody Heymann, M.D., *The Widening Gap: Why America's Working Families Are in Jeopardy and What Can Be Done About It* (New York: Basic Books, 2001).
[81]"Balancing Work and Family: Big Returns for Companies Willing to Give Family Strategies a Chance," *Business Week,* September 16, 1996, pp. 74–80; and "More Firms Compete to be Named on Lists as 'Family Friendly,' " *Wall Street Journal,* August 21, 1996, p. B1.
[82]Laura Nash and Howard Stevenson, *Just Enough: Tools for Creating Success in Your Work and Life* (New York: John Wiley, 2004).

encourages creativity and initiative and increases productivity and profitability — especially in high-growth companies.[83]

The fact-oriented manager may also have difficulty determining what his son or daughter is saying beneath either the quiet or the flurry of words. He has trained himself to look for the facts and so he takes the situation at face value. Furthermore, he might even lose patience with his wife and children for not saying what they mean. For him, it is not natural to sift through the words to determine what his wife, son, or daughter is really saying — often nonverbally. Moreover, in his impatience, he may not be able to be open enough to encourage them to communicate what they really are thinking and feeling. He is sometimes aware of this inability and the resulting conflict, and this causes additional tension and anxiety.

A person like the managers mentioned above has what is called a Type A personality, which is characterized by impatience, restlessness, aggressiveness, and competitiveness. Type A people also tend to have many irons in the fire and to be under considerable time pressure. Sixty percent of managers in the average organization are Type A. The Type A manager who is angry and cynical is two to five times more likely to have heart disease or a fatal heart attack than other managers. It is the quickness to anger and a habitual hostile outlook that contributes to heart problems. Children who do not get unconditional love from parents and considerable physical contact are more likely to become distrustful, easy-to-anger adults. Interestingly enough, it has been shown that although many Type A managers have the talent and attitude that enable them to rise in the organization, chief executive officers are generally not Type A; CEOs are more patient and more willing to examine the long-term ramifications of decisions.[84]

## Spirituality in the Workplace

Interest in spirituality in the workplace has increased dramatically in the last decade. The reason for this upsurge in interest is that spirituality is answering a need of businesspeople. Spirituality helps a person deal with the anxiety and stress that are characteristic of modern society. Spirituality helps to balance some of the major negative characteristics of our culture that cause this stress: materialism, depersonalization, the elevation of individual freedom over that of the community, and the inability to escape the 24/7 demands of the office. It is materialistic to say that the purpose of the market system is merely to create wealth, and not give priority to providing goods, services, and jobs; spirituality helps a manager to see the larger goal of business.

---

[83]Juan Florin, Michael Lubatkin, and William Schultz, "A Social Capital Model of High Growth Companies," *Academy of Management Journal,* 46, no. 3. (2003): 374–384; Francis J. Flynn, "How Much Should I Give and How Often? The Effects of Generosity and Frequency of Favor Exchange on Social Status and Productivity," *Academy of Management Journal,* 46, no. 5. (2003): 539–553; also Susan J. Lambert, "Added Benefits: The Link Between Work-Life Benefits and Organizational Citizenship Behavior," *Academy of Management Journal,* 43, no. 5 (2000): 801–815.
[84]Interview with Redford Williams, M.D., "Getting to the Heart of Type A's," *U.S. News & World Report,* May 15, 1989, p. 68.

Business managers can depersonalize individuals, and see them largely as workers to be paid or customers to be sold to. There is too little opportunity for businesspeople to see themselves as being intimately connected to other people (fellow workers, family, and neighbors), especially when they live in large cities and endure frequent career moves. Finally, the electronic aids for providing information globally link businesspeople. Cell phones often ring in restaurants, classrooms, social events, and even in church; this disrupts people's lives and leaves little time for enjoyment, quiet, and meditation. The pace and demands of business life often leave too little time to connect with the really important elements in one's life.[85] As one executive put it, "You get to the top of the ladder, and maybe find out that it is leaning against the wrong building."[86]

Spirituality can aid a person in providing balance and integration for all of one's life, including one's work life. Moreover, spirituality has advantages for the firm as well as for the person. It can help to make the workplace more ethical and humane, where believers and non-believers alike can find fulfillment. On the other hand, some fear that promoting spirituality in the workplace can lead to coercion and favoritism, and thus be divisive. This fear is greater when people bring religion into the workplace. Of course, any religious favoritism in hiring or promotion is unjust, and violates both American ideals and U.S. law.

What do we mean by spirituality? *Spirituality = a worldview + a path.* According to this broad definition, anyone who has the ability to reflect on his or her own life has a spirituality. A spiritual worldview is practical; it engages the person. It can be simple, sophisticated, religious, or even secular. By this broad definition, even materialism or achieving success can be a spirituality if it is the dominant worldview of that person. However, many question the adequacy of a spirituality with a goal of materialism or success. Most spiritualities acknowledge a supreme being or a higher power to whom one is dependant. Spiritualities often are rooted in a religion, with a belief in a supreme being, and those who practice them pray to that supreme being (e.g., God, Allah, Yahweh). Most spiritualities also emphasize our responsibility for each other.

A spirituality also involves a path; that is, a way of proceeding. For example, Muslims pray and prostrate themselves before Allah four times a day; a Zen Buddhist follows specific meditation practices. For a person who has a secular world view, the path might involve personal appreciation of nature and attention to preserving the environment. The path for many includes gathering in a church with people of similar beliefs where they are able to pray, form community, and do good works for others. There is even evidence that religious beliefs—for example, belief in hell and heaven—positively influence economic performance.

---

[85]Gerald Cavanagh, Bradley Hanson, Kirk Hanson, and Juan Hinojoso, "Toward a Spirituality for the Contemporary Organization: Implications for Work, Family and Society," in *Spiritual Intelligence at Work; Research in Ethical Issues in Organizations*, ed. Moses Pava and Patrick Primeaux (Amsterdam: Elsevier, 2003), pp. 111–138; see also Gerald F. Cavanagh, "Spirituality for Managers: Context and Critique" in *Work and Spirit*, ed. Jerry Biberman and Michael Whitty (Scranton, PA: University of Scranton Press, 2000), pp. 149–166.
[86]Marc Gunther, "God and Business: The Surprising Quest for Spiritual Renewal in the American Workplace," *Fortune,* July 9, 2001, pp. 58–80.

The authors of a large-scale study think that religious beliefs stimulate economic growth because they support individual values such as honesty, thrift, a work ethic, and openness to strangers, which are fundamental to business.[87]

On the other hand, some fear this new interest in spirituality and religion. They note the many acts of cruelty and discrimination that have been done in the name of religion (such as terrorist acts committed by Al Qaeda, the Crusades, the Spanish Inquisition, burning of "witches," treatment of women in Muslim countries, and genocide in Rwanda and Bosnia). However, the record shows that in most of these cases, religion has been the excuse for longstanding regional or tribal enmities. This raises an important question for contemporary peoples. Is it possible for a group to have strong spiritual and religious beliefs and practices, and yet include among those beliefs a respect and even love for peoples of other nations, tribes, and religions? The challenge of our modern world is to achieve such global understanding and respect.

Some Americans say they possess a spirituality, but they have little use for religion. Religion generally involves ritual, dogma, and group prayer, which they do not value. Such non-religious spirituality is in accord with American individualism. The person is not tied by liturgy, beliefs, or dependence on a congregation. However, such an attitude also bears the negative side of individualism: the reluctance to commit to other people, a group, or a pattern of living one's life.

Some firms have encouraged the formation of employee support groups, based on their common religious faith. Ford Motor Company began the Ford Interfaith Network in 2000. "The Company's global vision for diversity and worklife is to create an inclusive culture that respects the whole person and values all differences . . . since Ford Motor Company is an international, multicultural organization." Ford's objective is to become "a world-wide corporate leader in promoting religious tolerance, corporate integrity, family values, and human dignity."[88] The network links Hindu, Muslim, Catholic, Jewish, Evangelical Christian, and Mormon Ford workers. The Ford Interfaith Network has enabled Ford workers to gather to enrich their personal and shared spiritualities. In another example, Ricardo Levy, a Silicon Valley entrepreneur, considered selling a division of Catalytica, his 1,800-employee chemical firm. After doing the financials, Levy had many questions beyond whether the price was right. He was also concerned with whether the sale was good for employees and customers. Levy, who is Jewish, ultimately used a Christian discernment process developed by St. Ignatius Loyola to reach this most important decision to sell the division.

## A Career as a Vocation

People spend much time and effort determining their careers. A career can be part of a vocation, but it is not the same as a vocation. A vocation is larger and more

---

[87]Robert J. Barro and Rachel M. McCleary, "Religion and Economic Growth Across Countries," *American Sociological Review,* 58 (October 2003): 760; see also Patrick Primeaux and Gina Vega, "Operationalizing Maslow: Religion and Flow as Business Partners," *Journal of Business Ethics,* 38 (June 2002): 97–108.
[88]E-mail to all Ford employees, "Ford Interfaith Network," from Martin Inglis, April 12, 2001.

all-embracing. The word vocation is from the Latin word *vocare,* to call. It is a personal answer to the questions: Who am I? What should I do with my life? Where am I going in my life? Working out a vocation is not merely an individual task. A vocation is a calling, an invitation, and the answer to this invitation is generally worked out in prayer accompanied by at least some others of the relevant community. For many persons, that prayer is a careful, disciplined attempt to discern God's will for themselves and their lives. Hearing that call brings a greater freedom. In following the call, persons are able to follow their own talents, loves, and intuitions, and help others at the same time. People who do not believe in God can consider their vocations in relation to that which transcends the ego, such as a higher power or the world community. Nevertheless, the call is often hard to hear, and sometimes not welcome. Moreover, the voice is often drowned out by the busyness that surrounds us every day.

Recognizing that one is called to a particular line of work can give one assurance, courage, and security. When one finds his or her vocation, life is stirred; it engages the emotions. The very process of determining one's vocation enables one to be more self-reflective and to learn more about one's self. Such reflection also enables one to be more adaptable. Part of a vocation is an invitation to serve a community; it might result in work on behalf of the poor or the environment. Serving the community is an essential part of the tradition of every major religion. A principal benefit of finding one's vocation is that it brings a clarity of thought and action, and the inner peace that this provides.[89] Other people and families generally find that a person who has found and accepted a vocation is more centered, compassionate, and understanding. Determining their calling enables business executives to follow their own journey, to become better persons and better executives at the same time.[90]

Meditation is encouraged at many firms, and many businesspeople are engaging in this practice, sometimes joining an online meditation group. People who meditate find that it offers a number of benefits. New research shows that even short periods of meditation can have a profound influence on a person's mind and body both. Some find that meditation alleviates lower back pain, headaches, and arthritis; reduces absenteeism; increases brain wave activity; helps intuitive decision making; and benefits concentration.[91] A large-scale and well-publicized research study of Catholic religious sisters in the United States found that, while an active mind and body increased longevity, " . . . profound faith, like a positive outlook, buffers the sorrows and tragedies that all of us experience.

---

[89]Joseph Weiss, Michael Skelley, Douglas (Tim) Hall, and John C. Haughey, "Vocational Calling, New Careers, and Spirituality," in *Spiritual Intelligence at Work: Research in Ethical Issues in Organizations,* eds. Moses Pava and Patrick Primeaux (Amsterdam: Elsevier, 2003), pp. 175–201.
[90]James J. McGee and Andre L. Delbecq, "Vocation as a Critical Factor in a Spirituality for Executive Leadership in Business," in *Business, Religion and Spirituality,* eds. Oliver F. Williams, C.S.C. (Notre Dame, Ind.: University of Notre Dame Press, 2003); the 16 other articles in this volume are also excellent.
[91]"Meditation: New Research Shows That It Changes the Brain in Ways That Alleviate Stress," *Business Week,* August 30, 2004, pp. 136–137; and "Zen and the Art of Corporate Productivity: More Companies Are Battling Employee Stress with Meditation," *Business Week,* July 28, 2003, p. 56.

Evidence is now starting to accumulate from other studies that prayer and contemplation have a positive influence on long-term health and may even speed the healing process."[92]

However, caution is in order here. If spirituality, meditation, and even religion is embraced in order to achieve good health results, that spirituality, meditation, or religion is likely to be superficial and shallow. Many of the current books and conferences on spirituality are "limited in scope and avoid the hard issues. Death, suffering, injustice, the nature of the transcendent, worship, and awe are mostly overlooked in favor of mental techniques for reducing stress and achieving higher performance."[93]

Ten organizations from around the world were selected as winners of the 2004 *International Spirit at Work Awards*. These firms employ more than 150,000 people and are headquartered in India, the Philippines, and the United States. Two are chemical manufacturers, two are banks, and six are hospital systems. The largest of the awardees, Ascension Health, has 88,500 full-time employees and was honored for spirituality training programs, a Spirituality Symposium, a Spirituality Scorecard for each hospital, and a seven-step ethical discernment process. Medtronic and the *Times of India* are former winners of the International Award.[94]

Princeton University has set up a program jointly sponsored by their business and divinity schools to help businesspeople integrate their spirituality with their work. Its director, David W. Miller, is also president of The Avodah Institute, which has a mission "to help leaders integrate the claims of their faith with the demands of their work"[95] The Institute sponsors conferences, encourages research, and provides advice for businesspeople.

## Executives as Leaders

Executives bear a special responsibility to set the ethical tone of their organizations.[96] They should lead their organization in such a way that they provide a sense of integrity, accomplishment, and satisfaction, not stress, to their members. James Autry was senior vice president of Meredith Publishing, a Fortune 500 firm. He offers five guidelines for successful management. Three of these are: "Be honest," "Trust your employees," and "If you don't care about people, get out of management before it is too late." He emphasizes his last point by saying, "Save yourself a heart attack and save many other people a lot of daily grief." This parallels statements made earlier in this chapter. He points out that in the work setting, "friends and co-workers are the new extended family." He notes that younger workers are looking for good values in the workplace. This value-quest

---

[92]David Snowdon, *Aging with Grace: What the Nun Study Teaches Us About Leading Longer, Healthier, and More Meaningful Lives* (New York: Bantam Books, 2001).
[93]See Laura Nash, "A Spiritual Audit of Business Firms: From Tipping Point to Tripping Point," in *Business, Religion and Spirituality, op. cit.*
[94]For more information, see www.spiritatwork.org.
[95]For more information, see www.avodahinstitute.com.
[96]Terry Thomas, John Schermerhorn, and John Dienhart, Strategic Leadership of Ethical Behavior," *Academy of Management Executive,* 18 (May 2004): 56–83.

has produced, for the first time in the history of American publishing, a decade in which business books consistently have been on the bestseller list. Most of those books deal with values and relationships, not high finance. Autry finds that when the sports metaphor is used to describe business it is not helpful:

> By invoking the metaphor of sports teams these days, we imply that we in business are involved in a game in which there must be winners and losers, in which there are stars who play and benchwarmers who watch, in which our personal success is measured only by the numbers on the scoreboard and not by how well we played, and in which our value to society is transitory at best.[97]

Autry concludes by asking what kind of a CEO Jesus would be.

Max DePree was CEO of Herman Miller, Inc. and he underscores the same points and adds a religious viewpoint. For example, he writes about a business leader forming a "covenant" with the people in the firm. He says, "Covenants bind people together and enable them to meet their corporate needs by meeting the needs of one another." DePree emphasizes that leaders must take a role in developing, expressing, and defending civility and values. As examples, he lists some actions to be avoided:

> To be a part of a throwaway mentality that discards goods and ideas, that discards principles and law, that discards persons and families, is to be at the dying edge. To be at the leading edge of consumption, affluence, and instant gratification is to be at the dying edge. To ignore the dignity of work and the elegance of simplicity, and the essential responsibility of serving each other, is to be at the dying edge.[98]

Both Autry and DePree are examples of successful business managers who can be described as *servant leaders*. As leaders, they are servants of those they lead. They clear the way so that those who report to them are able to do their jobs even better. In the process, those subordinates grow as people, and also become healthier, wiser, freer, and more autonomous. The servant leadership movement is growing as this style of leadership is becoming more popular. It will be discussed further in Chapter 10.

Rapid technological change, information richness, and global competition require marshaling the best efforts of all the people in an organization. Executives can bring this about by encouraging teamwork, empowerment of workers, and open and distributed information systems. Such leaders encourage self-leadership—that is, each person takes initiatives and uses his best abilities. The *superleader* listens more, asks more questions, encourages learning, and uses less punishment. In short,

---

[97]James A. Autry, *Love and Profit: The Art of Caring Leadership* (New York: Avon Books, 1991), pp. 46, 156.
[98]Max DePree, *Leadership Is an Art* (New York: Bantam Doubleday, 1989), pp. 15, 21.

organizations can be better workplaces.[99] Clearly indicating the organization's goals, open communications, and development opportunities enables members to understand and do their job better, and thus enjoy it more. Moreover, organizations who adapt these policies are able to lower turnover, increase productivity, and generally perform better finanacially in both the short and long term. For example, national Baldrige Award winners such as Federal Express, Cadillac, and IBM Rochester provide a clear mission for all, solicit employee involvement in planning, emphasize teams in employee development and compensation, and communicate constantly with employees via face-to-face meetings, live in-house television, and a variety of other methods.

Other firms, such as PepsiCo, Silicon Graphics, and AT&T, encourage their people to become more reflective and prayerful. Executives in these firms judge that managers and workers alike will be more effective if they take time to reflect on and balance their own goals and activities.[100] Such firm initiatives come from ethical leaders and thus support the moral development of the members of their organization. We examined moral development in Chapter 2.

Recent examinations of organizations focus on *positive organizational scholarship,* which recognizes a virtuous organization as one that is characterized by compassion, integrity, forgiveness, trust, and optimism. "Organizations scoring higher in virtuousness were more profitable."[101]

## SUMMARY AND CONCLUSIONS

People's values are heavily influenced by business and the firm. During the working day, the expectations of supervisors impact the behavior of employees. In the evening and on weekends, products, corporations, and their values are sold through television programming and advertising.

Successful businesspeople generally are ambitious, achievement- and power-oriented, disciplined, and adaptable. Younger managers are intent on being "winners" and "self-developers," often at the expense of empathy for others. Many of these values are ingested when the business manager joins the firm. The prevailing values of free market, competition, and opposition to government intervention

---

[99]Charles C. Manz and Henry P. Sims, Jr., *The New SuperLeadership: Leading Others to Lead Themselves* (San Francisco: Berrett-Koehler, 2001); see also Linda Klebe Trevino, Kenneth Butterfield, and Donald McCabe, "The Ethical Context in Organizations: Influences on Employee Attitudes and Behaviors," *Business Ethics Quarterly,* 8 (July 1998): 447–476.

[100]Mark A. Huselid, "The Impact of Human Resource Management Practices on Turnover, Productivity, and Corporate Financial Performance," *Academy of Management Journal,* June, 1995, pp. 635–672; Richard Blackburn and Benson Rosen, "Total Quality and Human Resources Management: Lessons Learned from Baldrige Award–Winning Companies," *Academy of Management Executive,* 3 (1993): 49–66; Stratford Sherman, "Leaders Learn to Heed the Voice from Within," *Fortune* August, 22, 1994, pp. 92–100.

[101]Kim S. Cameron, Organizational Virtuousness and Performance in *Positive Organizational Scholarship: Foundations of a New Discipline*, eds. Kim S. Cameron, Jane E. Dutton, and Robert E. Quinn (San Francisco: Berrett-Koehler, 2003); also Fred Luthans, "Positive Organizational Behavior: Developing and Managing Psychological Strengths," *Academy of Management Executive,* 16, no. 1 (2002): 57–72.

are learned early, along with the specific values of the particular firm. Hence many of the goals of managers are determined for them—whatever goals must be accomplished for success within the firm become the goals of managers. Just as early in life the rules of the game were set by others, so now the economic rules of the game come from outside the firm.

People's personal goals are changing. Individuals now desire more than salary and status. They desire challenging work, participation in decision making, the respect and approval of friends, the ability to identify with their community, and a stimulating and fulfilling life. People are trying to balance the demands of work and those of their family. They find that spirituality, often grounded in their faith tradition, brings not only better physical and mental health, but also security, openness, and inner peace. Business firms whose senior executives direct them with wisdom can help in the achievement of many of these goals.

## DISCUSSION QUESTIONS

1. Does rational decision making rest on values and ideological assumptions? What might those assumptions be?
2. Because business managers often claim their actions are "value-free," why inquire about values?
3. What does the change in the nature of discipline problems in school (see Figure 7-1) tell you about American culture and values?
4. Is it acceptable for a firm to attempt to socialize its members? How does it do so? What are the unexpected costs of socialization?
5. When most college freshmen believe that it is more important to be very well-off financially than to develop a meaningful philosophy of life, what does that tell us? Is the prospect of wealth more important than a good education?
6. Do business managers tend to be more interested in people, power, or tasks? Are executives more conformist or more innovative?
7. Can you name a TV program or a film that pictured a businessperson as one who worked hard, produced a valuable product, supported teamwork among her colleagues, and was satisfied with her work? Is this the typical image of the businessperson in the media?
8. What do Solomon Asch's experiments on the influence of groups tell us?
9. What values develop as a person matures and becomes self-actualized? What role does concern for other people play in the set of values of a self-actualized person?
10. How does Maslow's description of the ethical values of the self-actualized person relate to Kohlberg's Level III moral reasoning?
11. What sort of upbringing do people with a high need for achievement tend to have? What in a culture encourages a high need for achievement? Are those elements present in your own culture?
12. If business is the major outlet for a contemporary need for achievement, as opposed to religion and art, does this indicate an impoverishment of spirit?
13. What special problems in achieving do many women have?
14. Is a high need for power a help or a hindrance to effective leadership? Explain.
15. What is the effect of authority on a person's willingness to inflict pain, or even the danger of death, on another? Describe an experiment regarding this subject. Do parallel situations occur in your organization? In your country? Explain.

16. Describe the family life and values of the mobile manager.
17. Outline the pros and cons to the individual of having salary and status as goals. Do managers "sell" themselves?
18. Are you concerned with making yourself more "marketable"? What sort of values does this engender in a person?
19. How do published lists of salaries affect your sense of equity?
20. Describe the values that are most important to someone in organizational life and the values that are developed in family life. Is there a conflict here? How can it be resolved?
21. Do you find a conflict between your goal of earning a good wage and your own satisfaction within a firm? Does the same firm provide both, or is there a tradeoff?
22. Describe some of the current strains on work-life balance. How does it affect men and women in their careers?
23. How have some firms helped their workers cope with the work-life balance?
24. In your experience, do most people possess a spirituality? What are the varieties of spiritualities that you notice? How do you characterize a spirituality that stems from a religious tradition, and one that does not? What are the advantages of each?
25. Is it possible for a group to have strong spiritual and religious beliefs and practices, and yet include among those beliefs a respect and even love for peoples of other nations, tribes and religions?
26. In your experience, do many people experience a calling in their life and career? What is the benefit of such a calling?
27. Describe some CEOs who have positively affected the humane, spiritual, and ethical tone of their firm for their workers. Is this common? Is it difficult? Does it pay off?

# CASES

## Case 7-1      The Purchasing Manager's Car

Jim Angot is the purchasing manager for Nihco, Inc. He is responsible for buying two $1 million computer workstations. Nihco has a written policy prohibiting any company buyer from receiving a gift in excess of $50 and requiring that all gratuities be reported. A salesperson for a computer manufacturer offers to arrange it so that Angot can purchase a $40,000 auto for $12,000. The auto would be bought through a third party.

1. Should Jim decline the offer?
2. Should he notify his superior?
3. Should he notify the salesperson's superior? ■

## Case 7-2      Top Management and Sex: Astra USA

CEO Lars Bildman ran Astra USA for 15 years, and is credited with making the Swedish pharmaceutical firm a success with 1,500 employees and $323 million in revenues. However, national sales meetings found Bildman and other top executives dancing with young sales reps. Bildman was "running his hands down her [one of the sales reps'] back and nibbling her neck." Another woman said, "If they felt like grabbing a woman by the boob or by the ass, that was O.K." Other women complained of either being fondled or solicited for sex by Bildman and other executives. An investigation found that Bildman was also using company funds for personal expenses. The CEO was fired and served time in jail.[102]

1. How could such flagrant sexual harassment take place?
2. What responsibility did Astra have for this environment?
3. Why did so few women complain?
4. What ethical norms are involved here? ■

---

[102]"Lars Bildman: Go Directly to Jail," *Business Week,* February 9, 1998, p. 48; "Firm to Pay $10 Million in Settlement of Sex Case," *New York Times,* February 6, 1998, p. A10.

# Case 7-3 The Boss's Work Time

You have a new job as first-level manager in an auto parts store. Your supervisor, the store manager, spends one third of his work week talking with his friends on the phone.

1. Would you work around your lazy supervisor, or would you inform the district manager?
2. What are the ethical norms that help most in this case? ■

---

## EXERCISE

### A Life Worth Living

Imagine yourself on your deathbed. You are able to collect your thoughts and memories. How would you complete the following:
I wish I had spent more time _____.
You may complete this thought in three paragraphs, if you like.

---

## EXERCISE

### Write Your Own Obituary

Write your own obituary that will appear in your city newspaper. Assume that it is written by your best friend who knows the real you in addition to your accomplishments. After you do a first draft, ask a good friend to make comments. Write a maximum of 300 words.

# CHAPTER 8

# *Rebuilding Trust in Business*

The only trouble with capitalism is capitalists. They're too damn greedy.
Excessive fortunes are a menace to true liberty.

HERBERT HOOVER, PRESIDENT OF THE UNITED STATES, 1928–1932

The market economy, if utilized rather than worshiped, is the best mechanism available for pursuing both economic dynamism and desirable social goals.

ADAIR TURNER, VICE CHAIRMAN, MERRILL LYNCH EUROPE

We see no conflict between business goals and social and environmental needs. I believe the distinction between a good company and a great one is this: A good company delivers excellent products and services; a great one delivers excellent products and services and strives to make the world a better place.

BILL FORD, CHAIRMAN AND CEO, FORD MOTOR CO.

The ethical and financial failures of so many business firms over the last decade have challenged business managers to rebuild trust in business. The goals and ethics of a person are best communicated by their actions. Let us examine an executive who is often taken as a model of business behavior, Jack Welch of General Electric. Welch was chairman and CEO of General Electric from 1981 to 2001, and during his tenure shareholders benefited greatly. When Welch took office, GE was number 11 in the United States in capitalization (total value of outstanding stock); by his retirement, GE was number 1. GE stock price rose 1,500 percent from 1982 to 1997. Reginald Jones, the CEO who chose Welch as his successor, recognized the young man's intellect, energy, intensity, and his absolute determination to get the job done.

Within the first few months on the job Welch presented his norm for success. For each business unit GE would be either number 1 or number 2 in that market or GE would sell or close the business. The goal was to increase profitability and share price. Welch totally reshaped GE. Prior to his term, most of GE's revenue came from manufactured products, such as appliances and electrical gear; now the principal sources of revenue are entertainment (RCA and NBC) and financial services. When Welch purchased NBC, he overruled the notion that a TV network provided a public service, and therefore had duties to present the news and other important national events. Welch saw TV news as just another profit center.

There is probably no other executive in the last 50 years about whom more has been written, and who is more admired for his skills as an executive. Veterans of Welch's GE management training are much sought after and have become CEOs of dozens of other firms. Welch became the model for many other CEOs in the United States. Robert Allen was trained and championed by Welch, and became CEO of AT&T. In 1996 Allen eliminated 40,000 jobs, and his personal compensation soared to $16.8 million.[1] Welch's own compensation during each years of the late 1990s ranged between $50 and $90 million.

Welch was made CEO to streamline GE, to shake up the bureaucracy, and to make GE a leader in profits. He accomplished all of that. He promised Wall Street analysts continually improved quarterly earnings. GE achieved that, too, "by smoothing the numbers"; that is, they would restate the financials at the end of the year until they achieved the smooth upward swing they wanted in the "final, final, final ledger."[2] In Welch's first few years on the job, he sold scores of businesses, most of them profitable. In that period he eliminated a total of 100,000 jobs from GE. Even as he fired those thousands of people, he lavishly refurbished an executive office in Manhattan that he used twice a month, and spent $75 million on a new training facility and housing for GE managers.

Welch sold the Housewares Division, which included toasters, clocks, coffee makers, and hair dryers. Housewares had been one of GE's very first businesses. Moreover, in each of these markets the product was number 1 in market share and was profitable, but not profitable enough. He fired executives, mid-level managers, and line workers, many of them veterans of GE who felt that their lifetime loyalty deserved more. However, Welch preached that loyalty was an old-fashioned value,[3] along with trust, tradition, and compassion. Loyalty got in the way of efficiency, risk-taking, and fast action, and thus it did not contribute to the new, flexible, "lean and mean" GE. Early in his job as CEO, colleagues dubbed Welch "Neutron Jack,"[4] after the neutron bomb that would only kill people but leave buildings intact:

> Welch was domineering, immature, abrasive, and competitive to a fault, but, at the same time, likeable in an unvarnished way. One of his charms

---

[1]"Gross Compensation? New CEO Pay Figures Make Top Brass Look Positively Piggy," *Business Week,* March 18, 1996, pp. 32–34.
[2]James Martin, S.J., *In Good Company: The Fast Track from the Corporate World to Poverty, Chastity and Obedience* (Franklin, WI: Sheed & Ward, 2000).
[3]Thomas F. O'Boyle, *At Any Cost: Jack Welch, General Electric, and the Pursuit of Profit* (New York: Knoff, 1998).
[4]Jack Welch with John A. Byrne, *Jack: Straight from the Gut* (New York: Warner Books, 2001).

was that he didn't try to sublimate his personality or his passions; what you saw was what you got. What you saw was a man whose forceful personality made him appear bigger that he was. He talked in machine-gun-like bursts, throwing out ideas in a verbal torrent.[5]

Many managers did not want to work for Welch using his new standards. Even though Welch urged him to stay, one who left GE said "I didn't respect him as a human being. Jack is a guy who uses and abuses people. That troubled me. I didn't want to be one of Jack's boys." Another executive who also quit because he did not like Welch's style also recognized his personal strengths: "He's funny, charismatic, recalls names, puts his arms around you, the kind of guy other guys like to hang around."

In addition, during Welch's tenure, GE experienced many ethical lapses:

- GE subsidiary Kidder Peabody was fined by the Securities and Exchange Commission (SEC) for reporting false profits and fabricated record keeping. The division lost $1 billion; what was left was finally sold.
- GE's jet engine division pleaded guilty in 1992 to stealing $42 million from the U.S. government, and using the money to bribe an Israeli general to purchase GE engines. Two years later that same division paid the U.S. government $7.2 million in penalties for selling Air Force engines that did not meet contract specifications to the United States.
- From 1985 to 1992 GE's arms manufacturers were involved in 15 criminal convictions and civil judgments, more than twice as many as the next largest arms manufacturer.
- After Welch said that the toxic non-biodegradable chemical PCB posed no health risk, the U.S. Environmental Protection Agency (EPA) ordered GE to clean up the PCBs it had dumped into the Hudson River at a cost to GE of $500 million.
- A report shown on NBC television's *Dateline NBC* contained "tests" in which General Motors trucks were shown to explode when they wouldn't have otherwise. GM sued for libel, and NBC acknowledged their fabrication.[6]

Welch arranged a lucrative retirement package for himself, although his personal assets totaled $450 million. His retirement provides a total *monthly* income of $1.4 million. He maintains that such an income is necessary to meet his expenses. He reports his total monthly expenses as $366,000; these include: $9,000 for beverages, $5,500 for country club memberships, $1,900 for clothes, and $52,000 for gifts. In addition, his five homes—two in Florida, two in Connecticut, and one on Nantucket Island, Massachusetts—cost $51,000 per

---

[5]O'Boyle, *At Any Cost,* p. 57. See also Phillip M. Thompson, "The Stunted Vocation: An Analysis of Jack Welch's Vision of Business Leadership," *Review of Business,* 25 (Winter 2004): 45–55.
[6]O'Boyle, *At Any Cost,* pp. 76–77.

month to maintain.[7] These figures were revealed during contentious divorce proceedings from his second wife. She filed for divorce after she learned that Welch had become intimately involved with Suzy Wetlaufer. Wetlaufer, as editor of the *Harvard Business Review,* had been interviewing him. As a result, Wetlaufer lost her job at HBR, but became Mrs. Jack Welch number three.

Jack Welch's famously successful career as a CEO of what is now America's largest corporation raises many questions. Who benefited from his tactics of "fix, sell or close" a business, even when it was profitable? Were these tactics, which resulted in many layoffs and business being sent overseas, good for the United States as a whole? Was his intimidation of subordinates an appropriate way of communicating his and GE's goals and values? What does his immense compensation, both while CEO and in retirement, tell us about Welch, the GE Board which approved it, and the prevailing American culture? What do his living expenses tell us about his values? What does his affair with Suzy Wetlaufer, while married to his second wife (Wetlaufer was also married at the time), tell us? Earlier chapters may help us to answer the questions on Welch's goals, values, and ethics. Executive leadership, compensation, and corporate governance issues will be discussed in greater detail in this chapter. Welch was certainly not alone in layoffs, shallow morality, and shady accounting. On the last point, the GE CEO following Welch, Jeff Immelt, said that if quarterly earnings continue on a smooth upward climb, shareholders and the public now think they have been manipulated. Immelt acknowledged the earlier slippery practices and began to release more detailed and transparent financial information.[8]

We understand much about a person by watching what that person does and how he acts. This is also true of a firm; the policies and the activities of a business firm are the clearest demonstration of its values and ethics. The aforementioned actions and those described in the rest of this chapter tell us more about business values than do executive speeches or self-promoting advertisements. We will now examine the policies, actions, successes, and failures of some other executives and their firms.

## LOSS OF INTEGRITY

Jack Welch's management style and his goal of increasing shareholder value were the model for many United States business executives. However the business scandals in the first few years of the twenty-first century cast doubt on businesses that operated using Welch's style and goals. The financial and moral collapse of Enron and its auditor, the old and revered accounting firm, Arthur Andersen, surprised many.[9] In both cases, tens of thousands of employees lost their jobs and also their

---

[7]"Here's the Retirement Jack Welch Built: $1.4 Million a Month: In Divorce Case, Ex-GE Chief Details a Lavish Lifestyle; Gifts Totaling $52,486," *Wall Street Journal,* October 31, 2002, pp. 1, 15.
[8]"General Electric: Big Game Hunting," *Economist* March 16, 2002, p. 64.
[9]Mimi Swartz and Sherron Watkins, *Power Failure: The Inside Story of the Collapse of Enron* (New York: Doubleday, 2003); Barbara Ley Toffler, *Final Accounting: Ambition, Greed and the Fall of Arthur Andersen* (New York: Broadway Books, 2003).

pensions. Global Crossing, WorldCom, Waste Management, Qwest, Computer Associates, Trump Hotels, and dozens of other firms deliberately overstated their revenues and understated expenses so that they could steadily increase their share prices to meet the expectations of Wall Street. Meeting "the numbers," that is, share price, and especially earnings per share, became the ultimate objective. In contrast, Medtronic is a very successful maker of pacemakers and other medical devices; its share value grew at 37 percent annually from 1985 to 2001. During that time, Medtronic's CEO Bill George would regularly tell shareholders and analysts alike that shareholders come third. According to George, "Medtonic is not in the business of maximizing shareholder value. We *are* in the business of maximizing value to the patients we serve. Shareholder value comes from giving superior service to customers because you have impassioned employees serving them." George points out that the Medtronic mission—restoring people to full life—transcends the everyday struggles and provides motivation to Medtronic's 25,000 workers.[10]

Meanwhile, accounting firms and financial analysts were involved in conflicts of interest of their own. The hired overseers of honesty for business, the outside auditors KPMG, Ernst & Young, Deloitte & Touche, PriceWaterhouseCoopers, and Arthur Andersen received most of their income from their consulting businesses. They often also had the auditing contract for the same firm. Hence the auditors felt pressure to provide a favorable audit in order to retain the more lucrative consulting business. In a parallel conflict of interest, the investment banking firms Merrill Lynch, Morgan Chase, and Goldman Sachs generated most of their revenue representing business firms in their merger-and-acquisition activities. Hence financial analysts at the investment banks felt pressure to give these firms favorable ratings on their share price and any new stock offerings in order to retain their investment banking business. This resulted in the dissemination to the public of false favorable information on the financial status of firms. Those misleading statements led to a collapse of integrity, stained reputations, and the ultimate financial failure of many firms.

What was the cause of these failures? One cause was the personal greed of many executives. During the period when so many business scandals were emerging, newspaper headlines told us of the excessive compensation and the regal high living of their executives. Jack Welch's personal compensation and his lavish refurbishing of an office that he rarely used, while at the same time firing 100,000 GE workers, suggests at least a short-sightedness, if not personal greed. Dennis Koslowski, CEO of Tyco, pocketed $170 million in compensation in 1999, yet still charged Tyco for artwork for his personal use. The Rigas family charged many of their personal expenses to their firm, Adelphia. Samuel Waksal, then CEO of ImClone, sold shares in the firm before unfavorable news on ImClone's new cancer drug was available to the public; Waksal has served jail time for this. It is probably true that everyone on the yearly list of the highest-paid CEOs seeks to be number one on the list. This list reveals the annual compensation packages that went to men such as Michael Eisner

---

[10]Ronald Heifetz and Marty Linsky, *Leadership on the Line: Staying Alive Through the Dangers of Leading* (Boston: Harvard Business School Press, 2002), p. 211.

at Disney, whose pay dropped from $96 million in 2002 to $7.3 million in 2003, and Sandford Weil of Citigoup, whose compensation dropped from $90 million in 2002 to $17.9 million in 2003. Both men left their firms under a cloud.

Another cause of this errant behavior is Wall Street's obsessive concern with quarterly earnings per share. We receive daily reports of a stock's movement.

In another scheme to make money at the expense of the average citizen, most of the major accounting firms have a tax division. A major role of that tax division is to "sell" tax avoidance by using creative financial structures. Moreover, the auditing firm will show internal auditors how to "manage data" to meet quarterly goals and to avoid taxes. They also recommend relocating where there is little or no corporate tax. Tyco rechartered itself in Bermuda, as did Arthur Andersen's consulting spin off, Accenture.

In this chapter we will examine the effect of values and ethics on a firm's performance. We will note some executives and firms who are excellent models of concern for people, along with others who seem to show little concern. We will then explore strategies for those managers and firms that seek to improve their performance.

## MANAGING FOR SELF OR FIRM

Let us consider different types of managers and management styles. We present good and effective behavior that can be imitated, and ineffective management styles that can be avoided. To place this discussion in context, recall from Chapters 4 and 5 the traditional values that have prevailed in the United States. The Protestant ethic (Figure 4-1) urges hard work, self-control, self-reliance, perseverance, saving and planning ahead, honesty, and observing the "rules of the game." These same values also characterize the entrepreneurial middle class in developing countries. The market system encourages and rewards these values. However, for some, these values may have shifted toward short-term goals, such as a high salary, high status, self-fulfillment, entitlement, and immediate satisfaction (See Table 8-1). Are the traditional values still predominant, or have a new set of self-fulfillment values been embraced by Americans? We will raise this question later in this chapter and again in Chapter 10.

**TABLE 8-1**   Changing Values That Undergird American Business

| *Protestant Ethic . . . Is Shifting to . . .* | *Entitlement and Self-Fulfillment* |
| --- | --- |
| 1. Hard work | 1. Salary and status |
| 2. Self-control and sobriety | 2. Self-fulfillment |
| 3. Self-reliance | 3. Entitlement |
| 4. Perseverance | 4. Short-term perspective (if not successful here, move on) |
| 5. Saving and planning ahead | 5. Immediate satisfaction (buy now, little savings) |
| 6. Honesty and observing the "Rules of the game" | 6. Obey the law (in any case, don't get caught) |

## Executive Compensation and Breach of Trust

The disproportionately high pay of American CEOs has been criticized for many years in the business press. For example, over the past 10 years, Sanford Weil of Citigroup has earned an average of $98 million per year, Lawrence Ellison of Oracle $88 million, and Michael Eisner of Disney $76 million. On the other hand, the annual compensation of very successful investor Warren Buffet of Berkshire Hathaway is but $100,000. Also compare the 2003 compensation of Costco CEO James Sinegal of $350,000 to that of Cendant CEO Henry Silverman of more than $17 million; for both firms the operating income has increased but the market value has decreased over the past 5 years.[11] Average compensation for 180 CEOs of large American firms in 2003 rose 23 percent to $5.9 million. In that same year the pay of the average American worker rose only 2 percent.[12] Hence CEO pay presents a conflict between the free market that claims to reward talent by compensation and a perception of a lack of justice in such disproportionate pay.

American top management and CEO salaries are higher than those of any other nation. As we have just seen, they are still rising much more rapidly than the wages of other workers. In 1980 the average CEO's salary was 42 times that of the ordinary factory worker, but has now risen to more than 120 times that of the factory worker. How does a CEO's salary become so huge? From the executive's perspective, the salary does not seem large; he often measures his self-esteem by comparing his salary to that of other CEOs. Moreover, the chief executive generally chooses the group of directors that decides his salary. In addition, some CEOs appear to be just plain greedy. While the ratio of the pay of the CEO in the United States to that of the average worker is 120:1; in Japan this ratio is 16:1, in Germany it is 21:1, and in the United Kingdom it is 33:1.[13] Boards of directors are treating CEOs as professional football or basketball players. What boards and CEOs seem to ignore is that the CEO is leading an organization, and the success of that organization demands the energy and commitment of all the people in the organization. It is interesting to note that almost all of the immense CEO salaries go to males. Highly successful female CEOs, such as Meg Whitman of eBay, receive salaries that are more in line with their responsibilities. Are males more prone to large egos, and so more apt to seek the outsized pay?

Moreover, compensation of some hedge-fund managers is even higher than that of CEOs. Bruce Kovner of Caxton Associates earned $600 million in 2002. James Simons of Renaissance Technologies received $287 million and Paul Tutor Jones II of Tutor Investment received $250 million in 2002. Hedge fund managers do not create new products or wealth; they merely speculate on already

---

[11]"Executive Pay: A Special Report," *New York Times,* April 4, 2004, Sec. 3, pp 1–10; see also "Wall Street's CEOs Still Get Fat Paychecks Despite Woes," *Wall Street Journal,* March 4, 2003, p. 1; "Executive Pay: CEO Pay Keeps Soaring—Leaving Everybody Else Further and Further Behind," *Wall Street Journal,* April 11, 1996, pp. R1–R18.

[12]*Ibid.,* pp. 1, 6; also research supported by the Century Fund summarized by Edward N. Wolff, *Top Heavy: The Increasing Inequality of Wealth in America and What Can Be Done About It* (New York: The New Press, 2002).

[13]"Does America Still Work," *Harper's,* May, 1996, pp. 35–47.

existing assets, and the immense rewards go to very few. A report sponsored by the Securities and Exchange Commission (SEC), the New York Stock Exchange (NYSE), and the National Association of Securities Dealers (NASD) charges that securities firms are not doing enough to police their own brokers.[14] This has been borne out by the scandals at Citigroup, Kidder Peabody, Merrill-Lynch, Morgan Stanley, and Salomon Brothers.

Efforts to build trust, cooperation and better communication are undermined by such huge compensation packages. When cutting costs, top managers urge hourly and salaried workers to settle for little additional pay. Many CEOs have closed plants, cut wages, urged early retirement for some, and fired others. Some of this is necessary, but immense executive compensation does not make the case to colleagues of the need to cut costs. Since CEO compensation is often public knowledge and is so clearly self-serving, it supports an attitude of "everyone for himself" and "get what you can, while you can, before the selfish guys get theirs."

Warren Buffet, one of the most successful investors in the United States, decries the typical immense CEO compensation. In the wake of the business scandals, he said, "What really gets the public is when CEOs get very rich and stay very rich and they [the public] get very poor." John Lauer, CEO of Oglebay Norton, thinks that most CEOs are vastly overcompensated. After doing his own careful research, he says that most CEO pay is not linked to performance at all; in fact, excessive compensation for top management erodes worker loyalty and productivity. The compensation is based on comparison to their peers. Receiving less than others injures their self-esteem. Since some short-term costs, such as environmental lawsuits and excessive warranty costs, can be hidden, a portion of CEO compensation could be deferred and paid out after a longer period. So Lauer has tied his own compensation to the long-term performance of his firm, and his bonus is capped at $200,000. His big payoff is a one-time option package that is redeemable three years into his contract.[15]

There are several potential justifications for such high executive compensation. It can be a reward for superior performance, the sum required to attract the talent, and a just return for contributions. In addition, whether intentional or not, such compensation is also a signal to others in the firm about the comparative worth of a person. The second two reasons for executive compensation are largely ignored. Therein lies the problem. Some of the extremely high CEO pay is tied to a rise in the firm's share price. But why should the CEO be the only person in the firm who receives a bonus on the basis of higher share price?[16] Some firms now reward the performance of everyone in the firm who contributed to the success.

---

[14]"The Bubble Lives On," *Business Week,* July 14, 2003, p. 12; "Brokerages Still Broken," *Business Ethics,* May 1996, p. 16.
[15]"A Buffett Warning on Executive Pay," *New York Times,* March 17, 2003, p. C3; see also Mel Perel, "An Ethical Perspective on CEO Compensation," *Journal of Business Ethics,* 43 (December 2003): 381–391; "A CEO Cuts His Own Pay," *Fortune,* October 26, 1998, p. 56.
[16]On the relationship between compensation and ethical behavior, see Nancy B. Kurland, "The Unexplored Territory Linking Rewards and Ethical Behavior," *Business and Society,* 34 (April 1995): 34–50.

Derek Bok, retired president of Harvard University, has often spoken, written, and acted on behalf of ethical issues. Bok says that such high compensation in business drains talented people away from teaching and public service at precisely the time when the public is asking for better education and better government. Bok also challenges the very high pay of specialized physicians, trial and corporate lawyers (he is a lawyer himself), and business CEOs.

He notes that in the period since World War I, the only times in which CEO salaries increased so dramatically (the 1920's and from 1980 on), were "two periods in which America's values moved sharply toward the celebration of material rewards." He also says that this is not inevitable, citing the fact that in the period from 1940 to 1965, CEO salaries moved up less rapidly than salaries of the average blue-collar worker even though the economy was doing well. Bok's solution is twofold: He urges a change in values away from blatant materialism, and he also supports a graduated income tax on those receiving such large pay.[17]

As long as it is so huge, CEO compensation will continue to receive attention as an example of inequity and greed. Negative reactions from shareholders is causing some boards of directors to examine their executive compensation more carefully to ensure that it is a reward for the long-term performance of the firm.

Let us now examine the ethical aspect of other management issues.

## American Supremacy Challenged

The United States has lost hundreds of thousands of jobs and entire industries in manufacturing and service. Shoes, clothing, toys, cameras, watches, radios, televisions, and video cassette recorders are almost all imported. Many service jobs, such as design of software and call centers, are now carried out in overseas centers. The United States has also lost many middle-management and high-wage factory positions. Because of globalization, nations that have lower wages attract these jobs.

Managers are essential for the success of any enterprise. They provide the vision, plans, and leadership for the organization. However, some managers are short-sighted. These executives invest little in worker training and research, and spend too much on acquisitions. A group of chief executives and strategy scholars met under the auspices of the Council on Competitiveness and the Harvard Business School to determine why this is the case. Chair of the panel and business strategy expert Michael Porter lays the blame on the way America's financial system allocates capital. In Porter's words, "the money doesn't go to the right companies for the right investments." In the external markets, the system underfunds firms that can deploy capital most productively. Internally, it directs funds to wasteful projects instead of toward research, training, and other initiatives that would aid a company's long-term prospects. The problem is worse in large firms; since managers do not know the details of operations, they "manage by the numbers," using as indicators of success short-term markers such as earnings, return on investment, return on equity, or market share. Hence,

---

[17]Derek Bok, *The Cost of Talent: How Executives and Professionals Are Paid and How It Affects America* (New York: The Free Press, 1993); also his "It's Time to Trim Hefty Paychecks," *New York Times,* Dec. 5, 1993, p. F13.

the panel recommended more than a decade ago a series of changes that would allow more productive use of capital.[18] This warning has yet to be heeded.

Bonus plans are generally based on last year's performance. However, managers often expect to be in their current job just a few years and then to receive a preferable position elsewhere. A newcomer who takes a manager's place would better the reward of superior long-term performance. Thus there is little financial incentive for a person to plan and budget for even a few years out. A better gauge would be to measure performance over perhaps a 5- or 10-year term. Substantial growth is best accomplished when managers plan for the long term.

The larger and more diversified a firm is, the more difficult it is for top management to know specific products, markets, and employees. Because of their distance from customers, production, new product ideas, and the public, managers often turn to what it can understand—the only "objective" control mechanism that is available—"the numbers." This encourages short-term thinking, and often results in reducing research, curtailing risk taking, and ultimately lessening productivity. Moreover, it also makes managers less likely to examine the ethics of management decisions. The ethical problems of General Electric under Jack Welch are an example. So we see that pressure to achieve short-term results "by the numbers" also fractures the ability to examine ethical issues.[19]

Perhaps compensation would be more equitable if firms asked employees to rate their own supervisors. Many of America's most admired companies do just that; they call it "upward evaluation" or "360-degree feedback." Among the firms that ask subordinates to rate their superiors, including the CEO, are: Alcoa, BellSouth, DuPont, Eaton, General Mills, Hewlett-Packard, Merck, Herman Miller, Morgan Stanley, Motorola, Procter & Gamble, and 3M.

To summarize, the principal cause of a lack of long-term planning is the pressure on managers to achieve short-term results. The same sort of motivation leads to unethical behavior. Managers often publicize measurable, short-term results so that they may appear to be doing their job well. However, other executives are noted for their ethical actions and they lead very profitable firms. Let us examine some of them.

## LEADERS IMPACT THE CULTURE AND ETHICS OF A FIRM

Executives have an immense influence on the corporate culture, climate, and ethics of a firm. That influence can be one that makes the firm successful financially, and at the same successful for its employees and other stakeholders.[20] Or that leadership can bring about the failure of the firm as a good place to work,

---

[18]Judith H. Dobrzynski, "A Sweeping Prescription for Corporate Myopia," *Business Week,* July 6, 1992, pp. 36–37.
[19]Alex Berenson, *The Number: How the Drive for Quarterly Earnings Corrupted Wall Street and Corporate America* (New York: Random House, 2003).
[20]Mark Bolino, William Turnley, James Bloodgood, "Citizenship Behavior and the Creation of Social Capital in Organizations," *Academy of Management Review,* 27 (October 2002): 505–522; Jacqueline Hood, "The Relationship of Leadership Style and CEO Values to Ethical Practices in Organizations," *Journal of Business Ethics,* 43 (April 2003): 263–273.

the failure to produce quality products, and often, ultimately, the failure of the firm itself.

**James D. Sinegal**, founder and CEO of Costco, was listed in a *Business Week* cover story as one of "The Good CEOs"[21] in the aftermath of the business scandals. When newspapers showed executives being led off in handcuffs, the magazine judged it important to identify some CEOs who were model leaders. Sinegal opened the first wholesale Costco store in 1983 in Seattle. His strategy is to offer lower prices by stripping away everything judged to be unnecessary. For example, CEO Sinegal answers his own phone, does not have an executive washroom or even an office that has walls, and his office has 20-year-old furniture.

Costco is a retailer that competes directly with Wal-Mart's Sam's Club. But, while Wal-Mart has been criticized for its low wages and poor retirement and health benefits, Costco treats its associates much better. The average hourly wage at Costco is $15.97, while at Sam's Club it is $11.52. Costco's annual health cost per worker is $5,735, and that is for 82 percent of the workers, while Sam's Club spends $3,500 each on only 47 percent of its workers. Sinegal is convinced that treating workers better pays off. Costco's employee annual turnover is only 6 percent, while Sam's Club is 21 percent. More revealing is that Costco's profit per employee is $13,647 while Wal-Mart's Sam's Club's profit is only $11,039 per employee. Nevertheless, Wall Street financial analysts object to the higher hourly and benefit costs per employee that Costco pays. Wall Street has the short-sighted view that lower labor costs are better for shareholders. However, CEO Sinegal puts it simply, "Paying your employees well is not only the right thing to do but it makes for good business."[22]

Two additional examples illustrate the integrity found at Costco. One of Sinegal's rules is to strictly limit markups to 12 percent on national brands. On one occasion they were selling Calvin Klein jeans for $29.99 when they obtained a batch at $22.99. While they were selling well at the higher price, Sinegal insisted on lowering the price and not taking the possible higher markup. On another occasion Costco was expanding in the U.K., and its bankers recommended structuring a borrowing transaction so that both principal and interest were tax deductible, instead of only interest being tax deductible. It would have given Costco a large tax savings. When Sinegal looked more carefully at the proposal, it became clear that it would be exploiting a loophole in the tax code, and Costco refused to do it.[23] With that sort of integrity, do you think Costco will be able to compete with Sam's Club in the marketplace?

## Executives as Moral Leaders

We will now spotlight a few additional business leaders because of their contributions to business, business values, and business ethics. They have been selected because their values and actions can serve as models for all businesspeople.

---

[21]*Business Week*, September 23, 2002, pp. 82–83.
[22]Stanley Holmes and Wendy Zellner, "The Costco Way: Higher Wages Mean Higher Profits. But Try Telling Wall Street," *Business Week*, April 12, 2004, pp. 76–77.
[23]Interview of John Dienhart, from "Strategic Leadership of Ethical Behavior in Business," *Academy of Management Executive*, 18 (May 2004): 61.

*Ray Anderson*, an engineer, began *Interface Carpet* in 1973 and is now CEO of the firm. Interface, a billion dollar business, is the largest producer of commercial floor coverings in the United States. It sells in 110 countries and manufactures on four continents. In 1994 Andersen realized that he and his firm were in his words "plunderer of the earth."[24] He read Paul Hawkin's book, *Ecology of Commerce: A Declaration of Sustainability,*[25] which changed his view of himself and his firm. Hawkins describes how most manufacturing firms eat through the earth's limited resources without regard for the poisons they leave behind for future generations to clean up. Hawkin argues that business is responsible for most of the damage, but it can also be a part of the solution. Andersen points out that business is the largest, wealthiest, and most pervasive institution on Earth, so business must take the lead in directing the Earth away from collapse and toward restoration.

Andersen says that reading the book "was like a spear in my chest . . . . That's the way I had been running my company . . . taking something that wasn't mine." Anderson decided to change. He pledged to work toward not using the earth's natural resources, and to eliminate all waste and harmful emissions by 2020. Anderson runs a firm whose floor tiles are petroleum based, yet he says that "if I can get it right, I will not take another drop of oil from the earth." He has plans for recycling used carpet, and has already contracted with numerous firms to "rent" them carpet. That is, he will provide any new floor covering they require; he will then take back and recycle the old so that it is not thrown into landfills, but rather used for new carpeting. Anderson is on his way to his goals for Interface. He has reduced waste by 80 percent, energy consumption by 31 percent, water intake by 78 percent, and use of petroleum by 28 percent. By doing so he has saved Interface $231 million.

Anderson went beyond making his own firm eco-friendly. He set out to convince other business executives of the importance of not trashing the earth. He has given talks throughout the country and the world on the importance of sustainability. He defines sustainability as: *meeting the needs of today without compromising the ability of future generations to meet their own needs.*[26] In those talks Anderson points out that two-thirds of humanity is starving, unemployed, or living on less than $2 a day, and are thus left out of our current economic system, except perhaps to be exploited. Calling himself a "recovering plunderer," Anderson says, "as we focus myopically on financial capital through the lens of a misbegotten economic system," human capital (social equity) and natural capital (the environment) are neglected.

Anderson has also made Interface a model for worker, supplier, and customer relations. In 2000 Interface began a "Stakeholder Dialogue," in which the company asks employees and suppliers for detailed opinions about the company in an anonymous annual survey. The results are mailed to and compiled by a third party. Interface has also been named as one of the top 100 companies to work for in America by *Fortune.*

---

[24]"In the Future, People Like Me Will Go to Jail," *Fortune,* May 24, 1999, pp. 190–200.
[25]Paul Hawken, *The Ecology of Commerce: A Declaration of Sustainability* (New York: HarperBusiness, 1994).
[26]Ray Anderson, *Mid-Course Correction: Toward a Sustainable Enterprise—The Interface Model* (Atlanta: Peregrinzilla Press, 1998).

*Gun Denhart* as a mother noted the lack of and the expense of high-quality, cotton children's clothes. She began a new mail order firm, *Hanna Andersson's* children's clothes. The firm was named for Gun's grandmother, since "Gun" did not sound appropriate for a children's clothing firm! Gun as CEO and her husband Tom as marketing director were initially the sole employees. Both were also struck by the excessive waste they noticed in the United States, far more than Gun had experienced in Europe. To emphasize the high quality of their clothes, and also to discourage throwing clothes away when they were outgrown, they began the "Hannadowns" program. A customer could return a used Hanna piece of clothing and receive a credit of 20 percent of the cost of the original product toward a new purchase. Hanna Andersson in turn donates the used clothing to charities for women and children.

Gun Denhart calls the Hannadowns program a win-win-win-win program. As she describes it, all parties benefit from the program:

> It is good for Hanna as a company because it is a way, marketing-wise, to show our customers that these are great products and can be used for more than one baby. It makes the customer feel good because they have all these clothes in their closets and the kids have outgrown them. They don't know what to do with them, and they feel good that they will be used again by someone who really needs them. Employees love it, and finally, but not least, it is just wonderful for the kids who get the clothes because, normally, they wouldn't have this kind of quality clothing.[27]

These quality clothes were so attractive that the firm grew to $35 million annual sales within 10 years, and is still growing. Hanna Andersson has a management team that is 80 percent female and that has a participative management style. Working mothers appreciate the flexible work schedules. The firm also funds one-half of day-care expense. Hanna Andersson subsidizes fitness classes, has formal wellness programs, and provides exercise equipment and showers on the premises. The firm also provides jobs to some who had received Hannadowns as homeless or battered women. Denhart received one of *Forbes* magazine's first business ethics awards.[28]

Gun Denhart is concerned with many problems in contemporary society: waste, poverty, homelessness, and the fact that many women and children are victims. She thinks that business has a responsibility, "I think you can't put all that burden on the government. I think individuals and corporations have to take some responsibility to help for a better world."[29]

*William Clay Ford, Jr.* is chairman and CEO of *Ford Motor Company*. Bill Ford, 43 years old when elected CEO, is the grandson of Henry Ford. He

---

[27]David Bollier, "Recycling Clothes While Building Customer Loyalty," *Aiming Higher* (New York: Amacom, 1996), pp. 23–36; the original quote is from *Social Entrepreneurship: The Story of Gun Denhart and Hanna Andersson* (Stamford, CT: Business Enterprise Trust, 1992), p. 6.
[28]"Interview with Gun Denhart," *Business Ethics,* July–August 1994, pp. 19–21.
[29]*Social Entrepreneurship: The Story of Gun Denhart,* p. 16.

took the job when Ford was losing billions of dollars annually and being sued by thousands of SUV drivers for Firestone tire blowouts. Bill Ford was able to assemble a superb management team encourage new auto design, and return Ford Motor to profitability. Ford Motor makes much of its profit on the Navigator, Excursion, and Explorer SUVs, so some criticize him for polluting the environment. Nevertheless his accomplishments are worth note here.

Bill Ford led the redesign of Ford Motor's historic 1927 Rouge complex, a two-square-mile collection of manufacturing plants, warehouses, and docks on the Rouge River. Rather than move and leave behind polluted and devastated land, the Rouge facility will remain the largest industrial complex in the world. Bill Ford hired the award-winning environmentally conscious architect William McDonough to design the complex. McDonough had received the United States Presidential Award for Sustainability and had been chosen as a "Hero of the Planet" by *Time* magazine.

The Rouge facility was finished and opened to the public in 2004 and features a new style of industrial architecture. The buildings have a green roof on which a variety of vegetation absorbs water and provides thermal insulation. Porous parking lots draw water into a landscape of trenches full of native plants that filter water, which then goes to underground retention beds. The system will eliminate much traditional sewage piping, and will save the city and Ford millions of dollars a year.[30] Environmentalists have been critical of Bill Ford and the Ford Motor for selling oil-guzzling and polluting SUVs and trucks. Bill Ford responds that U.S. citizens unfortunately want these heavy vehicles, and that he has a responsibility for hundreds of thousands of jobs. Moreover, he says that Ford Motor makes them in a more environmentally responsible way than do Ford's competitors. Ford Motor joins BP (U.K.) and Toyota (Japan) in seeing increasing fuel economy and reducing emissions as a business opportunity. Ford has an internal plan to reduce emissions by 80 percent by 2030. Bill Ford, along with the chief executives of the other major U.S. auto firms, have called for a significant gasoline tax to encourage fuel efficiency and hybrids. As Bill Ford put it, "Anything that can align the individual customer's purchase decisions with society's goals are the way to go."[31] Also to support fuel efficiency, Ford Motor has introduced a gas-electric compact SUV, the hybrid Escape, which averaged 38 miles per gallon in city driving.

Ford also unveiled a Model U concept car which is designed for total recycling. The car can be easily taken apart, so that its high-tech materials can be reused and its bio-materials can be returned to compost. Under Bill Ford's leadership, Ford Motor has won numerous awards from the Wildlife Habitat Council, National Geographic, and other international groups for re-establishing wildflowers, grasses, and trees on Ford sites on several continents. Bill Ford does

---

[30]William McDonough, "A New Era for Manufacturing: Newest Factories Mark a Trend Toward Green," *Detroit Free Press,* May 2, 2004, p. 7.
[31]"Ford: Hybrids Need a Boost from the U.S.," *Detroit Free Press,* April 8, 2004, pp. 1, 8; "A Fuel-Saving Proposal from Your Automaker: Tax the Gas," *New York Times,* April 18, 2004, p. 3; "Ford Lays Out a Move to Cut Auto Emissions." *New York Times,* October 2, 2004.

not pull rank. He and his family can be seen waiting in line for tickets to the historical Henry Ford Museum, which his grandfather built.

***Ryuzaburo Kaku*** was chairman of ***Canon Inc.***, a firm based in Japan that has annual global sales of more than $16 billion on Canon copiers and computer printers. Kaku's interests go well beyond copiers and Japan. He fears that humankind may not survive its current problems of lack of food, environmental difficulties, and the imbalance of wealth between the nations. As a result of these concerns, Kaku began to use solar energy at Canon. He also initiated an extensive recycling program of both copier ink cartridges and of the copiers themselves.[32] Such recycling saves manufacturing costs, and perhaps more importantly, dumps less waste into the environment.

Kaku has attained international stature as an active member of the Caux Roundtable of business leaders from Europe, Japan, and the United States. When the Caux Roundtable developed its *Principles for Business,*[33] a global code of business conduct, the value of "human dignity" from the Western tradition was agreed upon as one of the basic bedrock principles. Just as importantly, Kaku insisted that another of those basic values be "Kyosei" from the Eastern traditions. Kyosei means "living and working together for the common good," and managers at Canon recognize this vision. We will discuss the Caux Principles for Business again in Chapter 9. Kaku himself spends much of his time trying to change business attitudes in Japan. Kaku is convinced that we must work for the common good if our peoples, and indeed the planet itself, are to survive.

***Felix Rohatyn*** is still probably the best-known and best-connected investment banker in America. He was senior partner at ***Lazard Freres & Co.*** and served as United States Ambassador to France. For 30 years he has been the principal deal maker at Lazard. Rohatyn engineered a deal that enabled New York City to avoid bankruptcy. Lazard Freres reported three times the profit per employee as its closest rival. Rohatyn was one of the earliest and most skillful consultants to firms involved in giant financial deals. He is now stunned by the deliberate falsifications and breakdown of honesty on Wall Street. He points out that "our modern capitalistic system is based on disclosure and veracity." If foreign investors begin to doubt the integrity of the U.S. market, "it could have dramatic repercussions on the dollar, on domestic inflation, on the economy."[34]

Rohatyn is critical of many of his peers in investment banking. He says that the United States has done practically nothing to prevent a recurrence of a stock market bubble and crash. He notes that the primary purpose of the stock and bond markets is to provide investment funds for organizations that need capital. Yet the markets do not accomplish that well:

> The fundamental weakness in the securities markets, world-wide, is the result of excessive speculation, excessive use of credit, and inadequate regulation. This speculative behavior is not driven by individuals, as was

---

[32]"Interview with Ryuzaburo Kaku," *Business Ethics,* March–April 1995, pp. 30–33.

[33]The Caux Principals for Business are in Appendix A.

[34]"Felix Rohatyn on Wall Street's Corruption," *Business Week,* May 3, 2002; "The Last Emperor of Wall Street," *Business Week,* May 30, 1988, p. 65.

the case in the 1920s, but by institutions such as pension funds, banks, savings and loans, and insurance companies. In many cases, these institutions are backed by federal government guarantees. Curbing speculation and promoting investment must be the objective of reform.[35]

He points out that it is in the short-term self-interest of investment bankers and lawyers to complete "deals" (mergers or acquisitions); otherwise they do not receive their fees. They are paid even when the merger is not in the best interest of the client. Rohatyn also thinks that investment bankers' fees are much too large. Rohatyn feels that he has a "responsibility to save capitalism from itself—that greed, ideological rigidity, or the simple lack of competence outside their narrow arenas of expertise can blind the movers and shakers of the business world to the risks of financial instability they are promoting."

The following are among Rohatyn's suggestions for encouraging investment and cooling speculation:

- Impose a 50-percent tax on the profit of securities held for less than a year. This tax would apply to individuals, corporations, partnerships, and currently tax-free institutions. At the same time, reduce capital gains taxes on securities held for more than five years to 15 percent.
- Sharply limit the type and proportion of speculative investments held by federally insured institutions.

With regard to firms in general, being ethical often benefits a firm's sales. Surveys indicate that consumers prefer to purchase from a firm that has a good reputation; 55 percent of consumers say that "they always take a company's ethics and values into account when purchasing a product or service." Forty percent always consider "treatment of employees" and 23 percent always look at the company's environmental record. In a second survey, 78 percent of the respondents said that they would buy a product made by a firm that contributes to education and medical research. Two-thirds said they would switch brands to a manufacturer that supported a cause they deemed worthy. One-third said they were more influenced by a firm's social activism than by its advertising.[36]

There are hundreds of additional cases of firms cooperating with nongovernmental organizations to improve the lives of people in their community. These include Home Depot workers volunteering to build playgrounds for poor children, Microsoft providing funding and computers to set up Internet access in libraries in poor neighborhoods, Denny's helping Save the Children, and Bank of Boston working with the domestic peace corps for minority young people.[37] More than 800 firms that are attempting to be socially responsible belong to a group called *Business for Social Responsibility* (www.bsr.org). The group meets annually,

[35]Rohatyn, "Institutional 'Investor' or 'Speculator' " *Wall Street Journal,* June 24, 1988, pp. 14, 24.
[36]The first study is cited in John Adams, "Dissecting Corporate Goodness," *American Advertising,* Spring 1996, pp. 10–15. The second by Roper Starch Worldwide is quoted in "Good Stewardship Is Good Business," *Fortune,* March 21, 1994, p. 16.
[37]Shirley Sagawa and Eli Segal, *Common Interest, Common Good: Creating Value Through Business and Social Sector Partnerships* (Boston: Harvard Business School Press, 2000).

partially to support one another in their efforts to be socially responsible. Among these firms are Shorebank of Chicago, Newman's Own Inc., Tom's of Maine, and Glen Ellen Winery.[38]

Many others could be added to this group of talented and visionary CEOs. John Brown of BP has led the firm as it has become more concerned with renewable energy and the environment. On social and environmental measures, European firms are generally ahead of their American counterparts. One account edited by the CEOs of DuPont, Royal Dutch/Shell, and Anova Holding lists 67 cases of European, Japanese, and U.S. firms engaged in successful sustainable business operations.[39]

Executives that have been spotlighted here build an environment that, according to research, builds organizational wealth. The favorable relationships with suppliers, employees, customers and the community constitute that wealth, which in turn provides a difficult-to-copy competitive advantage for the firm in the global marketplace.[40] Moreover, Ray Anderson's vision for the planet and Rohatyn's suggestions for encouraging long-term investments provide a good introduction for the section later in this chapter in which we identify business strategies to make ethical decision making and good character integral portions of the fabric of the firm. But in spite of the rewards that integrity and cooperation bring, there are some businesspeople who look to their own self-interest. Let us examine some cases.

## Executives That Destroy Wealth and People

Most executives take their responsibilities to people and the community seriously. On the other hand, there are some executives who focus exclusively on dollar return or personal gain—and that hurts people and ultimately hinders the efficient operation of the firm. Some firms such as Lockeed, Philip Morris, Salomon Brothers, RJR, and General Dynamics have a decades-long reputation for self-interested behavior. Whether you are a customer, employee, or supplier of these firms, it is wise to check your contract closely and leave little to a handshake. Let us now examine some recent examples of selfish behavior.

***Frank P. Quattrone*** was the best known and most successful investment banker for high tech firms in Silicon Valley, California during the high-tech bubble of the 1990s. He made $120 million in 2002 working for ***Credit Suisse First Boston (CSFB)***. Among the firms that he took public are Cisco Systems and Amazon.com. Quattrone offered shares of firms that were about to go public (initial public offerings—IPOs) to executives known as "Friends of Frank" at a low price—that is, as a bribe to give CSFB their lucrative investment banking business. Such an action is unjust to the client who is selling shares because that

---

[38]Mary Scott and Howard Rothman, *Companies with a Conscience,* (New York: Citadel, 1994); for additional information on Business for Social Responsibility, as well as a list of members, see Joel Makower, *Beyond the Bottom Line* (New York: Simon & Schuster, 1994), pp. 311–321.
[39]Charles O. Holliday, Jr., Stephan Schmidheiny, and Philip Watt, *Walking the Talk: The Business Case for Sustainable Development* (San Francisco: Berrett-Koehler, 2002).
[40]James E. Post, Lee E. Preston, and Sybille Sachs, *Redefining the Corporation: Stakeholder Management and Organizational Wealth* (Stanford, CA: Stanford University Press, 2002).

client is not getting full price for the shares. Moreover, it is also unfair to the firm of the executive who purchases the low-priced IPO shares, because the bribing investment banker may not be the most capable or the lowest-cost person for the future job. CSFB Bank settled a charge related to similar claims for $100 million.

Quattrone was convicted in federal court of witness tampering and obstructing a grand jury investigation into the payment of high commissions to himself and his bank by hedge fund managers in exchange for shares in hot IPOs. He claimed that he had no knowledge of how IPOs were allocated, but the prosecutors found an e-mail from him that indicated otherwise; he had even asked his subordinates to "clean up" their files. The federal judge found Quattrone guilty and fined him $90,000 and sentenced him to 18 months in federal prison.[41]

***Conrad Black*** was CEO of publishing conglomerate ***Hollinger International***. The firm published the *Chicago Sun-Times* and dozens of smaller U.S. and Canadian newspapers. When wrongdoing was suspected, a Hollinger internal investigative committee was set up. They reported that Black designed the finances of the firm so that he and an associate were able to pocket $400 million, almost all of Hollinger profits for 1997–2003. Moreover, in addition to his regular salary, he charged extraordinary expenses to Hollinger: $1.4 million for a personal chef; maids and butlers for his four homes; $390,000 for taking care of his RollsRoyce and other cars, $24,950 for "summer drinks," and $42,870 for a birthday party for his wife.

The report accuses Sir Conrad Black (a Canadian who was knighted and made a member of Britain's House of Lords) of using the firm as a personal "piggy bank." The report goes on: "Behind a constant stream of bombast regarding their accomplishments as self-described 'proprietors,' Black and Radler (former chief operating officer) made it their business to line their pockets at the expense of Hollinger almost every day, in almost every way they could devise." Through an elaborate holding-firm scheme, Black paid "management fees" of roughly $218 million to two firms; and almost all of that money went directly to him and his friends.

Among the negligent board members were Henry Kissinger and Richard Perle. Perle served both the Reagan and the George W. Bush administration. At Hollinger, Perle reaped more than $3 million between 2000 to 2003 from Hollinger, in addition to his annual $300,000 salary and board fees. Even though a board member, he was also made CEO of Hollinger Digital and devised a scheme that gave him 22 percent of all profits, but no penalty if investments turned sour. Perle continues to be an influential voice in neo-conservative circles on federal policy in Washington, D.C.[42]

***Fausto Tonna*** was the CFO of the Italian firm ***Parmalat***, a grocery retailer and one of Europe's largest and best-known multinational firms. Parmalat had sales of $9.2 billion and 36,000 employees, but was forced into bankruptcy in

---

[41]"Ex-Banking Star Given 18 Months for Obstruction: Led High-Tech Offerings," *New York Times,* September 9, 2004, p. 1, C2; "Friendless Frank," *The Economist,* May 8, 2004, p. 75.

[42]"Lord Black's Board: A-List Cast Played Acquiescent Role," *Wall Street Journal,* September 27, 2004, p. 1; Geraldine Fabrikant, "Hollinger Files Stinging Report on Ex-Officials"; Floyd Norris, "Misdirected: The Trouble with Hollinger's Board," *New York Times,* September 1, 2004, p. 1, C6.

December 2003. When Parmalat defaulted on a $185 million loan, investigators found that a claimed $4.9-billion Bank of America account in the Cayman Islands never existed. Investigators are still trying to determine what happened to $8.5 to $12 billion in vanished assets. Parmalat used derivatives and other complex financial transactions to make its balance sheet look acceptable. The firm did this via investment banks such as Citigroup and Merrill Lynch. One of these used a Citigroup subsidiary called Buconero LLC, which means "black hole" in Italian. A Citigroup manager later apologized for the name.

The firm had two outside auditing firms during this period, Grant Thornton until 1999, and Deloitte for the four years since. Parmalat changed auditors because of an Italian law that seeks to prevent fraud and encourage transparency. Nevertheless, neither firm detected the fraud. Bankruptcy forced Parmalat to lay off thousands and to sell many of its subsidiary businesses. Parmalat's ex-CFO Tonna has now petitioned for $6 million in severance pay from the firm.[43]

***Charles Hurwitz*** is a Houston financier who controls ***Maxxam*** and through it ***Pacific Lumber***, ***Kaiser Aluminum*** and several other firms. Maxxam was cited as one of the ten worst polluters in the United States by the Council on Economic Priorities. Hurwitz's hostile takeover of Pacific Lumber has brought him considerable attention.[44] Pacific Lumber was a family-operated firm, and possesses 189,000 acres of redwood forests in northern California. For 100 years the firm provided steady work for generations of lumber workers in the area around Scotia, California. Moreover, it had selectively cut its timber; that is, cut no more than would be replaced naturally. Pacific Lumber also worked with conservation people to preserve its old-growth redwoods as a State Park. Pacific Lumber had set aside much of its own property as a preserve for when funds become available.[45]

Hurwitz's takeover was financed by $800 million in junk bonds. The junk bonds were floated by his friend, Michael Milken at Drexel Burnham Lambert. Milken later pleaded guilty to six felonies, served time in jail, and agreed to pay a total of $1.2 billion in penalties. Drexel Burnham paid $650 million in fines and restitution, and is now bankrupt.[46] Milken's friends Boyd Jefferies and Ivan Boesky both secretly and illegally parked large investments in Pacific Lumber stock until Hurwitz was ready to attack. Both Jefferies and Boesky were also later convicted and served jail terms for their fraudulent raider tactics. Once Hurwitz was in control of Pacific Lumber, he took $50 million of the $90 million employees' retirement fund to finance the debt. Hurwitz also tripled the rate of cutting the redwoods and began to cut the old-growth redwoods that had been set aside as a preserve.

---

[43]"Italy Widens Parmalat Inquiry to Foreign Banks," *New York Times,* January 8, 2004, pp. 10, C1; "How Parmalat Went Sour," *Business Week,* January 12, 2004, pp. 46–48.

[44]See David Harris, *The Last Stand: The War Between Wall Street and Main Street Over California's Ancient Redwoods* (New York: Times Books, 1996); "The Worst Polluters of 1995," *Business Ethics,* January 1996, p. 15.

[45]Lisa H. Newton, "Chainsaws of Greed: The Case of Pacific Lumber," in *Case Studies in Business Ethics,* eds. Thomas Donaldson and Al Gini (Upper Saddle River, NJ, PrenticeHall, 1996), pp. 86–106.

[46]John M. Holcomb and S. Prakash Sethi, "Corporate and Executive Criminal Liability: Appropriate Standards, Remedies and Managerial Responses," *Business and the Contemporary World,* 4 (Summer 1992): 81–105.

The actions of Hurwitz brought retaliation from environmental groups, including public protests and legal actions. In order to stop the clear cutting of redwoods, a radical group, Earth First!, began to drive spikes into the trees. The spikes would ruin chain saws, and made cutting those trees dangerous and unprofitable. Hurwitz has lost seven environmental lawsuits on his logging of the redwood forests. Nevertheless, his cutting the redwood trees forced the federal and California governments to pay him $450 million to acquire and thus preserve 9,500 acres of the Headwaters Redwood Forest.

Hurwitz was sued by the federal government for the 1988 failure of a Texas thrift that cost U.S. taxpayers $1.6 billion. In 2002 Hurwitz agreed to settle the case for $206,000. Among dozens of other lawsuits against him was a suit in 1971 by the SEC for stock manipulation, and he paid $400,000 to settle that case.[47] In 2004 Hurwitz canceled the medical and retirement benefits for Kaiser Aluminum employees.

***Gerald M. Levin*** was CEO of ***Time-Warner*** and then ***AOL Time Warner*** for 10 years. Levin was also instrumental in the ill-fated sell-out to AOL.[48] The $8-billion firm includes many old and valuable enterprises. But some of the firm's books, films, and music fail to respect people. Time Warner signed Geto Boys "who sing lyrically about slitting women's throats and cutting off their breasts."[49] Sony and BMG refused to sign Dr. Dre, but Time Warner did sign him. He is author of the line, "Rat-a-tat and tat like that/ Never hesitate to put a nigga on his back," which is a musical call for black men to kill each other. C. DeLores Tucker, chair of the National Political Congress of Black Women says that Time Warner is "one of the greatest perpetrators of this cultural garbage."

Time Warner sold a book of pornography by Madonna for $49.95, and then had its own Book of the Month Club declare it a selection. Warner also produced the cynical Oliver Stone film, *JFK,* and also wholesale killing graphically presented as fun in the film *Natural Born Killers.* All of these ventures are profitable for Time Warner. Gerald Levin defends them by citing the First Amendment and the freedom of expression. Under public pressure, Time Warner sold the worst offending record company. Does the fact that these businesses are profitable, legal, and meet some people's interests make them acceptable? Are they ethical? Does Gerald Levin have ultimate responsibility for the content of Time Warner's music, films and books?

Other examples of executive misbehavior are too common. In order to escape U.S. taxes, executives at Tyco, Accenture, and other firms have moved their headquarters to Bermuda; such actions increase profitability, but neglects their responsibilities to citizens. Each of the managers in this section had a profound impact on the ethics and the values of the firm he or she led. A manager's influence on peers and subordinates is proportionate to his or her responsibility in the firm. Let us now consider how a climate of responsible behavior is built and maintained in a firm.

---

[47]"Charles Hurwitz's Tough Raider Image Looms Large in Alumax Takeover Battle," *Wall Street Journal,* February 26, 1996, p. B8; "The Raiders Return," *Economist,* March 2, 1996, p. 68.

[48]Alec Klein, *Stealing Time: Steve Case, Jerry Levin, and the Collapse of AOL Time Warner* (New York: Simon & Schuster, 2003).

[49]John Leo, "The Leading Cultural Polluter," *U.S. News & World Report,* March 27, 1995, p. 16.

## THE CORPORATION SERVES SOCIETY

Corporations were initially chartered by the British crown to provide a service to society. The Hudson Bay Company, which was founded in 1670, explored, claimed land, and traded goods; the Massachusetts Turnpike Company was chartered to build toll roads. These were typical of early corporations. For two centuries thereafter the purpose of the corporation was primarily to serve the public good; for example, building and maintaining canals, bridges, roads, water systems, banks, and colleges. Investors were invited to participate and the incentive for that participation was a financial return. But it was clear to all that the primary purpose of the publicly chartered corporation was to perform a public service. This changed in the late 1800s when the primary purpose of the corporation shifted from serving the public interest to maximizing the wealth of investors. This purpose has now shifted to include increasing the wealth of hired executives.

The power of the global corporation in the United States and in other constitutional democracies comes from its legal position and its charter. And that power proceeds from the people; the government receives its power from the consent of the governed.

> The modern corporation has vast powers, and great benefits and privileges, legally bestowed by its charter. Very importantly, a corporation has the ability to disguise itself, to run and hide, or to reorganize into a whole new entity. It can sell off divisions and subsidiaries and rename itself, seemingly emerging as a completely different company. Today's corporation wasn't yesterday's and can't be counted on to be tomorrow's.[50]

Since a state charters the corporation, it also has the power to revoke that charter. When a corporation becomes a net liability to society, a state literally could put that firm out of business. Recently, a law professor led a court case asking California to revoke the charter of Union Oil Co., and a Circuit Court judge in Alabama sought to revoke the charter of the five major tobacco manufacturers. The criteria upon which a charter could be revoked could be set out very clearly. The mere threat of such action might bring more responsible behavior.[51]

The large publicly-held corporation now is sometimes said to be responsible primarily to its investors. The defense for this position is that the investors provide the funds that enable the firm to operate. But this is not true, except for IPOs and new stock offerings. Most stockholders merely purchase from other

---

[50]Ralph Estes, "Corporate Accountability: The Tyranny of the Bottom Line," in *The New Business of Business,* eds. W. Harman and M. Porter (San Francisco: Berrett-Koehler, 1997), pp. 111–120; see also Estes' *Tyranny of the Bottom Line: Why Corporations Make Good People Do Bad Things* (San Francisco: Berrett-Koehler, 1999). Thanks to Ralph Estes for the excellent research and insights in this section.

[51]Russell Mokhiber, "Death Penalty for Corporations Comes of Age," *Business* Ethics, November 1998, p. 7.

stockholders, and most capital for the firm's operation is obtained from retained profits and bank loans. This fact undermines the legitimacy and justice of the claim that investors should be the first beneficiaries of a corporation's actions. Note how putting investors first has influenced business to neglect social responsibilities and brought us the scandals, as in WorldCom, Adelphia, and General Electric. Pressing for greater profits and "smoothed" earnings was one of the causes of the problems at Enron, Computer Associates, Arthur Andersen, and so many other business tragedies of the last decade. The perceived need to satisfy shareholders forces managers to focus on profitability and growth. This has encouraged claiming false earnings, hiding losses, buying tax shelters, and the many other violations of people, property, and integrity. CEOs also have the ability to set their own compensation, which is often lavish. On the other hand, management is not required to make sacrifices themselves, even in difficult times when they are asking for sacrifices from others. Moreover, managers are generally shielded from financial harm by corporate law and the firm's insurance and legal staff.

Shareholders are not the only ones who invest in the corporation. Others often invest far more than merely their money. Employees invest their time, talent, and experience; their investment may be a decade or more of their work lives. Customers invest in a firm by purchasing its products. When these are "big ticket" items, this investment is similar to that of stockholders; and if they receive a defective product or service, their risk may be much more than that of financial investors. Suppliers often commit a large portion of their own time, equipment, and assets to large corporate customers; this investment and risk can also be greater than that of stockholders. Many now suggest that requiring corporations to report on their social and environmental impacts, in the same way as they report on their financial results, would provide more information and thus make the market system more fair. We will discuss these reporting initiatives later in this chapter.

## Role and Responsibilities of CEOs and Boards of Directors

The CEO of a firm is ultimately responsible for the firm's success or failure. The CEO, in consultation with others, sets policy, decides on new products or services, establishes budgets, and sets the mission and culture of the firm. The CEO is the person most responsible for the values, ethics, culture, and climate of the firm. Today the CEO is viewed as more responsible for employees and citizens than was his or her counterpart a generation ago.[52]

The responsibility of the *board of directors* is to (1) hire, evaluate the performance of, and when necessary, fire the CEO, and (2) approve major policies and actions recommended by the CEO. The oversight role of the board is essential if the corporation is going to be both effective and ethical. This oversight is effective when board members can exercise independent judgment—that is, if they

---

[52]For some practical suggestions, see Larry Johnson and Bob Phillips, *Absolute Honesty: Building a Corporate Culture That Values Straight Talk and Rewards Integrity* (New York: American Management Association, 2003).

| | |
|---|---|
| Inside Director: | A director who is in the full-time employ of the firm |
| Outside Director: | A director who is not in full-time employ of the firm |
| Independent Director: | An outside director who has no business relationship to the firm |
| Lead Director: | In companies whose CEO is also the chair, the lead director is an independent director who acts as chair at regularly scheduled meetings at which the CEO isn't present |

**FIGURE 8-1**  Types of Members of Corporate Boards of Directors

are independent directors (see Figure 8-1). Yet the constitution of corporate boards continues to present problems with many board members who have a conflict of interest. CEO Michael Eisner's Disney board was often criticized for having too many directors who are not independent. For two years in a row, it topped *Business Week's* annual list of the worst boards in the United States. Prior to 2002, the Disney board included Eisner's personal architect, a principal of a school his children attended, and an actor, plus three additional directors with strong financial ties to Disney. Moreover, three directors who were critical of Eisner's policies were not reelected to the board.[53] For decades Eisner himself has been one of the highest-paid CEOs in the United States, and the $150 million he used to induce his old friend Michael Ovitz to leave Disney's employ has been challenged by a shareholder suit.

There is considerable conflict of interest among members of other boards. For example, three directors of Tyson Foods are former Tyson executives who hold six-figure Tyson business contracts; another director has a 10-year $4-million consulting contract. Verizon, Bank of America, General Electric, Nike, and FedEx all have a number of board members who have similar conflicts of interest. It is much more difficult for directors who are not independent to ask hard questions of those executives who pay them. Moreover, even after Enron, boards of directors are doling out unearned compensation. For example, Gary Wendt, CEO of Conseco, was given an $8-million bonus in spite of the fact that he led his firm to just one profitable quarter in two years.[54]

Producing additional conflict of interest, in 80 percent of the largest firms in the United States the CEO is also the chairperson of the board. Harold M. Williams, a former chair of the Securities & Exchange Commission and CEO himself, said more than a decade ago, "The CEO should not be chairman of the board. Control of the agenda and pace of the meeting is a powerful control."[55] Board members are now being asked to bear much more responsibility for the integrity of the firm. The compensation for board members in 2003 at the largest

---

[53]David Lieberman, "Disney Tries to Work Magic with New Board Lineup," *USA Today,* March 18, 2003.

[54]"Directors Conflicts of Interest Often Buried Deep in Firms' SEC Filings," *USA Today,* March 5, 2002, pp. 1A-2A; "Look Who's Still at the Trough: Bonuses, Loans, Free BMWs—Boards Are Up to Their Old Games," *Business Week,* September 8, 2002, p. 58.

[55]"Chairman and CEO: One Hat Too Many," *Business Week,* November 18, 1991, p. 124.

200 firms in the United States increased 13 percent to an average of $176,000 per year for a part-time, albeit important, job. This large compensation presents yet another conflict of interest; board members are setting their own compensation.[56] In response to post-Welch shareholder and governance concerns, General Electric replaced stock options for directors and in their place provides "deferred stock units," which cannot be redeemed until at least one year after they leave the board. This encourages a longer-term perspective. In the United Kingdom, after 10 years on a board, a director cannot claim to be independent, and a board member that has significant stock holdings of that firm cannot be considered independent.[57]

The principal factors that enable board members to be effective are:

- All are "independent" board members.
- The chairperson of the board is an independent director, and not the CEO of that same firm.
- Directors are prepared, are sufficiently skeptical, and ask enough questions about proposals presented to the board (see Figure 8-2).

When these factors are not in place, a conflict of interest, which undermines the objectivity of the board, almost always results. First, inside board members are full-time employees of the firm and this makes it difficult for them to objectively evaluate and criticize company plans and proposals at board meetings. The

**FIGURE 8-2** Recommended Characteristics of Members of a Business' Board of Directors

- Board members should have top management experience and should represent a variety of perspectives.
- The optimum number of directors on a board is in the range 8 to 12.
- Board members should be independent of the firm, with few exceptions.
- The audit, nominating, compensation, governance, and ethics committees should consist of *only* independent directors.
- Board members should be prepared for board meetings, and also be skeptical and willing to challenge management on important issues.
- Independent directors should meet regularly without the CEO or other management present. For example, General Motors has a lead director, who then chairs these meetings.
- Directors should not micromanage or interfere with management.
- A director should not serve on more than 3 to 5 boards at the same time.

---

[56]*Business Week*, October 11, 2004, p. 18; Dan R. Dalton and Catherine M. Daily, "Director Stock Compensation: An Invitation to a Conspicuous Conflict of Interests," *Business Ethics Quarterly*, 11, no. 1 (2001): 89–108.

[57]"More Work, More Money" and "Where Europe Leads," *Wall Street Journal*, February 24, 2003, pp. R4, R6. This entire 12-page section of the *WSJ* is devoted to better corporate governance.

proposals come from the CEO, the very person who will decide their performance appraisal, increase in pay, and promotion. Outsiders, however, also have a limitation, since they often do not have the information to ask good questions. Moreover, some directors sit on too many boards, and thus do not give the time required to do the homework to ask intelligent questions.

Second, a CEO who is chair of the board thus directs the very body that is charged with evaluating his or her own performance. The chair of the board determines what is discussed at the meeting, what information is sent to the members, and the order and pace of the board's discussions. A primary role of the board is to assess the performance of the CEO, yet the CEO has vast influence over the very group that sits in judgment. In Japan, very few CEOs chair their own board.[58] Also note the contrast with university governance. In universities, an outsider is the chair, whereas in 80 percent of American business firms the CEO is still the chair. Yet, in businesses in which the profit motive is strong and large sums of money are involved, there is great danger of conflict of interest. Thus most argue that the CEO should not chair the board, and some go further and maintain that because of the conflict of interest the CEO should not be a member of the board. Finally, we now know that in the Hollinger, Enron, WorldCom, and other debacles, board members did not sufficiently question the CEO and management about their many fraudulent proposals.

## Federal Regulation: Sarbanes-Oxley and the SEC

Government regulation of corporations in the United States has been effective in many areas, but was unable to avoid the injurious actions of Computer Associates, Qwest, and many other firms. The U.S. Congress passed the Sarbanes-Oxley Act (SOX, as it is sometimes called) in 2002, in the wake of these failures. The new legislation attempts to correct some of the problems that allowed the deceit to take place.

One provision of SOX requires that both the CFO and CEO both personally certify quarterly financial reports. This will make it more difficult to claim ignorance, as did CEO Ken Lay of Enron, claiming he knew nothing of the complex and false Enron accounts. In addition, all the members of a board audit committee (which receives the outside audit) must be non-officers or outside board members. The outside auditing firm itself is not permitted to have both auditing and consulting business for a firm, in order to avoid being pressured to give a favorable audit in order to retain the more-profitable consulting business. The auditing firm must also rotate the lead auditor on a firm account every 5 years, lest the lead auditor become too closely tied to the firm being audited.

SOX also charged the SEC to write regulations to prevent conflict of interest of investment banks and their own investment analysts. The SEC has also set up a regulatory oversight board for the outside auditing firms. SOX did not address the conflict of interest when the CEO is also chair of the board. Doing what SOX demands is not cheap. One estimate is that firms with $5 billion revenue will

---

[58]Dan R. Dalton and Idalene F. Kesner, "Composition and CEO Duality in Boards of Directors: An International Perspective," *Journal of International Business,* Fall 1987, pp. 35–40.

spend an average of $4.7 million each implementing SOX; this comes to a nationwide total of $5.5 billion annually. However, citizens and investors contend that SOX was both necessary and worth the expense. They argue that SOX or something like it was essential if business is to rebuild its reputation and investors are to return to the markets. SOX has influenced board-governance procedures; from 2002, when the law was passed, to 2004, boards that evaluated themselves jumped from 35 percent to 90 percent. Also, boards that provide training for directors went from 14 percent to 80 percent.[59] Yet even after SOX, it is still possible to exaggerate income, hide losses, and avoid corporate income tax.

The SEC is the principal regulatory body overseeing these issues. During the scandals the SEC was hobbled by poor leadership and a lack of budget for adequate enforcement. The SEC has received much stronger leadership under Chair William H. Donaldson, and the budget for enforcement has increased. Donaldson was a founder of a Wall Street investment firm and later was chair of the NYSE.[60] He is trying to bring greater shareholder democracy to corporations and to make stock exchange fees more transparent. This experienced Republican Wall Street insider and now tough cop is presently trying to restore honest practices to business.

## STRATEGIC PLANNING AND ETHICS BUILD TRUST

No person, including a business executive, is able to develop a strategic plan without a clear goal. Given that goal, strategic planning and ethics are intimately linked.[61] Moreover, there is a new, strong external argument for encouraging the good behavior of members of a business firm.

The U.S. Sentencing Commission has established guidelines for the sentencing of organizations found guilty of violating federal laws. Penalties depend upon the steps that a firm has taken to avoid violations. Under the guidelines, penalties are greater if a firm has experienced previous violations, or if firm's managers were aware of the violations. On the other hand, company actions to avoid illegal and unethical acts will reduce penalties. This is a powerful incentive for business firms to take initiatives, such as developing an ethical code of conduct, educating members of the organization on ethical questions, appointing an ethics officer, and regularly auditing the ethical record of the firm.[62]

Successful firms such as Medtronic, 3M, Johnson & Johnson, Sony, Hewlett-Packard, and McDonald's have a strong set of values, a clear core mission, and

---

[59]"The Big Picture," *Business* Week, October 11, 2004, p. 15; "Companies Complain About Cost of Corporate-Governance Rules," *Wall Street Journal,* February 10, 2004, p. 1A; "Governance: Backlash in the Executive Suite," *Business Week,* June 14, 2004. pp. 36–39.

[60]"This Cop Means Business: Bill Donaldson Has an Ambitious Agenda," *Business Week,* June 23, 2003, pp. 110–112.

[61]LaRue Tone Hosmer, "Strategic Planning as If Ethics Mattered," *Strategic Planning Journal,* 15 (1994): pp. 17–34; Daniel R. Gilbert, *The Twilight of Corporate Strategy: Comparative Ethical Critique* (New York: Oxford University Press, 1992).

[62]O.C. Ferrell, Debbie LeClair, and Linda Ferrell, "The Federal Sentencing Guidelines for Organizations, *Journal of Business Ethics,* 17 (1998): 353–363; U.S. Sentencing Commission, "Sentencing Guidelines for Organizational Defendants," *Federal Register,* 1991, pp. 22786–22797.

employees dedicated to achieving that mission. Values and ethics are important to these firms. It is essential that CEOs and managers deal responsibly with ethical issues (for example, respect for colleagues, honesty in advertising, pollution, and relations with the local community). If an ethical work climate is achieved in the firm there is greater likelihood that members of that firm will act ethically and they are less likely to steal or act in other unethical ways.[63] Many firms have a high-level officer and staff that plans for and monitors these issues.

Firms have integrated ethical and social responsibility issues into planning and strategy. Most financially successful firms are also ethically successful. Several studies have shown that a firm that is socially responsible is more likely to have good financial performance.[64] Strategic planning is the beginning of the responsibilities of the CEO. Let us now examine the role of institutions that purchase equity shares in firms.

## The Influence of Institutional Investors

Institutional investors (pension funds, mutual funds, insurance companies, trust funds, banks, and university endowments) have a large and increasing influence on publicly-held corporations in the United States. This was not true a generation ago. In 1955 pension funds and mutual funds owned less than 5 percent of corporate stock; by 2000 they owned 57 percent. Institutional investors now hold more than $18 trillion in equity stock in U.S. firms.[65] In recent years, institutional investors have been active in attempting to influence corporate policy and the selection of directors. Institutional investors in many cases own well over 50 percent of the outstanding common stock of many firms.

Institutional investors have increasing influence on business executives in two ways: First, a fund's portfolio manager, seeking short-term financial gains, can push an executive into short-sighted actions. These actions include pressuring company management for short-term returns and supporting the takeover attempts when the expected result will be an increase in share price. Such actions can damage a firm, since a responsible executive must plan for the long-term, as we saw in Chapter 1.

Second, institutions are now more likely to vote their shares on annual issues on a firm's proxy ballot. Any shareholder, following SEC rules, can place an issue on the ballot for vote at the shareholder meeting of any publicly held firm. In 2003, the number of shareholder proposals at large firms was 668, an increase from 358 in 2000. Of these proposals, 159 proposals received a majority of

[63]James Weber, Lance B. Kurke, and David W. Pentico, "Why Do Employees Steal? Assessing Differences in Ethical and Unethical Employee Behavior Using Ethical Work Climate," *Business and Society,* 42 (September 2003): 359–380; James C. Collins and Jerry I. Porras, *Built to Last: Successful Habits of Visionary Companies* (New York: Harper Business, 1994).

[64]See Marc Orlitzky, Frank L. Schmidt, and Sara L. Rynes, "Corporate Social and Financial Performance: A Meta-Analysis," *Organizational Studies,* 24, no. 3 (2003): 403–444; also Samuel B. Graves and Sandra A. Waddock, "Institutional Owners and Corporate Social Performance," *Academy of Management Journal,* 37 (August 1994): 1034–1046.

[65]Lori Verstegen Ryan and Marguerite Schneider, "The Antecedents of Institutional Investor Activism," *Academy of Management Review,* 27 (October 2002): 554–573.

votes.[66] The proposal initiator generally tries to negotiate with management before placing the issue on a firm's ballot. In 2004 a General Electric investor objected to Kenneth Langone being on the GE board's compensation committee; Langone had been chair of the NYSE board committee that approved former NYSE chair Richard Grasso's $140 million compensation. General Electric removed Langone from its compensation committee and avoided having to defend him on the proxy ballot.[67] For shareholder resolutions that are placed on the proxy ballot, a majority vote is not binding. Nevertheless, a large shareholder vote does put pressure on management to take action. An example of the latter was when Walt Disney shareholders expressed a vote of no confidence in CEO Michael Eisner. The board then asked Eisner to step down as chair. A 2004 SEC regulation now requires mutual funds to reveal how they vote on shareholder issues, and this is causing an increase in voting and making the shareholder proposal a more effective instrument for reform.

Shareholders place on the ballot and vote on two types of issues, the first being governance issues (for example, making options for executives an expense, or annual election of board members). The second type encourages a firm to be more socially responsible on issues such as excessive executive compensation, diversity of members on the board, not advertising tobacco products to teenagers, global climate change, global reporting initiative, HIV/AIDS, and genetically modified organisms. The investing group often asks management to provide a report on its progress on the particular issue. By placing these issues on the ballot, the initiating group is able to focus top management's attention, inform the general public, and often negotiate an agreement with management that will achieve its ends.

Shareholder resolutions opposed by management often do not receive a majority vote. Nevertheless, even a small percentage can represent thousands of individual and institutional share owners who question management policy. The embarrassment of the possibility of these shareholders voting against management is often pressure enough for management to change policy. The Interfaith Center for Corporate Responsibility (ICCR) is the most active agent for placing social and environmental issues on shareholder ballots. The ICCR is a division of the National Council of Churches. It speaks for $110 billion of combined assets—mostly retirement funds—representing 25 Protestant denominations and 230 Roman Catholic orders and dioceses.[68]

To help institutional investors reach a judgment on the merit of the various proposals, the Investor Responsibility Research Center (IRRC) was set up in 1972 at the request of and with the help of grants from the Ford, Carnegie, and Rockefeller Foundations. The IRRC (not to be confused with ICCR) presents the position of both management and the group that introduced the proposal. The IRRC analyzes the proposal and poses critical questions that merit consideration.

---

[66]"Corporate Gadflies Are the Buzz," *Wall Street Journal,* June 10, 2004, p. C1.

[67]"Directors in the Crosshairs," *Business Week,* March 29, 2004, pp. 95–96.

[68]Lori Verstegen Ryan and Bryan Dennis, "The Ethical Undercurrents of Pension Fund Management: Establishing a Research Agenda," in a special issue on finance of *Business Ethics Quarterly,* 13 (July 2003): 315–336; "Following Your Conscience Is Just a Few Clicks Away," *Business Week,* May 13, 2002, pp. 116–118.

The IRRC does not recommend how to vote; that is the investor's decision. At the end of the proxy voting season, the IRRC publishes a summary of the season's voting. It lists the firms, the issues, and the percentage of shareholders supporting the proposal; it also often indicates which institutional investors supported or opposed individual proposals and why.

The shareholder resolution as an instrument for raising social policy issues is now accepted by most institutional investors. This reflects the fact that owning stock carries a responsibility to express judgment on major policy questions. The shareholder resolution can also be an aid to management. It brings to the attention of management many questions that might be overlooked. It provides an early warning system that alerts management that certain issues may become important in the future and deserve more attention. The ethical investor movement can help stakeholders catch the attention of management. Management thus receives important information that it would not otherwise have possessed.

Going a step further, some investors place their money in funds that use a "social screen" for their investments. That is, they invest only in firms that have a good social and/or environmental record. This movement has grown from investments of $40 billion in 1984 to $2 trillion today. Moreover, these socially responsible funds have performed as well and sometimes better than the S&P 500-stock index.[69] Now let us consider a means that a firm itself has for making explicit its own values and ethics: its code of ethics.

## Code of Ethical Conduct

Among large U.S. firms 78 percent have a code of ethics. Most of these codes have been introduced in the last three decades. They were established following the overseas bribery scandals of the 1970s and the introduction of the U.S. Sentencing Commission Guidelines in the 1990s. Early studies showed that two-thirds of managers thought a code of ethics would raise the ethical level of business practice.[70] These managers judged that a code would be welcomed by businesspeople to aid in specifying the limits of acceptable conduct; and they wanted a code of ethics to help them clarify their own ethical standards and decisions. Some did not know what was ethical and acknowledged that they needed help. Cases of overseas bribery (Exxon, Lockheed, ITT, Northrop) and of using privileged information for private gain (ImClone, Martha Stewart), as well as other transgressions, have underscored the problem.

When an ethical code is designed for a firm, the CEO is most often the initiator. However, implementation of that code is often delegated to the legal department.

[69]Pietra Rivoli, "Making a Difference or Making a Statement? Finance Researach and Socially Responsible Investment" *Business Ethics Quarterly,* 13 (July 2003): 271–287. For good overviews, see Curt Weeden, *Corporate Social Investing* (San Francisco: Berrett-Koehler, 1998), and James Melton and Matthew Keenan, The *Socially Responsive Portfolio* (Chicago: Probus, 1994); Peter D. Kinder, Steven Lydenberg, and Amy Domini, *Social Investment Almanac: A Comprehensive Guide to Socially Responsible Investing* (New York: Henry Holt, 1992), p. 11

[70]Gary R. Weaver, Linda Klebe Trevino, and Philip L. Cochran, "Corporate Ethics Programs as Control Systems: Influences of Executive Commitment and Environmental Factors," *Academy of Management Journal,* 42 (February 1999): 41–57; Raymond C. Baumhart, S. J., *Ethics in Business* (New York: Holt, Rinehart and Winston, 1968).

A code is more effective in influencing attitudes and actions when the CEO is actively engaged in that implementation. Firms that have model ethical codes and systems for monitoring them are Johnson & Johnson (see Figure 8-3), Cray, Caterpillar, and Weyerhaeuser.[71] Caterpillar's code is distributed to all managers worldwide, and these managers must report annually to the home office on "any events or activities that might cause an impartial observer to conclude that the code hasn't been fully followed." The code's provisions recognize the difference between what is legal and what is ethical: "The company's most valuable asset is a reputation for integrity. If that becomes tarnished, customers, investors, suppliers, employees, and those who sell our products and services will seek affiliation with other, more attractive companies. We intend to hold to a single standard of integrity everywhere. We will keep our word."

For Japanese managers, codes of conduct and company policy have a profound effect on their decisions. In Europe, research shows that the application of procedural justice increases compliance with firm policy, especially for managers of subsidiaries operating in global industries.[72] Within the United States, however, some codes have had little effect in bringing about ethical conduct in the firm. Recent business debacles show that some firms that possess a code are less ethical than some without. Enron and WorldCom had codes of conduct that were highly praised. This is partly explained by the fact that many corporate codes are considered to be necessary public relations, and are written to protect firms from their own employees. These codes generally cover issues such as kickbacks from suppliers, customer relations, keeping honest financial records, and conflicts of interest. On the other hand, fewer than one-fourth of the codes cover product safety, product quality, environmental issues, matters of personal character, and civic and community affairs—issues of concern to customers and outside stakeholders.[73] If a firm has only a code and nothing more, one suspects that the code is established because of the Sentencing Commission Guidelines, and it is seen as a cheap means of compliance. However, if the code is part of a program that includes an ethics office, ethics training and other initiatives, the ethics program is more likely to be effective.

## Planning for Ethics and Disclosure

In order to communicate its general goals, as well as to make clear the importance of ethics, a firm should develop a clear, motivating mission statement and conveys that mission to members of the firm. The mission statement will be

[71]For additional information about Johnson & Johnson and Cray, see Francis J. Aguilar, *Managing Corporate Ethics* (New York: Oxford University Press, 1994), pp. 61–71.
[72]Chiaki Nakano, "A Survey Study on Japanese Managers Views of Business Ethics," *Journal of Business Ethics,* 16, no. 16 (1997): 1737–1752; The European data is in W. Chan Kim and Renee Mauborgne, "Procedural Justice, Attitudes, and Subsidiary Top Management Compliance with Multinationals' Corporate Strategic Decisions," *Academy of Management Journal,* 36 (June 1993): 502–526.
[73]For valuable additional insights, see Max B. E. Clarkson, "A Stakeholder Framework for Analyzing and Evaluating Corporate Social Performance," and Thomas Donaldson and Lee E. Preston, "The Stakeholder Theory of the Corporation: Concepts, Evidence, and Implications," *Academy of Management Review,* 20 (January 1995): 65–91, 92–117.

# Our Credo

We believe our first responsibility is to the doctors, nurses and patients,
to mothers and all others who use our products and services.
In meeting their needs everything we do must be of high quality.
We must constantly strive to reduce our costs
in order to maintain reasonable prices.
Customers' orders must be serviced promptly and accurately.
Our suppliers and distributors must have an opportunity
to make a fair profit.

We are responsible to our employees,
the men and women who work with us throughout the world.
Everyone must be considered as an individual.
We must respect their dignity and recognize their merit.
They must have a sense of security in their jobs.
Compensation must be fair and adequate,
and working conditions clean, orderly and safe.
Employees must feel free to make suggestions and complaints.
There must be equal opportunity for employment, development
and advancement for those qualified.
We must provide competent management,
and their actions must be just and ethical.

We are responsible to the communities in which we live and work
and to the world community as well.
We must be good citizens—support good works and charities
and bear our fair share of taxes.
We must encourage civic improvements and better health and education.
We must maintain in good order
the property we are privileged to use,
protecting the environment and natural resources.

Our final responsibility is to our stockholders.
Business must make a sound profit.
We must experiment with new ideas.
Research must be carried on. Innovative programs developed
and mistakes paid for.
New equipment must be purchased, new facilities provided
and new products launched.
Reserves must be created to provide for adverse times.
When we operate according to these principles,
the stockholders should realize a fair return.

*Johnson & Johnson*

discussed further in Chapter 10. However, the development of a mission statement and code is just the beginning of management's job. In addition, managers must hire people who embody those values, and provide them rewards to encourage desired actions—perhaps prizes and publicity. The message is reinforced when the CEO sets a good example, gives occasional ethical pep talks, and tells inspirational stories of real people within the firm.[74]

Firms that are transparent in their operations encourage ethical conduct and discourage misconduct. Unethical business behavior thrives in secrecy. Disclosure requires communication of the mission, values, policies and models of behavior to members of the firm, and communication of successes and yet-to-be-achieved goals to external stakeholders. We discussed internal communication earlier. Let us now focus on external disclosure.[75]

The case for disclosure to external stakeholders (customers, employees, suppliers, and the community, in addition to stockholders) is that such information enables free markets to operate more efficiently. Without accurate information, there is poor allocation of resources and inefficiencies. As Thomas Clausen, former CEO of Bank of America and the World Bank put it, "a company's actions simply cannot be judged efficient, responsive, accountable, or consistent with the public interest, unless sufficient information about its activities is available." He adds that if government regulation becomes burdensome, it will be because business leaders were not sensitive to the needs of their stakeholders.[76] The Sarbanes-Oxley Act, which was triggered by the ethical failures of business, underscores Clausen's point.

Cynthia Cooper was head of internal auditing at WorldCom. In March 2002 she and the internal auditing team received word of $400 million taken from a reserve account to boost WorldCom's revenues. They examined accounts more closely; by May they found that the firm had charged expenses as capital costs, which enabled the firm to shift a $660 million loss into a $2.4 billion profit in 2001. Cooper confronted WorldCom CFO Scott Sullivan with the data; he was furious with her and told her to back off. Instead she presented her findings to the audit committee of WorldCom's board, and they in turn fired the CFO. The news was out, and WorldCom's stock collapsed. Although she was named a *Time magazine Person of the Year—2002,* Cooper refuses to be called a hero. But she is surely an excellent example of an internal auditor with integrity and courage—exactly the qualities that one would choose in an internal auditor.[77]

---

[74]Sandra A. Waddock, Charles Bodwell, and Samuel B. Graves, "Responsibility: The New Business Imperative," *Academy of Management Executive,* 16, no. 2 (2002): 132–147. For examples of ethical behavior in the rank and file, see Bill Fromm and Len Schlesinger, *The Real Heros of Business* (New York: Currency, 1993); see also Francis J. Aguilar, *Managing Corporate Ethics,* pp. 72–86.

[75]On the importance and means of disclosure, Eliane Ciulla Kamarck and Joseph S. Nye, Jr., eds. *Governance.com: Democracy in the Information Age* (Washington: Brookings, 2002).

[76]Thomas Clausen, "Voluntary Disclosure: An Idea Whose Time Has Come," in *Corporations and Their Critics,* eds. Thornton Bradshaw and David Vogel (New York: McGraw-Hill, 1981), pp. 61–70.

[77]Amanda Ripley, "The Night Detective," *Time,* January 6, 2002, pp. 45–50; Arthur Brief et al., "What's Wrong with the Treadway Commission Report? Experimental Analyses of the Effects of Personal Values and Codes of Conduct on Fraudulent Financial Reporting," *Journal of Business Ethics,* 15 (1996): pp. 183–198. See also, "U.S. Congress Looks at Internal Auditors," *Internal Auditor,* October 1987, pp. 4–7.

A firm's internal auditor, its external auditor, and the audit committee of the board have the responsibility to oversee financial reporting to insure honest disclosure, and this information should be communicated in the annual financial report. An internal auditor such as Cynthia Cooper must decide whether information that has been ignored or even hidden by management should be brought to the attention of outside auditors. The willingness of the internal auditor to report fraudulent behavior depends on many variables, especially the ethical climate of the firm. The success of an ethics program depends on the cooperation of the people involved. If the firm is perceived as fair in dealing with its workers, the program is much more likely to achieve its goals of establishing an ethical climate. Punishing a manager for violations of a code should be a last resort. Nevertheless, if it is perceived to be just, that punishment can positively influence the behavior of both the person being punished and others in the organization.[78]

As we indicated earlier, among the more important means of implementing socially responsible policies and adequate disclosure is oversight by the board of directors. The board's job is made easier when it has an ethics or social policy committee. Among the firms that have active ethics or social policy board committees are Toyota, PPG, General Electric, NEC, Levi Strauss, and General Motors. These committees oversee the implementation of the corporate ethics program. The good reputation that results when a firm is known to have good ethics is a positive benefit. Given current rapid communications, this is important for building trust with customers, suppliers, and other stakeholders. Planning begins with the firm's vision and mission statement, and this mission is then translated into goals. The firm's stakeholders now ask that these goals and the firm's performance on social, environmental, and financial issues be stated, measured, and reported.[79]

## Ethics Programs: Training, Audits, and Reports

Cummins Engine, Citibank, Boeing, and General Dynamics sponsor ethics training for all managers. Top managers initially spend a day, and middle managers several hours, in ethics training, and there are periodic follow-up programs. About 67 percent of workers in large firms and 41 percent in small firms report some ethics training. Moreover, 77 percent of workers in large firms and 47 percent in smaller firms report that there is a mechanism in place to anonymously report misconduct. In addition, 51 percent of large firms have established

---

[78]Gary R. Weaver, "Ethics and Employees: Making the Connection," *Academy of Management Executive,* 18, no. 2 (2004): 121–125; Linda Klebe Trevino, "The Social Effects of Punishment in Organizations: A Justice Perspective," *Academy of Management Review,* 17 (October 1992), pp. 647–676. See also Gail Ball, Linda Trevino, and Henry Sims, "Just and Unjust Punishment: Influences on Subordinate Performance and Citizenship," *Academy of Management Journal,* 37 (April 1994), pp. 299–322.

[79]See the detailed discussion of these issues by Sandra Waddock, *Leading Corporate Citizens: Vision, Values, Value Added* (Boston: McGraw-Hill, 2002); see also Kevin T. Jackson, *Building Reputational Capital: Strategies for Integrity and Fair Play That Improve the Bottom Line* (Oxford: Oxford University Press, 2004).

an ethics hotline and/or an ombudsman with whom any employee can speak anonymously about ethical issues.[80]

A social report enables a firm to state its social and environmental goals and to articulate the firm's impact on society. Firms that provided reports on social performance jumped from 7 in 1990 to 487 in 2001. Moreover, 40 percent of these reports now are externally audited.[81] Social reporting is also provided in annual financial reports and on firm Web sites.

A corporate social report discloses corporate activities that have a social impact (for example, energy saving, environmental actions, diversity in the firm, support of the community, and education) and assesses the success of these activities. Diversity in the firm and environmental issues can be quantitatively measured and reported. Specific targets and measurable results can be obtained, since it is possible to count the number of people in various jobs and the parts per million of pollutants. A report in these two areas is mandated by the government for many firms. Reporting other issues is often in the form of a description of activities.

Among the hundreds of global firms that now produce a detailed report on their social and environmental activities are Hewlett-Packard, Intel, General Motors, Honda, Philips, McDonald's, NEC, and UPS.[82] The reports are prepared internally and provide detail on what the firm is doing on social issues. For example, Ford Motor Company's *Connecting with Society* is published annually and is available in print form and on the Web. It discusses Ford's position on such issues as: stakeholder relations, sustainability, global climate change, and corporate citizenship. These environmental and social reports provide information to shareholders and other stakeholders.

However, it is difficult to compare one firm to another, since there is not yet a standard format for reporting, such as the U.S. SEC requires for financial reports. And there is also no standard repository of reports, although Boston College's *Center for Corporate Citizenship* has a good collection of reports available on their Web site, www.bc.edu/corporatecitizenship. The Global Reporting Initiative (GRI) has set standards for reporting, especially in the areas of human rights and the environment; we will discuss GRI in the next chapter. U.K.-based AccountAbility (www.accountability.org.uk) has rated the Fortune 100 companies for their impact on society and the environment. Their 2004 rating of the top 10 included only one U.S. firm, Hewlett-Packard, plus seven European and two Asian firms. The highest rated firm was BP (British Petroleum or Beyond Petroleum, as they now call themselves). U.K.-based SustainAbility (www.sustainability.com) has also organized conferences and done consulting on social issues for almost 20 years

A few firms have asked outside auditors to prepare their social performance report. Of the major accounting firms only KPMG provides ethical consulting and auditing. Their Integrity Management Services has helped Royal Dutch/Shell and

---

[80]*National Business Ethics Survey—2003* (Washington: Ethics Resource Center, 2003); Gary R. Weaver, Linda Klebe Trevino, and Philip Cochran, "Corporate Ethics Practices in the Mid 1990s: An Empirical Study of the Fortune 1000," *Journal of Business Ethics,* 18, no. 3 (1999): 283–294.

[81]John Ruggie, "Managing Corporate Social Responsibility," *Financial Times,* October 25, 2002; "The New Accountability: Tracking the Social Costs," *New York Times,* March 24, 2002, p. 4BU.

[82]These and hundreds of other reports can be accessed at www.cswire.com.

The Body Shop with their social reports. They also helped Home Depot with its sustainable wood sourcing.[83] Toy maker Mattel asked Dr. Prakash Sethi to visit and examine its overseas suppliers, focusing especially on working conditions and child labor. Sethi independently wrote his report on Mattel. Ben & Jerry's Homemade Ice Cream published an outside audit of their firm for several years. The Body Shop, a British-based cosmetics firm, chided by criticism of its environmental claims, published an outside audit of its social activities. Because of the U.S. sentencing guidelines and other pressures, some expect such external audits to become more common.[84] When a firm acknowledges its failures and publishes assessments that are critical of its own activities, its reports gain credibility, more so than when it reports only positive accomplishments. The Dow Jones Sustainability Index (DJSJ) for 2004 includes more than 300 companies; it is based on each firm's economic, social, and environmental performance. According to DJSJ (www.sustainability-index.com) Japanese firms are in the lead on environmental performance, European firms are best on labor indicators, human capital development, and social and environmental reporting, and U.S. firms lead in codes of conduct and compliance.

The Council on Economic Priorities has for decades done comprehensive, objective reports on the social policies and actions of firms. Considerable voluntary disclosure is involved in providing information for the book, The 100 *Best Companies to Work for in America*. The authors give background on each firm and also rate each on the following specific criteria: pay and benefits, opportunities for promotion, job security, pride in work and company, openness and fairness, and camaraderie and friendliness.[85]

Many large firms have a corporate ethics officer who is designated to oversee the firm's ethics initiatives. This person generally monitors and oversees the firm's legal, ethical, and social responsibility issues. The ethics officer is often asked by the CEO to help write and communicate the firm's code of conduct. Therefore, this person must have intimate knowledge of the firm, and must have good people skills.

In order to provide education and support for corporate ethics officers, the *Ethics Officer Association* began in 1992 and has grown to more than 800 members. Sponsoring members include American Express, BASF, Dow, EDS, General Electric, Hershey Foods, Honeywell, Hughes, Merck, Northrup Grumman, Novartis, Prudential, Sears, Shell, Siemens, Sony, Texas Instruments, UPS, and

---

[83]Mary Miller, "In Search of Business Ethics Among the Big Five Accounting Firms," *Business Ethics* (March-April 2002): 6.

[84]S. Prakash Sethi, *Setting Global Standards: Guidelines for Creating Codes of Conduct in Multinational Corporations* (Hoboken, NJ: John Wiley, 2003); Meinholf Dierkes, "Corporate Social Reporting and Performance in Germany," in *Research in Corporate Social Performance and Policy,* ed. Lee E. Preston, vol. 2 (Greenwich, CT: JAI Press, 1981). A classic for preparing a social audit is American Institute of Certified Public Accountants, *The Measurement of Corporate Social Performance* (New York: American Institute of Certified Public Accountants, 1977).

[85]Robert Levering and Milton Moskowitz, The *100 Best Companies to Work for in America,* (New York: Penguin, 1994); Peter D. Kinder et al., *Social Investment Almanac: A Comprehensive Guide to Socially Responsible Investing* (New York: Henry Holt, 1992), pp. 745–788; See also Steven Lydenberg, Alice Tepper Marlin, and Sean Strub, *Rating America's Corporate Conscience* (Reading, MA: Addison-Wesley, 1986).

Westinghouse. The organization sponsors annual meetings to provide information to the ethics officers, and also publishes a regular newsletter to update them on current issues (see www.eoa.org). Each of the aforementioned strategies depends on the initiatives of managers within the firm. But outside stakeholders, especially shareholders, can also have an influence on the values and ethical performance of those inside the firm.

## Growth and Narrow Interests

Indicators provide conflicting signals on the moral health of American society. On the healthy side, we highly value family, honesty, and integrity. Church attendance is higher in the United States than in other industrialized countries. While we have witnessed lying, fraud, and conflict of interest among some executives, such actions still cause scandal and outrage. Yet there is also evidence of selfish attitudes among many businesspeople. Moreover, our society suffers from a high incidence of bribery, alcoholism, drug addiction, street crime, and murders.

When facing such large problems, many people focus on protecting themselves. Special-interest lobbying groups in politics have fractured society into competing camps. Witness, for example, the success of gun owners, used car dealers, tobacco farmers, trial lawyers, specific business firms and entire industries in achieving their goals—even when their goals are contrary to the good of the community. Too often it is difficult to discuss political issues, because people have already taken a position and are not open to hear new evidence and balanced, intelligent discussion. Often political leaders nourish such attitudes by engaging in slogans and negative comments about opponents. Thus it is perhaps not surprising that among world democracies, the United States has one of the lowest rates of voting. Ronald Reagan, Bill Clinton, and George W. Bush were elected by less than one-third of the voters. About half of Americans didn't even bother to vote.

Most of the challenges required in society (for example, confronting terrorism, balancing the budget, rebuilding crumbling cities, helping poor and underprivileged people, limiting our voracious use of energy, and decreasing the hostility between nations) will require careful planning and visionary leaders who listen, but also an open mind, humility, and sacrifice on the part of all. History tells us that little can be accomplished without sacrifice, but we now hear little discussion of costs. In order to create a better society we are aware of and must use our strengths as a people, but few are willing to acknowledge and counterbalance our personal and national weaknesses. We will discuss how globalization is affecting individuals and firms in Chapter 9.

## SUMMARY AND CONCLUSIONS

The goals, values, and ethics of a person and of a firm are communicated by their actions. Values and ethics are communicated verbally and by actions to members and outside stakeholders. Most executives have as a goal the long-term good of the firm and society. Humane, cooperative, and ethical values create a more participative, attractive, and effective culture. In such a culture, employees are more likely to use their abilities to achieve the goals of the firm. Some executives, however, seek their own financial gain, which harms other people, the firm and society. Individualism and the Protestant ethic have carried Americans fast and far, but now delayed gratification has given way to the consumer ethic of "buy now, pay later." Individualism encourages "get rich quick" schemes that rarely benefit either individuals or society.

Traditional American flexibility and some changes offer signs of hope. Social concerns are now a part of corporate strategic planning. Pension and mutual funds, endowments, and foundations now exercise more influence, and often bring pressure on management through voting on social issues at shareholder meetings.

Boards of directors now take their responsibilities more seriously, some of this because of new legislation. Implementation of social policy and ethics brings a code of ethics. Moreover, most firms consider social issues in evaluating the performance of managers, and provide information to stakeholders about their social and ethical activities.

Executives recognize that stakeholders want more than return on investment from a firm. Quality products, planning for the long term, and involvement with local communities are but a few of the expectations citizens have of firms. To the extent that firms do not respond willingly, government will legislate or regulate. The alternative is for management to voluntarily initiate policies to ensure that its obligations are met, and we are seeing much of this today.

## DISCUSSION QUESTIONS

1. Who benefited from Jack Welch's tactics of selling or closing a business, even when it was profitable? Were these tactics good for the United States? How do you judge Welch's intimidating management style? What does his personal lifestyle and compensation tell us about his own values and ethics? Use the ethical norms developed in Chapter 3.
2. Is Bill George more correct than Welch when he says that Medtronic is not in the business of maximizing shareholder value?
3. Do you think that American values have shifted as indicated in Table 8-1? How does this affect the values of managers?
4. Is the compensation of Dennis Koslowski, Michael Eisner, and Sandy Weil reasonable? Are CEO salaries a problem in the United States today? Do you agree with Warren Buffet's assessment of CEO compensation? Is such compensation just?
5. Why is U.S. CEO compensation so disproportionately high compared to CEOs in other countries? Is the lesser compensation of female CEOs a result of them having a better sense of justice and community or is it sexual discrimination?
6. Is there a lack of incentive for managers to plan for the long term? Explain.
7. Given higher labor costs and the integrity of James Sinegal and Costco, do you think they will be able to compete with Sam's Club in the marketplace?
8. How would you characterize the values, ethics, and management style of Bill Ford and Ray Andersen (Interface Carpet)? What of the values of Gun Denhart and Ryuzaburo Kaku?
9. Do people consider a firm's ethical reputation when they purchase a product? Do you?

10. How would you characterize the values, ethics, and management style of Frank Quattrone (CSFB) and Lord Conrad Black (Hollinger)? Examining his overall record, is Charles Hurwitz a winner or a loser?

11. Does Gerald M. Levin bear any responsibility for undermining American values?

12. Is a corporation a servant of society? Does a corporation receive more benefits than it has responsibilities in society? Does civil society have the ability to revoke a corporate charter for serious misdeeds? Should this be a civil policy to protect the public interest?

13. What is the difference between an independent director and an outside director? What is a lead director? What problems arise when a board is made up mostly of insiders? What conflicts of interest arise when the CEO is also chair of the board?

14. Why should board members be skeptical when proposals are brought to board meetings for their approval? Why should independent board members meet periodically without any of the firm's managers present?

15. How has the Sarbanes-Oxley Act influenced the responsibility of the CFO and CEO for financial statements? How has the same Act influenced auditing firm policies?

16. How has the U.S. Sentencing Commission influenced how managers treat ethics within the firm?

17. Are the mission, goals, values, and ethics of a firm integral to corporate planning? Describe how to make ethics an effective part of planning.

18. Describe what influence institutional investors have on firms in which they hold stock. What are the advantages and disadvantages of this involvement from the standpoint of the firm? From the standpoint of society?

19. Why do firms have a code of ethical conduct? What is the difference between a code that is for public relations and one that is effective?

20. What is the argument for disclosure of financial information? What is the argument for social issue disclosure? Describe the ways in which social issue disclosure is made. What outside groups provide help in assessing social and environmental reports?

# CASES

## Case 8-1     Ebola Virus and Entertainment

The 1995 film *Outbreak* is based on a real-case outbreak of the Ebola virus in Zaire (now Congo), Disease Control (CDC) in Atlanta sent a team to a "hospital deserted save for a few patients dying the ugly, bloody death of Ebola . . . no running water, no telephones . . . "[86] and contained the disease.

Dustin Hoffman played the movie lead role. C. J. Peters, M.D. is chief of Special Pathogens, Centers for Disease Control. Peters is fighting budget cuts for his unit. Note the comparative data.

| CDC's Pathogens Branch | | Warner brothers *Outbreak* | |
|---|---|---|---|
| Salary: Dr. C.J. Peters: | $ 125,000 | Dustin Hoffman: | $ 6,000,000 |
| Budget: CDC FY 1995: | $7,200,000 | Production: | $54,000,000 |
| Spending on Ebola: | $1,800,000 | Gross in 3 months: | $67,000,000 |

1. What do these comparative expenditures tell us about American values and priorities?

2. Is there an inequity in these figures? Why or why not?
3. What ethical norms help you to deal with the case? ■

## Case 8-2     Stock Purchase Deal

Kenneth McGinty is an investment banker working with Maco Corporation on acquisitions. He learns that Maco is about to purchase Digital Optics. Digital is a small publicly held firm that has had an unprofitable year and its stock is undervalued. The price of the stock is certain to rise when the buyout is

announced. Set aside legality and look only at the ethical issues:
1. Can Ken purchase some stock for himself?
2. May he tell a good friend?
3. What ethical norms are most helpful here? Explain. ■

---

[86]"The Point Man in Germ Warfare," *Business Week*, August 21, 1995, pp. 72–73.

# Case 8-3 Company Controller

Carol Goudreau, company controller, is asked by the CFO to "manage earnings" in such a way as to present more favorable financial results for this quarter.

The CFO does Carol's performance appraisal. Why?
1. What should Carol do?
2. Why? ■

# Case 8-4 Home Depot and Certified Wood

An independent, not for profit, international organization called the Forest Stewardship Council has been established with input from loggers and environmental groups. It has developed a list of environmentally sound logging practices. The practices include "harvesting lumber at a rate sustainable indefinitely, maintaining old-growth forests and maintaining biodiversity." Timber firms may then request certification and they are inspected to determine if they adhere to the practices. Home Depot, the largest buyer and retailer of forest products in the United States, decided that would eliminate sales of wood products from environmentally sensitive areas, and it would give preference to certified wood.

1. What reasons could you give for this new policy of Home Depot?
2. Will this new policy provide better service to customers?
3. Will this new policy provide better service to shareholders?
4. What ethical norms are most helpful here? ■

# EXERCISE

## Business for Social Responsibility

The following firms have a record of exemplary business behavior. They are all described in the book *Companies with a Conscience*.[87] For this exercise, compare one of these companies with one other in the same industry not on the list on such issues as: employment diversity, pollution, attitudes toward and programs for employees, and any other special issues that you note.

---

[87]Mary Scott and Howard Rothman, *Companies with a Conscience: Intimate Portraits of Twelve Firms That Make a Difference* (Denver: The Publishing Cooperative, 2003).

| Firm | Industry |
|------|----------|
| Ben & Jerry's | Ice Cream |
| Shorebank | Banking |
| Patagonia | Clothing designer and distributer |
| America Works | Employment agency |
| Interface | Floor carpeting |
| Kansas City Chiefs | Professional athletics |
| Sunrise Medical | Wheelchair manufacturer |
| Greystone Corp | Bakery, construction |
| Birkenstock Footprint | Make and distribute sandals rule |

# CHAPTER 9

# Globalization's Impact on American Values

Global financial markets are beyond the control of national or international authorities. . . . Market fundamentalism has rendered the global capitalist system unsound and unstable.

GEORGE SOROS, CRISIS OF GLOBAL CAPITALISM

Riches are not from an abundance of worldly goods, but from a contented mind.

PROPHET MUHAMMAD

A few decades ago it was only large firms that operated across borders. Today every business must be aware of its opportunities to sell overseas, and also be prepared to defend itself from global competition. Globalization thus has an immense influence on American business and American business values. By globalization we mean the integration of communications, markets, and technologies such that individuals, corporations and nations are able to operate internationally more easily, coupled with a consciousness of world interdependence. Let us examine some varying examples of this global marketplace.

Jurgen E. Schrempp, Chair of DaimlerBenz, and Robert Eaton, Chair of Chrysler, in 1998 announced a "merger of equals." Several years later, Schrempp, then Chair of DaimlerChrysler, acknowledged that he always intended that Chrysler be merely a division of the German firm. He said he deliberately misled people about it at the time; otherwise he felt that the deal would have failed. The Chrysler division is financially doing better now, but after the merger it was not profitable, and in the wake of Schrempp's disclosure, morale and profits plummeted at the United States division.[1]

---

[1]"Chrysler: Not Quite So Equal," *Business Week,* November 13, 2000, p. 14.

**292**

Muhammad Yunus received his Ph.D. in economics at a United States university, and returned to his native Bangladesh to teach. He then noticed the poverty of the people around him. So two decades ago he began to provide loans of $10 to $30 that enabled illiterate poor women to purchase raw materials and set up their own home-based small businesses. One woman makes stools, another has a photo-developing shop, and others rent cell phones to neighbors. He chose to loan to women rather than men because he found that they were more apt to repay the loan, and the fruit of their entrepreneurial work would more likely aid their children. Yunus founded Grameen Bank to provide these microloans, and the Bank has loaned $3 billion to 2.3 million borrowers, and now employs 12,000 people. Because the venture has been profitable, it has spawned numerous imitators that have helped more than 60 million poor, illiterate women in dozens of other countries.[2]

Retailers in Thailand and China sell thousands of pirated DVD movies and music from sophisticated catalogues. Prices are low, and they ship the item the next day. The shop in Bangkok has a catalogue of classic films from around the world not available in regular stores. Despite arrests by the local authorities, the business is expanding rapidly. The film industry estimates losses in 2003 from piracy in 15 Asian countries at $719 million.[3]

The global economy is successful in providing low-cost goods. In the process there is pressure for lower prices and thus lower wages. There are increasing links between rich and poor nations and dramatically increased investment in poorer nations by global corporations.[4] Owners, investors, and speculators have reaped billions of dollars. The two major players on the world stage are global corporations and nations. If we arrange the 100 largest "economies" of the world in rank order, including nations and corporations, we find that 53 are global businesses. For example, ExxonMobil has annual revenues that are greater than the Gross Domestic Product of all but 20 of the world's 220 nations.[5] Because of their economic and political power, global corporations have vast influence on individual nations.[6] The French, Arabs in the Middle East, and many others complain of an Americanization and cultural homogenization of values across the world because of globalization.[7]

The George W. Bush administration initially came to office in 2001 pledging that it would be less involved in global issues than prior administrations. Bush withdrew from mediating peace talks in North Korea and Israel-Palestine, and withdrew the United States from the Kyoto Treaty on global warming. However,

[2]Muhammad Yunus, *Banker to the Poor: The Autobiography of Muhammad Yunus, Founder of Grameen Bank* (Karachi: Oxford University Press, 2001); Joshua Kurlantzick, "Muhammad Yunus: With a $27 Loan, He Started a Revolution," U.S. *News & World Report*, August 27, 2001, p. 51.
[3]Stan Sesser, "Smooth Operators," *Wall Street Journal Online,* August, 27, 2004.
[4]Jeffrey Sachs, "International Economics: Unlocking the Mysteries of Globalization," in *Globalization and the Challenges of a New Century,* eds. Patrick O'Meara et al. (Bloomington: Indiana University Press, 2000), pp. 216–217.
[5]Archie B. Carroll, "Managing Ethically with Global Stakeholders: A Present and Future Challenge," *Academy of Management Executive,* 18, no. 2 (2004): 114.
[6]John Cavanagh and Jerry Mander, *Alternatives to Economic Globalization: A Better World Is Possible* (San Francisco, Berrett-Koehler, 2002).
[7]Benjamin R. Barber, *Jihad vs. McWorld* (New York: Ballantine Books, 1996); Peter L. Berger, "Four Faces of Global Culture," in *Globalization and the Challenges of a New Century,* eds. Patrick O'Meara et al. (Bloomington: Indiana University Press, 2000).

the crash of three hijacked U.S. airliners into the World Trade Center and the Pentagon in September 2001 pushed the United States into renewing its concern with global affairs.

The United States, its economic health, moral status, and its future are inextricably intertwined with the other nations of the world. People in wealthy nations are able to purchase low-priced goods because of the lower costs of manufacturing overseas. Moreover, markets for goods and services from any nation are now global. The Internet has made communication and trade around the world much easier; a housebound maker of shirts in India can sell her work directly to a purchaser in Chicago. In addition, steel mill pollutants in China and cutting trees in Brazil's Amazon rain forest can shorten lives in Europe and the United States. Let us now examine the extent to which American firms depend on other peoples.

## MULTINATIONAL FIRMS AS CORPORATE CITIZENS

Global corporations such as Cisco Systems (United States), Toyota (Japan), and Shell (Netherlands) not only sell their products but also have operations in most of the countries in the world. These firms are but examples of the hundreds of businesses that affect our lives every day. They and the countries they represent are members of the global economy. The North American Free Trade Agreement (NAFTA) binds Canada, Mexico, and the United States even closer together economically. The European Union (EU) goes even further in joining the many European countries. We are becoming a world without economic borders where capital, products, services, and managers move easily from one country to another. The notion of a major product produced entirely by people of any one country is becoming obsolete.

The global corporation provides a multitude of benefits to billions of people around the world: jobs, goods, and income. Global firms hire local people, and provide them with training and sometimes education. Moreover, global firms have a vested interest in stability. Terrorism, wars, and revolutions disrupt business, even as they bring anguish, injury, and death to people. The global firm bridges nations, cultures, and peoples. Even when political institutions—individual countries and even the United Nations—are burdened by bureaucracy and nationalism, the global corporation is able to cross boundaries and deal with people where they live. From the standpoint of values, the global firm brings the great advantages of jobs, person-to-person contact of people of different cultures, and the *necessity* that one understand and work with people of another cultures. What we refer to here as the global corporation is sometimes also called the multinational corporation (MNC) or the transnational corporation (TNC).

If a firm tries to export its own national values and business practices to its overseas operations, it will not be successful; managers must be attentive to local needs and values. An experienced consultant outlined the stages of development of values for the global firm; in the final stage, the firm must "create a system of values shared by company managers around the globe to replace the glue of nation-based orientation once provided."[8] This system of building trust and shared values is difficult and takes time. However, it is doubtful whether a firm's shared values can substitute for the values learned in family, neighborhood, and nation. In any case, building shared values is aided when one understands one's own values and is aware of the processes that reinforce or undermine values.

## Worldwide E-Commerce

Doing business globally demands that one understand the culture of other nations, and also involves using e-mail and the Internet.[9] The Internet enables businesspeople to communicate globally, selling goods and tracking the global supply chain. It even provides the poor women in Bangladesh described at the beginning of the chapter the ability to sell their products to first-world purchasers. The Internet offers a powerful ease of communication between peoples and nations. The number of people using the Internet went from 1 million in 1988 to more than 750 million in 2004 and continues to grow at a very rapid rate. Internet communication is cheap, accurate, direct, and can span continents in moments. It is used by firms for billing, ordering from suppliers, planning, and advertising.

At present there is very little law that applies to the Internet. Net purists maintain that there should be no regulation at all. It is true that whatever law there is would probably be easy to circumvent. It is simple to replicate copy-righted work, as we saw with the pirated DVD movies and music discussed at the beginning of the chapter. A person who would never break a car window to steal a stereo thinks little of punching the enter key to copy $300 worth of software, music, or films, and it is hard to detect such theft. Scam artists can obtain credit card numbers from unsuspecting customers, and operate offshore to avoid the law. Pornographic material can be brought into the home by a 5-year-old. The Internet is a powerful tool, and we have not yet determined the ethical and legal boundaries for its use. Indeed, it is doubtful, given the variety of nations involved and the fragility of global codes, that any boundaries can be set. Global business activity has brought three additional troublesome issues to the fore: sweatshops, pollution, and speculation.

## Sweatshops Around the World

Today's American consumer demands low-cost goods. Consequently, U.S.-based firms such as Wal-Mart, Nike, and GE view themselves less as American firms and more as competitors in a global market, and therefore necessarily free of any one nation's political or social ideology. In this view people and nations simply provide resources to meet a firm's needs. This philosophy results in outsourcing manufacturing and service jobs because it is cheaper. Subcontracting firms will receive those contracts only if they cost less, and the overseas firms then most

---

[8]Kenichi Ohmae, *The Borderless World: Power and Strategy in the Interlinked Economy* (New York: Harper, 1990), p. 91.

[9]John Cullen, Praveen Parboteeah, and Martin Hoegl, "Cross-National Differences in Manager's Willingness to Justify Ethically Suspect Behaviors: A Test of Institutional Anomie Theory," *Academy of Management Review,* 47 (June 2004): 411–421.

often feel compelled to use sweatshops to meet the demands for cutting costs. U.S. firms are faced with the competition of low-priced goods from Asia, and thus feel forced to send their labor-intensive operations to low-wage countries. China, for example, has more than a half billion workers and has wages so low that they constitute a threat to every other country.[10]

From the standpoint of people in poor countries, any work that provides income is generally welcome. Child labor, long hours worked, and poor working conditions are secondary concerns. As a result, the International Labor Organization (ILO) estimates that in developing nations 250 million children between the ages of 5 and 14 are working—almost half working full-time. Close to a billion children between the ages of 14 and 18 are fully employed in poorer countries, and "there are upwards of 125 million young people who have never had the opportunity to attend school at all."[11] At the other end of their work life, ". . . most manufacturing operations . . . do not keep them beyond the ages of 20 or 21, only to replace them with another wave of 16- to 19-year-old workers. The older workers with few skills are then thrown out to join the armies of the destitute and unemployed."[12] Workers who are thus exploited in China are now protesting these workplace and social inequities, official corruption, and the lack of ability to air grievances.[13]

*Sweatshop* is the popular term describing the manufacturing facilities in which these people work—often 10 to 12 hours a day, 7 days a week, with few toilet facilities and no rest breaks. Moreover, many of these manufacturing facilities demand that people work at machines that can cause physical injury, and they must breathe glue that is carcinogenic.

A 22-year old woman from Bangladesh reported that she worked 19-hour shifts for eight cents an hour making caps and garments for U.S. universities and retailers. She said "We need to keep jobs in Bangladesh, but we also need to improve conditions." Workers can become indentured servants, who fall into debt and have no alternative but to continue working. "For the privilege of working 12-hour shifts seven days a week making plastic bags for Motorola cellphones, Mary, 30, will be in debt for years to come." The promised salary of $460 a month was five times what she could earn in her native Philippines, so she paid $2,400 to a labor broker to get her to Taiwan where the factory was located. Mary did not have the cash, as is most often the case, so she was forced to borrow the money at 10 percent per month to pay that broker. Once she arrived in Taiwan a second labor broker met her at the airport and demanded another $3,900 to deliver her to her new job. In addition, Mary must now pay living and other expenses plus taxes in Taiwan, so it will take her a decade or more to pay off her debts. This practice is legal; the firms in Taiwan need the labor and so encourage the brokers. Mary is at

[10]"The China Price," and "Shaking Up Trade Theory: For Decades Economists Have Insisted That the United States Wins from Globalization. Now They're Not So Sure," *Business Week,* December 6, 2004, pp. 100–120.
[11]Frank Vogl, "Forward," in *Rising Above Sweatshops: Innovative Approaches to Global Labor Challenges,* eds. Laura Hartman, Denis Arnold, and Richard Wokutch, (Westport, CT: Praeger, 2003), p. xix.
[12]S. Prakash Sethi, *Setting Global Standards: Guidelines for Creating Codes of Conduct in Multinational Corporations* (Hoboken, NJ: John Wiley, 2003), p. 10.
[13]Kathy Chen, "China Faces Rash of Protests: Officials' Abuses of Power and Social Inequities Provoke Unrest," *Wall Street Journal,* November 5, 2004, p. A10.

a disadvantage, since firing workers who attempt to organize a union is common in developing countries.[14] The only workers' union in China is a state-sanctioned monopoly, which ensures worker discipline and output. Protecting the interests of workers is only a secondary function of unions in China.[15]

Students at universities throughout the United States have protested sweatshop conditions, and have pressed their university administrations to make sure that their university logo caps and garments are manufactured under humane conditions. A labor union was formed at a supplier plant in the Dominican Republic with the help of this pressure. The students and other consumers have had some success in pressing national brands to supply information on the status of working conditions in their supplier plants, and in pressuring for better wages and working conditions. Some brands, such as, Mattel, Nike, Adidas, Reebok, Phillips-Van Heusen, Levi Strauss, and Liz Claiborne, now publish on their Web sites a report on conditions at their supplier factories. Gap goes still further in its candor. Its 2004 report tells of conditions at 3,000 supplier factories around the world. Among the items revealed was that in Mexico, 23 percent of the factories paid less than the minimum wage. In Africa, over 50 percent of factories did not have adequate safety devices for workers. A majority of the Chinese factories inadequately disposed of toxic materials. The report sets a new high-water mark for honesty in social reporting. The report was a risk for Gap, but it has won praise from analysts and an award for its social report.[16]

However, many other major retailers and brands, such as Wal-Mart and Disney, either have not done an audit of their suppliers or refuse to release the results of that audit.[17] A recent study of global firms operating in developing countries focused on how to achieve business efficiencies and national growth, as well as decent wages and conditions for workers. The authors concluded that, while government regulations are important, the ultimate responsibility rests with executives of the multinational firms themselves—as they put it, "responsibility cannot be outsourced." It is up to these retail and brand executives to set the standards for suppliers, and then audit those suppliers to ensure that the standards are observed. In addition, it is increasingly important for the global firm to empower and encourage local talent.[18]

The market system seeks the lowest cost. This puts downward pressure on wages, as we have seen throughout history. In Chapter 5 we saw that in the

---

[14]Nicholas Stein, "No Way Out: Competition to Make Products for Western Companies Has Revived an Old Form of Abuse: Debt Bondage," *Fortune,* January, 2003, pp. 102–108; "Special Report About Life on the Job," *Wall Street Journal,* October 30, 2003, p. 1.

[15]Jill Murray, "The Global Context: Multinational Enterprises, Labor Standards and Regulation," in Hartman et al., *Rising Above Sweatshops,* p. 29.

[16]Peter Asmus, "Gap, Inc.: Social Reporting Award," *Business Ethics,* Fall 2004, p. 9.

[17]David Gonzalez, "Latin Sweatshops Pressed by United States Campus Power: Dominican Plant Sings Labor Pact," *New York Times,* April 4, 2003, p. 5; Amy Merrick, "Gap Offers Unusual Look at Factory Conditions: Fighting Sweatshop Tag, Retailer Details Problems Among Thousands of Plants," *Wall Street Journal,* May 12, 2004; Aaron Bernstein, "Sweatshops: Finally Airing Their Dirty Linen," *Business Week,* June 23, 2003, pp. 100–102.

[18]Tatiana Kostrova and Kendal Roth, "Social Capital in Multinational Corporations and a Micro-Macro Model of Its Formation," *Academy of Management Review,* 28, no. 2 (2003): 297–319; Hartman et al., *Rising Above Sweatshops.*

United States, child labor and inhuman working conditions were common until only a few generations ago. As discussed in Chapter 6, Karl Marx demonstrated how the dynamics of the free-market system naturally bring about such conditions unless there is some outside pressure or countervailing power.

## The Earth's Environment

The environment affects everyone. Unlike the sweatshops that are a burden to poor workers in developing countries, environmental degradation can effect the lives of rich and poor alike.[19] As a result, France and the U.K. have mandated that business firms report on their use of resources and the amount of pollution they generate. A case worth examining is the problem of global climate change.

Data show us that the earth is gradually warming, and almost all scientists agree that the burning of fossil fuels is the major factor behind this warming of the earth.[20] It is caused by a "greenhouse effect," the result of carbon dioxide pollution that is emitted from the burning of coal, oil, and natural gas. This warming is likely to produce flooding, droughts, loss of crops, animal extinctions, and more violent storms; and this warming could proceed rather rapidly and bring on sudden and catastrophic change.

Viewing the data, delegates from 160 nations met in Kyoto, Japan in 1997 to write a pact in an attempt to lessen the causes of global warming. Europe, Japan, and the United States pledged to reduce carbon dioxide emissions by 6 to 8 percent below their own 1990 levels. The United States, with less than 5 percent of the world's population, produces almost 25 percent of the greenhouse gases. In his 2000 presidential campaign George W. Bush acknowledged the problems posed by global warming and promised to reduce carbon dioxide emissions; nevertheless, in the year following his election, he withdrew the United States from the Kyoto Treaty, rather than try to renegotiate it. He said that the goals for the United States were too stringent, the cost of compliance was too high, and developing nations were not included in the efforts to reduce greenhouse gases. Yet even without the United States, 178 nations hammered out an agreement to implement the Kyoto Treaty in July, 2001. The developed nations pledged to reduce carbon emissions and pay penalties if goals are not met, to establish a system to trade credits for emissions reductions and for investing in energy-efficient projects overseas, and to set up a fund to help developing nations adapt.

Many American business firms are ahead of the U.S. President and Congress in planning to reduce carbon dioxide emissions. This is surprising to some, but consistent with these firm's own goals and values. DuPont has cut its greenhouse gas emissions 65 percent since 1990; Alcoa, Entergy, Pfizer, FPL Group, and International Paper are also among those voluntarily reducing their carbon dioxide emissions.

---

[19] Vernon Ruland, *Conscience Across Borders: An Ethics of Global Rights and Religious Pluralism* (San Francisco: University of San Francisco, 2002).

[20] Molly O. Sheehan, "Carbon Emissions and Temperature Climb," in *Vital Signs—2003*, ed. Linda Starke (New York: W.W. Norton, 2003), pp. 40–41.

In addition, General Electric, General Motors, and Ford are planning renewable energy sources. Even American Electric Power, a principal user of coal, is accumulating worldwide credits for reducing carbon dioxide.[21] Global climate change threatens food sources, livelihoods, and future generations. A firm in California, Hyperion Solutions, is offering its workers $5,000 each toward the purchase of a "green" car that gets 45 mpg or better.[22] In these cases, businesses are doing better long-term planning than the government is. There are business opportunities in alternate energy sources, but developing these new sources is expensive, though it benefits people worldwide. Looking to the common good of all people is commendable for business but is the responsibility of government.

However, not all firms are as responsive to global concerns. Government regulation is essential because of those firms that do not act voluntarily. ExxonMobil and coal-mining firms, for example, have resisted attempts to limit carbon dioxide emissions and thus slow global climate change. In another case illustrating the power of global firms, the California petroleum firm Unocal built a natural-gas pipeline in the dictator-led nation of Myanmar (Burma). Unocal is accused of cooperating with the Myanmar military to force men from villages to work at no pay to clear jungles and build roads for the pipeline. Villagers said that those who refused to work, or were too weak to continue, were executed by the military. In a parallel case, ChevronTexaco is being sued on behalf of 30,000 indigenous people in Ecuador for dumping "over four million gallons a day of toxic waste-water, contaminated with oil, heavy metals and carcinogens into open pits, estuaries and rivers," between 1971 and 1992.[23]

## Speculation in Global Markets: The Casino Economy

A champion of the free market and an entrepreneur on his own, Edward Luttwak points out some of the dilemmas of the current market:

> They call it the free market, but that is shorthand for much more than freedom to buy and sell. What they celebrate, preach, and demand is private enterprise liberated from government regulation, unchecked by effective trade unions, unfettered by sentimental concerns over the life of employees or communities, unrestrained by customs barriers or investment restrictions, and molested as little as possible by taxation. What they insistently demand is the privatization of state-owned businesses of all kinds and the conversion of public institutions from universities and botanic gardens to prisons, from libraries to schools to old-age homes, into private enterprises run for profit. What they promise is a more dynamic economy that will generate new wealth—while saying nothing

---

[21]John Carey, "Special Report—Global Warming: Consensus Is Growing Among Scientists, Governments and Business That They Must Act Fast to Combat Climate Change," *Business Week*, August 16, 2004, pp. 60–69, 108.
[22]"Drive Green and Get Some Green," *Business Week*, December 13, 2004, p. 14.
[23]Marianne Lavelle, "The Court of Foreign Affairs: U.S. Corporations Face a Slew of Lawsuits Alleging Human-Rights Abuses," *U.S. News & World Report*, June 23, 2003, p. 31; Abby Ellin, "Suit Says ChevronTexaco Dumped Poisons in Equador," *New York Times*, May 8, 2003, p. C8.

about the distribution of any wealth, old or new ... they call this the free market, but I call it turbo-capitalism.[24]

The current state of markets in the United States and overseas is an example of the free market that works disproportionately to the advantage of the already wealthy; it consists more of speculation than of long-term investment.

An initial public offering (IPO) is an investment. Warren Buffett, an exemplary investor, does a careful assessment of any firm into which he places his money; it is as if he were going to purchase the firm. His investment is for the long term. Contrast this with the person who watches for hourly reports on the stock markets. Moreover, if analysts predict that a firm's earnings are going to increase by 8 percent this quarter, and if they increase by only 7 percent, that firm's stock will take a tumble. This is not investment for the long term. Indeed, can one call it investment at all, or is it merely speculation? Many say that what we now have is a "casino economy" rather than an economy that encourages investment. George Soros, who made billions in such speculation, points out that such a practice does not bring stability to domestic and world markets, but rather inefficiencies and even chaos. To bring more stability to global markets, Nobel prize-winning economist James Tobin proposed a small tax on foreign currency trades. Tobin's purpose was to shield poor countries from financial speculators.[25]

## Corruption and Transparency

Businesspeople who deal regularly with people of other cultures must understand the values of those other cultures if they are to operate successfully. Some cultures possess characteristics that make them less attractive for business. Corruption impedes development when government officials demand payments to obtain permits to build or to turn on the electricity. Corruption is very common in Russia. Pervasive corruption in the Japanese construction industry in the form of bid rigging may be one of the principal reasons for the current lack of health of Japan's economy and political process.[26] Not only does the money not go to suppliers, workers, or local investors who deserve it, but business planning becomes difficult, since one does not know when an arbitrary new demand may be made. The World Bank has called corruption the single greatest obstacle to economic and social development. It undermines development by weakening local institutions and the rule of law. The poor especially suffer from corruption, because they are the most reliant on public services and the least capable of paying the extra costs stemming from bribery and fraud.

There is evidence that corruption may be increasing in some developing countries. Three of the largest and fastest-growing Asian nations, China, India,

---

[24]Edward Luttwak, *Turbo-Capitalism: Winners and Losers in the Global Economy* (New York: HarperCollins, 1999).
[25]See Barry Eichengreen, "Financial Instability," in *Global Crises, Global Solutions,* ed. Bjorn Lomborg (Cambridge, MA: Cambridge University Press, 2004); George Soros, *The Crisis of Global Capitalism: Open Society Endangered* (New York: Public Affairs, 1998); on the "Tobin tax" see "Economic Forum: A Worldly Philosopher," *Economist,* March 16, 2002, p. 78.
[26]William K. Black, "The *Dango* Tango: Why Corruption Blocks Real Reform in Japan," *Business Ethics Quarterly,* 14 (October 2004): 603–623.

and Indonesia harbor pervasive corruption. Bribes, kickbacks, and "grease" money are the most noticeable forms of corruption, although they are not always the most serious.[27] Friendship, sharing information, and gift-giving pervade all cultures; such practices support a society's social capital. Such relationships become corrupt when the giver provides a "gift" that is substantial, and expects a specific favor (for example, a permit or a large contract) in return. That gift may be to a government official who has the power to award a contract or to a private-sector purchasing agent who can purchase the briber's product. In China, for example, *guanxi* is a reliance on relationships, and it can be mistaken for corruption. People depend on people they know because of a general lack of trust and the inadequacy of the legal system. On the other hand, in spite of official warnings of "this spreading cancer of corruption," it is still rampant in China. A county chief has been threatened and his wife bombed because of his attempt to get to the bottom of corruption among high government officials.[28]

Corruption sometimes becomes even more prevalent as global firms begin operations in various developing countries. In some countries, corruption reaches the highest levels of government, and is supported by what is called "crony capitalism." Business managers sometimes claim that bribery is a part of the culture of a particular country. However, "bribery is illegal and criminal under the laws of virtually every country, even those with cultures that supposedly support corruption."[29] Most people do not support corruption. Generally the only people who defend bribery are those who benefit from the bribes. When they hear about it, ordinary working people are outraged at the injustice of powerful officials taking huge sums of money in return for "favors." Bribery violates almost every local religious norm of how a public official should act, whether this religious norm be Islamic, Buddhist, Judaic, Christian, or Confucian. Moreover, developed nations share much of the blame for corruption, since most bribes come from business-people in developed countries.[30] U.S. law prohibits overseas bribery, but as we will see later, U.S. firms can be clever in circumventing the law. In many countries, there is now also a reaction against corruption. With popular support, South Korean courts sentenced four corporation presidents, including the Chairman of giant Daewoo and a former president of Korea, to jail for corruption.[31]

Crony capitalism, rampant in many Asian countries such as Thailand, Indonesia, China, India, and Malaysia means that who you know and the connections you have

---

[27]Jonathan Doh et al., "Coping with Corruption in Foreign Markets," *Academy of Management Executive,* August 2003, pp. 114–127.

[28]"Corruption in China: Shooting the Messenger," *Economist,* September 4, 2004, p. 43; John Boatright, "Exporting American Ethics," *Loyola Magazine,* Spring 2004, p. 17.

[29]Kathleen A. Getz, "International Instruments on Bribery and Corruption," in *Global Codes of Business Conduct: An Idea Whose Time Has Come,* ed. Oliver Williams (Notre Dame, IN: University of Notre Dame Press, 2000), p. 143; Duane Winsor and Kathleen Getz, "Regional Market Integration and the Development of Global Norms for Enterprise Conduct," *Business and Society,* 38 (December 1999): 415–449.

[30]Lawrence E. Mitchell, *Corporate Irresponsibility: America's Newest Export* (New Haven, CT: Yale University Press, 2001).

[31]"Unfinished Business: Kim Sends the Chaebol a Message," *Business Week,* September 9, 1996, pp. 56–57.

are more important than price or quality. Political, ruling, and military family groups require cash payments for permission to invest. In sum, where there is widespread bribery of officials, it is difficult to do business in that nation, since costs often are increased by 10 to 30 percent, and one can never be certain when one has seen the end of the demands for money. Moreover, the illegal payoffs do not go to legitimate targets, but to people who are already wealthy—those who have power.

Transparency International (TI) is a non-governmental agency based in Berlin which for more than a decade has been effective in trying to reduce corruption. TI estimates that the "amount lost due to bribery in government procurement is at least $400 billion per year worldwide." TI's principal vehicle for discouraging corruption is to publish an annual list of countries that are rank ordered from least corrupt to most corrupt. TI used 18 surveys of businesspeople and country analysts which asked about a country's corruption, and then averaged those polls to develop the 2005 TI list. For the full Corruption Perception Index, see the Transparency International Web site for the ranking of countries, the methodology used in determining the ranking, and additional information on each of the 146 countries: www.transparency.org.

TI found that corruption is rampant in 60 countries, and that the public sectors in those countries are plagued by bribery. These 60 countries scored less than 3 compared to a clean score of 10 on the TI list. A larger number, 106 out of 146 countries, on the index scored less than 5. Peter Eigen, Chairman of TI, points out that corruption seems to be most acute in Bangladesh, Haiti, Nigeria, Chad, Myanmar, Azerbaijan, and Paraguay, each of which has a score of less than 2. Most of the oil-producing countries also have very high levels of corruption. Countries at the top of the list, countries that have very low rates of perceived corruption with a rating of 9 or higher—Finland, New Zealand, Denmark, Iceland, Singapore, Sweden, and Switzerland—are wealthy countries. The United States, with a mediocre score of 7.5, is tied for 17$^{th}$ place with Belgium and Ireland. Hong Kong, Germany, Luxembourg, Austria, Canada, U.K., Netherlands, Australia, and Norway have progressively better scores than does the United States But the poorest countries, most of whom are in the bottom half of the list, have the greatest need for help in their fight against corruption.

TI also measures the countries in which corruption seems to be increasing and those countries in which it is decreasing. The fair, but not excellent, ranking of the United States may be due partially to the U.S. election system. In the 2004 elections more than a billion dollars were gathered from wealthy Americans and firms who contribute to political campaigns, expecting legislative and regulatory favors in return; people overseas view this as a form of corruption. Although it is illegal for a firm to directly contribute to political candidates in the United States, individuals and firms have found ways around the law.

In sum, all political officials must attempt to reduce the influence of private wealth on public power; otherwise wealthy interests dominate the public good. Corruption is a symptom of such failure. Private individuals then pay government officials to obtain permits, reduce their taxes, avoid costly regulations, and obtain contracts. The result is a loss of confidence in government, and the diversion of taxpayers' money away from public goals and goods into the hands of wealthy individuals.[32]

## Impact of Global Firms

With its global operations, the business firm produces goods, services, jobs, technology and wealth. Less widely acknowledged are the values that are communicated. The global firm brings the values of wealthy societies to developing ones. Values of discipline, individual responsibility, a regulated workday, and rewards for work under the direction of another come with working in a factory. As modernization proceeds, so too do the perceived values of the importance of money, goods, image, and advertising. These imported values often conflict with values of care for extended family, tribe, and village, and local cultural and religious values. This often causes misunderstanding and resentment in poor countries. Global managers are immersed in specific local cultural values and must understand and build on these values.

People in developing countries seek a better life. For them this normally means jobs, increased income, and more goods and services. Education and health care is vital for poor people, as are clean water and sanitary facilities, and their availability varies widely from country to country. The World Bank has spelled out the strategies that are most effective at making these services available.[33]

In spite of the efforts of the World Bank, the global economy is largely unregulated and thus unstable:

> The global economy with its momentum, inconsistency, and amorality, is developing much more rapidly and substantially than the sense of global community with which to moderate, interpret, and ground it. Put another way, the global economy unleashes all that is selfish about human nature without a global sensibility necessary for the well being of humans and our natural environment.[34]

One of the specific problems raised by the unbridled competition in the global economy is that the disparity of incomes between the richest and the poorest peoples of the world has increased in recent years. Between 1980 and the late 1990s, inequality increased in 48 of 73 countries for which good data are available, including China, Russia, and the United States. Moreover, these 48 countries account for 78 percent of the gross world product and 59 percent of world population. The former Communist nations had a dramatic surge in inequality. Among the industrialized nations, the United States has the most unequal distribution of income. Over 30 percent of income goes to the richest 10 percent, while

---

[32]Susan Rose-Ackerman, "Governance and Corruption," in *Global Crises, Global Solutions,* ed. Bjorn Lomborg (Cambridge, MA: Cambridge University Press, 2004), pp. 301–344.
[33]*World Development Report—2004: Making Services Work for Poor People* (Washington, D.C.: World Bank and Oxford University Press, 2003).
[34]John Della Costa, *The Ethical Imperative: Why Moral Leadership Is Good Business* (Reading, MA: Addison-Wesley, 1998), p. 20.

the poorest 10 percent receive only 1.8 percent. The richest 5 percent of the United States population has experienced the greatest percentage gain in income; and the top 1 percent gained more than the next 4 percent of the population.[35] We have seen how this disparity has caused envy, anger, terrorism, and wars in many nations; this could lead to serious instability in the future. In sum, the global corporation can be a major factor in assisting the economic development of poorer countries, but it also brings problems with it (see Table 9-1).

Acknowledging the strengths and weaknesses of globalization, economist Jagdish Bhagwati, an expert on world trade and defender of globalization, says that "globalization will yield better results [than isolationism] if it is managed." He then makes specific suggestions, among them encouraging International Labor Organization labor standards, compensating for layoffs in poor as well as

**TABLE 9-1** Pros and Cons of Global Firms Aiding Poor People

| Pros | Cons |
|---|---|
| 1. Provides jobs, income, capital, technology, and managers for poor people. | 1. Seeks low cost and encourages sweatshops—low wages, long hours, unsafe working conditions. |
| 2. Provides training and develops leadership for local people. | 2. Closes plants when wage rates rise, workers organize, or regulations become burdensome. |
| 3. Pays taxes and reinvests some of its profits in the local economy. | 3. Seeks nations with lenient environmental standards. |
| 4. Provides business for local firms and so creates jobs, both through purchasing from local suppliers and through workers' purchases. | 4. Encourages urbanism and the resultant uprooting of people, families, and villages. |
| 5. Provides mechanization, fertilizers, and other aids to agriculture. | 5. Bribes government officials and retards reform. |
| 6. Produces foreign exchange by exporting goods. | 6. Widens the gap between the few very rich and the many poor in the host country. |
| 7. Aids the host nation's development plans. | 7. Sends profits from operations back to richer home nation. |
| 8. Encourages the development of technical and professional skills among local people. | 8. Often supports authoritarian over democratic government because it is more stable. (E.g., China, Saudi Arabia, Malaysia, and Singapore.) |
| 9. Contributes to local and shared ownership projects. | 9. Advertises and sells expensive, unnecessary, and sometimes dangerous consumer goods. (E.g., cigarettes, alcohol, and weapons.) |

---

[35]Radhika Sarin, "Rich-Poor Divide Growing," in *Vital Signs—2003: The Trends That Are Shaping Our World,* ed. Linda Starke (New York: W.W. Norton, 2003), pp. 88–89.

rich countries, managing trade so it benefits people, and enacting and enforcing healthy national environmental standards.[36]

## BUSINESS AND GLOBAL POVERTY

There is no issue that uncovers our personal and business values more readily than our response to global poverty. Many are convinced that one of the principal tests of global business is whether it will pull people out of poverty in developing nations. It is true that jobs and opportunities have increased in poorer nations. However, the evidence also demonstrates that most of the financial rewards of globalization go the people who already have the resources: investors, owners, and managers are the principal winners both in wealthy and in poor countries. Both within countries and between countries, the gap in incomes between the rich and the poor is growing wider.

Data on world poverty show:

- 1.2 billion people in the world live on less than a dollar a day.
- 1 billion people do not have access to clean water.
- 1.3 billion people, mostly in cities in the developing world, are breathing air below the standards considered acceptable by the World Health Organization.
- 700 million people, mostly women and children, suffer from indoor air pollution caused by indoor stoves, which is equivalent to smoking three packs of cigarettes per day.
- Hundreds of millions of poor farmers have difficulty maintaining the fertility of soils from which they eke out a meager living.[37]

As populations grow, more people move to cities and add to the polluted environment, and so the problem becomes more difficult. The population of urban areas is expected to triple over the next two generations. In 47 of the least-developed nations, 10 percent of the world's population lives on less than 0.5 percent of the world's income. Illustrating the disparities, the wealthiest 20 percent of the world's population receive 85 percent of world's income. Meanwhile, the remaining 80 percent of the world's people live on 15 percent of the income, and the bottom 20 percent live on 1.3 percent of the world's income.[38] A telling way of describing the disparity: "The richest 3 people on the planet have more wealth than the combined GDP (gross domestic product) of the 47 poorest countries. The richest 15 people have more wealth than the combined GDP of all of sub-Saharan Africa with its 550 million people."[39]

This disparity has increased over the past generation. From 1960 to 1995, the disparity in per capita income between the world's 20 richest and 20 poorest

[36]Jagdish Bhagwati, *In Defense of Globalization* (New York: Oxford University Press, 2004).
[37]Data from Ismail Serageldin, "World Poverty and Hunger—The Challenge for Science," *Science*, 296 (April 2002): 54–58.
[38]*Ibid.*, p. 54.
[39]Ismail Serageldin, "World Poverty and Hunger . . . ," p. 55.

countries more than doubled, increasing from 18 to 1 to 37 to 1. In addition, because inequality has also risen within countries, the gap between those at the top and those at the bottom is even more glaring.[40] The former president of the World Bank, James Wolfensohn, says, "Despite years of relative peace and prosperity in industrialized countries, global poverty is getting worse. More troubling still is the massive and widening gap between rich and poor."[41]

Nobel Prize-winning economist, Joseph Stiglitz, summarizes:

> Globalization today is not working for many of the world's poor. It is not working for much of the environment. It is not working for the stability of the global economy. The transition from communism to a market economy has been so badly managed that, with the exception of China, Vietnam, and a few Eastern European countries, poverty has soared as incomes have plummeted.[42]

Stiglitz criticizes the International Monetary (IMF) fund for demanding economic policies for troubled poor countries that hindered their recovery; he claims that it is only because China and Korea ignored the IMF that they succeeded. On the other hand, Thailand followed the IMF policies, and has not recovered. Even though the IMF was established to aid poor nations, its policies are actually geared to supporting the financial institutions that provide the loans. Just as IMF policies are dominated by financial institutions, he maintains that the World Trade Organization (WTO) has been dominated by global corporations. The WTO can overrule an individual nation's labor or environmental regulation as a restraint of trade, and it can do this without appeal. Stiglitz's solution is to have appropriate national and international government intervention, so that all people, including the poor, gain the advantages of economic growth.

## Toward International Stability

The goal of the World Bank is to alleviate poverty and to stimulate growth in poor nations. After conversations with 60,000 poor people in 60 countries, James Wolfensohn and the World Bank staff conclude that in addition to sound economic policies, it is necessary to support education, health, good governance, the fight against corruption, legal and judicial reform, and environmental protection. According to them, fighting poverty has become a global concern; the stability of the world depends upon it. Much of this work must be done within the developing nations themselves, so that these nations can develop the necessary civic and legal institutions and rid themselves of corruption. In this effort, resources and experts from wealthier nations can be of help.[43]

In most of the developing countries, a large percentage of the population works on small farms. These developing countries have agreed to open markets, but they

---

[40]Michael Renner and Molly Sheehan, "Poverty and Inequality Block Progress," Starke, *Vital Signs—2003,* pp. 17–24.

[41]James D. Wolfensohn, "A Call to Global Action," *America,* January 8–15, 2001, pp. 8–12.

[42]Joseph E. Stiglitz, *Globalization and Its Discontents* (New York: W.W. Norton, 2003), p. 214.

[43]"Special Report-Global Poverty: There's No Panacea But Here Are Strategies That Work," *Business Week,* October 14, 2002, pp. 107–118.

find that their best potential export, agricultural products, cannot be sold. Europe, the United States, and Japan together spend $300 billion a year to subsidize their own farm products. These subsidies lower production costs for wealthy country producers, and make it impossible for farmers from poor nations to sell their products on the world market. Moreover, much of the U.S. subsidy goes to agribusiness, which has access to better equipment, seeds, and irrigation. In spite of wealthy nations' call for open markets, their own subsidies crush, for example, the cotton growers of Pakistan, the rice farmers of Indonesia, and the sugar producers of Africa. Compare $300 billion spent on agricultural subsidies for developed nations to the total of $50 billion spent annually to financially aid poor countries.[44] While wealthy countries urge open markets on poor countries so that they can purchase finished goods from them, these same affluent countries refuse to open their own markets. On this vital issue globalization is a one-way street: It benefits the wealthy nations and penalizes poor nations.

One method of helping poor nations is to focus development assistance on the needs of the poor peoples; for example, on education, health, clean water, and technical skills. Table 9-2 shows the amount of foreign aid that has been provided in recent years by the primary contributing countries, as measured both in total

**TABLE 9-2**  Development Assistance of Top-15 Contributors, 1992 and 2000

| Country | 1992 | | 2000 | |
|---|---|---|---|---|
| | *Total* | *Share of GNP* | *Total* | *Share of GNP* |
| | *(million 2000 dollars)* | *(percent)* | *(million 2000 dollars)* | *(percent)* |
| Denmark | 1,583 | 1.02 | 1,664 | 1.06 |
| Netherlands | 3,132 | 0.86 | 3,075 | 0.82 |
| Sweden | 2,798 | 1.03 | 1,813 | 0.81 |
| Norway | 1,448 | 1.16 | 1,264 | 0.80 |
| Belgium | 984 | 0.39 | 812 | 0.36 |
| Switzerland | 1,296 | 0.46 | 888 | 0.34 |
| France | 9,407 | 0.63 | 4,221 | 0.33 |
| United Kingdom | 3,659 | 0.31 | 4,458 | 0.31 |
| Japan | 12,685 | 0.30 | 13,062 | 0.27 |
| Germany | 8,613 | 0.39 | 5,034 | 0.27 |
| Australia | 1,107 | 0.35 | 995 | 0.27 |
| Canada | 2,861 | 0.46 | 1,722 | 0.25 |
| Spain | 1,727 | 0.26 | 1,321 | 0.24 |
| Italy | 4,689 | 0.34 | 1,368 | 0.13 |
| United States | 13,319 | 0.20 | 9,581 | 0.10 |
| All Countries | 68,808 | 0.33 | 53,058 | 0.22 |

*Source:* Worldwatch Institute, State of the World, 2001, www.worldwatch.org.

---

[44]"Mowing Down Farm Subsidies," *Business Week,* August 16, 2004, p. 108; "The Rigged Trade Game," *New York Times,* July 20, 2003, p. 10wk.

dollar amount and as a percentage of each country's Gross National Product (GNP). Note that most aid contributions have fallen rather substantially by both measures. The United States is no longer the largest aid contributor, and as a percentage of GNP the United States trails every one of the contributor nations.

Compare the U.S. foreign aid of $9.6 billion to the military budget of $280.6 billion before the increases after September 11, 2001. "The U.S. military budget is larger than the defense budgets of the next nine nations below us *combined.* And the United States will pull away even further with the increase next year of some $50 billion, as much as the entire defense budget of the next biggest spender, Japan."[45] There was much discussion during the 2004 U.S. presidential elections of how best to keep the world safe in the coming years. A strong military and aid to poorer nations are the two most important means.

Given a limited amount of aid resources, a group of politicians and economists, including three Nobel prize winners, met in Copenhagen in 2002 to discuss how best to help poor nations. After evaluating dozens of worthy issues, the panel reached a consensus, and recommended investment in the following 10 projects: climate change, communicable diseases, civil conflicts, access to education, financial instability, governance and corruption, malnutrition and hunger, migration, subsidies and trade barriers, and sanitation and access to clean water.[46] Would shifting a portion of developed nations' military budget tax dollars from jet aircraft, tanks, and rockets to civilian aid for education, health, clean water, and combating malnutrition for people in poor nations be a better investment in peace?

## GLOBAL ETHICAL CONDUCT: LAWS, CODES, AND REPORTING

We pointed out in Chapter 3 that the ethical norms described there are also useful in other cultures. In Chapter 8 we discussed the importance of a firm having its own mission and code of ethical conduct and offered some models of excellent codes. The increasing influence of global business, which is being expedited by the North American Free Trade Agreement (NAFTA), the EU, and the organization of Asian nations (ASEAN), makes it apparent that individual company codes are not sufficient.[47] Bribery of government leaders for permits and purchases is still common. In many countries workers are paid less than it takes to live, and their government forbids them to organize to seek

---

[45]David Gergen, "Military Expenditures," U.S. News & World Report, March 4, 2002, p. 84.
[46]See the final report of the group, Bjorn Lomborg, ed., *Global Crises, Global Solutions* (Cambridge, MA: Cambridge University Press, 2004); "Putting the World to Rights: What Would Be the Best Way to Spend Additional Resources Helping the Developing Countries?" *The Economist* (June 5, 2002), pp. 63–65; for a more comprehensive view with cases, see Lee A. Tavis, *Power and Responsibility: Multinational Managers and Developing Country Concerns* (Notre Dame: University of Notre Dame Press, 1997).
[47]Janice M. Beyer and David Nino, "Ethics and Cultures in International Business," *Journal of Management Inquiry,* 8 (September 1999): 287–297; Akira Takahashi, "Ethics in Developing Economies of Asia," *Business Ethics Quarterly,* 7 (July 1997): 33–46.

better pay and working conditions. Moreover, air, water, and solid waste pollution is killing tens of thousands in poor countries daily. Global codes could set similar expectations among firms in different nations, and provide an "even playing field" for all business.

International bodies some time ago attempted to state basic principles of just business transactions across national boundaries. The United Nations agreed in 1948 on the *Universal Declaration of Human Rights,* and the International Labor Office (ILO) in 1977 codified the basic rights of working people in the *Tripartite Declaration.*[48] On a more specific product issue, because of widespread abuse, the World Health Organization (WHO) prodded major infant formula manufacturers such as Nestlé, American Home Products, and Abbott Laboratories to agree on international guidelines for marketing infant formula.[49] With regard to the environment, 70 firms, including American Airlines, Bank of America, Coca-Cola, Consolidated Edison, Ford, General Motors, Interface, and Nike have endorsed the Coalition for Environmentally Responsible Economies (CERES) Principles. These endorsing firms pledge to follow the 10 CERES Principles and to preserve and protect the environment in some cases at levels beyond what is required by local law. Being an endorser is a two-way process. At least once every 5 years CERES does an independent report to certify that the firm is following the 10 principles. For example, CERES did a Performance Review of General Motors in 2002 and found that "GM made significant progress in cleaning up and reducing factory emissions, conserving resources, and eliminating waste, and has led the way on corporate disclosure and stakeholder engagement." The review of product improvements was less positive, since GM has not increased the fuel economy of its fleet of cars and trucks. The entire report, along with an executive summary, is publicly available.[50] CERES also founded, along with the United Nations Environment Programme (UNEP) the *Global Reporting Initiative* (GRI), which we will discuss later in this chapter.

The United States in 1977 attempted to make international business conduct more fair through domestic legislation. In the 1970s many American firms bribed foreign leaders to obtain preference for doing business in that country or so that country would purchase the firm's products. Executives of Lockheed paid more than $22 million to leaders of Japan, Netherlands, Saudi Arabia, Korea, and other nations to purchase their aircraft. United Brand's executives paid $2 million to the president of Honduras to reduce taxes on bananas, and Gulf Oil paid the South Korean president $4 million to give it a permit to build an oil refinery. These bribes caused a government to fall in Japan and major embarrassment for the leaders of the other nations. In order to reduce this bribery of foreign leaders by U.S. executives, in 1977 the U.S. Congress passed the Foreign Corrupt Practices Act (FCPA).

The FCPA does not prohibit "expediting," "grease," or tip (to insure promptness) payments to customs or other minor officials to cut through red tape.

---

[48]For an overview of the content and impact of international compacts, see William C. Frederick, "The Moral Authority of Transnational Corporate Codes," *Journal of Business Ethics,* 10 (1991): 165–177. We should note that the United States stands alone in not ratifying the Universal Declaration of Human Rights.

[49]Again, the United States is the only nation that has never agreed to these international guidelines.

[50]See: www.ceres.org/pdf/gm_exec.pdf.

Payments are allowed if the official has no impact on the final decision, and the payment merely makes the transaction move more quickly. But the FCPA does prohibit a major payment to an official to influence that official's judgment, for example, to obtain access or to purchase a product. The firm is also required to keep detailed records and accounts of all payments so that auditors may inspect and judge them. When Congress passed the FCPA, they presumed that other developed nations would soon follow with similar legislation to prevent bribery, so as to make international operations fairer. It has taken two decades for other nations to enact legislation that prohibits bribery.

The Organization for Economic Cooperation and Development (OECD) is the major economic policy-making body for the industrialized nations. The OECD finally issued guidelines by which member nations were expected to change their domestic legislation to criminalize bribery beginning in 1997. The European Union had been reluctant to prescribe legislation for member states, but finally agreed to support the OECD guidelines.[51]

There has also been criticism of firms doing business in China, Myanmar (Burma), Sudan, and other countries that have poor records in respecting human rights. As we discussed earlier, in many countries children sometimes labor 80-hour weeks for two dollars a day to make consumer goods for U.S. customers. These workers are most often forbidden to organize to ask for better pay or working conditions. Because of this, firms such as Levi Strauss, Reebok, and Nike have developed their own principles of how workers should be treated and they monitor their suppliers. In addition, some business executives have organized to fashion global codes of business conduct. Let us now examine two of the best known.

### The Caux Round Table Principles for Business

The Caux Round Table (CRT), founded in 1986, is an organization of senior executives of firms from Europe, Japan, the United States, Lebanon, Thailand and many other countries. Their *Principles for Business* were written in 1994 by executives from firms including Siemens, 3M, Canon, Chase Manhattan Bank, Matsushita, Dana, Nissan, Ciba Geigy (now Novartis), Ambrosetti Group, Philips Electronics, Sumitomo, and others. The CRT took a set of principles that had been developed by Minneapolis-St. Paul executives and added two major basic principles. The first, from the Eastern tradition is the principle of "kyosei," a Japanese word, that means living and working together for the common good, enabling cooperation and mutual prosperity to coexist with healthy and fair competition. The second principle underlying CRT Principles, from the Western tradition, is "human dignity," which refers to the sacredness or value of each person as an end, not simply as a means to the fulfillment of other's purposes. The principles include a preamble, seven "general principles," and specific sets of stakeholder principles, covering customers, employees, owners/investors, suppliers, competitors, and

---

[51]For an overview of the problem and the possible solutions, see James Weber and Kathleen Getz, "Buy Bribes or Bye-Bye Bribes: The Future Status of Bribery in International Commerce," *Business Ethics Quarterly,* 14 (October 2004): 695–711.

**TABLE 9-3**  Origin of Global Business Conduct Codes and Reporting Mechanisms

| Author of Code | Code | Year Initiated |
| --- | --- | --- |
| Business Executives from EU, Japan, and U.S. | Caux Round Table Principles for Business | 1996 |
| Kofi Annan and global business executives | United Nations Global Compact with Business | 2000 |
| Coalition for Environmentally Responsible Economies (CERES) and UN Environment Programme (UNEP) | Global Reporting Initiative (GRI) | 2002 |

communities.[52] The CRT Principles are found in Appendix A. For the origins of the codes and reporting initiative discussed here, see Table 9-3.

The Principles are offered as a benchmark for a firm in developing, updating, or improving its own mission and code of behavior. The Principles have considerable support, since they were written and sponsored by a prestigious group of senior business executives. The Bank of America, along with executives from Australia, Malaysia, China, Russia, Netherlands, Lebanon, and many other countries, used the Caux Principles as a model for their own firm's code. The CRT meets regularly and are particularly concerned about alleviating world poverty and attempting to make it possible for poor nations to share in global prosperity.[53] The Caux Principles have been taught in dozens of universities worldwide. For example, at a 1995 meeting in Indonesia, members of the International Association of Jesuit Schools of Business, a group of 60 business schools from 20 countries on six continents, voted to support and teach the Caux *Principles for Business.*

The CRT has now developed a Self-Assessment and Improvement Process (SAIP) to help business address the growing public expectations that corporations will conduct their activities in an ethically responsible manner. The SAIP "allows senior leaders to 'score' the firm's conduct in relation to an acknowledged global standard for responsible behavior."[54] The scoring is done privately, so executives are able to be more forthcoming with information, and have less fear of embarrassment because of their data. However, those who formulated the SAIP expect that soon executives will seek to compare their scores with at least some other firms, so as to learn from them. At the CRT meeting of executives in Mexico in 2002, a major item on the agenda was the *United Nations Global Compact with Business.* At that meeting the CRT agreed to cooperate with this newer effort.

---

[52]Kenneth Goodpaster, "The Caux Round Table Principles: Corporate Moral Reflection in a Global Business Environment"; Gerald Cavanagh, "Executives' Code of Business Conduct: Prospects for the Caux Principles," in *Global Codes of Business Conduct: An Idea Whose Idea Has Come,* ed. Oliver F. Williams, C.S.C., (Notre Dame: University of Notre Dame Press, 2000), pp. 169–195.

[53]See www.cauxroundtable.org.

[54]Kenneth Goodpaster, Dean Maines, and Michelle Rovang, "Stakeholder Thinking Beyond Paradox to Practicality," *Journal of Corporate Citizenship,* no. 7 (2002): 93.

## The United Nations Global Compact with Business

World business and political leaders in 1999 invited Secretary General of the United Nations Kofi Annan to address them at the World Economic Forum in Davos, Switzerland. In that presentation, Annan warned that "we have underestimated the fragility of the global economy." He pointed out that many people are suspicious of the global economy since "the spread of markets outpaces the ability of societies and their political systems to adjust to them, let alone guide the course they take. History teaches that such imbalance between the economic, social, and political realms can never be sustained for very long." Until people have confidence in the global economy, it "will be fragile and vulnerable—vulnerable to backlash from all the 'isms' of our post-cold war world—protectionism, populism, nationalism, ethnic chauvinism, fanaticism, and terrorism." To avoid a backlash, Annan invited leaders of large corporations to join with the United Nations in a "global compact" to "support and enact a set of core values in the areas of human rights, labor standards and environmental practices." In return, he offered United Nations support for "the open global market."[55]

Annan's challenge and suggestion struck a responsive cord with the corporate leaders and they fashioned what is now called the *United Nations Global Compact with Business.* The Compact consists of 10 simple principles that seek to protect human rights, worker rights, and the environment. The Compact is reprinted in Appendix B. If a firm decides to participate in the Compact, the firm first submits a letter of intent from the firm's chief executive officer, and then agrees to publish in its annual report, or a similar corporate report, a description of the ways in which it is supporting the Global Compact and its 10 principles.[56] The goal is to make the principles of the Global Compact part of the firm's business strategy, culture, and day-to-day operations.[57]

By 2004 more than 800 firms on six continents had joined the Global Compact, among them BP, Cisco Systems, DaimlerChrysler, Deloitte & Touche, Dupont, Hewlett-Packard, Novartis, Schell, Unilever, and Volvo. Annan also set up an advisory council for the Compact consisting of senior business executives, international labor leaders, and leaders of key non-governmental organizations (NGOs). The Global Compact helps firms that sign the Compact to adhere to the basic principles and to write their annual report through "Learning Forums," which provide an opportunity for firms to share their experiences and successes with each other. The Learning Forum "is a mechanism to stimulate action, to enhance transparency and encourage information sharing." A learning forum was held in China and discussed human and worker rights. To lessen the anxiety of firms, the Compact declares that it "does not 'police,' enforce or measure the behavior or actions of companies. . . ." The Compact does not accept corporate funding for Global Compact activities, to

---

[55]Kofi Annan, "Business and the U.N.," *Vital Speeches,* February 15, 2000, pp. 260–261.
[56]Georg Kell, "Do Corporations Threaten Globalization?" *Business Ethics in a Global Economy Conference,* Santa Clara University, February 20, 2003; Georg Kell and David Levin, "The Evolution of the Global Compact Network: An Historic Experiment in Learning and Action," *Working Draft: UN 8–2002,* Academy of Management Conference, Denver, August 13, 2002.
[57]*The Global Compact: Corporate Citizenship in the World Economy* (United Nations: Global Compact Office, 2003); see also www.unglobalcompact.org/Portal/Default.asp.

forestall accusations of being "bought" by business. Through the Learning Forums, the Global Compact encourages collaboration. An outcome of collaboration is that firms share information, undertake change cooperatively, and individually work actively on change.[58]

On the other hand, the Compact has been charged with "bluewashing," that is, signing up firms and allowing them to display the blue United Nations (UN) logo in spite of the fact that some firms do not file their annual reports and do little to implement the Principles. They become "free-riders." Compact officers are trying to address these difficulties with several initiatives to make signatory firms' actions more transparent.[59]

Some firms that have signed the Global Compact have been criticized by CorpWatch, a U.S. non-profit organization (NGO), for violating the principles of the Compact. They include: Aventis, Bayer, Nike, Unilever, Norsk Hydro, Rio Tinto, and the International Chamber of Commerce. CorpWatch called for greater accountability for firms that sign the Compact.[60] A non-UN, non-governmental unit acting as a watchdog helps to increase the integrity and transparency of the Compact activities. Many NGOs are also affiliated with the Compact, with a complete list of those signing the Compact listed on the Compact's Web site. Firms based in the United States have been more reluctant than European or Asian firms to participate in the Global Compact.

## Global Reporting Initiative

The Global Reporting Initiative (GRI) began in 1997 through a partnership of the Coalition for Environmentally Responsible Economies (CERES), which we discussed previously, and the United Nations Environment Programme (UNEP). Its purpose is to develop globally applicable practical guidelines for reporting on the economic, environmental, and social performance of corporations, governments, and NGOs. GRI proposes to "elevate sustainability reporting practices worldwide to a level equivalent to financial reporting." The intention is to produce corporate "triple bottom line" reports that are as comparable on environmental and social issues as are current financial reports. GRI brought the various stakeholders together to develop the guidelines and the instruments for measuring the progress of organizations in meeting those guidelines. GRI's *Sustainability Reporting Guidelines* were field tested in draft form, and since 2002 have been in widespread use by firms. Some of those guidelines are specific to particular industries. The Guidelines are the first global reporting device for measuring progress on the "triple bottom line;" that is, environmental and social, as well as economic, issues.

---

[58]Peter Senge, "Collaboration of Firms Within the UN Global Compact," Academy of Management Conference, Denver, August 12, 2002.
[59]For the status of the Compact, see Oliver F. Williams, "The UN Global Compact: The Challenge and the Promise," *Business Ethics Quarterly,* 14 (October 2004): 755–774; Pete Engardio, "Global Compact, Little Impact: Four Years in, the UN's Voluntary Corporate Responsibility Plan Is Falling Short," *Business Week,* July 12, 2004, pp. 86–87.
[60]Kenny Bruno and Joshua Karliner, *Earthsummit.biz: The Corporate Takeover of Sustainable Development* (Oakland, CA: Food First Books, 2002); for an overall assessment, see Claude Fussier, Aron Cramer, Sebastian van der Vegt, *Raising the Bar: Creating Value with the UN Global Compact* (Sheffield, UK: Greenleaf, 2004).

The GRI guidelines are followed by firms that report their triple bottom line results. GRI has about 45 sponsoring organizations worldwide, and many times that number have used the guidelines and reported their results. Sponsoring organizations include Baxter International, BP, Canon, Ford, GM, Heineken, Nike, and Philips. The firm's reports are listed on GRI's Web site.

Some people and institutions have asked for these reports. Analysts at leading socially responsible investment firms, representing $147 billion in assets, have urged firms to do GRI-based reporting, thus enabling analysts to make more intelligent buy and sell decisions. They suggest that publicly-traded firms report annually on environmental, labor, and other social issues using the standard and tested guidelines of GRI. These analysts are looking for higher-quality disclosure from each firm, which in turn provides a better sense of opportunities and risks associated with environmental and social issues. As one analyst put it, "A company's GRI report should be the first place investors and research institutions consult for information."[61]

## Effectiveness of Global Codes and Reporting

The Caux Principles, the Global Compact and the Global Reporting Initiative have each had some success. The Caux Round Table Principles for Business were written by business executives, have the top executives of the Round Table to support it, and are more detailed, covering many more stakeholder responsibilities than does the UN Global Compact. In addition, it was one of the first of the global codes, and thus has received favorable attention among some business executives and business school faculty. The United Nations Global Compact has the advantage of the prestige of Kofi Annan and the global reach of the United Nations itself. It is the most recent, and the simplicity and transparency of the reports that the Global Compact requires may make it more attractive and increase its long-run effectiveness. The Global Reporting Initiative was devised to obtain comparable triple bottom line data for each firm. In the few years it has been in place, it has been rather successful for firms reporting their triple bottom line. Ultimately, codes such as these will be trusted and thus be effective instruments to bring transparency, which will occur when firms report on their own actions following a commonly accepted format, and the reports are audited by outsiders. The global corporation is such an important player in the twenty-first century that it must be trusted; in order to be trusted, it must be transparent.[62]

Each of these global instruments has been more popular with firms in Europe and Asia than in the United States The UN Global Compact requires CEOs to sign a statement saying that they will abide by the code. GRI requires reporting. In overly litigious U.S. society, corporate lawyers advise executives that to sign a compact or make a report increases exposure to lawsuits. A firm might be sued if it does not appear to be acting as it pledges or reports. As a result, U.S. corporations have been more reluctant to become involved in any of these codes and reporting mechanisms. In an attempt to avoid expensive lawsuits, NAFTA set up an intra-national judicial process which is outside the U.S. legal system, and whose decisions cannot be appealed, in order to assure that free markets are protected and enforced. Are American business

---

[61]See www.globalreporting.org/about/brief.asp.
[62]S. Prakash Sethi, *Setting Global Standards: Guidelines for Creating Codes of Conduct in Multinational Corporations* (Hoboken, NJ: John Wiley, 2003).

executives thus more willing to submit to international law in order to support the free market than to ensure fair working conditions or lowering toxic pollution?

A free market is most efficient and effective when it is open, transparent, and has commonly accepted "rules of the game." Each of these codes and reports attempts to achieve that.[63] Hence most business executives support these instruments, at least in theory. There are short-term costs to abiding by a global code and reporting economic, environmental, and social activities. But there is a long-term benefit for all citizens in providing better wages and working conditions and inflicting less environmental damage. When firms do not participate in a voluntary code or reporting mechanism, it undermines the best vehicle for encouraging voluntary cooperative action. Moreover, only two other opposing and less-desirable options are then available: individualistic actions that provide short-term rewards to sweatshops and polluters because of their lower costs, or global legal restraints. Are global legal restraints, such as treaties and regulation, the most feasible solution, given the damage and chaos caused by individualistic actions and the limited success of global codes? For a comparison of the various strategies, see Table 9-4.

**TABLE 9-4**  Global Ethical Guidelines for Business: Advantages and Disadvantages of Alternate Strategies

| Strategies | Advantages | Disadvantages |
|---|---|---|
| Treaties and Regulation | Provides clear guidelines, applicable to all Provides enforcement methods Lessens advantages of "free-rider" | Difficult to negotiate Ineffective without monitors and sanctions Managers' dislike for regulations A nation can remain outside agreement |
| Codes and Reports | Focuses managers' attention on ethical issues Easier to support because not coercive Initiates cooperation and communication | Many countries and firms do not participate U.S. executives fear costly lawsuits No mandatory reports or sanctions |
| Self-Restraint | Enables stakeholders to identify ethical norms Managers able to anticipate regulation Imposes no red tape or limiting restrictions Useful if no regulation or code in place | Inadequate to deal with some issues Provides spotty long-term results Gives financial advantage to unethical firms |

*Definitions*

| | |
|---|---|
| *Regulation:* | *Multilateral treaties and international agreements.* |
| *Codes and Reports:* | *Global codes and reporting of business conduct.* |
| *Self-Restraint:* | *Voluntary self-restraint of individual executives and firms.* |

---

[63]For a more detailed comparison, see Gerald F. Cavanagh, "Global Business Ethics: Regulation, Code, or Self-Restraint," *Business Ethics Quarterly,* 14 (October 2004): 625–642.

## CHALLENGES FOR THE MULTINATIONAL FIRM

Business will continue to be the source of jobs and hope for a brighter future for poor peoples. The pressure to lower costs will continue in the global market place. For the business manager, this poses a dilemma, since the lower cost method often places larger costs on others. Earlier in this chapter we examined working conditions and pollution in developing countries. The challenge for the manager is to continue to provide low-priced goods and services and jobs at living wages, and to do it in a fashion that will benefit and not penalize people now and in the future.

### Sustainable Development

The last two decades have been sobering, not only to Americans but to all peoples. In addition to the constant threat of terrorism, citizens in the United States, Japan, and Europe now realize that they will never again attain the supremacy in world markets or the growth rate that they had in the latter part of the twentieth century. In addition, rainforests are being cut down in Latin America, Africa, Indonesia, and India, and we are losing farmland even as world population grows.[64] Housing for millions without electricity or running water plagues Mexico City, Jakarta, Bombay, and hundreds of other cities. Moreover, we anticipate up to 1 billion people in China and India who will own autos that use petroleum and add to pollution. All of this provides new opportunities for the creative entrepreneur. We realize that our development and growth must be such that generations following us may also enjoy a decent standard of living and a livable world.[65]

In the United States, 15 percent of citizens have family incomes below the poverty level. In the last chapter we cited the huge compensation of top executives. This gap between the rich and the poor is widening each year, and it is large and apparent in many Asian, Latin American, and African countries, also.[66] Thus it will be more difficult for business to prosper in the long term, both because potential markets are thus limited, and also because of the danger of social instability.[67] Moreover, many of the new service jobs and even some high-tech jobs are not challenging and pay less. They do not provide the opportunity for expanding one's skills or for advancement, as we note at Burger King, McDonald's, and retailing. In addition to the above, resources are becoming more expensive, since non-renewable resources, such as petroleum and metals, are being used at a non-sustainable rate.

---

[64]Linda Starke, ed., "Farmland Quality Deteriorating," and "Forest Loss Unchecked" in *Vital Signs—2002: The Trends That Are Shaping Our Future* (New York: W. W. Norton, 2002), pp. 102–106.
[65]Petra Christmann, "Multinational Companies and the Natural Environment," *Academy of Management Review,* 47 (October 2004): 747–760; Lester R. Brown, *Plan B: Rescuing a Planet Under Stress and a Civilization in Trouble* (New York: W.W. Norton, 2003); Brown, *Eco-Economy: Building an Economy for the Earth* (New York: W.W. Norton, 2001); *Academy of Management Review,* 20 (October 1995): 873–1089, which analyzes seven ecologically sustainable organizations.
[66]"Rich-Poor Divide Growing," in *Vital Signs—2003: Trends That Are Shaping Our Future,* ed. Starke (New York: W.W. Norton & Co., 2003), pp. 88—89.
[67]Paul Krugman, *The Age of Diminished Expectations* (Cambridge, MA: MIT Press and Washington Post, 1994).

Most manufacturing and services add to pollution, and the cost to clean up pollution places a burden on others and increases the cost of living.

On the other hand, many business firms are taking the lead in shifting to a sustainable economy. Hewlett-Packard and IBM collect and recycle many of their old computers. Computers contain toxic metals, such as lead, mercury, cadmium, and bromine, which can get into the ground water and poison people; moreover, those and other materials are recyclable. In 2004, Dell, the leading computer manufacturer, announced that it would aggressively recycle. It runs a low-cost pick-up service, and its goal is to collect and reuse the materials from 50 percent of the computers it has manufactured.[68] Dell's initiative is aimed at people in the United States and in many other countries as well.

## A Nation Among Nations

In this world of increasing population, faster transportation and communication, and more choices in lifestyles, people are becoming more interdependent. On the individual level, we depend on each other and we require interaction to develop as persons. For example, when people flee the problems of the city, their affluent children, without parks, libraries, and corner stores within walking distance, find little to do and become bored. Bus service is often not available in these communities, leading to isolation for anyone who does not drive. Many children then turn to alcohol or drugs, drop out of school, and run away from home. On the international scene, terrorists attacks and wars and revolutions in the Middle East, Latin America, or Asia touch us within hours. Information about starvation among refugees in Africa comes into our living rooms by means of TV, along with the fact that our use of dog food, lawn fertilizer, and red meat may play a role in depriving those Africans of life-giving grain. No nation's peoples can assume that what is good for them is therefore good for other peoples. If one group of people ignores another group, they do so at their peril. In this small world, we are linked together. We are interdependent, whether we like it or not.[69]

Most problems that face the world cannot be solved by any single nation acting alone. Consider, for example, terrorism, global climate change, malnutrition, toxic waste, dwindling finite resources, and even a balance-of-trade deficit.[70] Too often, we in the United States and our government officials are insensitive to world-wide reaction to U.S. policies. America's invasion of Iraq, lone vote against the Kyoto Treaty on Global Climate Change, withdrawing from the World Health Organization's code for marketing infant formula, and our repudiation of the Law of the Sea Treaty has lost the United States much international respect and support. Business managers know that nationalistic attitudes that might have been tolerated a generation ago can now cause problems for the United States and U.S. business.

---

[68]Peter Asmus, "Dell, Inc.: Environmental Progress Award," *Business Ethics,* Fall 2004, pp. 10–11.
[69]Amitai Etzioni, *From Empire to Community: A New Approach to International Relations* (New York: Palgrave-Macmillan, 2004)
[70]Global climate change is first issue that requires a solution, according to the Copenhagen consensus. See William R. Cline, "Climate Change," in *Global Crises, Global Solutions,* ed. Bjorn Lomborg (Cambridge, MA: Cambridge University Press, 2004), pp. 13–38.

We operate in global markets and must be responsible citizens of more than one country.[71] As the world gets smaller, all people depend more on each other. Yet, paradoxically, new nationalism, provincialism, and even fundamentalism is afoot around the world. The United States often stands with those few nations that are unwilling to limit their sovereignty or their self-interest. Hence we see individualism and nationalism clash with the reality of interdependence. This is an unsustainable posture.

Sociologist Robert Bellah thinks that America's failure lies in its emphasis on the atomistic self and on rational self-interest, and in its break with the basic understandings of the Founding Fathers. In early America, there was a strong social, collective emphasis: Citizens together were responsible for the state. Bellah demonstrates how this emphasis derived from the biblical covenant between God and God's people and from the gospel notion of a loving community based on membership in the common body of Christ. Bellah is convinced that the economic system of contemporary industrial America no longer is based on the early American view that economic interdependence is the foundation of the political order.[72] Respect for other peoples' positions, cooperation, and negotiation are necessary in this interdependent world. The urgency and importance of the problems that face the peoples of the world demand that leaders work together for solutions.

## Global Corporate Citizenship

A major challenge for twenty-first century business managers is to see themselves as citizens with multiple responsibilities. Then the corporation becomes a constructive player, providing products, services, jobs, income, and leaving behind a healthier world. A firm must be a good corporate citizen at the same time that it maintains its competitive edge.

Employees' ownership of stock in the firms where they work (employee stock ownership plan-ESOP) and socially responsible investing are two growing movements that help a firm and executives to align their own goals with those of citizens. With an ESOP, workers have an ownership stake in the firm and are more likely to look to the long-term benefit of customers and fellow workers, as well as be interested in the firm's profitability. Socially responsible investment is growing, and both the Domini and Calvert socially responsible funds have outperformed the market during the past 15 years.[73] These issues have been discussed earlier in Chapters 6 and 8 of this book.

Becoming a good corporate citizen requires vision and humane values, neither of which should be taken for granted in any firm. The vision and values of a firm

---

[71]For a comprehensive collection of expert views on the challenges of globalization, see Patrick O'Meara et al., eds., *Globalization and the Challenges of the New Century* (Bloomington, IN: Indiana University Press, 2000).

[72]Robert N. Bellah, *The Broken Covenant: American Civil Religion in Time of Trial* (New York: Seabury, 1975).

[73]William Greider, *Beyond Scarcity: A New Story for American Capitalism* (New York: Simon & Schuster, 2003); see also Greider's *One World, Ready or Not: The Manic Logic of Global Capitalism* (New York: Simon & Schuster, 1997).

will lay a foundation for the future direction of that firm.[74] For decades, executives have planned globally in financing operations and marketing of products. A new global structure is emerging, a patchwork of institutions that will help the firm. These institutions include treaties, codes, reports, and initiatives to educate and help poor peoples to live a decent and better life and even to get a start in business.[75] These institutions and initiatives were discussed earlier in this chapter.

## SUMMARY AND CONCLUSIONS

Fast and easy movement of information, goods, services, and people has enabled business to operate around the globe. To grow, a firm must sell and operate overseas. To be competitive, that firm must reduce costs as much as possible. A developing country seeks to attract jobs, investment, and technology. To lower costs, a global firm is inclined to choose the country that offers it lower wage rates and one that will allow it to dump its refuse in the local air, water, or landfill. So the free market encourages and we thus witness both sweatshops and environmental pollution in many countries—especially in the poorer countries of the world. In addition, because of fluctuating values of local currency, a country may attract speculators who are able to make millions of dollars in a quick exchange. Bribery and corruption of public officials is also a problem whenever large sums of money are in play. Seeking contracts and important permits for operating in poorer countries often leads to payoffs of officials in those countries by agents of global firms.

Business deals in developed countries are generally covered by local legislation and regulation. Investors have long called for transparency and openness in financial reporting. European nations are in the forefront in seeking transparency and also reporting on a firm's environmental and social impact. Transparency International (TI) annually ranks the nations of the world according to the level of perceived corruption in each country. In addition, several voluntary codes and reporting schemes have been developed in order to bring greater transparency and justice to global business. These plans have received considerable attention and are used by many business firms. *The Caux Round Table Principles for Business* were written by an international group of business executives, and are widely acclaimed and used. *The United Nations Global Compact with Business* is shorter and focuses on workers' and environmental issues; it has the advantage of the global outreach of the United Nations. The Global Reporting Initiative (GRI) provides an instrument for a firm to report on its "triple bottom line" performance: environmental and social, as well as economic, results. The GRI has been more widely accepted and used in Europe than in the United States.

---

[74]Sandra Waddock, *Leading Corporate Citizens: Vision, Values and Value Added* (New York: McGraw Hill, 2002), pp. 83–140.
[75]Archie B. Carroll, "Managing Ethically with Global Stakeholders: A Present and Future Challenge," *Academy of Management Executive,* 18, no. 2 (2004): 114–120. See the several examples of successful business initiatives from four continents in Maria Cecilia Arruda and Georges Enderle, eds., *Improving Globalization* (Rio de Janiero, Brazil: International Society of Business, Economics and Ethics—ISBEE, 2004).

Most of these initiatives are voluntary, so some question their effectiveness. Voluntary actions place costs on ethical firms, while unethical firms ("free riders") are able to save money in the short-term at the expense of the health, safety, and lives of people in poor countries. In Chapter 5 we discussed that these problems occurred in the United States prior to legislation on wages, hours, safety, and the environment. Some then claim that the only solutions are fair international standards on wages, working conditions, health, safety, and also the environment. Would global minimum wage, safety regulations, and environmental standards be acceptable and effective? Many multinational or transnational corporations have annual sales that are greater than the total gross domestic products of most nations. The global corporation is thus in a dominant position to influence the policies of national and global bodies.

In domestic as well as in global operations, most business executives realize that whatever development takes place, it is not just or wise to lay the bill on the doorstep of future generations. This is true in the use of resources, pollution of earth, air and water, and global climate change. Many native Americans planned keeping in mind the seventh generation to come. Will my descendants be better off and thus thank me for how I have thought about and prepared for them? Or am I leaving them and the earth with fewer natural resources and greater pollution than I originally inherited?

## DISCUSSION QUESTIONS

1. Describe how communication and transportation has enabled global business to thrive. In what way is this an ethical good? How does it bring ethical problems?
2. In what way are international business firms good corporate citizens? How are some global firms not good citizens?
3. Describe how the free market encourages sweatshops. What are the advantages of sweatshops to purchasers of goods? What are the problems of sweatshops for people who work in them and the workers' home countries? Are sweatshops just? What distinctions are necessary?
4. How have students and other purchasers had influence on the conditions under which products are made in developing countries?
5. Describe how global climate change presents a danger to the world. Why do you think that some U.S. firms possess more enlightened policies on carbon dioxide emissions than do other firms or the U.S. government?
6. What is the difference between global investment and speculation? What is the danger of the latter?
7. What sort of bribery is outlawed by the U.S. Foreign Corrupt Practices Act and the OECD Guidelines? What is "crony capitalism"? Why are both (bribery and crony capitalism) unjust?
8. What is Transparency International and what is TI's principal method? (See TI's Web site, www.transparency.org). Why do you think are some countries more corrupt than others? Why is the United States only 17th on the 2004 list? Other things being equal, would you prefer to invest in a country that is less corrupt? Why?
9. Outline the overall contributions and the overall costs of global firms.
10. Roughly how many of the world's people are caught in poverty? How is that poverty manifested?

11. What is the significance of the data on the gap in income between the rich and the poor? How could this lead to instability or even a war—within a nation and in the world?
12. How are subsidies to agriculture in United States, Japan, and Europe unfair to farmers in poor countries?
13. How does the amount of development assistance to poor nations compare with military expenditures? How might development assistance help to make the world safer?
14. How effective have been international bodies in developing binding treaties to regulate global business? What are the advantages of international treaties and regulations? What are the advantages and disadvantages of voluntary international codes and reports?
15. What are the advantages and disadvantages of the Caux Round Table Principles for Business? Describe the SAIP.
16. What are the advantages and disadvantages of the UN Global Compact? What does it require to join? What sort of annual report does it require?
17. What are the advantages and disadvantages of the Global Reporting Initiative? Describe the report that the GRI requires.
18. Is American business more willing to submit to international law ensuring the free market under NAFTA than to ensure fair working conditions or lowering toxic pollution?
19. Why do you think that the aforementioned codes and reports are more popular in Europe than in the United States? What sort of future business environment will the codes and reports bring?
20. Are global binding treaties the most feasible way to regulate global business, given the limited success of global codes and the damage caused by individualistic actions?
21. What personal lifestyles will enable us to pass on a more healthy earth to future generations?
22. Why is it becoming more difficult for one nation to believe that it can make decisions for other nations? Are there limits to economic and political power?
23. To repeat the questions from the summary: Will my descendants be better off because of how I have used the earth? Or am I leaving the earth with fewer natural resources and greater pollution than what I inherited from my parents?

# CASES

## Case 9-1      Merck and River Blindness

In the wake of their problems with Vioxx, it is worth remembering an earlier case. Merck developed a drug for treating parasites in domestic animals. River blindness among people in Equatorial Africa is caused by a larvae deposited by the bite of a fly, and the larvae grows and moves through the human body until it causes blindness. After years of testing, Merck and the World Health Organization (WHO) found that a variation of the drug would kill the larvae if it is taken once a year. WHO agreed to deliver and administer the drug; however, the people who need the drug have no money to purchase it. Merck was not successful in their efforts to persuade foundations, world organizations, or U.S. foreign aid to purchase it for these poor people. If Merck gave the drug away, it could not recoup its research or even its production costs.[76]

What would you recommend to Merck management? Do you think that Merck management should give it away? What ethical status would you give the poor Africans who suffer from the disease: Do they deserve the drug? Would it be fair to shareholders to give it away? What ethical norms are of most help here?

(Merck's decision is given in the book noted in the endnote 76 and in *American Business Values*, 4th ed., pp. 235–237.) ∎

## Case 9-2      ExxonMobil and Global Climate Change

As we have seen in the chapter, data show that the earth is gradually warming, and almost all scientists now agree that the burning of fossil fuels, forming greenhouse gases, is the cause. Global climate change is breaking up the world's ice packs, which threatens to raise ocean levels perhaps by as much as three feet in 50 years, thus swamping many coastal areas and islands around the world. Climate change also threatens to cause increased storm damage

---

[76]David Bollier, "Quandaries in Developing a Wonder Drug for the Third World," in *Aiming Higher: 25 Stories of How Companies Prosper by Combining Sound Management and Social Vision* (New York: American Management Association, 1996), pp. 280–293. Although Merck has had problems with its drug Vioxx, its $789 million is the second largest of U.S. firms' contributions to charities; see "How Companies Hand It Out," *Business Week*, November 29, 2004, pp. 86–104.

because of warmer oceans. ExxonMobil, the largest of the petroleum firms, sponsored the Global Climate Coalition, a now defunct industry lobbying group, that was formed to lobby for U.S. rejection of the Kyoto Treaty. BP, Shell, Ford, and GM quit the Coalition, once the data on global climate change became clear. ExxonMobil still takes the position that there is not enough certainty to make policy decisions. ExxonMobil is also the owner of the Exxon Valdez, which ran aground in Prince William Sound in Alaska in 1989, and spilled 11 million gallons of crude oil that covered fish, fowl, mammals and 1,200 miles of coast. ExxonMobil is still held

responsible by citizens and the state of Alaska for the accident and for not doing a thorough job of cleaning up the spill.

1. Does ExxonMobil bear responsibility for the production of greenhouse gases?
2. What would lead them to be the last to support the dying Global Climate Coalition?
3. What responsibility did ExxonMobil have for the cleanup of Prince William Sound?
4. Did the firm take responsible action on these two issues?
5. What ethical norms help you decide these two cases? ■

---

# Case 9-3      Made in the United States or Asia

Hutchinson Technology makes more than half of the suspension assemblies for computer disk drives. Asian firms purchase 98 percent of its assemblies, but it resists pressure to move manufacturing from Minnesota and Wisconsin to Asia. Hutchinson requires precision manufacturing and these skills are scarce. It can also more easily introduce labor saving equipment in the United States. Moreover, Hutchinson

also fears that having a facility in Asia would make it easier for competitors to steal their manufacturing trade secrets.[77]

1. Is Hutchinson recognizing globalization or is it being nationalistic?
2. Is the firm's lack of trust of others overseas a lack of respect for them?
3. What ethical norms are most useful here? ■

---

[77]Timothy Aeppel, "Still Made in the U.S.A.," *Wall Street Journal,* July 8, 2004, p. B1.

# CHAPTER 10

# Business Values for the Future

Given existing technology and products, for all six billion people on the planet to live like the average American, we would require the equivalent of three planet Earths to provide the material, create the energy and dispose of the waste.

CHARLES O. HOLLIDAY, JR., CHAIRMAN AND CEO, DUPONT

The change is fast and fierce, replete with opportunities and dangers. The issue is: Do we shape it or does it shape us? Do we master it, or do we let it overwhelm us?[1]

TONY BLAIR, PRIME MINISTER, UNITED KINGDOM

We do not see the poor of the world's faces, we do not know their names, we cannot count their number. But they are there. And their lives have been touched by us. And ours by them. George Bernard Shaw put it perfectly: "You see things, and say why? But I see things that never were, and I say why not?"

ROBERT S. MCNAMARA, CONCLUSION OF HIS LAST ADDRESS AS PRESIDENT OF THE WORLD BANK

In the final analysis, the purpose of business is to serve the best interests of people by efficiently providing people with products, services, jobs, and family income. Although some call creating profits and shareholder value a purpose, it is only a measure of the financial success of the firm. The focus of business, as with almost all human endeavors, is (or should be) on the welfare of people. This is the foundation for both successful business planning and a healthy society.[2]

Planning for the future is essential for business success. Planning in turn is based on projections of what to expect in the coming decades, coupled with a consensus on an organization's mission and capabilities. Corporate planning determines markets for new products and requires determining the expectations

---

[1]Tony Blair, "Traditional Values for the Digital Age," *Responsible Community,* Fall 2000, p. 53.
[2]S. A. Cortright and Michael J. Naughton, eds., *Rethinking the Purpose of Business* (Notre Dame: Notre Dame Press, 2003).

of a firm's various stakeholders. But note that both demand for products and expectations depend upon people's values. Thus, being alert to changing values enables a firm to formulate better business plans in such a way as to be a better corporate citizen. This chapter probes current planning conditions, examines why having a coherent business ideology is important, investigates future scanning for business, and projects changing values and ethics over coming decades.

## TODAY'S BUSINESS VALUES

How values of businesspeople develop and how those values influence business practices have been examined in previous chapters. However, business is not an isolated institution. It operates in society and is influenced by cultural values and government. A reciprocal relationship exists between business and government. Government's role is to ensure that all citizens have an equal opportunity and are treated fairly. Government regulates business in order to achieve this common good, and business provides goods and services to government and lobbies government to purchase products and to grant favorable regulations.

How extensive government regulation should be—and how much an individual firm should work for the common good even when it is not regulated and it is costly to do so—is disputed. Some maintain that each firm should pursue its own profit exclusively. As we have seen in earlier chapters, these proponents of free enterprise say that more efficient markets and lower price goods mean that people are better off as a result. On the other hand, most hold that a responsible corporation will explicitly consider the well-being of others, even in cases where it is costly. In spite of this disagreement, almost all agree that free enterprise is the most productive, efficient, flexible, and innovative socioeconomic system yet devised. Nonetheless, free markets do not in themselves provide social goods that are costly to business; for example, clean air, safe drugs, and truthful advertising. Moreover, there is widespread agreement on the many strengths and limitations of the economy of the United States. This consensus allows us to more objectively examine the major business and global problems that face us.

### Free Markets Triumph

Almost all countries around the world today have some form of a free market economy. Russia, Eastern Europe, and China now have market systems that encourage market exchange, and hence also benefit from innovation and efficiencies.[3] Recognizing that markets are now global is both an opportunity and a challenge to people in every country. If a firm anywhere in the world is able to produce high-quality goods at low cost, that firm has an opportunity to be a success and to create jobs. But we also know that empowerment, loyalty, and efficiencies come to firms in which people deal with each other honestly and justly.

---

[3]Jared Diamond, "The Wealth of Nations," *Nature,* June 10, 2004, pp. 616–617.

People in every nation also know that government must provide the vital public services that a market system does not provide. Free markets do not provide parks, libraries, street lighting, art museums, or clean air and water. Without government regulations, free markets encourage businesses to cut costs by dumping pollutants in local streams. Moreover, in spite of the rhetoric we often hear, economic systems are not democratic; each person does not have only one vote.

## Aristocratic Markets

Many claim that free markets are much like a democracy. That is, each of us "votes" with our dollars on what we want, and in that way we set priorities for ourselves and for our society. This is called "consumer sovereignty," and it places the consumer in the role of decision maker and policy maker. In the very act of purchasing goods, each consumer sets priorities for him- or herself, for others, and for society. Nevertheless, when we consider purchasing power, the markets of free enterprise nations are not democratic, but rather aristocratic; that is, wealthy people have more influence on goods available and on our nation's priorities than do others. Some people earn one hundred times the annual income of others, and as a result they possess one hundred times the economic "votes." They may spend their discretionary income on expensive jewelry, a second huge house, a third SUV, or on investing in entrepreneurs in the inner city or education for the poor.

Many who work harder than some who make ten times as much find it difficult to pay the rent or the food bills. Although we say that becoming wealthy is a reward for hard work, we also know that good fortune—especially birth into an affluent family—is even more important. A child born to college-educated parents in the United States has many advantages over one born, for example, to poor parents in Bangladesh.

Making consumer sovereignty the basis for setting market priorities is more defensible than making it the basis for setting social goals. Using consumer sovereignty to set social goals is convenient; it is parallel to our successful economic system, and it distributes responsibility. But then who is responsible for solving the many problems that we have "voted for" with our dollars in past decades, such as the trade and federal deficit and the excessive use of petroleum, along with air, water, and solid-waste pollution? In setting social goals, consumer sovereignty leads to unplanned, promiscuous, often damaging economic growth, including waste and pollution. In addition, it is also a convenient principle for those who claim to be value-free, for it enables them to dodge important questions about the common good. But note that an adherence to consumer sovereignty is not value-free; it is based on a choice of values. It values the individual over community, encourages self-centered behavior, and rewards funding special interest groups to sway government. This in turn leads to short-term, narrow-minded divisiveness and stalemates, as these special interest groups pull in opposite directions.

Exclusive reliance on consumer sovereignty and free enterprise to choose our society's priorities enables us to avoid the difficult process of choosing what kind of society we want. That is, we avoid the tough questions until crises are upon us, flexibility is gone, and options have been narrowed. For example, decades ago we waited until Lake Erie died before we realized the costs of water pollution. The nuclear power plant disasters at Three Mile Island and Chernobyl had to take place before we acknowledged the costs and dangers of nuclear power plants. It took the collapse of Enron and WorldCom to alert us to the need for new regulations to bring about better financial accountability and corporate governance. We wait until a crisis has hit us before we take action.

A major inequity within contemporary American capitalism is that a dispro-portionate financial reward goes to those who possess capital—that is, those who are already wealthy. They are called investors, but most of their dollars do not go into innovation and new businesses; rather, they speculate in the market. It is "income detached from productivity."[4] Free enterprise can also encourage selfish activities. According to its ideology, free markets and competition—guided by Adam Smith's "invisible hand"—result in the most efficient and profitable use of resources. Looking after one's own self-interest benefits the general good. Or, as an early observer put it, "Private vices make public profit." At least in the short term, capitalism can reward those who are selfish. In addition, it provides an ideology that promotes and often blesses self-seeking, self-centered behavior.

Capitalism in the United States was built on self-interest and rugged indi-vidualism. In the nineteenth century, huge fortunes were amassed before social legislation was enacted. Workers and small businesspeople were injured by the actions of men such as John D. Rockefeller, Andrew Carnegie, and J. P. Morgan. Nevertheless, many of these wealthy men later used that wealth to benefit the public. In fact, Andrew Carnegie's defense of large fortunes was based on his claim that rich people can more wisely use the wealth created by industry for public purposes (see Chapter 5). John D. Rockefeller built the University of Chicago, Carnegie funded libraries across the United States, and Collis P. Huntington built a rail-based rapid transit system for Los Angeles (which was torn down in the 1950s by a combine of GM, Firestone, Phillips Petroleum, and Standard Oil of California). Foundations were set up by wealthy men such as Ford, Carnegie, and Rockefeller to serve the public, and these foundations have continued to fund valuable new programs. Bill Hewlett and David Packard used their wealth to fund education, the arts, and other public institutions. Yet many multi-millionaires today rarely consider the needs of their fellow human beings. When people are rich simply because huge fortunes have passed from generation to generation, there is a strong case for inheritance taxes. Bill Gates' father favors a steep inheritance tax, just as Andrew Carnegie did; Gates, Sr. maintains that the wealthy should pay a larger portion of their income in taxes. According to him, shifting the tax burden away from the wealthy is opposed to American values. Progressive taxation protects American democracy against the massing of excessive power by the very wealthy.[5] Both Gates and Carnegie think that the next generation should also have the motivation to work, and

---

[4]Marjorie Kelly, *The Divine Right of Capital: Dethroning the Corporate Aristocracy* (San Francisco: Berrett-Koehler, 2003).
[5]William Gates, Sr. and Chuck Collins, *Wealth and Our Commonwealth: Why America Should Tax Accumulated Fortunes* (Boston: Beacon Press, 2003).

should experience the thrill of earning their own million dollars. Moreover, both also argue that inherited wealth establishes an aristocracy whose members oppose many democratic values. Will billionaires Warren Buffet, Sandy Weil, Michael Eisner, Donald Trump, and others who make a fortune in this generation use their wealth to help other people?

## Democracy and the Threat of Special Interests

We know how essential planning is for business. However, during the past three decades there has not been similar planning in the United States in the public sector. Not enough libraries, museums, or parks have been established, and what we have are not well maintained. Moreover, suburbs sprawl haphazardly, paving over farmland that a generation ago provided food and might have been set aside as parks or rapid transit right-of-ways. Many suburban housing tracts do not have sidewalks for children and the elderly, and for pedestrians and cyclists. Vision and planning are required to make cities, neighborhoods, and communities livable and attractive, and, in general, they are lacking today. Attention is focused on economic growth: new businesses, new offices, and new homes. Meanwhile, cities continue to deteriorate; many of our roads, public transit facilities, libraries, and parks were built 50 or more years ago. When individuals pursue their own self-interests, the community as a whole is made poorer.

It takes time to agree upon national priorities, since this must be done primarily through open discussion, negotiation, voting, and legislation. On public interest issues, Americans are generally committed to an open system and to consensus. However, it generally takes a catastrophe to alert us to inadequacies in our social or business goals. Millions of birds died from pesticides before we learned how we were poisoning them.[6] It took the Los Angeles riots and white supremacists to force us to face continued racial and job discrimination. Add to this the death of Lake Erie, the nuclear disaster at Chernobyl, and the barely averted disaster at Three Mile Island, and it is no wonder that many Americans are impatient with and distrust government. Widespread lack of trust in government makes it difficult to plan and work out national policies for the common good.

A democracy works slowly and often requires a crisis to awaken its citizens to new public needs. Men and women must personally feel a need before they are willing to work to meet that need. Thus long-range planning for a city, a nation, or the globe is extremely difficult. Legislators feel pressure to vote on issues to benefit those who contribute money to their election campaigns. Attempts to regulate campaign spending have been thwarted. In spite of the McCain-Feingold law, 2004 federal races for Congress and the White House cost a record $3.9 billion. President Bush raised a record $273 million and his challenger Senator John Kerry raised a record for a challenger of $240 million.[7]

A few firms, at some risk to their relations to the incumbent government, now refuse to make any political "contributions," because they see them as a veiled

---

[6]Rachel Carson, *Silent Spring* (Boston: Houghton Mifflin, 1962).
[7]Glen Justice, "Even with Campaign Finance Law, Money Talks Louder Than Ever," *New York Times,* November 8, 2004, p. A16.

form of bribery. BP chair John Browne announced its decision not to contribute, saying "We'll engage in policy debate, stating our views and encouraging the development of ideas, but we won't fund any political activity or political party."[8] Most major political contributors expect favors in return, which is what we mean by bribery. Under such circumstances, there is a disincentive for legislators to sacrifice present benefits for future goals. Yet any investment policy, whether it be related to money, cities, land, or the environment, is precisely such a tradeoff. Special interests, lobbyists, money, and felt needs back home all militate against the kind of long-term investment of time and resources in planning that will pay off a generation from now. Moreover, many of the problems we face are serious and long-term; for example, broken families, poor education, urban decay, pollution, dwindling resources, and distrust among nations. When a crisis erupts before we understand how serious the problem is, there is little time left to find solutions. This may be the most serious flaw of democracy.

As an alternative to financial capitalism, democratic capitalism features worker ownership, cooperation in the workplace, and humble, self-effacing executives.[9] It is true that women and men are amazingly imaginative and flexible. If we look to the welfare of our grandchildren, it will be easier to acknowledge our long-term needs. If we can marshal the imagination, talent, and initiative that we possess, we can find solutions.

## Lack of Clear Values

A survey some years ago found that, when young people were critical of the beliefs of their parents and other elders, they were not so much critical of what they believed but of their seeming lack of beliefs and convictions. Their elders' values, they said, seemed to be absorbed passively from the surrounding culture; they had few thought-out, internalized goals and values.

Many of us are victims of homogenized mass education and passive entertainment. Not only does mass education directly influence thinking, but it also indirectly influences values through the clothes, food, and TV programs that are popular or "cool." Mass education substitutes tastes and fads for critical thinking and reflection on personal goals and values. Often we escape thinking by turning on the TV or radio. Thus people's moral and intellectual fiber is softened by being pounded for decades by violence, sex, and quick solutions to every problem.

The confusion, apathy, and cynicism that are often found in younger people challenges their elders to articulate their own values and ethics. If adults, with more experience, are unclear about their own life goals and aspirations, young people are left with no one to help them. They are left with no rudder, and are pushed by events from one job or problem to another. Without values and goals, people are not in control of their own lives, careers, or destinies. Opportunities, challenges, and crises come rapidly, and individuals who have not reflected on why and how they live, what they do, and why they do it are unable to deal with events.

---

[8]"BP Will No Longer Make Any Political Donations," *Wall Street Journal,* March 1, 2002, p. B4.
[9]Ray Carey, who was CEO of ADT, makes a cogent argument in his *Democratic Capitalism: The Way to a World of Peace and Prosperity* (Bloomington, IN: AuthorHouse, 2004).

Such people become confused, frustrated, and hurt. If they were to gain ownership of their roots and goals, these people would be able to choose and grow.

Minds are like parachutes: They work only when they are open. Yet in a critique of American society entitled *The Closing of the American Mind*,[10] the author maintains that people of all great civilizations were steeped in knowledge of other times and other thinkers. But American universities have virtually stopped conveying traditions. Since we are not taught any better, we become a pragmatic, unreflective people, who rarely examine the most important questions, such as: What kind of person do I want to be? What is my goal in life?

## An Aid to Core Beliefs and the Work Ethic

People whose personal values and goals are clear tend to have greater self-esteem, and thus are better able to work with others. Hence both individuals and organizations benefit when people probe their basic values, and articulate answers to basic questions such as the following:

- What is my fundamental purpose in life?
- Are people basically self-seeking or are they basically good and generous?
- Do people have a spiritual end, or is this present life with its pleasures and material satisfactions all there is?
- Are there moral goods and evils—for example, charity and murder—or is everything relative?
- Does society exist for people or do people exist for society? What is the purpose of the business firm? What is the purpose of the state?
- Are human beings moving toward long-term progress or toward decline and perhaps collapse?

The responses to such questions have an effect on the goals of organizations and also on government legislation and regulations.

If you reflect on questions such as these, and answer them, you will learn much about yourself. This will complement the "Personal Goals and Values" paper from Chapter 1 that you wrote. Your answers to these questions may show that you have a concern for others and are sometimes willing to sacrifice your own interests for their sake. On the other hand, your responses may show that you are focused on your own interests and that you see other people as instruments to attain your own goals. To gain another perspective, consider what responses you would prefer from a potential spouse or from a future business partner. If you were hiring a person, which attitudes of a person would incline you to consider that person as a future employee?

As for choosing a job, what sort of a firm you would like to work for—a firm whose workers are more focused on themselves and their own careers, or a firm whose people are also concerned about others? In which sort of firm are you likely to do better work and be happy? In which would you likely be more successful?

---

[10]Allan Bloom, *The Closing of the American Mind* (New York: Simon & Schuster, 1987).

A recent, thorough, nationwide study of business firms that far outperformed peers in their industry examined those firm's top leadership. They found that they were led by CEOs who were not motivated by their compensation. The study "found no systematic pattern linking executive compensation to the process of going from good to great." These executives elicited the best from all the people they worked with. They did not come up with the solutions and give directions, but rather "led with questions, not answers." Moreover, in a surprise to the investigators, these executives were not only not motivated by their pay, but demonstrated "a compelling modesty, shunning public adulation; [and] were never boastful."[11]

Business firms sometimes provide ethics education for their people, and they stress practical skills. This is helpful, but it does not go far enough. Ethics training programs at business firms most often do not stress critical thinking and self-assessment such as we have described here, which is essential to personal maturity and moral development.

## A VIABLE BUSINESS CREED

The most salient and precious American business value is freedom: free markets, free competition, free movement of people and capital, and most especially, freedom of the individual. But as important as personal freedom is in American society, it is not unlimited. An individualistic freedom that is not conscious of other people leads to mistrust, inefficiencies, and ultimately chaos. One does not have the freedom to shout "Fire!" in a crowded theater, unless there actually is a fire. Traffic lights are restrictions that were objected to by libertarians. A business firm does not have the freedom to mislead in its product advertising or to dump its waste in a lake. As people live closer together and become more dependent on one another, freedom must be limited by both self-control and external checks. In fact, real freedom paradoxically emerges only when people have developed internal constraints. Freedom is endangered if a free society's shared values are no longer sufficiently vigorous to preserve the moral cohesion on which the discipline of free people rests. Although individualists find it hard to understand, limitations based on a consideration for others (for example, driving on the right side of the street or truth-in-advertising laws) introduce even greater freedom for all. People have less fear and greater trust in the safety of driving and in what is claimed for a product, and thus they can act more freely.

One of the strengths of American business has been its pragmatism—getting the job done while avoiding theoretical and ideological issues. The ideology of American business is its ability to perform. The justification of the corporation is not in the natural right of private property, but in its ability to provide more goods to more people. Pragmatism thus leads us to accept values and goals simply because they work and often regardless of undesirable by-products and inequities.

---

[11]Jim Collins, *Good to Great: Why Some Companies Make the Leap and Others Don't* (New York: HarperCollins, 2001), pp. 36, 49, 64, 74.

Any valid defense of the values of business and the economic system cannot rest merely on the importance of freedom and efficiency because the following questions then arise: Freedom for what? Efficiency for what? Freedom, efficiency, and the business system they support should not be ultimate goals on their own, but rather means that allow people to pursue more important goals. Greater freedom and productivity allows a society to provide more jobs, goods, and services with less effort, but this greater productivity should be considered a major benefit, not the goal, of society.

## Problems for Future Managers

Some of the problems that now hinder business in the United States have a potential for creating even more trouble in future years. The United States had a trade deficit of $489 billion in 2003, up from $418 billion the year before. We purchase that many more goods and services from overseas than we are able to sell. Moreover, we must borrow from overseas to buy these additional goods and services. The largest single commodity we purchase from other countries is petroleum. Even though the United States is one of the largest petroleum producers in the world, that is not enough to satisfy us. We now purchase almost two-thirds of the petroleum we use from overseas, at a cost of more than $100 billion each year. Thus, we are on the slippery slope of borrowing foreign money to purchase foreign goods, all the while increasing our outstanding foreign debt. The United States was the largest creditor nation in the world until 1985. We financed many activities beyond our borders and received interest on those loans. Having a large foreign debt is characteristic of poor nations, who need to borrow capital from wealthier nations to finance their own development programs. However, currently the United States is the largest debtor nation in the world; we now borrow more capital from other nations than any other country. This increases the cost of investment capital for entrepreneurs in the United States.

In addition to the balance-of-trade deficit, the United States had a record budget deficit in fiscal year 2004 of $413 billion. This brings the accumulated federal debt to $7.4 trillion or $7,400,000,000,000.[12] The annual interest on that debt is $380 billion. To get a better idea of what is owed, consider that it comes to $23,000 for every man, woman, and child in the United States, and that to pay the interest on it costs each person about $1,300 per year. So it costs a family of four $5,200, for which we have nothing to show. Much of the debt is owed to Europeans, Japanese, and petroleum producers. The real problem with the huge federal deficit now is that when the large number of boomers begin to draw on Social Security and Medicare in a decade, we will not have the dollars to fund what we have promised. It would be wiser to be fiscally prudent and save now. Are we willing to sacrifice today to meet our promises to the next generation?

If we are not more fiscally prudent now, how will this affect business in the future? To pay for the spending of our generation will require increased taxes,

---

[12]See the Congressional Budget Office Web site: www.cbo.gov/showdoc.cfm?index'5773&sequence'2 (accessed November 9, 2004).

which will add to the cost of doing business. It thus adds additional costs when we must be competitive in world markets. In addition, the trade and federal deficits illustrate a new American value: If you can obtain goods today without paying full price, do so, even if your children must pay later. Ted Turner, founder of CNN and other cable networks, illustrates our spending habits by the following: "In the United States we have 2.5 percent of the children of the world, but we spend 60 percent of all that is spent in the world on toys."[13]

## Mission Statement and Core Ideology

Firms that have a clear and strong vision or mission statement tend to outperform their rivals in the marketplace. Put another way, the most successful and profitable firms have a much stronger vision than their competitors. An investigation established that the best companies in a field have a clear and strong vision that is expressed in their mission statement and is acted on by the people in the organization.[14] The firms that were studied were well established and highly successful. These visionary companies include: 3M, American Express, Citicorp, Ford, General Electric, Hewlett-Packard, IBM, Johnson & Johnson, Marriott, Motorola, Nordstrom, Procter & Gamble, Sony, Wal-Mart and Disney. Each of these firms is outstanding in its industry, is widely admired by businesspeople, has made an indelible imprint on the world in which we live, and was founded before 1950. Their stock has outperformed the market by a factor of more than 12. Moreover, from the standpoint of people who work there, they find more satisfaction with their jobs, *if* they agree with the vision.

Each of these visionary companies "more thoroughly indoctrinate employees into a core ideology than do comparison companies." The visionary companies more carefully nurture and select senior management. Visionary companies selected their chief executives from inside the company in 96.5 percent of the cases, while comparison companies selected their chief executives from inside in only 78 percent of the cases. An organization's mission statement and goals reflect the core values of those who formulate the statement. The Johnson & Johnson credo (see Figure 8-3) reflects the core values of the firm, values that have endured for over 50 years. It is "the glue that holds the organization together," in the CEO's words.

The mission statements of these firms stress elements such as the importance of integrity, respect for the individual employee, service to the customer, and responsibility to the community. However, each mission is unique. What is common is the authenticity of the ideology; that is, the extent to which the firm's actions are consistent with what it claims in its mission statement.[15] These businesses have higher ethical and spiritual ideals. The resulting culture then attracts like-spirited people to the organization. A test for such an organization is to institutionalize those values so they remain after the retirement of those

---

[13]Ted Turner's address at the University of Detroit, November 25, 1985.
[14]James C. Collins and Jerry I. Porras, *Built to Last: Successful Habits of Visionary Companies* (New York: Harper Business, 1994).
[15]*Ibid.*, p. 87.

who created the statement of ideals. It is essential that all members of the orga-nization have ownership of the mission.[16] Each of these firms passed this test.

Collections of some of the best business mission statements have been gathered and analyzed. Moreover, the collectors also provide historical background on the firm and how the statement was developed. The firms that are discussed include General Mills, Georgia-Pacific, Gillette, Hallmark, Honda, IBM, Johnson & Johnson, Kellogg, Merck, Motorola, Saturn, Southwest Airlines, and many more. These statements speak of values and a credo, and always include the principle that customers and employees are treated with respect. They are written in an attempt to articulate a vision for the firm.[17]

## Spiritual Business Vision

The re-election of George W. Bush as President of the United States in 2004 is credited by many to Evangelical Christians who supported him. Evangelicals seek to have their Christian values influence business, communities, attitudes, and legislation. Many Christian entrepreneurs support Republican causes and political candidates. Christian Evangelicals do not always stand for the moral and Gospel values of peace, respecting diversity, eliminating the death penalty, concern for the poor and disadvantaged, and the human dignity of *all* people.

In this newfound national strength of the Christian Evangelicals, other Americans fear that we are thus leaving behind many of the values of the Enlightenment. There is some truth to this, since the Enlightenment encourages, "critical intelligence, tolerance, respect for evidence, [and] a regard for the secular sciences."[18] However, in recent years, we have also become aware that the most serious problems that we face in the world cannot be solved by rational solutions alone. Consider, for example, terrorism, the widening gap between the rich and the poor, the dangers of famine, depletion of non-renewable resources, AIDS, and the shallowness and crassness of news and entertainment media.

In an attempt to go beyond rational insights, leaders in business ethics have re-introduced the wisdom of various religious traditions to enable us to better grasp solutions to the problems that face us.[19] Religion historically was central to the marketplace in the West and remains central for most cultures today. Medieval Europeans planned their cities with their cathedral on a hill and at the center of the city. They regularly expected the church to set standards for trade and norms of fairness, bring disputants together to adjudicate those disagree-ments, and finally to ensure that the interests of the poor and the disadvantaged were not forgotten. Such an active role of religion was not limited to medieval

---

[16]Burt Nanus stresses the importance of discussing the mission statement with the entire group in his "Leading the Vision Team," *Futurist,* May–June 1996, pp. 21–23.

[17]Patrick E. Murphy, *Eighty Exemplary Ethics Statements* (Notre Dame: University of Notre Dame Press, 1997); Jeffrey Abrahams, *The Mission Statement Book: 301 Corporate Mission Statements from America's Top Companies* (Berkeley, CA: Ten Speed Press, 1996).

[18]Garry Wills, "The Day the Enlightenment Went Out," *New York Times,* November 4, 2004, p. A31.

[19]Steward W. Herman, ed., *Spiritual Goods: Faith Traditions and the Practice of Business* (Bowling Green, OH: Philosophy Documentation Center, 2001).

Europe. For Native Americans, religion was generally central. Religion was a principal integrating force in the lives for both Mayan and Aztec peoples, and they designed their religious temples as the largest and most important buildings in their cities. Medieval Europeans and Native Americans are not exceptions. The role that they gave to religion is typical of most societies. Note the major function of religion in the Middle East, Africa, Latin America, and in many Asian countries. However, there is only one dominant religion in most of those societies; they are not pluralistic.

The Enlightenment at the beginning of the 1800s greatly influenced modern Western states. The legitimacy of the state and all other social structures was reformulated on non-religious principles to which all rational thinking individuals could subscribe. Thus the U.S. Constitution separated church and state. Religion became a private matter. Although the immediate effect of this was negligible, over time this separating of religion from business and public life had a profound effect. The separation is underscored when we consider the great influence the early theologian John Calvin had on the Protestant Ethic, and the fact that the first economist, Adam Smith, was a professor of *moral philosophy* (see Chapter 4).

Western peoples seldom have outright hostility to religion. However many tend to trivialize religion, to treat it as a hobby or a "mystical irrationality." It is all right to make polite references to God at public events. But this reference to God should not be substantive; it should not be a foundation for public policy. Yet religion is likely to survive as a major influence on people and policy, as the 2004 United States elections prove.[20]

While the European Enlightenment had a profound influence on western values, there is nevertheless a new interest in spirituality in the workplace. But this spirituality is not restricted to Evangelical Christianity. Spirituality in the workplace generally is a spirituality that welcomes people of every faith—including Muslims, Jews, Hindus, and others. In the wake of downsizing, working people feel more pressed, and ask themselves "Why do I feel so unfulfilled?" Firms such as AT&T, Boeing, Ford, Lotus, and Medtronic have programs of prayer and reflection within the firm. Other firms hire "spiritual" consultants, including poet David Whyte, Tom's of Maine founder Thomas M. Chappell, former senior vice president of Meridith Magazine Group and author James A. Autry, and corporate culture scholar Terrance Deal. Much has been written recently about spirituality in the workplace.[21]

Management scholar Charles Manz writes about Jesus as a model of excellent leadership: "The last shall be first," "Lead other with compassion," "Gather the lost sheep," and "Lead without blindness"–with each section containing explicit

---

[20]Stephen L. Carter, *The Culture of Disbelief* (New York: Basic Books, 1993); also relevant are Carter's *Integrity* (New York: Basic Books, 1996), *Civility: Manners, Morals, and the Etiquette of Democracy* (New York: Basic Books, 1998).

[21]Oliver F. Williams, C.S.C., *Business, Religion and Spirituality* (Notre Dame: University of Notre Dame Press, 2003; Jerry Biberman and Michael D. Whitty, *Work and Spirit: A Reader of New Spiritual Paradigms for Organizations* (Scranton, PA: University of Scranton Press, 2000).

citations from the Gospels. Manz, in a prayerful and respectful fashion, cites Jesus as a leadership model.[22] Spirituality builds upon traditions that include St. Augustine and Thomas Merton, but it also includes New Age followers who find God everywhere and give "expression to the being that is in us; it has to do with the feelings, with the power from within, with knowing our deepest selves and what is sacred to us."[23]

At the grassroots, groups of businesspeople in many cities of the United States gather weekly or monthly at prayer breakfasts, and discuss and pray over their faith, families, and firms. Several of these groups, such as the Woodstock Business Conference and Legatus, are organized nationally.[24] An annual conference on spirituality in business has been held for more than a decade.

The Protestant Ethic has had a profound effect on business values. As discussed in Chapter 4, the Protestant Ethic emphasizes self-interest and achievement. Note that this ideology has its roots in Calvinist Protestantism, but it is now a secular description of the American ideology of work. Some have identified another spirituality that has even deeper roots in Christianity and provides a balance to the Protestant ethic. To distinguish it, they call it the Catholic ethic:

> The Catholic ethic views the world through the lenses of family and forgiveness. The Protestant ethic views it through the lenses of individualism and immutability. In the Catholic ethic, life in this world is a process, a journey, in which forgiveness is always possible. In the Protestant ethic, one's efforts to "succeed" may help in this world but have less influence in the next. . . .
>
> The merciful culture of the Catholic ethic has many elements that make the sharing of resources natural and ordinary, and that temper hostility toward the needy, and these elements guide the daily decisions of those who are influenced by this ethic.[25]

In sum, those who bring spirituality, prayer and reflection into the workplace range from Evangelical Christians to New Age practitioners. These are ordinary people who are trying to better understand themselves and their work lives. They would like to break down the compartments in their lives, and better integrate their work life, their family life, and their religious faith.

---

[22]Charles C. Manz, *Leadership Wisdom of Jesus: Practical Lessons for Today* (San Francisco: Berrett-Koehler, 1998). For excellent books by Christian business executives, see James A. Autry, *Love and Profit: The Art of Caring Leadership* (New York: Avon Books, 1991); also Max DePree, *Leadership Is an Art* (New York: Dell, 1989).

[23]Jay A. Conger, *Spirit at Work: Discovering the Spirituality in Leadership* (San Francisco: Jossey-Bass, 1994), p. 9.

[24]The national offices are Woodstock Business Conference, Woodstock Theological Center, Georgetown University, Washington, D.C. 20057-1097, phone: (202) 687-6565. Legatus is c/o Domino Farms, 30 Frank Lloyd Wright Dr., P.O. Box 997, Ann Arbor, MI 48106-0997, phone: (313) 930-3854.

[25]John E. Tropman, *The Catholic Ethic in American Society* (San Francisco: Jossey Bass, 1995), p. 99.

## PLANNING AND FORECASTING

Managers know the importance of strategic planning. But strategic planning can be done only when one has some notion of what to expect in the future.[26] Much information is available from public sources: demographics, availability and price of resources, employment skills, and ecsonomic forecasts. Also needed are forecasts of what public policy issues will emerge in the future. Public policy issues were discussed in Chapters 1, 6, 8, and 9.

### Organizing for the Future

A firm may ask in-house staff, a trade association, or a consultant to prepare materials for strategic planning. They obtain, analyze, and report information on future trends. Various sources of information and techniques for gathering information are available. For example, considerable information is readily available on population, economic trends, production in various industries, use of food and energy, transportation, and perceptions with regard to what constitutes quality of life.[27] The advantages of obtaining the required information and using it for planning are that it

- Enables the firm to design a business map for the future.
- Reduces the possibility of unpleasant surprises.
- Enables the firm to focus on opportunities and get ahead of issues.
- Enables the firm to engage in consensus building.[28]

Capital-intensive firms in stable industries have more need of advance warning of future developments, because of their large investment and lack of flexibility.[29] Firms that are adaptable with respect to resource deployment have more opportunity to respond quickly to new trends. One way of obtaining educated estimates on forthcoming sociopolitical issues is to use the Delphi technique, which is a structured method for arriving at a consensus of opinion among a panel of experts.

### Trend Analysis

A second technique used by many firms is called *trend analysis.* Using this technique, certain critical issues are followed in an effort to determine the direction and speed of their future development. Sometimes the CEO or a group of top managers

---

[26]See, for example, Adam Aston, ed., "Hold On to Your Hat: A Raft of Ideas That Could Change Your Life," *Business Week,* October 11, 2004, pp. 128–134.
[27]See the excellent sources, Brian Halweil, Lisa Mastny et al. *State of the World—2004* (New York: W. W. Norton & Co., 2004); Linda Starke, ed., *Vital Signs—2003* (New York: W. W. Norton & Co., 2003). These two reports are issued annually.
[28]Burt Naus, "Visionary Leadership," *Futurist,* September–October 1992, pp. 20–25. For an excellent presentation of corporate planning in an ethical context, see LaRue T. Hosmer, *Strategic Management* (Englewood Cliffs, NJ: PrenticeHall, 1982).
[29]John E. Fleming, "Public Issues Scanning," in *Research in Corporate Social Performance: A Research Annual,* ed. Lee E. Preston, vol. 3 (Greenwich, CT: JAI Press, 1981): 155–173.

initially determines which issues will be followed. At other times, corporate staff poll managers or scan media sources to determine which issues are emerging.

Print media can provide early indications of new trends. Firms can obtain the results of periodic examinations of selected "opinion leaders" from, for example, the *Wall Street Journal, New York Times,* or *Washington Post.* Either corporate staff or a consultant can do a brief summary of articles on the specified public policy issues— for example, instability in an overseas region, or potential new government regulations. Over time, interest in a certain issue may increase, as measured by the number of column inches devoted to it in a particular print media. This may indicate new opportunities for products, services, or strategies for the firm, new pressures on the firm, or potential government oversight. The scanning of public issues provides an early warning system for discovering future developments. The life insurance industry has engaged in trend analysis since 1970, and considers it to be essential for planning. General Electric has been a leader in such forecasting for decades.[30]

## Careers with a Future

The global marketplace, electronic communication, and the new importance of knowledge and information are having a profound effect on jobs and new employment needs.[31] Workers can do more work from a computer workstation, and often that can be at home or other locations. Firms now hire more people to do jobs on contract; and more are hired part-time to work on specific tasks.[32]

There are fewer jobs in manufacturing. However, contrary to popular belief, manufacturing output has constituted roughly the same percentage of the U.S. gross national product over the last 50 years, and this percentage will probably be maintained. In order for developed countries to maintain manufacturing, greater productivity and innovation will be required. More jobs are now in the service sector: hospitality, health care, education, banking, insurance, transportation, and a wide variety of other services. However, many of these jobs are not as high paying as those lost in manufacturing.

With more electronic equipment being used in manufacturing and services, there is a need for people to design, manufacture, and maintain this equipment. Biotechnology requires people with skills in biochemistry, microbiology, and molecular biology. Hazardous waste disposal skills are also in demand, along with skills in energy conservation, solar energy, and laser technology. Engineering and business skills will continue to be important as work and society become more complex. There will continue to be a demand for people in information processing, including those who can design hardware and software, and operate and maintain these systems.

The dramatic increase in the importance of knowledge and innovation skills will increase the demand for quality education. There will be less emphasis on rote

---

[30]John Stoffels, *Strategic Issues Management: A Comprehensive Guide to Environmental Scanning* (Elmsford, NY: Pergamon, 1994). and Sheila Moorcroft, ed., *Visions for the 21st Century* (England: Adamantine Press, 1992).

[31]Brian Halweil et al., *State of the World—2004;* Linda Starke, ed., *Vital Signs—2003;* Robert Barner, "The New Millennium Workplace," *Futurist,* March–April 1996, pp. 14–18.

[32]See Charles Handy, *The Age of Paradox* (Boston: Harvard Business School Press, 1994).

learning in large groups and more emphasis on encouraging understanding and creativity among individuals and small groups of learners. Institutions of higher learning serving college-age students will be more oriented towards individuals so as to better meet students' needs. Business will sponsor a wide variety of education and training programs for its own people, both in-house and off site.

However, a caution is in order here. Currently, U.S. tax laws encourage exporting high tech research and design work to lower-wage countries. If such high-tech work continues to be exported, there will be less demand for well-educated engineers and scientists in the United States, and so fewer will undertake these difficult and time-consuming career paths. This, in turn, could have a negative effect on future American innovation, productivity, and employment.

# FUTURE BUSINESS VALUES

American business and its values have shifted over the last decade; earlier chapters of this book charted these shifts. Changes continue at a rapid rate, so it is imperative that we understand the direction and the substance of those shifts.

In this final section of the book we will review the changes that are taking place and assess their potential impact on American business. We will identify emerging values that will significantly affect people, firms, and American business ideology. Note that these emerging values are extensions of traditional American values; there are fewer sharp breaks than one would think (see Table 10-1). We will attempt to make projections by using data and expert opinion.

## Central Role of the Person

The importance of the individual person pervades American life, literature, and thought. Individualism is increasingly important also in China, Singapore, South Korea, Japan, and other Asian countries. The central role of the person provides

**TABLE 10-1**  Traditional American Values Lead to Future Business Values

| *Traditional American Values* | *Future Business Values* |
|---|---|
| Personal rights, helping neighbors, labor unions— values stemming from dignity of the individual | Central role of the person |
| Growth and progress | Technology and innovation |
| Planning ahead, entrepreneurship and democratic spirit | Long-range perspective |
| Self-reliance and respect for the land | Sustainable development |
| Business as a provider of goods and services | Business for people |
| Frontier and self-sufficiency | Local control in a global economy |
| Influence of religion and spirituality on American life | Spiritual roots of the new business mission |
| Centrality of the person, the family, and the local community | Human measures of success |
| Optimism and openness | Vision and hope |

the impetus for individualism, democracy, human rights, the free market, and a court system built on the dignity of the individual person. Demands for greater productivity, coupled with the central role of the person, stimulate upgrading of skills and management development, along with flexibility in people's workday, workweek, and career. In addition, most recognize that teams and loyalty bring success and satisfaction. The family is again being recognized as the bedrock of America's social structure.

A firm in which the talents of each person are challenged, in which co-workers communicate, and in which supervisors provide feedback on work is one in which each individual will grow in skills, satisfaction, and as a person. For a business firm to succeed, its workers must be committed to a quality product or service. The firm will enlist the efforts of all workers in pursuing its goals by communicating its mission, creating a cooperative climate, and rewarding groups and individuals that contribute to reaching the goals.

Managers recognize that the best way to succeed is to draw on the full talents of all workers. Workers feel that they are part of the team when they are asked their opinion of products and processes. Workers then develop a sense of ownership with respect to the job and the firm, and they work better, experience less fatigue, and enjoy greater satisfaction as a result.[33] Most people find that liking their co-workers aids job satisfaction. If co-workers are friendly, cooperative, and interested in each other, people are able to look forward to work.

Many American firms have programs designed to increase employee involvement and satisfaction. For example, Ford reduced the number of defects in its vehicles by 48 percent in a two-year period by enlisting the insights of workers. Where labor relations are not adversarial, management is able to ask employees to help improve quality by monitoring the product as it is made and by suggesting better manufacturing processes. Ford engineers took a prototype of a pickup truck to line workers and asked for their suggestions. An assembly-line worker who had worked on a previous model pickup suggested that the design be altered to allow assemblers to bolt the pickup cargo box from above rather than from below. When bolting from below, assemblers had to lift heavy pneumatic wrenches over their heads from a pit beneath the truck. Bolts were not firmly tightened, and customers complained. Engineers used the worker's suggestions to redesign the assembly process, resulting in easier assembly and far fewer consumer complaints.

People who are loved develop into more mature persons, are less turned in on themselves, and more concerned about others. Self-centeredness and insularity are vices of the immature, as we saw in Chapter 2. Love for others is a basic human virtue. Expressing love is a matter of giving—often without consideration of return. Altruistic love is possible for anyone, although it is more readily achieved by those who have been loved. It is essential for the development of persons, families, and society, yet it is not always easy. Speaking of this sort of love, economist Kenneth Boulding said:

---

[33]Gerald F. Cavanagh, "Evolution of Corporate Social Responsibility: Educating Stakeholders and Virtuous Entrepreneurs," in *Is the Good Corporation Dead?—Social Responsibility in a Global Economy,* eds. John W. Houck and Oliver F. Williams (Lanham, MD: Rowman & Littlefield, 1996), pp. 169–199.

It always builds up, it never tears down, and it does not merely establish islands of order in a society at the cost of disorder elsewhere. It is hard for us, however, to learn to love, and the teaching of love is something at which we are still very inept.[34]

Much of the energy of the poor is spent on obtaining the necessities of life. Once a person's basic needs are reasonably satisfied, that person is more inclined to consider the needs of others in society. Thus, material security is often a foundation for loving and giving. Having food and shelter enables people to reach beyond themselves and their own problems to other human beings and to realize the interdependence of people, institutions, and nations.

Concern for others is an important part of the organizational climate at Hewlett-Packard and IBM. Aetna, L.L. Bean, Dow, Steelcase, and Johnson & Johnson have all established model programs to improve the health of their employees. These programs result in less illness and injury, and therefore also save money for the firm.[35]

## Technology and Innovation

Reliance on technology has been the principal means of increased business productivity over the decades. In the future, technology will continue to be a generator of business "progress."[36] However, what is seldom realized is that the sort of technology chosen reflects the values of the one who chooses, and, perhaps more importantly, that same technology has a profound influence on the values and lifestyles of all who use it. The choice of electrical power generation grids and large manufacturing plants influence the hours that we work and the way we live, even outside of work. Asbestos insulation and chlorofluorocarbon aerosol propellants are examples of choices whose costs we later learned were far greater than their benefits. The promotion of the automobile with a tax-supported freeway system rather than public rapid transportation is a choice that reflects a "triumph of individualistic over communal values."[37]

In the future, telecommuting—doing work from a computer work station at home—will increase flexibility and freedom, but will decrease teamwork and the sense of community that is found at a central work site. Computers and their ability to store data also pose ethical questions of how these data are found and used. TRW holds credit records on each of us that can be obtained for a fee. Some of

---

[34]Kenneth E. Boulding, *The Meaning of the Twentieth Century* (New York: Harper & Row, 1964), p. 146. The importance of the manager's love and caring was reinforced in the 1995 study by Kouzes and Posner, *The Leadership Challenge* (San Francisco: Jossey-Bass, 1995).

[35]Jeremy Rifkin, *The European Dream: How Europe's Vision of the Future Is Quietly Eclipsing the American Dream* (New York: Penguin, 2004); Shawn Tully, "America's Healthiest Companies," *Fortune,* June 12, 1995, pp. 98–106.

[36]William Halal, Michael Kull, and Ann Leffmann, "Emerging Technologies: 2001–2030" in *Globalization and the Challenges of the New Century,* ed. Patrick O'Meara et al., (Bloomington, IN: Indiana University Press, 2000).

[37]John M. Staudenmaier, S.J., "Technology," *A Companion to American Thought,* eds. Richard W. Fox and James T. Kloppenberg (Oxford: Blackwell, 1995).

these records are personal, and some are in error, yet people use this information to make decisions on hiring, lending, and for many other purposes. The Internet, with its extraordinary advantages for swift, global communications, also gives hackers access to very sensitive and personal data.

Emerging technologies make available to firms and individuals personal data that many would prefer remain private. Are there any limits to using this information to sell products? It is essential that we use our moral and ethical skills in deciding how this information can be used.

The technology that one adopts and how one uses it depend upon the values of those who make those decisions. The technological systems themselves are generally selected by elites; that is, leaders of business and government. Hence it is even more essential for justice and the stability of society to keep in mind the needs of *all people,* including those without a voice: the poor and disadvantaged.

## Long-Range Perspective

Business executives agree that business planning must include a long-range perspective. New products and new business depend on research and development, but cost-cutting and short-term thinking often result in too little time and money being devoted to research. A study of effective business leaders found that:

> Traditional management teaching focuses our attention on the short term, the Wall Street analysts, the quarterly statements, and the annual report. Yet all the effective leaders we've seen have had a long-term, future orientation. They've looked beyond the horizon of the present.[38]

The survival and growth of American business demands an increased attention to long-term concerns. Pressure resulting from short-term financial interests makes long-term planning in a publicly-held firm difficult, but does not alter its importance for the future.[39] To reduce this pressure, some suggest that the corporation should be viewed as a community, not something to be owned; "rewards for performance would take the form of bonuses approved by the board."[40] This issue was also discussed in Chapters 1 and 8.

## Sustainable Development

In the course of meeting people's needs, business firms will operate with greater respect for the natural environment. Pollution, undesirable by-products, and scarcity of resources place constraints on the direction and pace of economic and business growth. These physical constraints will become more pressing, and citizens' expectations that firms will respect those constraints will become more

---

[38]James M. Kouzes and Barry Z. Posner, *The Leadership Challenge,* p. 15.
[39]Henry Mintzberg, *Managers, Not MBAs: A Look at the Soft Practice of Managing and Management Development* (San Francisco: Berrett-Koehler, 2004); "Restorative Development: Economic Growth Without Destruction," *Futurist,* July–August, 2003, pp. 23–27.
[40]Russell C. Ackoff and Sheldon Rovin, *Redesigning Society* (Stanford, CA: Stanford Business School Press, 2003).

pronounced.[41] Hazardous industrial waste looms as an increasing problem during the coming decade. The cost of its transportation and disposal, as well as the effort to determine liability, will increase; this, in turn, poses costly problems for business in the future.[42]

Given the free market, is it surprising that West Africa is the dumping ground for American and European toxic waste? The cost of waste disposal is large; the cheapest thing to do with it is to pay Morocco, Congo, or Niger to bury it on their land. For example, in 1988, American and European private waste disposal firms offered Guinea-Bissau $120 million annually to bury 15 million tons of toxic waste from tanneries and pharmaceutical companies. This is slightly less than the African country's gross national product of $150 million. This practice created a furor in West Africa, with many people in these nations demanding that the contracts be repudiated.

Because of better worldwide communication, we are now more aware of global environmental problems. In contrast to the "cowboy economy" of the 1980s in which gross production and consumption measured success, the newer "spaceship economy" of the twenty-first century realizes that all men and women live together on the same fragile planet. This planet has only finite resources and a limited ability to cleanse itself of pollution. Since this is true, if human needs and desires could be met with less use of resources, less production, and less consumption, would that economy not be superior? To suggest this is, to some people, economic heresy. However, if we can meet human needs with fewer resources, less waste, and reduced pollution, are we not better off? We see around us that unlimited consumption and production harms people and the environment, and therefore consumption and production are not reasonable goals in themselves.[43]

The reformulation of goals and the new criteria of success require that we make judgments on the type of growth we allow, the products we want, and the tradeoffs and costs we are willing to accept. Such judgments require discussion, common understandings, and consensus-building—a difficult task in a fractured and polarized democracy. There is resistance to this reformulation of goals and to the new criteria of success that this requires. It suits some people's ideology and it is easier to allow the "free market" to decide which path we take. However, this gives more influence to individual decisions and less to community interests. Moreover, it wastes resources, arable land, and human lives. Can it therefore be a responsible policy?

---

[41]See, for example, "Reaping the Wind: GE's Energy Initiative Is a Case Study in Innovation Without Borders," *Business Week*, October 11, 2004, pp. 201–202; "How to Market a Groundbreaker: Ford Is Pitching Its Gas-electric SUV to Techies, As Well As Greenies," *Business Week*, October, 18, 2004, pp. 104–106.
[42]Dennis A. Rondinelli and Ted London, "How Corporation and Environmental Groups Cooperate: Assessing Cross-sector Alliances and Collaborations," *Academy of Management Executive*, 17, no. 1 (2000): 61–71.
[43]Jared Diamond, *Collapse: How Societies Choose to Fail or Succeed* (New York: Viking, 2004); John de Graaf, David Wann, and Thomas H. Naylor, *Affluenza: The All-Consuming Epidemic* (San Francisco: Berrett-Koehler, 2001).

As for work and home life, many would prefer a simpler and less stressful day. For example, note transportation. In addition to the workday becoming longer, today more time is lost in driving to and from work, schools, church, and stores. In older neighborhoods one could walk to each; now many suburbs do not even have sidewalks. This total reliance on the automobile wastes not only time but also petroleum and other natural resources. It constitutes a loss of freedom and so is not progress. Similarly, time is lost in filling out income tax returns, medical insurance forms, questionnaires, and in listening to advertisements. Some urge that wherever there is a choice between making more money and simplifying life, the latter road be taken.

Recall the comments of the Chairman and CEO of DuPont at the beginning of the chapter. A new series of cultural "thou shalt nots" may be required in the future. Humankind will not be able to survive if we individual humans do not set limits to our appetites, do not develop a habitual willingness to conserve and preserve, and do not maintain a conscientious concern for others. Although these attitudes are difficult to achieve, they are essential if we are to prevent terrorism, war, mass starvation, and chaos.[44] It is essential to develop spiritual and human values that are integrated into everyday life and institutional decision making. Developing countries, especially Asian nations, are also experiencing these dilemmas. Fortunately, most of these nations still have their traditional religions and respect for family to support concern for future generations. On this shrinking planet, economic and political planning must consider the welfare of future generations.[45]

There are numerous success stories of firms that plan, produce, and make profits in a sustainable manner.[46] The recognition of the need for a sustainable economy and society are more apparent in Europe and Japan than in the United States. These opportunities and constraints will have a major impact on firms and people's lives. The successful leader is alert to changes in attitudes and will direct policies and actions to the new needs. Future jobs, products, government policy, and personal values will be heavily influenced by the coming era of new opportunities in sustainable development.[47]

## Business for People

The free market model views a person and the business firm as isolated, independent, and competing with others to survive and grow. As long as a firm

---

[44]See special reports on the consumer society, *State of the World—2004,* Linda Starke, ed. (New York, W.W. Norton, 2004).

[45]Mark P. Sharfman, Teresa M. Shaft, Laszlo Tihanyi, "A Model of the Global and Institutional Antecedents of High-Level Corporate Environmental Performance," *Business and Society,* 43 (March 2004): 6–36.

[46]See dozens of cases involving global firms in Charles O. Holliday, Stephan Schmidheiny, and Phillip Watts, *Walking the Talk: The Business Case for Sustainable Development* (San Francisco: Berrett-Koehler, 2002).

[47]Rogene A. Buchholz, "The Natural Environment: Does It Count," *Academy of Management Executive,* 18, no. 2 (2004): 130–133; excellent data for sustainable economic development can be found in Lester R. Brown, *Eco-Economy: Building an Economy for the Earth* (New York: W.W. Norton, 2001); Brown, *Plan B: Rescuing a Planet Under Stress and a Civilization in Trouble* (New York: W.W. Norton, 2003). See also the classic, Paul Hawken, *The Ecology of Commerce: A Declaration of Sustainability* (New York: HarperCollins, 1993).

shows a profit, financial analysts and *Forbes* call it a success. The firm is thus judged successful whether it makes high-quality, energy-efficient necessities with less pollution, for example, HP (printers) and Novartis (medications), or dangerous, trivial products such as Altria and Philip Morris (cigarettes). The firm's "success" might be at the cost of unsafe working conditions (sweatshops in the United States and overseas) and the pollution of neighborhoods. The models and ideology of old-school economists and businesspeople urged profit-making, production, and consumption. For some people even to this day, any increase in gross national product indicates success. However, note that the manufacture of cigarettes and the hospital expenses for those with lung cancer or heart disease due to smoking all add to gross national product (GNP). An auto accident that causes serious injuries, and placing pollutants in the air, also lead to an increase in GNP—the cost of repairing the damage to humans and the physical environment. Is not the goal of business to provide for people— whether that be jobs, family incomes, products and services—and also to make lives happier, safer, and healthier?[48] How useful are our economic measuring criteria when we count unnecessary hospital bills, accidents, or pollution as success?

In this period of rapid technological change, information overload, and global competition, the best leadership is that which empowers others. Self-leadership enables each person to most effectively contribute to the project. Superleadership involves listening more and talking less, asking more questions, and encouraging learning.[49] An innovative and related perspective on leadership has been developed by the servant-leadership movement. The movement shows how a leader is most effective when the leader is able to elicit the best efforts from each member of the group. The leader empowers all workers to do their best and thus be a "servant of the group." This now popular viewpoint is aided by the writings of Robert Greenleaf, who had been an executive at AT&T and had taught at MIT and later at the Greenleaf Center.[50] The Greenleaf Center holds seminars and publishes books and a newsletter. Community volunteer work develops leadership skills and encourages service of others, and builds upon servant-leadership theory. Programs for providing service at non-profit organizations are now common in business firms, universities, and secondary schools.

---

[48]William Greider, *The Soul of Capitalism: Opening Paths to a Moral Economy* (New York: Simon & Schuster, 2003); "Humanizing Economy Is Theme of Conference Held by Bishops," *America,* February 18, 2002, p. 4. For a plan to achieve a just economic order, see John Paul II, *Centesimus Annus (On the Hundredth Anniversary of Rerum Novarum)* (St. Paul: Media Books, 1991). For an assessment of the influence of this plan see, S. Prakash Sethi and Paul Steidlmeier, "Religion's Moral Compass and a Just Economic Order: Reflections on Pope John Paul II's Encyclical *Centesimus Annus,"* *Journal of Business Ethics,* 12 (1993): 901–917.

[49]See the explanation of superleadership in Charles C. Manz and Henry P. Sims, Jr., *The New Superleadership: Leading Others to Lead Themselves* (San Francisco: Berrett-Koehler, 2001).

[50]Larry Spears and Michelle Lawrence, eds., *Practicing Servant Leadership: Succeeding Through Trust, Bravery and Forgiveness* (San Francisco: Jossey-Bass, 2004); see also Robert K. Greenleaf, *The Servant as Leader* (Newton Center, MA: Greenleaf Center, 1970). *The Servant Leader* and is a newsletter published by The Robert K. Greenleaf Center for Servant-Leadership, 921 E. 86th St., Suite 200, Indianapolis, IN 46240. See www.greenleaf.org.

Conscientious corporate executives have long acted on the notion that the firm should serve society. Many CEOs and boards have redirected their firms to ensure that social objectives are met. Many developing industries that have high-growth potential are geared to genuine human needs, such as biotechnology, robotics, solar power, office technology, and energy conservation.

A major criterion of the worth of any skill or work up to the time of the Industrial Revolution was the relative value of the good or service to society. As we have seen in earlier chapters, in recent generations an ideology developed that bestowed value on any work regardless of its outcome. Financial return became more important than what was accomplished. However, a growing number now question this criterion, and thus also doubt the value of some work no matter what wage it provides. Some will not work for a strip-mining firm, a hard-sell advertiser, a manufacturer of automatic weapons, or a manipulative financial advising firm. On the other hand, individual transportation vehicles serve the legitimate needs of people, and thus an auto worker's efforts have a value beyond the paycheck. Thus we reintroduce criteria that had been pushed aside. The value of a job or position is judged both by the contribution of the worker to a product or service *and* by the contribution that product or service makes to society. One problem here: It is easier to measure my relative worth against others on a wage scale and decide who is number one than it is to measure the value of a grade school teacher compared to that of a software salesperson. Does it make any difference whether one is helping to produce electricity, municipal bonds, tractors, cigarettes, throw-away bottles, nutritious foods, or Coca-Cola? Are all goods of equal value to society, and we are thus unable to judge the relative value of these goods? In a small, primitive economy, these questions do not arise, since there is only enough time and energy to provide necessities. Our society has more people, many goods, diminishing and more expensive resources, and the problem of pollution, so questions about relative values face us. It is becoming necessary to determine which goods are more valuable to society. A principle might help in developing these criteria: Goods and services might be judged more valuable insofar as they support life, families, and neighborhoods, and provide freedom, joy, and happiness.

## Local Control in a Global Economy

The entrepreneur and the small firm have been respected, encouraged, and often preferred to the large firm in the United States. In a time when there are many new and changing needs, the flexible entrepreneur has an important role. Pierre Omidyar worried in 1995 that big corporations would take over the Web and most business. So he designed eBay, saying "I wanted to give the power of the market back to individuals." He set up the Web site to empower people. Its success in providing an opportunity for every person to be a buyer or seller is demonstrated by the fact that it has 125 million members and, as a business, grossed $34 billion in 2004.[51]

Small businesses are encouraged in the United States by lower tax rates. Large size is necessary when economies of scale are required for the purpose of competing

---

[51]"The Web for the People," *Business Week,* December 6, 2004, p. 18.

in large international markets, for example autos and computers. Nevertheless, encouraging entrepreneurs and keeping the government's role limited are traditional American values. Even in providing human services, such as education and health, the independent sector can generally deliver better services at a lower cost than can the government. However, the global market can concentrate wealth in the hands of a minority, and democracy can inspire the outcast majority to violence, as we have seen in much of the world. The World Trade center disaster can be seen as merely envy on the part of the poor at the extravagance and arrogance of the rich; but this sort of violence against a wealthy minority has taken place in dozens of nations on every continent.[52]

As long as the poor and disadvantaged have access to necessary services, local control in both the public and private sectors has several advantages:

- It gives people more control over their work and lives and thus provides increased personal involvement.
- It more clearly locates responsibility.
- It eliminates layers of organizational bureaucracy.
- It is less costly.
- It is in the American tradition of self-reliance.

The global economy gives many local cultures the opportunity to compete globally. Both China and India have innovative, efficient, and well-financed entrepreneurs in the global marketplace.[53]

## Spiritual Roots of the New Business Mission

Evangelical Christianity is having a major influence on American policies in the twenty-first century. In the 2004 U.S. elections the winning rallying cry of Evangelicals was about being anti-abortion and anti-gay marriage. Commentators have pointed out that fundamentalist Muslims share some of the same attitudes as fundamentalist Evangelicals: "a rage at secularity, religious intolerance, fear of and hatred for modernity."[54] The opposing political position, which favors listening, peace, care for the disadvantaged, and respect for people regardless of race, sex, creed, and sexual orientation is also based on the moral high ground of the respect for every human person.[55] Personal and national goals in the United States have been strongly influenced by religion and spirituality, especially Christianity. We live on a foundation provided by the Judeo-Christian culture. Although it became secular, the Protestant ethic stemmed from Calvinist Puritan Christianity.

---

[52]Amy Chua, *World On Fire: How Exporting Free Market Democracy Breeds Ethnic Hatred and Global Instability* (New York: Doubleday, 2003).
[53]Manjeet Kripalani, "Getting the Best of the Masses: A Wave of Innovation Is Yielding High-quality Goods That India's Poor Can Afford"; Bruce Einhorn, "Huawei: More Than a Local Hero: The Telecom Gear Maker Aims to Be a Player in Global Innovation," *Business Week,* October 11, 2004, pp. 174–184.
[54]Garry Wills, "The Day the Enlightenment Went Out," *New York Times,* November 4, 2004, p. 31.
[55]James Martin, "The Business of Belief: Living a Spiritual Life in a Corporate World," *America,* July 1–8, 2000, pp. 16–19.

Religious values are now having a greater influence on civic attitudes and choices. What influence will these religious and spiritual ideals have on business in the future?

There has always been a strong streak of religion and moralism in American culture. Note the seeming paradox:

> How is it, then, that a nation as prosperous, as hardworking, and as governed by the quest for economic profits as the United States can also espouse an overwhelming religious faith, claim near-universal belief in God, and devote itself regularly to the teachings of its numerous churches, synagogues, meeting places, and fellowship halls?[56]

Witness our condemnation of buying votes in government, the sexual infidelities of Bill Clinton and other political leaders, and the self-seeking activities of corporate executives such as Conrad Black, Martha Stewart, Charles Hurwitz, and Frank Quattrone. In the nineteenth century, the powerful antislavery (abolition) and antitrust (muckraking) movements were morally motivated and received their inspiration from the Gospels.

The civil rights movement in the United States was led by Rev. Dr. Martin Luther King, Jr., a Baptist minister. He preached "love for the oppressor" and espoused Mahatma Gandhi's nonviolent methods to gain equal opportunity and social justice for blacks. The record shows how effective the movement and his leadership were. The role of churches in political life is increasing, and polls indicate that most Americans want that. Many of the most committed social activists are inspired by the Gospels. Ralph Nader comes from a religious family with high ideals, and Common Cause appeals to the generosity and moral qualities of Americans. Mahatma Gandhi was an inspiration to many people in India and around the world, and he said he was inspired by the life of Christ. Moreover, his nonviolent approach to gaining India's independence from England was successful.

In Poland and other Eastern European countries, religious convictions moved people to overthrow dictatorships. Many priests and sisters have defended the interests of the poor, and as a result have been murdered in Guatemala, El Salvador, Brazil, Bolivia, Chile, and other Latin American countries.[57] Their inspiration comes from Jesus, His love for the poor, and His commitment to bring justice to those at the bottom of the socioeconomic ladder (Matthew 5:3; Luke 6:20). The goal of these Gospel-inspired leaders is freedom. They want the poor, ordinary citizen to have sufficient freedom to own land, to vote, and to be a self-respecting citizen, as well as the freedom to work and earn a fair day's pay. They seek self-determination for peoples

---

[56]Robert Wuthnow, *Poor Richard's Principle: Recovering the American Dream Through the Moral Dimension of Work, Business and Money* (Princeton, NJ: Princeton University Press, 1996), p. 293.
[57]"Roman Catholic Priest Has Struggle Changing Lives in Rural Brazil: Father Ricardo Resende Faces Violence, Makes Enemies in Fight to Aid Landless," *Wall Street Journal,* August 28, 1986, pp. 1, 16. For additional examples, see Martin Lange and Reinhold Iblacker, *Witness of Hope: The Persecution of Christians in Latin America* (Maryknoll, NY: Orbis, 1981).

around the world. Thus they often find themselves in opposition to global business firms or military governments. Muslim and Hindu fundamentalist groups are having a profound influence in Asia, Africa, and the Middle East. They reject the Western values they see in our films and exported TV. Westerners, who have been influenced by the Enlightenment, have difficulty understanding the appeal of the fundamentalists.

It is no accident that 11 of the 100 *Best Companies to Work for in America*[58] are located in two areas of the United States that are heavily influenced by religious values. The 100 firms are rated on pay and benefits, opportunities, pride in work, job security, openness and fairness, and camaraderie and friendliness. Minneapolis-St. Paul is home to Medtronic, General Mills, H.B. Fuller, 3M, and other firms with long outstanding records in social responsibility. The area, where firms have a clear sense of social responsibility, is strongly Lutheran and Catholic. Western Michigan is home to Kellogg, Steelcase, Donnelly, and Herman Miller and is much influenced by the Calvinist Dutch Reformed Church.

Spirituality often views the manager or owner as a steward. Thus wealth and power constitute a trust that is held for others. Based on the understanding that the world and all its goods come from and ultimately belong to God, the individual businessperson holds all this in stewardship—in trust for others.[59] Numerous organizations and prayer groups now meet to enable businesspeople to better understand faith, family, and firm. Religion has traditionally urged concern for others, especially poor people in other nations and future generations.

## Human Measures of Success

A goal of most people is to obtain happiness, and for many this is measured by more compensation and wealth. However, for people who have met their basic needs, evidence shows that personal goals of greater wealth, although quite common, do not lead to happiness. We discussed this and presented the evidence in Chapter 2. People are happy when they can say they have enough.[60]

In a parallel fashion, to be successful, a business firm must be efficient and profitable. However, business leaders no longer claim that profit maximization is the only goal of business or that such a goal automatically benefits society. Chapters 1 and 8 describe numerous cases where actions and policies that made money for shareholders were not good for society. New measures of success for business firms are needed, especially when we consider that business firms ideally operate to benefit people.[61] Businesses are instruments of service to people—all kinds of people. Those who benefit include customers and shareholders, but also

---

[58]Robert Levering and Milton Moskowitz (New York: Penguin, 1994).
[59]See Oliver F. Williams, C.S.C., "Religion: The Spirit or Enemy of Capitalism," *Business Horizons,* November–December 1983, pp. 6–13; Williams, "Who Cast the First Stone?" *Harvard Business Review,* September–October 1984, pp. 151–160.
[60]See Robert E. Lane, *The Loss of Happiness in Market Democracies* (New Haven, CT: Yale University Press, 2002); Tim Kasser, *The High Price of Materialism* (Cambridge, MA: MIT Press, 2002); Richard C. Haas, *We All Have a Share* (Chicago: ACTA Publications, 1995), p. 32.
[61]See the alternate definition of productivity in Hass, *We All Have a Share,* p. 12.

employees, suppliers, and citizens of the local community. Business is not a zero-sum game; benefits to one constituency are generally not at the expense of another group. When Johnson & Johnson acts on its Credo (Figure 8-3), which says that its first obligation is to customers and its last to shareholders, the shareholders do better than they would otherwise.

Just as a financial audit sketches a firm's financial performance, a social audit outlines the impact of the firm's operations on its other constituents. Criteria for judging social performance are crucial if we are to accurately decide the degree of success achieved by a firm.[62] Business executives are aware of the need for corporate social performance measures. Many firms now prepare annual environmental and social reports on their activities. We described two examples of structures for reporting, the "triple bottom line" and the Global Reporting Initiative (GRI), in Chapters 8 and 9.

These new measures of success focus on the benefits that accrue to people— *all* the stakeholders of the firm. The achievement of environmental and social goals is now accepted as an important criterion for measuring the success of business managers. Hence social and environmental issues now have a greater impact on the values and perspectives of managers.

Global economies should operate for the long-term welfare of all people, not just to the financial benefit of a minority. If only a minority benefits, such economies are not only unjust, but also foster envy, instability, and violence. The objective should be to design the economy so that people have freedom from hunger, illiteracy, premature death from lack of health care, and the tyranny of undemocratic governments, which tend to ignore the poorest. A market economy can accomplish these human goals, but it requires government regulations to make the marketplace an even playing field for all.[63]

## Vision and Hope

The problems that we face—trade and budget deficits, outsourcing jobs and technical work, terrorism, culture divides, failing schools, broken families, pollution, refugees, and corrupt governments—are so immense that many of us find it easier to deny them. These problems often stem from trying to achieve narrow, short-term goals, and blindly disregarding the welfare of other people. Let us then ask: Am I willing to alter my actions to be more considerate of other people? Am I willing to seek solutions that might cost me something? Can we as a society build the values and institutions necessary for justice and peace at home and throughout the world?

Vision and hope have always been American virtues. Ever since the days of the frontier, we have always been optimists. Nevertheless, it would be foolish to underestimate the problems before us. Many people today are concerned primarily with

---

[62]See S. Prakash Sethi, *Setting Global Standards: Guidelines for Creating Codes of Conduct in Multinational Corporations* (New York: John Wiley, 2003); James F. Post, Lee E. Preston and Sybille Sachs, *Redefining the Corporation: Stakeholder Management and Organizational Wealth* (Stanford, CA: Stanford University Press, 2002).

[63]Amartya Sen, *Development as Freedom* (New York: Alfred A. Knopf, 1999). Sen is a Nobel Prize–winning economist.

their own personal lives and careers, and care little about what they can do to help others solve their problems. There are practical and detailed suggestions on how to fashion free markets that are beneficial for all people.[64] Moreover, as we have seen in earlier chapters, a single individual or a small group of talented, generous people can have a profound impact on the lives of others and on the world as a whole.

## SUMMARY AND CONCLUSIONS

The challenge of the future is to provide products, services, jobs, and a reasonable standard of living for all people, and at the same time not exploit finite natural resources or leave the world in worse shape than we found it. Business firms have achieved unprecedented efficiency, productivity, and growth. Nevertheless, on its own, the free market is not able to provide clean air and water, safe products, or even fair competition. A firm that provides jobs and goods sometimes also despoils the earth and harms people's health. A firm's operations may be demeaning, dangerous, use nonrenewable resources, or cause pollution.

Encouraging cooperation and providing benefits to people are appropriate goals for business and government. Americans have been pushed into many sterile and expensive traps by advertising and special-interest pressure, coupled with people's apathy and lack of clear goals. Note, for example, defective and dangerous products, collapsing railroads and urban public transportation systems, disappearing farmlands, defective nuclear power plants, and expensive and wasteful defense systems. Exacerbating the problem is the fact that traditional business ideology justifies and rewards selfishness. Humane personal values and acknowledging the common good helps to balance these costly blunders. Business firms forecast future values so that they can initiate product planning, employee participation, and advertising to meet new needs. Future planning is even more important for government.

Future business opportunities require business to be efficient and innovative. Moreover, citizens now demand that business decisions contribute to the overall good of society. A business firm is not merely a *private* enterprise; it is chartered by the state to serve the needs of society. If business firms do not choose to act responsibly, legislation or tax incentives will encourage such behavior.

In the shadow of large corporations and big government, Americans want greater independence. Individuals prefer autonomy, personal responsibility, and the ability to share decisions. Businesses will be structured to encourage such self-reliance and responsibility.

Spirituality and religion has in the past, and will in the future, provide a foundation for business values. Traditional spiritual values run counter to self-interest and the consumer ethic. The Protestant ethic required moderation, planning, and self-sacrifice. Budget deficits, pollution, anxiety, crime, and substance abuse demonstrate the failure of current values. Yet now there is almost no talk in the United States

---

[64]See, for example, Paul Hawken, Amory Lovins, and L. Hunter Lovins, *Natural Capitalism: Creating the Next Industrial Revolution* (Boston: Little, Brown & Co., 1999).

of the need to sacrifice for the sake of a larger purpose. Most would sacrifice a vacation in Cancun or a third automobile if it meant that they would have a more satisfying job, a happier life, better relationships, and that their grandchildren would not inherit a world ravaged by deforestation and cancer-causing wastes. Spirituality directs people's attention beyond themselves. As we regain this perspective, we will share expertise and resources with poorer peoples of the world so that they, too, may enjoy some of the humane fruits of business. The spirituality of all the major religions urge self-discipline and generosity toward neighbors, even the stranger, based on a reverence for God and a loving concern for others.

A person who grows to maturity must clarify and internalize his own values and goals. Especially during times of rapid change, internalized values provide a firm foundation on which to build a stable, challenging, and satisfying life. Furthermore, personal values and personal needs will be the building blocks of future business goals and policies. The process of articulating society's values and goals requires leadership. The problems are pressing and complex. Nevertheless, leaders in business, religion, government, and education, as well as all citizens, have the opportunity to inspire confidence, and help set goals to meet the challenges of tomorrow.

## DISCUSSION QUESTIONS

1. What are the issues on which there is general agreement between business managers and business critics? What is the major issue on which they disagree?
2. Outline the current major domestic and international evidence on the success of free markets.
3. What does it mean to say that free markets are aristocratic? To what extent is this true? Explain. How does an inheritance tax help to solve this problem?
4. What are the strengths and weaknesses of a democratic society in meeting new social needs—for example, public transportation, pollution control, or renewable energy sources?
5. How do special interests undermine the performance of a democracy? Give examples. How does anti-government rhetoric impact the effectiveness of government?
6. Do you think Warren Buffett, Donald Trump, and others who make a fortune in this generation will use their wealth to help other people?
7. How did you answer the questions in the section "An Aid to Core Beliefs and the Work Ethic"?
8. How do some limitations of personal freedom bring greater freedom? Give examples.
9. What are some of the problems we have created for managers in the coming decades?
10. How would you describe "visionary companies"?
11. What role has religion had in the formation of values? What influence are spiritual values now having on business values?
12. Outline the techniques of future forecasting. What is public issues scanning? What career skills will be needed in the future?
13. Which of the "future business values" listed in Table 10-1 do you think is likely to become prevalent? If they do become operative, what significance would each have for your organization?

14. If these business values became prevalent, would it increase or decrease the quality of life? Explain.
15. Are "cookies," which provide information on your Internet purchasing for advertisers and firms to use to sell to you, an invasion of your right to privacy?
16. Is an increase in gross national product a mark of success for an economy? Why or why not? Can you suggest additional criteria for the success of an economy?
17. What is the difference between the "cowboy economy" and the "spaceship economy"? Which model is more appropriate for the future? Why?
18. Would people be better off if they could meet their needs with less consumption, less pollution, and less use of finite resources?
19. Does it make any difference whether one's job is to help to produce cell phones, styrofoam packaging, automobiles, cigarettes, throw-away bottles, nutritious foods, or Coca-Cola? Are all goods of equal value to society?
20. Americans need to save more to provide for investment and to reduce foreign borrowing. How much do you save of your take-home pay? How much does your family save? Why?
21. What is servant leadership? Does it make sense to you? Explain.
22. If we are becoming more interdependent, what does this mean for a firm? For you as a citizen?
23. Upon what basic values might it be possible to build a domestic and foreign policy consensus for the future? Will spiritual values have a role in articulating this consensus?
24. Are you willing to alter your actions to be more considerate of other people? Are you willing to seek solutions that might cost you something? Can we as a society build the values and institutions necessary for justice and peace at home and throughout the world?

# CASES

## Case 10-1      Canon Keeps Manufacturing Jobs at Home

Japanese companies have moved manufacturing to Thailand, Malaysia, and China. But Canon decided that it can make its digital cameras faster and more efficiently at home, and will thus keep 60 percent of its manufacturing in Japan. Although 2003 monthly wage rates were $3,737 in Japan vs. $126 in China, Canon is improving innovation by keeping research close to manufacturing. Canon has also eliminated the traditional assembly line, and replaced conveyer belts with "cells" where workers perform multiple tasks. In these cells, workers feel more responsible for the process and talk about how to improve it. Although Canon knows it cannot compete on price, it feels its customers will pay more for a better quality camera.[65]

1. Is this strategy of Canon realistic?
2. Is it a strategy that could be viable for other firms?
3. What are the advantages and disadvantages of such a policy?
4. What ethical norms would help you judge this case?
5. Does Canon's strategy respect human dignity? Explain. ■

## Case 10-2      Local Manager in Trouble

You are the U.S.-based head of overseas operations for Star Electronics. You learn that one of your plant managers has been arrested in Kenya. His alleged "crime" is that goods found in your warehouse lack the proper customs stamps and papers.

But you learn that the truth is more complicated. For years, "grease" has been a way of life in Kenya's bureaucracy, and your plant manager has been paying gratuities to the customs officers. But he knows that it is against home office policy, so he stops doing so. The price for dropping all charges is $40,000.

1. What would you do? Would you pay the "fine"? Or would your let the plant manager be put in jail? ■

---

[65]Sebastian Moffett, "Separation Anxiety: Japan's Canon, Inc. Believes the Secret to Innovation Is Keeping Most of It at Home," *Wall Street Journal,* September 27, 2004, p. B11.

# Case 10-3 Betty Vinson, Accountant at WorldCom

Betty Vinson joined the international accounting division of a small long distance company that was to become WorldCom, in Jackson, Mississippi in 1996 at a salary of $50,000 per year. A few years later, her supervisor asked her to make false accounting entries to hide expenses to bolster the profits of WorldCom. At first she refused, but then she relented. Each quarter she hoped it would be the last time she was asked to make the false entries. For six quarters she helped to post $3.7 billion in false profits for the firm. She confessed what she had done to federal agents in Jackson in the hopes of avoiding prosecution, but prosecutors in New York decided to put her on trial. Vinson was not the only person who was involved in entering false information. At her trial she said that since her job was at stake, it was very difficult to say no to her boss. On the contrary, the U.S. prosecutor said that just following orders is not an excuse for breaking the law. Vinson pled guilty. She could face 15 years in federal prison; she has agreed to provide information to prosecutors at the trial of Bernie Ebbers, the former CEO of WorldCom.[66]

1. Does Vinson's boss bear responsibility for the false accounting entries? Does Vinson bear responsibility herself, even though she was merely following orders?

2. What ethical principles help to understand this case?

3. What lessons does this case have for you? ∎

---

[66]Susan Pulliam, "A Staffer Ordered to Commit Fraud Balked, Then Caved: Pushed by WorldCom Bosses, Accountant Betty Vinson Helped Cook the Books," *Wall Street Journal*, June 23, 2003, pp. 1, A6.

# Caux Round Table Principles for Business[1]

As a statement of aspirations, this document aims to express a world standard against which business behavior can be measured. We seek to begin a process that identifies shared values, reconciles differing values, and thereby develops a shared perspective on business behavior acceptable to and honored by all.

These principles are rooted in two basic ethical ideals: *kyosei* and human dignity. The Japanese concept of kyosei means living and working together for the common good—enabling cooperation and mutual prosperity to coexist with healthy and fair competition. "Human dignity" refers to the sacredness or value of each person as an end, not simply as a means to the fulfillment of other's purposes or even majority prescription.

The General Principles in Section 2 seek to clarify the spirit of kyosei and "human dignity," while the specific Stakeholder Principles in Section 3 are concerned with their practical application.

## Section 1. Preamble

The mobility of employment, capital, products, and technology is making business increasingly global in its transactions and its effects. Laws and market forces are necessary but insufficient guides for conduct. Responsibility for the policies and actions of business and respect for the dignity and interests of its stakekholders are fundamental. Shared values, including a commitment to shared prosperity, are as important for a global community as for communities of smaller scale.

For these reasons, and because business can be a powerful agent of positive social change, we offer the following principles as a foundation for dialogue and action by business leaders in search of business responsibility. In so doing, we affirm the necessity for moral values in business decision making. Without them, stable business relationships and a sustainable world community are impossible.

## Section 2. General Principles

### Principle 1. The Responsibilities of Businesses: Beyond Shareholders Toward Stakeholders

The value of a business to society is the wealth and employment it creates and the marketable products and services it provides to consumers at a reasonable price commensurate with quality. To create such value, a business must maintain its own economic health and viability, but survival is not a sufficient goal.

Businesses have a role to play in improving the lives of all their customers, employees, and shareholders by sharing with them the wealth they have created. Suppliers and competitors as well should expect businesses to honor their obligations in a spirit of honesty and fairness. As responsible citizens of the local, national, regional, and global communities in which they operate,

---

[1]Reproduced with permission.

businesses share a part in shaping the future of those communities.

## Principle 2. The Economic and Social Impact of Business: Toward Innovation, Justice and World Community

Businesses established in foreign countries to develop, produce or sell should also contribute to the social advancement of those countries by creating productive employment and helping to raise the purchasing power of their citizens. Businesses also should contribute to human rights, education, welfare, and vitalization of the countries in which they operate. Businesses should contribute to economic and social development not only in the countries in which they operate, but also in the world community at large, through effective and prudent use of resources, free and fair competition and emphasis upon innovation in technology, production methods, marketing, and communications.

## Principle 3. Business Behavior: Beyond the Letter of Law Toward a Spirit of Trust

While accepting the legitimacy of trade secrets, businesses should recognize that sincerity, candor, truthfulness, the keeping of promises, and transparency contribute not only to their own credibility and stability but also to the smoothness and efficiency of business transactions, particularly on the international level.

## Principle 4. Respect for the Rules

To avoid trade frictions and to promote freer trade, equal conditions for competition, and fair and equitable treatment for all participants, businesses should respect international and domestic rules. In addition, they should recognize that some behavior, although legal, may still have adverse consequences.

## Principle 5. Support for Multilateral Trade

Businesses should support the multilateral trade systems of the World Trade Organization and similar international agreements. They should cooperate in efforts to promote the progressive and judicious liberalization of trade, and to relax those domestic measures that unreasonably hinder global commerce, while giving due respect to national policy objectives.

## Principle 6. Respect for the Environment

A business should protect and, where possible, improve the environment, promote sustainable development, and prevent the wasteful use of natural resources.

## Principle 7. Avoidance of Illicit Operations

A business should not participate in or condone bribery, money laundering, or other corrupt practices: indeed, it should seek cooperation with others to eliminate them. It should not trade in arms or other materials used for terrorist activities, drug traffic, or other organized crime.

## Section 3. Stakeholder Principles

### Customers

We believe in treating all customers with dignity, irrespective of whether they purchase our products and services directly from us or otherwise acquire them in the market. We therefore have a responsibility to:

- provide our customers with the highest quality products and services consistent with their requirements;

- treat our customers fairly in all aspects of our business transactions including a high level of service and remedies for their dissatisfaction;
- make every effort to ensure that the health and safety of our customers, as well as the quality of their environment, will be sustained or enhanced by our products and services;
- assure respect for human dignity in products offered, marketing, and advertising; and
- respect the integrity of the culture of our customers.

### Employees

We believe in the dignity of every employee and in taking employee interests seriously. We therefore have a responsibility to:

- provide jobs and compensation that improve workers' living conditions;
- provide working conditions that respect each employee's health and dignity;
- be honest in communications with employees and open in sharing information, limited only by legal and competitive restraints;
- listen to and, where possible, act on employee suggestions ideas, requests, and complaints;
- engage in good faith negotiations when conflict arises;
- avoid discriminatory practices and guarantee equal treatment and opportunity in areas such as gender, age, race, and religion;
- promote in the business itself the employment of differently abled people in places of work where they can be genuinely useful;
- protect employees from avoidable injury and illness in the workplace;
- encourage and assist employees in developing relevant and transferable skills and knowledge; and
- be sensitive to serious unemployment problems frequently associated with business decisions and work with governments, employee groups, other agencies and each other in addressing these dislocations.

### Owners/Investors

We believe in honoring the trust our investors place in us. We therefore have a responsibility to:

- apply professional and diligent management in order to secure a fair and competitive return on our owners' investments;
- disclose relevant information to owners/investors subject only to legal requirements and competitive constraints;
- conserve, protect, and increase the owners/investors' assets; and
- respect owners/investors' requests, suggestions, complaints, and formal resolutions.

### Suppliers

Our relationship with suppliers and subcontractors must be based on mutual respect. We therefore have a responsibility to:

- seek fairness and truthfulness in all of our activities, including pricing, licensing, and rights to sell;
- ensure that our business activities are free from coercion and unnecessary litigation;

- foster long-term stability in the supplier relationship in return for value, quality, competitiveness, and reliability;
- share information with suppliers and integrate them into our planning processes;
- pay suppliers on time and in accordance with agreed terms of trade;
- seek, encourage, and prefer suppliers and subcontractors whose employment practices respect human dignity.

**Competitors**

We believe that fair economic competition is one of the basic requirements for increasing the wealth of nations and, ultimately, for making possible the just distribution of goods and services. We therefore have a responsibility to:

- foster open markets for trade and investment;
- promote competitive behavior that is socially and environmentally beneficial and demonstrates mutual respect among competitors;
- refrain from either seeking or participating in questionable payments or favors to secure competitive advantages;
- respect both tangible and intellectual property rights; and
- refuse to acquire commercial information by dishonest or unethical means, such as industrial espionage.

**Communities**

We believe that as global corporate citizens, we can contribute to such forces of reform and human rights as are at work in the communities in which we operate. We therefore have a responsibility in those communities to:

- respect human rights and democratic institutions, and promote them wherever practicable;
- recognize government's legitimate obligation to the society at large and support public policies and practices that promote human development through harmonious relations between business and other segments of society;
- collaborate with those forces in the community dedicated to raising standards of health, education, workplace safety, and economic well-being;
- promote and stimulate sustainable development and play a leading role in preserving and enhancing the physical environment and conserving the earth's resources;
- support peace, security, diversity, and social integration;
- respect the integrity of local cultures; and
- be a good corporate citizen through charitable donations, educational and cultural contributions and employee participation in community and civic affairs.

## Support for Caux Principles for Business from the International Association of Jesuit Business Schools

The International Association of Jesuit Business Schools, at its 1995 meeting in Yogyakarta, Indonesia, elected to present to member schools, their alumni, and local business leaders the *Caux Principles for Business* for consideration.

## A Statement of Support[2]

The International Association of Jesuit Business Schools (IAJBS) welcomes this opportunity to provide a statement of support, in the form of a rationale reflective of the values of our own Jesuit institutions, for the *Principles for Business* issued by the Caux Round Table in 1994. The Caux Principles are intended to serve as a framework within which individual organizations operating in foreign countries can draft their own freely-chosen codes of business conduct.

The Caux Round Table (CRT) is an international group of business leaders formed in 1986. Participants from Japan, Western Europe, and the United States meet at regular intervals in Caux, Switzerland, for discussions aimed at reduction of international trade tensions and fostering development of an improved international business climate. The Caux Principles are, in our judgment, worthy of favorable and widespread consideration, especially in Jesuit-sponsored programs of education for business. We take this position for the following reasons:

1. Collaborative economic activity is not only compatible with, but essential to the protection of individual human dignity in economic affairs. Responsible cooperation is preferable to destructive competition in both the workplace and the marketplace, domestic and international.
2. Respect for human dignity is an inviolable principle of socially responsible business activity.
3. Communitarian concerns are characteristic of the socially responsible person or organization in business.
4. A "stakeholder" outlook—i.e., a point of view with a focus wider than shareholders or owner interests—is appropriate for any management at any time, if management is to be at all times ethical and socially responsible in business decision making. The Caux Principles explicitly and individually address the interests of customers, employees, suppliers, owners/investors, competitors, and communities (understood in sufficiently broad terms to include the physical environment and the local culture). All of these are "stakeholders" in the organizations that managers manage.
5. Other Caux principles direct managerial attention to an organization's responsibility to (a) advance social development and protect human rights in foreign lands where the organization produces or markets its products and services; (b) go beyond the letter of the law to what is ethically required, although not legally prescribed; (c) respect both international and domestic rules; (d) support multilateral trade; (e) protect and improve the environment; (f) avoid all corrupt practices while refusing to trade in armaments or other materials that assist terrorism, drug traffic, or organized crime. Underlying these principles is an understanding of and commitment to the common good.

---

[2]By William J. Byron, S.J., former President, Catholic University of America, for IAJBS.

IAJBS welcomes the Caux initiative. We support the Caux Principles because they succeed in extending to the context of international trade the following general principles to which we, as business educators in the Jesuit tradition, freely subscribe: (1) the principle of human dignity; (2) the principle of participation and association; (3) the principle of subsidiarity; (4) the principle of preference for the poor (expressed, in the present instance, by means of trade-based economic development in less developed areas of the world).

The principle of human dignity is the bedrock of all the principles we promote under the twin rubric of business ethics and social responsibility. Human dignity is the natural endowment of every human person. But human dignity does not exist in a disembodied, abstract state. It requires association and participation with others in many ways, including trade. It also requires protection by the principle of subsidiarity, which assigns to a higher level of organization only those tasks that cannot be reasonably and effectively met at lower levels. It is in the spirit of subsidiarity that the Caux

Principles are offered as a framework within which any economic participant in international trade can compose and adopt its own code of conduct.

## Origin of Caux Principles for Business

The Caux Round Table is composed of business executives from Europe, Japan, and the United States. They recognized the need for some common understandings to provide the basis for the conduct of global business. They worked on the formation of global principles of business conduct with other executives. By 1994 they developed the Caux Principles for Business to outline conduct for international business. The Caux Principles have been translated into dozens of languages.

Executives from the following firms serve or have served on the Steering Committee of the Caux Round Table: Siemens, Honeywell, Chase Manhattan Bank, IBM, Shell, ABC Telecommunications, Canon, Matsushita, Ambrosetti Group, Timken, Prudential, 3M, Dana, Nissan, Novartis, Philips Electronics, Sumitomo, and others.

## QUESTIONS ON THE CAUX PRINCIPLES FOR BUSINESS

1. Do you think that a code of international ethics would be good for business?
2. Would a code of global ethics also benefit individual workers, families, and people in general? Why?
3. Would such a code benefit developing countries? Why?
4. Do you think the Caux Principles for Business have an application in the U.S.? What would that be? Would they be useful to executives in other countries? Why?
5. What advantage would there be to a firm if it used the Caux Principles as the basis for its own code of ethics?
6. How would you use the Caux Principles in designing a code of conduct for your firm?
7. Is there any way in which you would like to qualify or change any of the principles for the purposes of your firm?
8. Would you support the wide publication and implementation of the Principles?

# United Nations Global Compact with Business[3]

At the World Economic Forum in 1999, UN Secretary-General Kofi A. Annan challenged world business leaders to "embrace and enact" the Global Compact, both in their individual corporate practices and by supporting appropriate public policies. The Global Compact's operational phase was launched at UN Headquarters in 2000. During the first Global Compact Leaders Summit in 2004, the Secretary-General announced the addition of a tenth principle against corruption.

The Global Compact's ten principles in the areas of human rights, labor, the environment, and anti-corruption enjoy universal consensus and are derived from:

- The Universal Declaration of Human Rights
- The International Labor Organization's (ILO) Declaration on Principles and Rights at Work
- The Rio Declaration on Environment and Development
- The United Nations Convention Against Corruption

The Global Compact asks companies to support and enact, within their sphere of influence, a set of core values in the areas of human rights, labor standards, the environment, and anti-corruption:

**Human Rights**

Principle 1: Businesses should support and respect the protection of internationally proclaimed human rights; and

Principle 2: The refusal to participate in or condone human rights abuses.

**Labor Standards**

Principle 3: Businesses should uphold the freedom of association and the effective recognition of the right to collective bargaining;

Principle 4: The elimination of all forms of forced and compulsory labor;

Principle 5: The effective abolition of child labor; and

Principle 6: The elimination of discrimination in employment and occupation.

**Environment**

Principle 7: Businesses should support a precautionary approach to environmental issues;

Principle 8: Undertake initiatives to promote greater environmental responsibility; and

Principle 9: Encourage the development and diffusion of environmentally friendly technologies.

**Anti-Corruption**

Principle 10: Businesses should work against all forms of corruption, including extortion and bribery.

---

[3]Reproduced with permission.

# Selected Web Sites for Business Ethics

## University-based Sites with Links to Other sites

Markkula Center for Applied Ethics, Santa Clara University:
www.scu.edu/ethics

Center for Corporate Citizenship, Boston College:
www.bcccc.net

Zicklin Center for Business Ethics Research, Wharton, PA:
www.zicklincenter.org

University of St. Thomas Business Ethics Center, TX:
www.stthom.edu/cbes

Beard Center for Business Ethics, Duquesne University:
www.bus.duq.edu/Beard

John A. Ryan Institute for Catholic Social Thought, University of St. Thomas, Minneapolis:
www.stthomas.edu/cathstudies/zwebindex

## Non Governmental Organizations (NGOs) Sites

Caux Round Table Principles for Business:
www.cauxroundtable.org/principles.html

United Nations Global Compact:
www.unglobalcompact.org/Portal/Default.asp

Transparency International (combating global corruption):
www. transparency.org

Triple Bottom Line (Brooklyn Bridge):
www.tbli.org

Sustainability and Accountability:
www.accountability.org.uk

Ethics Officer Association:
www. eoa.org/home.asp

Ethics Resource Center:
www.ethics.org

AACSB Ethics Education Resource Center:
www.aacsb.edu/eerc

## Workplace Spirituality: Integrating Faith, Family, and Firm

Woodstock Theological Center, University:
www.georgetown.edu/centers/woodstock

Avodah Institute, Yale University:
www.avodahinstitute.com

Workplace Spirituality Information:
www.workplacespirituality.info

## Business Sites on Social Responsibility

Business for Social Responsibility:
www.bsr.org/index.cfm

Dow Jones Sustainability Index:
www.sustainability-index.com/htmle/assessment/review2004.html

## Sites for Academics

Social Issues Div., Academy of Management:
www.pitt.edu/~rorst6/sim/SIMmain.htm

International Association for Business and Society:
www.iabs.net

Society for Business Ethics:
www.societyforbusinessethics.org

# Index